Review Essays in Israel Studies

A PUBLICATION FROM *THE ASSOCIATION FOR ISRAEL STUDIES*

SUNY series in Israeli Studies
Russell Stone, editor

REVIEW ESSAYS
IN ISRAEL STUDIES

Books on Israel, Volume V

Laura Zittrain Eisenberg
and Neil Caplan, Editors

State University of New York Press

Published by
State University of New York Press, Albany

© 2000 State Univesity of New York

All rights reserved

Printed in the United States of America

No part of this book may be used or reproduced in any manner whatsoever without written permission. No part of this book may be stored in a retrieval system or transmitted in any form or by any means including electronic, electrostatic, magnetic tape, mechanical, photocopying, recording, or otherwise without the prior permission in writing of the publisher.

For information, address State University of New York Press, State University Plaza, Albany, N.Y., 12246

Production by Diane Ganeles
Marketing by Fran Keneston

Library of Congress Cataloging-in-Publication Data

Review Essays in Israel Studies / edited by Laura Zittrain Eisenberg and Neil Caplan.
    p. cm. — (Books on Israel : v. 5) (SUNY series in Israeli studies)
    ISBN 0-7914-4421-X (hc : alk. paper). — ISBN 0-7914-4422-8 (pbk. : alk. paper)
    1. Israel Book reviews. 2. Israel—Intellectual life, Book reviews. 3. Israel—Foreign public opinion, Arab Book reviews. I. Eisenberg, Laura Zittrain, 1960– . II. Caplan, Neil, 1945– . III. Series. IV. Series: SUNY series in Israeli studies.
DS102.95.B66 1998 vol. 5
956.94—dc21   0020388
                                                                                     CIP

10 9 8 7 6 5 4 3 2 1

Contents

Introduction   1

1. Ivory Tower and Embassy: Interview with Itamar Rabinovich   7

Part I: History, Economics, and Politics

2. The Yishuv's Early Capabilities: Organization, Leadership, and Policies   29
   Tobe Shanok

3. The Transition to a Market Economy: The Road Half Taken   47
   Ofira Seliktar

4. Israel as a Liberal Democracy: Civil Rights in the Jewish State   63
   Ilan Peleg

5. "Normal" or "Special"? Israel's Relationships with America and Germany in Historical Perspective   81
   David Rodman

Part II: Society and Culture

6. Mythmaking and Commemoration in Israeli Culture   99
   David C. Jacobson

7. Prophecy of Wrath: Israeli Society as Reflected in Satires for Children   119
   Yaakova Sacerdoti

8. Women's Issues in the Literary Marketplace: Anthologies of Israeli Women Writers   137
   Hanita Brand

9. Yemenite Jews on the Zionist Altar 153
   Nitza Druyan

Part III: Israel in the Region

10. Policy Transformation in the Middle East: Arms Control Regimes and National Security Reconciled 173
    Hemda Ben-Yehuda

11. Palestinian Sovereignty and Israeli Security: Dilemmas of the Permanent-Status Negotiations 193
    Naomi Weinberger

12. The Domestic-International Confluence: The Challenge of Israel's Water Problems 221
    Jeffrey Sosland

Part IV: Views of Israel from the Arab World

13. On Opposite Sides of the Hill: Syrian and Israeli Perspectives 241
    Eyal Zisser

14. Egyptian Representation of Israeli Culture: Normalizing Propaganda or Propagandizing Normalization? 263
    Deborah A. Starr

15. Arab-Israeli Economic Relations and Relative Gains Concerns 283
    Maen F. Nsour

16. The Debate over Normalization: Adonis and His Arab Critics 309
    Muhammad Muslih

Contributors 317

Introduction

This collection of critical essays constitutes the fifth volume in the Books on Israel (BOI) series, published by the State University of New York Press in conjunction with the Association for Israel Studies (AIS). The purpose of the series, begun in 1988, is to introduce readers to some of the best cutting-edge scholarship about Israel and the issues currently engaging the interdisciplinary field of Israel studies. Following in the fine tradition set by previous volumes, contributors to volume 5 represent a variety of disciplines: anthropology, sociology, history, political science, economics, and literature. Taken together, their review essays offer original examinations of the state of scholarship about Israel, along with insightful assessments of the nature of contemporary Israeli society, politics, economy, and culture. Readers of varied backgrounds are sure to find several essays that address their immediate interests, as well as others that open doors to a broader understanding of Israel through the prism of complementary areas of study. The current selection joins the four previous volumes in providing a unique brand of cross-disciplinary critical studies focusing on Israel.

The fifteen essays of volume 5 are grouped under the following broad headings: (1) History, Economics, and Politics; (2) Society and Culture; (3) Israel in the Region; and (4) Views of Israel from the Arab World. The volume opens with a new feature: an interview with a leading Israeli scholar, Itamar Rabinovich, who speaks about the evolution and current state of the field of Israel studies—including the ongoing debates over the "revisionist" work of Israel's "new historians" addressed in earlier BOI volumes;[1] the more recent concern for Arab-Israeli "normalization"; and his own special interest in diplomacy, both as a subject for academic analysis and as practiced in the real world of international relations.

The first section, *History, Economics, and Politics*, begins with Tobe Shanok's fresh look at the early days of the yishuv, making a strong case for a reevaluation of the traditional conception of the Jewish population as a completely helpless and leaderless community. Ofira Seliktar contributes the very first strictly economics review essay to the BOI series, assessing recent literature on Israel's unfinished journey along the road from a socialist to a market-style economy. Furthering the theme of the continual search for an ideal balance among the individual, society, and the state addressed in previous BOI essays,[2] Ilan Peleg takes a critical look at current literature pointing to the shaky status of civil rights in Israel. Rounding out the discussion in this section and continuing an earlier BOI discussion of Israel's international relations,[3] David Rodman reexamines the nature and evolution of two of Israel's "special" relationships: the frequently discussed one with the United States and the less frequently analyzed one with Germany.

Under *Society and Culture*, David Jacobson focuses on the current academic fascination with the role of myths and legends in the making and remaking of Israeli culture. Yaakova Sacerdoti carries forward the tradition of earlier BOI volumes that offered provocative essays on the wide range of Israeli literary and cultural output[4] with her analysis of Efraim Sidon and Meir Shalev's stories for children as tools of political satire aimed at the general public. Adding to an earlier BOI study of gender issues in Israel,[5] Hanita Brand writes on Israel's women writers' unfinished battle for recognition. Concluding this section, Nitza Druyan makes a valuable contribution to previous BOI discussions of Israel's rich ethnic diversity[6] with her review of recent publications highlighting the cultural sectarianism, embraced or enforced, of the Israeli Yemenite community.

Section 3, *Israel in the Region*, focuses on Israel's relations with the Palestinians and with the neighboring Arab states. Essays by Hemda Ben-Yehuda and Naomi Weinberger carry forward earlier BOI discussions on policy-making, strategic studies, and national security[7] into the radically different post-Oslo context, and focus on very contemporary dilemmas facing Israeli (and Palestinian) decision-makers. Jeffrey Sosland updates a recent BOI contribution[8] with his essay on the problems of sharing scarce water resources in a region plagued by hostility and mistrust.

The fourth and final section, *Views of Israel from the Arab World*, constitutes an exciting innovation, showcasing recent scholarship about Israel by prominent Arab writers. Its inclusion at this time reflects the breaking down, to a certain degree, of previously impervious intellectual barriers. Over ten years ago, the first volume of BOI featured an essay by Nissim Rejwan, a veteran Israeli analyst of Middle Eastern affairs. Rejwan reviewed forty years of Arab writing on the subject of Israel, in which he traced an evolution of Arab thinking through three periods:

1. "catastrophology," a dwelling on the shock of the 1948 defeat or "catastrophe" (*al-nakba*);
2. an official anti-Zionist phase during the 1950s and 1960s, tinged with imported anti-Semitic motifs, demonizing and delegitimizing the Jewish state as an intolerable aberration;
3. an increasing tendency since the 1967 war to speak of Israel "as part of the global order of things, a phenomenon—hostile and objectionable to be sure—but a state among other states with which one has to deal in the wider context of world politics and using the generally accepted means of diplomacy and war and hard bargaining."[9]

Today it appears that we are in a fourth stage, an era in which "normalization" is the yardstick by which the state of Arab-Israeli relations is measured. The essays in this section focus on cultural, economic, and political normalization between the Arab world and the Jewish state, and offer a new look at how Arab scholars talk among themselves and to their Arab readers, in Arabic, about Israel. Eyal Zisser, Deborah A. Starr, Maen F. Nsour, and Muhammad Muslih share their insights in their respective specialized domains, and together combine to present an authentic assessment of trends in Arab thinking about Israel in the post-Oslo 1990s.

The Association for Israel Studies (AIS) was established in 1985 by scholars from diverse disciplines for whom Israel serves as a common research interest. For further information about the activities of, or membership in, the AIS, please visit the AIS website at www.aisisraelstudies.org

Laura Zittrain Eisenberg
Carnegie Mellon University
Pittsburgh, PA

Neil Caplan
Vanier College
Montreal, Canada

Notes

1. Steven Heydemann, "Revisionism and the Reconstruction of Israeli History," in *Critical Essays on Israeli Society, Politics and Culture: Books on Israel, vol. II*, eds. Ian S. Lustick and Barry Rubin (Albany: State University of New York Press, 1991), 3–25—hereafter: *BOI II;* Jerome Slater, "The Sig-

nificance of Israeli Historical Revisionism," in *Critical Essays on Israeli Social Issues and Scholarship: Books on Israel, vol.III*, eds. Russell A. Stone and Walter P. Zenner (Albany: State University of New York Press, 1994), 179–99—hereafter *BOI III*.

2. Myron J. Aronoff, "The Ambiguities of a 'Binational' Israel," *BOI II*, 27–40; Stewart Reiser, "Sovereignty, Legitimacy, and Political Action," ibid., 63–73; Uri Ben-Eliezer, "Testing for Democracy in Israel," ibid., 75–90; Ilan Peleg, "Human Rights in Israel's Territories: Politics and Law in Interaction," ibid., 167–83; Yagil Levy and Yoav Peled, "The Utopian Crisis of the Israeli State," *BOI III*, 201–26; Peleg, "The Arab-Israeli Conflict and the Victory of Otherness," ibid., 227–43; Efraim Inbar, "The Intercommunal Dimension of the Arab-Israeli Conflict: The Intifada," ibid., 245–63; Efraim Ben-Zadok, "Neighborhood Renewal through the Establishment and through Protest," *Critical Essays on Israeli Society, Religion, and Government: Books on Israel, vol.IV*, eds. Kevin Avruch and Walter P. Zenner (Albany: State University of New York Press, 1997), 53–73—hereafter *BOI IV*; Samuel Krislov, "Israeli Courts and Cultural Adaptation," ibid., 74–92.

3. Asher Arian, "American Public Opinion toward Israel and the Palestinians," *BOI II*, 185–92.

4. Donna Robinson Divine, "Political Discourse in Israeli Literature," in *Books on Israel, vol.I*, ed. Ian S. Lustick (Albany: State University of New York Press, 1988), 37–46—hereafter *BOI I*; Aliza Shenhar, "National Neurosis in Israeli Literature," *BOI II*, 109–28; Eve Jacobson, "Exploring Answers to Zionism's Decay: Two Israeli Authors Rediscover Happiness," ibid., 145–63; Aviad E. Raz, "Rewriting the Holocaust: An Israeli Case Study in the Sociology of the Novel," *BOI III*, 9–29; Walter P. Zenner, "Espionage and Cultural Mediation," ibid., 31–42; Abraham Marthan, "An Authentic Human Voice: The Poetry of Amnon Shamosh," ibid., 43–61; Shmuel Bolozky, "On *The Schizoid Nature of Modern Hebrew*," ibid., 63–85; Nancy E. Berg, "Transit Camp Literature: Literature of Transition," *BOI IV*, 187–207; Nurith Gertz, "Historical Memory: Israeli Cinema and Literature in the 1980s and 1990s," ibid., 208–26.

5. Madeleine Tress, "Does Gender Matter?" *BOI III*, 89–105.

6. Walter P. Zenner, "Ethnic Factors in Israeli Life," *BOI I*, 47–54; Walter F. Weiker, "Studies on Ethnicity," *BOI III*, 107–20; Abraham Marthan, "An Authentic Human Voice: The Poetry of Amnon Shamosh," ibid., 43–61; Zvi M. Zohar, "Sephardic Religious Thought in Israel: Aspects of the Theology of Rabbi Haim David HaLevi," *BOI IV*, 115–36; Walter P. Zenner, "Remembering the Sages of Aram Soba (Aleppo)," ibid., 137–51; Nancy E. Berg, "Transit Camp Literature: Literature of Transition," ibid., 187–207.

7. Avner Yaniv, "The Study of Israel's National Security," *BOI I*, 63–82; Barry Rubin, "Israeli Foreign Policy," ibid., 55–61; Giora Goldberg and

Efraim Ben-Zadok, "Governing in a Turbulent National Policy Environment," *BOI III,* 161–75; Mohammed Abu-Nimr, "Dialogue and National Consensus in the Pre-Madrid Period: Dilemmas of Israeli and Palestinian Peace Activists," *BOI IV,* 30–50; Pnina Lahav, "Israeli Military Leadership During the Yom Kippur War: Reflections on the Art of Reflections," ibid., 171–86.

    8. Ofira Seliktar, "Water in the Arab-Israeli Struggle: Conflict or Cooperation?" *BOI IV,* 9–29.

    9. Nissim Rejwan, "Arab Writing on Israel: From Catastrophology to Normalcy," *BOI I,* 91–105. Quotation is from pg. 93.

1. Ivory Tower and Embassy: Interview with Itamar Rabinovich

This extensive discussion with Ambassador/Professor Rabinovich focuses on the intersection of his experiences as scholar and political practitioner, and on the merits of academic training and a scholarly career as preparation for the actual practice of diplomacy. Professor Rabinovich also shares his unique perspective on the state of theoretical and practical scholarship about Israel, with particular reference to U.S.-Israeli relations, Arab-Israeli relations, polarization within the field of Israel studies, and the peace process. Coeditors Eisenberg and Caplan conducted the interview in New York in April 1997 for this volume of Books on Israel (BOI). A list of bibliographic references for the works mentioned during the interview appears at the chapter's end.

BOI: Were there any particular facets of your experience in academia that served, in retrospect, as good preparation for your role as negotiator and ambassador?

Itamar Rabinovich is President of Tel Aviv University; Yona and Dina Ettinger Professor of Contemporary Middle Eastern History, Department of Middle Eastern and African History; senior research fellow, the Moshe Dayan Center for Middle Eastern and African Studies, Tel Aviv University; and Andrew White Professor at Large, Cornell University. From 1990 to 1992, he served as rector of Tel Aviv University, from which post he was called to head Israel's delegation in the peace talks with Syria (1992–95) following the Madrid Peace Conference. From February 1993 to September 1996, he was ambassador of Israel to the United States.

He is the author and editor of a dozen books, including *The War for Lebanon* (New York: Cornell University Press, 1984), *Israel in the Middle East*, coedited by Jehuda Reinharz (New York: Oxford University Press, 1984), *The Road Not Taken: Early Arab-Israeli Negotiations* (New York: Oxford University Press, 1991; winner of the Jewish Book Award); *The Brink of Peace: The Israeli-Syrian Negotiations* (Princeton, NJ: Princeton University Press, 1998); and, most recently, *Waging Peace: Israel and the Arabs at the End of the Century* (New York: Farrar, Straus and Giroux, 1999).

Rabinovich: Yes. I studied Middle Eastern history and general history at the Hebrew University and then I did my military service as a junior officer and spent six years in Israeli Military Intelligence as an analyst. As you know, part of the subtext of Edward Said's *Orientalism* and other attacks on Western and Israeli scholarship on the Middle East is the charge that much of the research has been in the service of colonial governments, or the Israeli government. I bring this up at the outset, and lay it on the table fairly and squarely because it so happens that the most important analytical work in Israel on the Arab world and the Middle East for many years was done by military intelligence, which predominates in this analysis work over the Foreign Ministry's research outfit. But there is nothing to hide in this sort of work, which is done in every country.

For the next twenty years at Tel Aviv University, my academic activity and writing focused on two issues: British and French policy in Mandatory Syria and Lebanon in the 1920s and 1930s, based on research in the British and French archives, and work on the contemporary Middle East, in what was then the emerging world of Israeli think tanks. The latter offered many opportunities to meet policymakers, diplomats, and visiting dignitaries from other countries. All three experiences—traditional historical scholarship, writing on the modern Middle East, and my work at the Shiloah Institute (subsequently the Moshe Dayan Center)—turned out to be pertinent to my diplomatic assignments in 1992–96. For example, working in diplomatic archives I imbibed many diplomatic techniques. After reading thousands of diplomatic despatches and the minutes written on them, and after following the careers of ambassadors and consuls and bureaucrats in London and in Paris, I came to know how foreign policy establishments work, inside and out.

BOI: Were there any specific readings or research which proved especially useful for your later diplomatic postings?

Rabinovich: Writing a book about early Arab-Israeli negotiations, *The Road Not Taken*, gave me even more preparation than working in the archives. I got a very clear sense of negotiations, of how [Israeli officials Reuven] Shiloah and [Eliyahu "Elias"] Sasson implemented [Prime Minister David] Ben-Gurion's instructions. Of course, one doesn't walk into a room with the Syrians and try to replicate what Sasson did with [Jordan's king] Abdallah, but if you ask me how that research compares with a two-year cadet course in the Israeli Foreign Ministry, I would say it's certainly not inferior to

Itamar Rabinovich. Courtesy F. Leslie Barron.

the Israeli Foreign Ministry, I would say it's certainly not inferior to the latter kind of training.

BOI: Can you elaborate upon the topic of "think tanks"? Are they something of a bridge between academia and policy-making?

Rabinovich: For some historical perspective, we have to speak about Chatham House, the American context of policy-making for the Middle East, and then about the Israeli environment.

Focusing on the interaction between intellectuals and policy-makers, Elie Kedourie's [seminal essay,] "The Chatham House Version," correctly identified the Royal Institute of International Affairs, also known as Chatham House, as the most important nongovernmental forum for shaping British policy in the Middle East. After World War II, power shifted to America. The Council for Foreign Relations and places like the Middle East Institute established a new environment for U.S. foreign policy-making. The American government also stepped into the picture with the National Defense Educational Act, by which it hoped to produce area experts.

Israel had its own small tradition, dating back to the Jewish Agency and its Political Department, partially staffed by academic experts on the Middle East, like David Ayalon, Uriel Heyd, and Pessah Shinar. There were also people who did not become academics in the sense of university professors, but were nevertheless experts, like Eliahu Elath, or Asher Goren, who for many years was the leading Arabist at the Foreign Ministry. Yaacov Shimoni was a very important intellectual force, while Eliyahu Sasson was the practitioner; both worked in the Jewish Agency and later in the Foreign Ministry. Shimoni also wrote books, lectured at the Hebrew University on Asia, and with others founded the journal *Yalkut ha-Mizrah ha-Tikhon*, the "Middle East Journal" of the yishuv which eventually became *ha-Mizrah he-Hadash* (The New East).

Notice that when people like Heyd and Ayalon took up careers in the university, they made a very clear decision to have nothing to do with the contemporary Middle East, drawing a distinction between their political work and their scholarship. The underlying assumption was that one could not do genuine scholarly work on yesterday's political event in Egypt or the next coup in Syria. The result was that the Hebrew University, which was for all intents and purposes the only university in the country for many years, did not have an institute or a center working on the modern Middle East. Also, remember that Israel of the early fifties was a very poor state, without independent sources of support for journals, institutes, or think tanks. Research was in the government, in the university, or not at all.

When the Israeli establishment finally decided to create an Israeli equivalent of a Chatham House or a Middle East Institute, they named it after Reuven Shiloah, a veteran policymaker and practitioner from the days of the Jewish Agency and subsequently the "father" of Israel's intelligence services. It was government supported and rather ineffectual until the mid-1960s, when Tel Aviv University invited Shimon Shamir, then a young faculty member at the Hebrew University, to come to Tel Aviv to set up a new department. Shamir's very creative vision was to insist that the university establish not just a department, but also an institute, to focus on the modern period. So Tel Aviv University took over the Shiloah Institute and this is how research on the contemporary Middle East was brought into the Israeli university world.

Leaping forward to our own day, there is now enough of a civil society in Israel to support institutes, think tanks, and forums that have nothing to do with the university, such as the Van Leer Institute. Still, the main theater of activity for foreign policy analysis is the university scene in Israel.

BOI: To what extent do these academic think tanks focusing on the contemporary Middle East inform actual policy?

Rabinovich: The dominant view at the Moshe Dayan Center is that we are a research institute, not a policy institute. Now I don't want to belittle advocacy institutes, which are very important and have their place and function, and are now emerging in Israel. But at the Dayan Center our work is to inform policy and the public debate about contemporary Middle Eastern issues, but not propose policy.

However the Jaffee Center at Tel Aviv University, which is quite different from the Dayan Center, published its famous study of six options for an Arab-Israeli settlement, and then advocated its own choice. The Dayan Center would never advocate specific policies. Privately, of course, if a member of government invites one of us for a discussion and asks "What do you think we should do?" we give him or her our opinion—like any other Israeli would.

One must remember that everything concerning the contemporary Middle East and also classical Islam can be politicized. Take the word *"jihad,"* for example, which Yasser Arafat used in his [May 1994] speech in South Africa and which caused an immediate hue and cry: "The man is inciting to war." Some replied, "No, *jihad* can also be a form of spiritual exertion." Now, when a scholar of Islamic studies is asked: "What is *jihad?*" his or her response in this case is necessarily politically charged. I don't wish to suggest that a scholar has to get politically involved; one can be an Orientalist at the Hebrew University and work on ninth-century Sufism and decide to have nothing to do with politics and policy. But anyone who is an active member of society may easily be drawn into these discussions—especially if one works on the twentieth century, and certainly if one works on the present.

The expression "inform public debate" raises the interesting issue of the media, where much of the public debate now takes place. In Israel, as in America, academics are often asked to be on public-affairs programs or to write op-ed pieces. It was all new in the early seventies, and at the Dayan Center we fumbled to find our place by trial and error. Someone would call from the radio and ask for a comment on a coup in Sudan or the outbreak of the Iran-Iraq war, and all of us, myself included, wanted to do everything. We were given opportunities and we grabbed them. But we made mistakes. It is a mistake for the academic expert to confuse his or her work with that of the journalist, the politician, or the policy-analyst.

BOI: So academics contribute the broader perspective, a historical or long-term view, as opposed to the policy-analyst who says "This is what we should do"?

Rabinovich: Yes. It's unnecessary for an academic to go on television or on radio and say, "Well, yesterday's coup in Sudan was carried out by Major so-and-so who is the brother-in-law of the former minister of defense, and who used the Seventh Battalion to capture the broadcasting station, and tomorrow he's likely to do this and that." Nobody needs academics for that. We need academics for the perspective, for the underlying analysis of what Sudan is, of what a military coup means in Sudan. The academic should not compete with the journalist on his or her turf. Once an academic has made that decision and learns to live comfortably with it, he or she can have a much more comfortable relationship with people in the government.

BOI: How did you find the reorientation from your academic role, dedicated to research, to your political roles, which were by definition "advocacy" aimed to influence and advance policy?

Rabinovich: It was a big change, of course. Let me say a word about having an "influence" on policy-making. Often academics say, "In addition to my scholarly work, I also want to have an impact on policy." And there are many ways one can do so, depending on the discipline. For instance, people who work in areas like modern or contemporary history, international relations, or political science may want to help shape national security policy. My very clear-cut advice is: if you really want to have an influence, join the government. By writing position papers, or by going to see the decision-makers on a random basis, your contribution is very limited.

If, for example, someone who works on Jordan wants to advance a specific cause that has little to do with scholarship, such as a closer relationship between the Hashemite family and the State of Israel, he or she should join the fray. Talking to the policymakers every so often has limited influence. But the rules of the political fray are substantially different than those that govern academia. Political actors engage in advocacy and partisanship, because they work for a political leader and are duty-bound to promote the agenda as set by the politician. Then they engage in policy-making, in policy formulation, implementation, advocacy, partisanship—all of it. One certainly doesn't have to stoop to the lowest level of the political gutter, but if you don't play by the rules of the political game, you are going to be "out," or insignificant.

There is evidence that occasionally the academic can have a degree of influence by writing an important book which shapes the climate of opinion in which public opinion is formed and policy made. Edward Said had a great deal of influence on current affairs with his *Orientalism*—although not with *The Question of Palestine*. Bernard Lewis, through many articles and books over the years had a tremendous impact on how outsiders view the Arab and Muslim worlds. Publishing a seminal work is a very significant way of making a contribution, maybe truer to the calling of the scholar than having day-to-day influence on policymakers.

BOI: There have been substantial changes in the political climate, albeit with highs and lows, since 1991. Do you see evidence of serious Arab scholars, research institutes, and think tanks prepared to undertake joint projects with Israeli scholars and institutions?

Rabinovich: There is a long distance to be covered. Until recently, Israel was a taboo subject among Arab scholars, who could justify studying Israel and learning Hebrew only under a "know-thine-enemy" approach. That, of course, is a very skewed way of studying another society. We are beginning to see changes. When I went to Jordan for the second time, in 1996, I spent an evening with a group of Jordanian intellectuals and was very glad to be questioned about the most minute details of the difference between Shas and Degel ha-Torah, or the Agudat-Yisrael and Degel ha-Torah parties. I said to myself, "We have reached a very positive phase; they are not just interested, but also knowledgeable about the subject matter, which is good."

I think that one of the instructive aspects of the work of Israeli academics and researchers is that we produce scholarship about the Arab countries that is significant in absolute terms; a number of our publications are used throughout the scholarly community, including Arab academics, as basic works. I've yet to see work of comparable quality about Israel written by Arab scholars.

BOI: So the Syrians read Moshe Ma'oz's work on Hafiz al-Asad, and they take his analysis seriously?
Rabinovich: Yes, they do.

BOI: But there isn't an equivalent Syrian scholar writing about Yitzhak Rabin?
Rabinovich: Right. Exactly. And a related point is, there isn't a running discussion in Syria on what Moshe Ma'oz writes. People don't organize or attend seminars in Damascus on "Asad's leadership style." The use they can make of Ma'oz's work is limited by the constraints on public discourse in Syria.

BOI: What about Arab scholars and institutions outside of the Middle East, such as the Institute of Palestine Studies (IPS), which has an office in Washington? It seems to combine research with advocacy. Do you have any experiences, either from watching this organization in action or from personal dealings?
Rabinovich: I know the main actors in the Washington office, and I used to meet with them. At one time the IPS reflected the quasi state the Palestinians had in Lebanon prior to 1982 and was quite important; I think that since then its significance has declined immensely. But the *Journal of Palestine Studies* still has interesting material: an important interview with Syrian ambassador Walid Moualem, a recent piece by Patrick Seale on the Israeli-Syrian negotiations . . . it's a good journal. I think the IPS is in a transitional period. If the Palestinian Authority becomes consolidated, there will be a new wave of production from places like the Palestinian universities in the West Bank. But this has yet to happen.

BOI: When thinking about the reversibility or irreversibility of the peace process, we look for signs of "normalization" of relations between Israel and the Arab world. What can you say about normalization between Israeli and Arab scholars and academics who meet each other outside of the Middle East? Can we see the frequency and openness of those encounters as a barometer of how well, or poorly, the peace process is going at any given time?

Rabinovich: Let's not talk about reversibility or irreversibility; this is based more on hunches than sound scholarship. As for normalization, the former debate about "peace" has been telescoped into a debate about "normalization." What's happened is that the Arab world has accepted "peace"—to the same extent that the Israeli consensus has, by and large, accepted the notion of a Palestinian state. Arabs have accepted the word "peace" and the notion of signing peace treaties and opening diplomatic relations with Israel. But all their remaining opposition and misgivings that were formally invested in the word "peace" are now tranferred to the word "normalization." All the arguments that used to be marshaled against *peace* are now marshaled against *normalization*. And that, I think, is an issue with which we are only beginning to grapple, and an area where much work needs to be done.[1]

BOI: Do you see Israeli and Arab scholars who meet each other outside of the Middle East, perhaps at annual conferences like MESA [the Middle East Studies Association], playing a role in advancing normalization?

Rabinovich: I feel that Arab scholars and Israeli scholars should be among the first to grapple with "normalization." My first meetings with Arab academics at international conferences, dating back to 1979 at the Orient Institute in Hamburg, established relationships that have lasted until today. We spent many hours talking together, forming an informal "network" and a way of understanding each other, and I'm very much for it. It has certainly become more comfortable since the late seventies, although this process is pegged to the latest headlines in the sense that the tendency of Arab participants to show up or not to show up depends on the political situation at home, and how comfortable they can feel "consorting" with Israelis at any particular time.

I might add that I, personally, stopped going to MESA meetings a long time ago. The Association for Israel Studies [AIS] annual meeting has become, in many respects, a much more constructive place to go. In the late 1970s, Jehuda Reinharz and I began working on a college reader, *Israel in the Middle East*, which grew out of a discussion about what was wrong with MESA and the "establishment" in Middle East studies. Jehuda proposed that scholars interested in Israel and Arab-Israeli relations need not be "stepchildren" of MESA, but should foster a recognized area of "Israeli studies" which would be institutionalized like other areas of scholarly activity.

BOI: Were there important American books or authors who helped prepare you for your ambassadorial work outside the Ivory Tower?

Rabinovich: In my career as practitioner, there were two very different areas: ambassador in Washington, and peace negotiator with Syria. The ambassador needs to work with the administration, with Congress, with the media, and with the American Jewish community, each of which requires different skills and different areas of expertise. They can, of course, be mutually reinforcing. One can be effective with the administration because one has a standing in Congress, and one may have a standing in Congress because one knows how to work with the Jewish community, or one may have some clout in Congress because one has something interesting to say to a senator with whom a good relationship has developed. Senator Byrd, for example, is interested in Roman history; others are interested in foreign affairs and love to hear about Arab-Israeli negotiations. I built a very interesting relationship with Speaker Newt Gingrich, based on common academic interests; that, needless to say, was a very important relationship to have. I believe that, being an academic myself and able to have an "intellectual" discussion with him, was significant.

And, in this sphere, the books one needs to read are books about American politics: Hedrick Smith, *The Power Game*; Sidney Blumenthal, *The Rise of the Counter-Establishment*; Robert Caro's biography of Lyndon Johnson; David McCullough's biography of Truman. One needs to read these in order to feel comfortable with the American political tradition, not just to know the technicalities.

BOI: What about the traditional political literature on American-Israeli relations?

Rabinovich: It's good work and one needs to know it. One needs to know the history, for example, of the use of American pressure on Israel: Eisenhower's pressure on Ben-Gurion to retreat from Gaza in 1956 and early 1957; Carter and Reagan's relationships with Begin; the Bush administration's influence over Shamir at Madrid.

Questions arise: Does it make sense to try to mobilize the American Jewish community through AIPAC [the American-Israel Public Affairs Committee] in order to arm-wrestle with the president? What is the relative weight of the State Department in the scheme of things? What is the relative weight of the secretary of state and the national security advisor? Is the Pentagon important for policy-making? How important is the CIA? How does one work with all these factors?

Survey books don't include that. Bernard Reich, Nadav Safran, and William Quandt give insights into the nature of the relationship and how things work, and they give the chronology. But the real know-how comes from some of the "manuals" on how Washington works, and from the transmitted knowledge of veterans in the field. For example, I spent a lot of time—not with any deliberate plan—talking with Ephraim "Eppie" Evron, a great Israeli diplomat, a master of building networks and relationships as minister during the Johnson administration and ambassador during the Carter administration. In the years before I actually went to Washington, I learned a lot simply by talking to practitioners. Samuel Lewis [U.S. ambassador to Israel, 1977–85], was someone from whom I learned a great deal.

BOI: What can you say about some of the authors who have become the "standard work" in their fields, such as William Quandt on Camp David, Saadia Touval on mediators, and Harold Saunders on the peace process?

Rabinovich: These are the standard works and we all need to read them as we go along, either for teaching courses in modern Middle East history or diplomatic history, or if we want to be practitioners. But let's never underestimate the frequent superiority of practical knowledge over book-learning. I am reminded of an incident when Prime Minister Rabin recalled a minute detail of the 1974 Disengagement Agreement with Syria which I, his "expert," had to look up! Rabin, Peres, Dayan all became experts through practice. Asad has been at this business for almost fifty years. In Egypt, Osama El-Baz and Hosni Mubarak have been on the scene forever. And of course there's King Hussein in Jordan. They know their history firsthand; they have become real "experts."

BOI: Do journalists have a role in contributing to scholarship? David Shipler and Thomas Friedman [*New York Times*] and David Makovsky [*Jerusalem Post*] have written books which students appreciate for their interesting and anecdotal treatment, despite a lack of scholarly rigor.

Rabinovich: The media has become a very important part of diplomacy today. The journalist, as the author of serious books, offers us a different form of scholarship. Patrick Seale's first book on Syria was originally written as an Oxford Ph.D.—though it does not read like a dissertation. David Shipler's work [*Arab and Jew*] is an account of a journalist who has lived through interesting experiences. Friedman's book [*From Beirut to Jerusalem*], to some extent, is the same. They share their experiences, often with some very profound insights, some pieces of information, and some creative writing. It's a different form of knowledge than what we call "scholarship," but it's legitimate, important, and has its place.

What Makovsky did [*Making Peace with the PLO*] is journalism in the sense of "high journalism," which oftentimes is not well respected by social scientists, who sometimes also look down on historians for an alleged lack of scientific or methodological rigor. And there is something in these accusations. Let's look at this "high" journalism and "low" history. I think we do well to use works like Tom Friedman's in the classroom. He's a man who knows a lot and has a particular gift for saying things that graphically catch the main point. He's also someone who speaks to everybody involved, from [President Bill] Clinton to [Secretary of State] Warren Christopher to [U.S. special Middle East coordinator] Dennis Ross to [Syrian ambassador] Moualem.

Similarly, anyone wanting to know about what goes on in Israel should read Nahum Barnea, who is a very significant source. He's very smart; everybody talks to him; he's the most influential journalist in the country. Ehud Yaari is also very good, very knowledgeable. Again, he speaks to many Israelis, to many Arabs, to many Americans; he is friendly with Martin Indyk [U.S. ambassador to Israel, 1995–97] and Dennis Ross, and he's a very authoritative source. Yaari is an area specialist, while Barnea gives both a very good X-ray and a photo of Israeli reality, which makes him somebody scholars and teachers should want to use in the study of Israel. Sometimes instructors must choose between a dry academic study of an important social phenomenon and brilliant insights offered by a journalist, or by an author like Amos Oz, in his *In the Land of Israel*—a very significant collection of reportages. Another such book is by Israeli journalist Daniel Ben-Simon, whose *Another Land*, a study of what happened in the 1996 elections, is a message to the traditional Israeli elites: "Ladies and gentlemen, you don't realize it, but you are living in another country."

At the same time, we must remember that journalists—whether in their books or in their columns—don't have to answer to the same rigorous criteria that we use in scholarly work.

BOI: What can you say about the politicization of Israel studies by scholars promoting left- or right-wing agendas? What is your opinion of the "revisionists" and "new historians" on the left who have recently generated a great deal of heated scholarly debate?

Rabinovich: I draw a distinction between "revision" and "revisionism." Revision is part and parcel of what we do and what we have to do; there is no point in you or I writing another biography of Lincoln if we are not going to revise the standard picture; otherwise, what's the point?

Revisionism, I think, is an exercise that begins with the determination that one is going to change the view of a particular past before even beginning one's research. Secondly, it's always grounded in a present perspective. For example, the American revisionist historians of the Cold War began with an animosity toward the Vietnam War. They believed that if America behaved so badly during the Vietnam War, it might not have been so "good" when the Cold War began, and therefore the Russians may not have been the "bad guys" and the Americans may not have been the "angels." And so they looked at the evidence through that lens in order to produce a different history. In a way, the conclusion was predetermined before the work began.

Thirdly, the revisionists mostly work with the source material only of their side. When writing history only through the Israeli archives, there is a built-in inaccuracy or twist. Let's say one writes about the expulsion/flight of the Palestinian refugees. If one were to write about it based only on the Jordanian archives, one would see the problem through the eyes of the Jordanian officers and some of the Palestinians, with their own dilemmas, particularly the dilemma of flight. If one writes it through the eyes of the Israeli officers, the dilemmas are the dilemmas of exclusion. There is a certain deformation built into the research. Ideally, one would consult Israeli archives, Arab archives, British archives, etc., requiring many years of sifting through the files and coming up with an integrated picture, as seen from four or five perspectives. Now many revisionists, since they already know the answer, don't look at the whole range of evidence. That is another flaw that is built into that school.

BOI: What is your assessment of the likely long-term impact of the current wave of revisionist Israeli history?

Rabinovich: First, there are elements of substance. I myself have written that the state-inspired, self-serving Zionist orthodoxy had to be corrected. This is a definite contribution that the revisionists and others have made. In every intellectual endeavor there is a danger of staleness; people may become too comfortable doing what they have been doing for too many years, resting on conventional wisdom. Anyone who stirs the waters, I would credit them with doing something very positive. Definitely, the revisionists have stirred the waters, asked important questions, and generated important debates. Some of the work they did also stands on its own and should be welcomed. But some of it, I think, needs to be criticized along the lines that I mentioned.

BOI: It sounds as if you credit them with asking fresh, hard questions, but challenge their interpretations and conclusions.

Rabinovich: What I tried to do in writing *The Road Not Taken*, as you [Caplan] noted in your review article in *Israel Affairs*, was to bridge the traditional and revisionist schools. I read Avi Shlaim's 1986 piece on Husni Za'im and had two reactions: First, Shlaim had clearly found some extremely important and interesting material in the archives and, second, I sensed that he was wrong in his interpretation. My own look at this subject took me to the Israel State Archives in Jerusalem, where I read the files that Shlaim cited in his footnotes and confirmed my intuition that Shlaim was wrong. I subsequently wrote a paper on Ben-Gurion and Husni Za'im (which eventually became the Syrian chapter in *The Road Not Taken*) and then I thought of expanding the study to look also at the Jordanian and Egyptian negotiations at the time. I devoted several months of work in the Israel, American, and British archives, and then took a summer sabbatical to write the book. So, I am grateful to people like Shlaim and Tom Segev for generating this research interest.

But I think that the "new historians" picked on some very weak opponents. The people who wrote the traditional histories of the War of Independence were, for the most part, nonacademic historians. It's very easy to say that they were given access to the archives when others were not and therefore felt somewhat timid. These people were intellectually ill-equipped to debate with scholars versed in the latest Oxford or Berkeley vocabulary and academic styles. Elhanan Orren, for example, has a Ph.D., but it is difficult for him to debate with Avi Shlaim, in English, in an academic setting. Shabtai Teveth, on the other hand, is not an academic historian but is intellectually powerful, and, I think, gave the "new historians" a fair fight [during a 1989 symposium at the Dayan Center]. Efraim Karsh, in his new book, *Fabricating Israeli History*, offers a frontal attack on the "new historians," and he may be the first intellectually equipped scholar to tackle them on their own ground. He may be the first manifestation of what will become a counterweight to them. Avraham Sela, a young historian who works on the 1948 period, is less explicit than Karsh. He works with the intellectual tools and language skills that some of the "traditional" historians lacked, so his research will definitely become a valuable resource for the next wave.

BOI: Could you elaborate on this issue of a counteraction from the scholarly right?

Rabinovich: Yes, there is now an attempt to create an intellectual right-wing revisionism in Israel. The "Shalem Institute" in Jerusalem is a neoconservative think tank, financed by Ronald Lauder (of Estee-Lauder cosmetics). It seems to be a direct response to Benjamin Netanyahu's call for the creation of a right-wing intellectual tradition—as if intellectual traditions are created—because, as he correctly observes, in the USA and in France there are some very impressive right-wing intellectuals. Irving Kristol and Bernard-Henri Levy don't have their Israeli equivalents, but I don't think one can simply manufacture them. Maybe at some point they will write their own revisionist history of the creation of the state or of the peace process. But, so far, the "new historians" are revisionists with a left-wing ideological bent.

BOI: What about Daniel Pipes and Efraim Karsh, whose argument that the Syrians never intended to make peace in the post-Madrid talks has been embraced by the right wing? Your take on the Syrian position, based on four years of negotiating with them, is quite different. What are their sources? How should readers choose between the different theses in their books and yours?

Rabinovich: I happen to be privy to a lot that will never be in any archive, information that I will put at the reader's disposal in my new book, *The Brink of Peace*, saying: "Here are the facts; here is my analysis; here is my hypothesis." Now this, of course, does not exclude other forms of knowledge or scholarship. What can the other authors offer? It's not as though Pipes or Karsh has been given the American record or the Syrian record to read, and they are therefore offering a different interpretation. Each of them is saying, "Based on my understanding of the Syrians, I think that Asad is not interested in peace and is only interested in the peace process." I, on the other hand, am saying that Asad was interested in, but not anxious about, making a very specific form of peace. Let's argue about it.

Pipes and Karsh's approaches are legitimate, but you will not find anyone on the liberal side of the spectrum making their argument. It happens to be a conservative argument. This raises another interesting issue. What happens when one writes scholarship in an honest and professional manner, and then people vulgarize or politicize it? Take the book by Shmuel Katz, *Battleground*. He rips through Bernard Lewis, Elie Kedourie, and others and vulgarizes them to say that there's no point in making peace with Muslims and Arabs. Scholars are in the public domain. They write their books and anyone can use them to promote their own interests. But certain arguments and theses are taken up either by the right wing or by the left wing. The Pipes version of Syrian intentions happens to suit the Golan settlers. They also like to argue that Asad doesn't want peace, because this is what they would like to believe. The center of their universe is the Golan Heights, and their question is, "How do we stay here?" If they can arrange "reality" around the argument that "Asad is not interested in making peace, therefore there will not be peace, therefore I can continue to live here," that's just fine for them.

BOI: This is the first book that you have written since you ceased being ambassador. Do you find that you are writing differently than you did prior to your government service? Do you write differently knowing that there will be a government censor reading your work?

Rabinovich: The main difference that I notice now is that I write more freely. Having worked a lot with the media in those years "liberated" me. I hope that I write better, more vividly. *The Brink of Peace* is a short account of a very powerful personal experience. I include portraits of the other negotiators. Part of the historian's work here is to recreate reality as well as possible, and I would like the reader to come away from the book actually feeling how it felt in the negotiating room.

The book will have both advantages and drawbacks. I intend to be fair-minded and decent, but I cannot claim to be objective, not just because I am involved in the story, or because it may be the most significant thing I have done in my life. I'll also be limited in the sense that I am not free to write everything. As a former government official, I have to submit the book for review, and there are also constraints that I impose upon myself. I don't intend to write a "kiss-and-tell" book; I don't believe in working with people and then turning around and spilling all the beans.

BOI: Based on your experiences in both the academic and political realms, do you see any gaps or underdeveloped areas of scholarly inquiry pertaining to Israeli foreign policy, and especially the peace process?

Rabinovich: I think there is much more to be done. I would love to see a biography of Elias Sasson. I know that Uri Bialer has written on early Israeli foreign policy, but much more needs to be done. We still haven't got a book, written by an Israeli, that covers the terrain that Ian Lustick covered on Israeli Arabs. I think we can take a fresh look at 1967. There is room for an Israeli treatment of Camp David, to go along with the definitive work by Quandt. I could go on and on; the good news is, there is plenty to be done.

Note

1. Essays in this volume by Zisser, Starr, Nsour, and Muslih contribute important first steps in this direction. For an indication of how far the terms of the debate have changed since 1948, see Nissim Rejwan, "Arab Writing on Israel: From Catastrophology to Normalcy," in *Books on Israel, vol. I*, ed. Ian S. Lustick (Albany: State University of New York Press, 1988), 91-105.

List of Works Cited

Ben-Simon, Daniel, *Another Land*, Tel Aviv: A. Nir, 1997. (Hebrew)

Bialer, Uri, *Between East and West: Israel's Foreign Policy Orientation, 1948–1956*, Cambridge: Cambridge University Press (LSE Monographs), 1990.

Blumenthal, Sidney, *Our Long National Daydream: A Political Pageant of the Reagan Era*, New York: Harper and Row, 1988.

———, *The Rise of the Counter-Establishment: From Conservative Ideology to Political Power*, New York: Times Books, 1986.

Caplan, Neil, "Israeli Historiography: Beyond the 'New Historians'," *Israel Affairs* 2:2 (Winter 1995), 156–72.

Caro, Robert A., *The Years of Lyndon Johnson*, New York: Knopf, 1982.

Friedman, Thomas L., *From Beirut to Jerusalem*, New York: Doubleday Anchor, 1990.

Jaffee Center for Strategic Studies, *Israel, the West Bank and Gaza: Toward a Solution* (Report of a JCSS Study Group),Tel Aviv: Tel Aviv University, 1989.

——, *The West Bank and Gaza: Israel's Options for Peace* (Report of a JCSS Study Group),Tel Aviv: Tel Aviv University, 1989.

Karsh, Efraim, *Fabricating Israeli History: The 'New Historians,'* London: Frank Cass, 1997.

Katz, Samuel, *Battleground: Fact and Fantasy in Palestine,* new updated ed., introduction by Menachem Begin, New York: Bantam, 1977.

Kedourie, Elie, *The Chatham House Version and Other Middle-Eastern Studies*, London: Weidenfeld & Nicolson, 1970.

Lustick, Ian, *Arabs in the Jewish State: Israel's Control of a National Minority*, Austin: University of Texas Press, 1980.

McCullough, David, *Truman,* New York: Simon & Schuster, 1992.

Makovsky, David, *Making Peace with the PLO: The Rabin Government's Road to the Oslo Accord*, Boulder: Westview Press, 1996.

Ma'oz, Moshe, *Asad: The Sphinx of Damascus: A Political Biography*, New York: Grove Weidenfeld, 1988.

Middle East Contemporary Survey (MECS), Tel Aviv: The Moshe Dayan Center, Tel Aviv University, and Boulder: Westview Press. Annually. Various editors.

al-Moualem, Walid, "Fresh Light on the Syrian-Israeli Peace Negotiations," interview with Ambassador Walid al-Moualem, *Journal of Palestine Studies* 26:2 (Winter 1997), 81–94.

Oz, Amos, *In the Land of Israel*, New York: Harcourt, 1983.

Pipes, Daniel, *Greater Syria: The History of an Ambition,* New York: Oxford University Press, 1990.

Quandt, William P., *Camp David: Peacemaking and Politics*, Washington DC: Brookings Institution, 1986.

——, *Decade of Decisions: American Policy Toward the Arab-Israeli Conflict, 1967–1976*, Berkeley: University of California Press, 1977.

——, *Peace Process: American Diplomacy and the Arab-Israeli Conflict since 1967*, Washington, DC: Brookings Institution, 1993.

Rabinovich, Itamar, *The Brink of Peace: The Israeli-Syrian Negotiations,* Princeton: Princeton University Press, 1998.

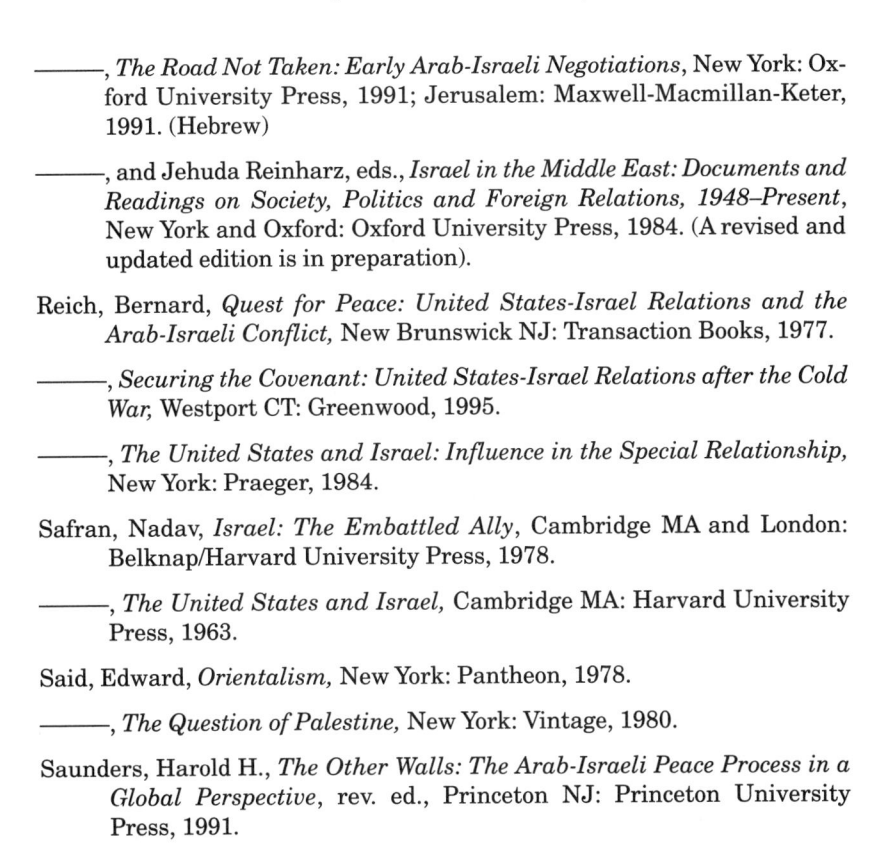

———, *The Road Not Taken: Early Arab-Israeli Negotiations*, New York: Oxford University Press, 1991; Jerusalem: Maxwell-Macmillan-Keter, 1991. (Hebrew)

———, and Jehuda Reinharz, eds., *Israel in the Middle East: Documents and Readings on Society, Politics and Foreign Relations, 1948–Present*, New York and Oxford: Oxford University Press, 1984. (A revised and updated edition is in preparation).

Reich, Bernard, *Quest for Peace: United States-Israel Relations and the Arab-Israeli Conflict*, New Brunswick NJ: Transaction Books, 1977.

———, *Securing the Covenant: United States-Israel Relations after the Cold War*, Westport CT: Greenwood, 1995.

———, *The United States and Israel: Influence in the Special Relationship*, New York: Praeger, 1984.

Safran, Nadav, *Israel: The Embattled Ally*, Cambridge MA and London: Belknap/Harvard University Press, 1978.

———, *The United States and Israel*, Cambridge MA: Harvard University Press, 1963.

Said, Edward, *Orientalism*, New York: Pantheon, 1978.

———, *The Question of Palestine*, New York: Vintage, 1980.

Saunders, Harold H., *The Other Walls: The Arab-Israeli Peace Process in a Global Perspective*, rev. ed., Princeton NJ: Princeton University Press, 1991.

Seale, Patrick, "Asad's Regional Strategy and the Challenge from Netanyahu," *Journal of Palestine Studies* 26:1 (Autumn 1996), 27–41.

———, *The Struggle for Syria: A Study of Post-War Arab Politics, 1945–1958*, London: Oxford University Press (Royal Institute for International Affairs), 1965.

Segev, Tom, *1949: The First Israelis*, New York and London: Free Press/Collier Macmillan, 1986; in Hebrew: *1949: ha-Yisra'elim ha-Rishonim*, Jerusalem: Domino, 1984.

Sela, Avraham, "Arab Historiography of the 1948 War: The Quest for Legitimacy," in *New Perspectives on Israeli History: The Early Years of the State*, ed. Laurence J. Silberstein New York: New York University Press, 1991, 124–54.

———, "Transjordan, Israel and the 1948 War: Myth, Historiography and Reality," *Middle Eastern Studies* 28:4 (October 1992), 623–88.

Shipler, David K., *Arab and Jew: Wounded Spirits in a Promised Land*, New York: Times Books, 1986.

Shlaim, Avi, *Collusion Across the Jordan: King Abdullah, the Zionist Movement, and the Partition of Palestine*, Oxford: Clarendon Press, 1988.

———, "Husni Za'im and the Plan to Resettle Palestinian Refugees in Syria," *Middle East Focus* ([Toronto], Fall 1986), 26–31; also in *Journal of Palestine Studies* 15:4 (no.60) (Summer 1986), 68–80.

Smith, Hedrick, *The Power Game: How Washington Works*, New York: Random, 1988.

Teveth, Shabtai, "The Palestinian Refugee Problem and Its Origins," *Middle Eastern Studies* 26:2 (April 1990), 214–49.

Touval, Saadia, *The Peace Brokers: Mediators in the Arab-Israeli Conflict, 1948–1979*, Princeton: Princeton University Press, 1982.

Part 1

History, Economics, and Politics

2. The Yishuv's Early Capabilities: Organization, Leadership, and Policies

Tobe Shanok

This essay questions some of the starting assumptions about the yishuv's image and self-perception as a completely helpless and leaderless community prior to, during, and immediately following the First World War. The author suggests that the integration of as-yet-untapped primary sources into the corpus of relevant research materials would result in a fundamentally new appreciation of the yishuv, with implications for Israeli society's contemporary self-perception and perception of "the other."

Efrati, Nathan, *From Crisis to Hope: The Jewish Community in Eretz Israel During World War I*, Jerusalem: Yad Yitzhak Ben-Zvi, 1991. (Hebrew)

Eliav, Mordechai, ed., *Siege and Distress: Eretz-Israel During World War I*, Jerusalem: Yad Yitzhak Ben-Zvi, 1991. (Hebrew)

Kolatt, Israel, ed., Vol. I. *The History of Eretz Israel Since the First Aliyah, The Ottoman Period*, Jerusalem: Daf Noy, 1989. (Hebrew)

Lissak, Moshe, ed., Vol. 2, Part I. *The History of the Jewish Yishuv in Eretz Israel Since the First Aliyah; The British Mandate Period*, Jerusalem: Daf Noy, 1993. (Hebrew)

Lissak, Moshe, Anita Shapira, Gavriel Cohen, eds., Vol. 2, Part II. *The History of the Jewish Yishuv in Eretz Israel Since the First Aliyah, The British Mandate Period*, Jerusalem: Daf Noy, 1994. (Hebrew)

*H*istory is the business of re-creating the past, but may be done in various ways and may be used for many purposes. This essay delineates the ways in which a number of contributors define the history of the Jewish community in Eretz-Israel (Palestine)—known as the yishuv—during World War I, and how these histories have been transferred to the public domain.[1]

A close look at five volumes reveals two visions of history. One concludes that the external world (outside of the Palestinian Jewish community) was the major factor of the community's survival, while the other view recognizes the participation of yishuv elements in its survival during the war. This raises important questions about how the Jews, inside and outside of Palestine, defined their role and identity during the war and how this history is being passed down. These are questions that go to the heart of the debate between "traditional" versus "new historians," and that are relevant to continuing research on the Jewish community in Palestine, Jewish history, and Diaspora Jewry.

This review of the five volumes chosen will focus on the main thesis of each, and how each relates its history and what kind of history is created. Another important issue is the usage of source material. Are the sources well-grounded, and do they span a wide range of opinions and ideas? Have any sources been left aside? Have information and material been integrated so as to form a broad scope of historical development? Does the work under review change previous assessments and conclusions? And, most importantly, how is this history being utilized in educating the younger generations?

The first part of this essay will delineate the main points of each volume, focusing specifically on those articles or books that deal with the organization, capabilities, and leadership of the yishuv during World War I. The second section will offer a comparison of the editors'/author's title and thesis to the contributors' conclusions, raising the questions: What may be learned from this comparison? Is there a binding theme throughout these volumes? The third section of the article will use examples from the five volumes as a basis for a critical analysis of the present state of early yishuv historiography. The discussion will center on internal yishuv development and why there needs to be a thorough reassessment and reevaluation of present historiography of the period. Concluding the essay, thoughts will be offered on some key issues that may bear reassessment and thus change perceptions of the yishuv's wartime capabilities.

While a number of books concentrate on the Diaspora Jewish communities and on Great Power politics, my ongoing research into yishuv history makes it evident that the First World War Jewish community merits a deeper and more intense scrutiny. During this period, the existence of institutions, bodies, policies, and leadership may be envisioned as a continuation of prewar development; this would help explain the community's survival and the rapid postwar organization of the yishuv under the British Mandate.

Main Themes

Mordechai Eliav's *Siege and Distress: Eretz-Israel During World War I* is a collection of articles which describes the Jewish community's dire situation during the war years (1914–18). The contributions cover topics on the demographic decline of the yishuv, medical aid and health issues, education, Great Power intervention on behalf of the Jewish community in Eretz-Israel, and military campaigns in Palestine. An epilogue consists of the translation of a Carmelite priest's wartime diary.

The three-volume series, *The History of the Jewish Yishuv Since the First Aliyah*, begins with the volume edited by Israel Kolatt (1990), which covers the late Ottoman prewar period, until 1914. There are five specific areas of interest: Great Power activities within the Ottoman Empire (political, economic, and cultural consequences of the powers' interests and competition within the crumbling empire); Arab-Zionist contacts; Zionist policy in Turkey; early experiments in settlement; and education.

The next two volumes in the series, edited by Moshe Lissak, Anita Shapira, and Gabriel Cohen (1993), relate the yishuv's political and social development during the British Mandate period. The first part is concerned with the external relations of the Jewish community; the "development of the network of political relations between the World Zionist Organization and the institutions of the yishuv and between the British Government, the Mandate Government, the Arab population and its organization" during the 1920s (Lissak, part 1, introduction, p. 23). The second part of this edited volume focuses specifically on internal factors within the Jewish community; "the process of the political party map of the yishuv, the splits within the movements and parties and the formation of a political culture" in the 1930s (ibid.).

These three volumes are included in this review not so much for their data, but for some of their specific conclusions about the yishuv's existence during the war period as a starting point for

British rule. In the single major article directly related to the topic, "The Question of Eretz-Israel During the First World War Period," Isaiah Friedman discusses the political development of Zionism and the role of the Great Powers in the yishuv's survival.[2]

In the final volume under review, *From Crisis to Hope: The Jewish Community in Eretz-Israel During World War I* (1991), Nathan Efrati discusses the organization of the yishuv from the beginning of the war in early 1914 (before the Ottoman government's secret treaty with Germany became public knowledge) until the British occupation of Palestine in late 1918. Efrati analyzes the impact of the war on the process of internal yishuv development and the attempts of various personalities to deal with the problems faced by the Jewish community. In addressing these issues, he examines internal, communal, diplomatic, financial, and organizational activities carried out by its leaders.

Intentions and Conclusions

There are two major factors that define historiographic works: first, the thesis that the writer chooses to convey and how this is transferred to the reader; and second, the source material that is utilized and how one evaluates its importance. In comparing the themes of the four edited volumes, it becomes apparent that there are discrepancies between some of the editors' introductions (theses) and the conclusions reached by some of the contributors.

The titles and introductions of the books set the tone and direction of this historiography. Whereas Eliav's title is *Siege and Distress*, Efrati uses the optimistic title *From Crisis to Hope*. These titles connote a particular historical direction that is followed through in the volumes' respective introductions. The three-volume series edited by Kolatt, Lissak, Shapira, and Cohen, maintains a more neutral title: *The History of the Jewish Yishuv in Eretz-Israel Since the First Aliyah*.

Beyond the titles of the chosen volumes, the central themes portray a mind-set of historical perceptions. Eliav opens his introduction to *Siege and Distress* with the following words: "You cannot have a more fitting title which defines the Jewish community's expression of misfortune than in that of 'Siege and Distress,' siege—from the outside and distress—from within" (p.11). The division of Eliav's first two topics illustrate this theme: part 1, the yishuv under siege, and part 2, the Great Powers' aid to the Jewish community in its dis-

The Yishuv's Early Capabilities

tress. He deals with the yishuv as a single unit, considering its distress as intense and all-pervasive. The yishuv's existence is saved by Great-Power intervention, actions that involved external elements.

This particular point is underlined in Isaiah Friedman's article "German and American Intervention Concerning the Subject of Exile from Jaffa in December 1914 and April 1917," where the author describes the survival of the Jews as "simply in the hands of Turkey and her ally, Germany" (p.171), as well as from American financial support: "And thanks to this aid [American warships bringing additional money] the yishuv survived" (ibid.).

But a number of contributors to this book portray a very different picture than that of the editor's introduction. In spite of the distressing situation of the yishuv, elements of leadership within the Jewish community, networking with outside help, used the opportunity of challenge and change during the war to gain authority over certain aspects of the yishuv's resources, molding them into a Hebrew national political/education system. Rahel Elboim-Dror, in her article "The War as an Opportunity to Conquer Hegemony in Education," takes as her point of departure the recognized phenomenon of leaders who use war situations to their advantage (in Eliav, pp. 49, 50, 51, 60). She then examines how some yishuv leaders utilized the war's uncertainties and changes in order to form an all-yishuv education system. She points to two crucial factors in the attainment of a national Hebrew educational system: leadership and money (pp. 53-54). Two points are relevant for this discussion. First, this changes the historical view from a sudden "Jewish miracle" occurring to one of sociopolitical phenomena based on financial strength as the key to political power. Second, we have the view that this phenomenon occurred during the war *within* the local Jewish communal leadership, and not just among external Zionist organization leaders. Another major point put forward by Elboim-Dror is that the emergency situation brought about cooperation among all sectors of the Jewish community working toward a common goal (p. 59).

Another piece that appears in Eliav's volume and that also points in the same direction of internal communal organization is Zvi Shiloni's article "Medical and Hospital Service in Jerusalem during the War." "A fact worthy of emphasis," writes Shiloni, "is the outstanding endurance of the Jewish medical facilities and hospitals in Jerusalem during the years of crisis and distress" (p. 83). While Ottoman and foreign medical teams and services collapsed under the strain, the Jewish sector in Jerusalem maintained its ability to work and even expanded its health and medical personnel and services.

This type of work could only proceed with organization, personnel, and money—all of which Shiloni claims were present within the Jewish community. "The strong and special support that the medical service and hospitals received from the *Jewish population and leadership in the city* and Jews in the Diaspora" (ibid., emphasis mine) was central to the ability of the medical services to overcome the crisis.

Further proof of the Jewish community's ability to organize itself emerges from the conclusions of other contributors to Eliav's volume who deal with fiscal and military matters in the yishuv. Efrati's article on Eliezer S. Hoofien, Yaakov Markovsky's piece on the yishuv's mobilization on behalf of the Ottoman army, and Yaakov Goldstein's article on the ha-Shomer organization and role in World War I all conclude, intentionally or not, that Jewish communal activities during the war were instrumental in forming the nucleus of a national Jewish entity in financial and security matters by the end of the war.[3] Efrati determines, in his study of the Dutch immigrant-banker, that Hoofien was a central figure in the financial survival of the community during the war and that he turned the Anglo-Palestine Bank into a central financial tool over and above its general purpose as a banking branch.[4]

Although both Eliav and Isaiah Friedman's articles in the Eliav collection concentrate on Great-Power intervention on behalf of the Jewish community as the key to yishuv survival, Friedman turns his thesis of the yishuv's physical deterioration upside down when quoting from a letter from Sir Reginald Wingate to the British Foreign Office dated 21 November 1917. He notes that, to the astonishment of the British forces arriving to occupy Palestine, the Jewish colonies (apart from Jaffa) were intact, and even Jerusalem was not seriously damaged.[5] This offers a view of the difference between perception and reality and strengthens the need for a reexamination of the yishuv's position during the war. Whereas both Friedman and Eliav support the thesis that the powers' intervention was the only means for communal survival, negating the existence of internal yishuv capabilities, other contributors point to the existence of internal Jewish communal activity and resources that have not been fully explored.

In contrast to the articles in Eliav's collection discussed above, the three-volume series edited by Kolatt, Lissak, Shapira, and Cohen brings to the fore a traditional view of a Jewish community completely divided, weak, devastated, and leaderless. This has some serious consequences for how one views the Jewish community, its organization, and its place in both Jewish and general history. Although Kolatt does not divide the essays in his volume, "The Ottoman Period," into sections of "Old" and "New" yishuv, the contributors use this dichotomy as a point of departure for their conceptualization of the yishuv. The Jewish community, at this point, was a multiethnic, multi-cultural mosaic, rather than a flat polarized conceptualization of Orthodox-Secular, or Old-New, entities. The latter tends to oversimplify the population's composition and distorts the complex cultural-ethnic networks within the community.

Unlike many previous researchers, Efrati in his book *From Crisis to Hope* is willing to consider and critically analyze source material that has been underutilized. He examines the influence of different groups within the yishuv upon each other, their relationship to the community as a whole as well as to the Arab-Jewish issue, and its influence upon Jewish communal activities. Instead of ducking the issues of population figures and the relationship of Jemal Pasha to the Jewish community, Efrati faces them squarely. He approaches the source material with care and when necessary utilizes novel approaches to unsolved questions. For example, even though Efrati realized that essential Ottoman source material on Jemal Pasha's relations with the Jews was not available, he attempted to draw some conclusions in that sphere by creatively examining Jemal's relations with other communities within the empire, as well as Ottoman relations with the powers.

Reassessment

In order to reexamine and reassess the yishuv's organization, leadership, and capabilities, it is necessary to revise the historiographic framework within which the yishuv has, until now, been viewed.

One of the aspects of Jewish communal organization that does not appear to have been fully linked to the development of an autonomous Jewish community is the transformation of the Ottoman "millet" system and its impact on communal organization. It was this structure, and the manner in which it was utilized by the Jewish community, which aided the Jews in slowly evolving a semi-autonomous communal framework with its own organization, leadership, and institutions separate from Ottoman government institutions.[6] It was through this framework that the communal organization could function independently during the war when local committees were formed to help relieve hunger, seek employment for refugees, and expand political and economic activities from within, undisturbed by the government.

A topic that has been a focal point for the view of a weak and divided community has been the determination of the Jewish community's population, or more correctly, the depopulation of Eretz-Israel by the end of the war. The figure of 56,000 Jews remaining in the yishuv has been used by many scholars as the starting point of the political and social reorganization of the yishuv during the British Mandate period.

There are reasons for hesitation about using the number 56,000, or any number, as a basis for the designation of the postwar yishuv population. There are various estimates of the prewar population (ranging from 85,000 to more than 100,000) upon which the postwar numbers are based. Uziel Schmeltz, in his article, "The Decreasing Population of Eretz-Israel" (in Eliav, pp. 17–47), questions the accuracy of this count of the Jewish community, because both the length of time taken (it took three years) and the inexperience of the census-takers resulted in critical errors in the calculations. Another glaring problem is the absence of birth and death records, which do not seem to have been factored in, and the lack of consideration given to population movements during the war.[7]

Additional problems arise when using the demographic figures registered by those who were alive at the time. Davis Trietsch's work (*Palæstina Handbuch,* 1911) predates the large Ottoman Jewish population movements during and following the Balkan uprising of 1912–13.[8] The latter, surprisingly, has not always been considered in the demographic calculations. Arthur Ruppin's figures may be suspect (and are strongly criticized by Justin McCarthy), since his position as head of the Palestine Office of the Zionist Organization (ZO) may have motivated him to show a large prewar immigration total (in order to showcase Zionist success) and to exaggerate wartime catastrophe (in order to maximize financial contributions to the yishuv).[9]

Even contemporary demographic studies by Kemal Karpat, Justin McCarthy, and Joan Peters are not without their problems. Karpat's article on Jewish population movements in the Ottoman Empire—although utilizing a large amount of Ottoman documentation and mindful of the Jewish population movements in the Balkans—ends in 1914, just before the outbreak of the war.[10] McCarthy's work is problematic in that he attempts to base the bulk of his work on birth and death rates—going back, readjusting the prewar demographic statistics in order to correct and recalculate wartime figures, but without taking into consideration changes and movements during the war.[11] Peters's work raises different problems. She expresses wariness of early statistics because they discounted, in her view, the presence of Jews in the area of Palestine; in addition, the soundness of her scholarship has been the object of some challenges.[12] While the work of the latter three overlap at various points, none of them completely covers all the elements of a demographic study, which should include births/deaths, emigration/immigration, Ottoman citizens and non-Ottoman residents, people who refused to register, and migrations within the Ottoman Empire. Furthermore, the populations being measured need to be clearly delineated within consistent geographic boundaries, something that many demographic studies of Eretz-Israel fail to do.

Further proof of the difficulty of establishing, with any real accuracy, the population of the yishuv during and at the end of the First World War may be realized through a careful perusal of the American Joint Distribution Committee (AJDC) papers, and the diary of Mordechai Ben-Hillel HaCohen.[13] Both sources clearly indicate that, due to the chaos that occurred during Jewish population movements in 1914 and 1917, time did not allow for any accurate counting of those who departed; nor was any record kept of those who returned. The very fact that these population movements are still being researched offers a clue to their importance in any proper reassessment of the development of the yishuv.

Questions arise not only as to how and on what basis this calculation of 56,000 was made, but why researchers have decided to base their conceptions of a weak and disoriented Jewish community on a computation that has not been thoroughly investigated or substantiated.[14] Since the wartime view of the yishuv has been conceptualized according to this questionable figure, the very assumption of a sharply depopulated community at the end of the war with an immediate postwar "formative " period under the British Mandate as the foundation of an all-yishuv organized political arena needs to be carefully reexamined.

Two additional documents add further doubt as to the validity of the presently used demographic figure of 56,000 for the postwar yishuv population. One document, dated 26 October 1917 in the David Yudelowitz files, is a hand-written estimate, in French, of the population of the Ottoman administrative district of Jerusalem.[15] The figure given for the Jews in the Ottoman Jerusalem administrative district area is 83,360, and does not include those who had moved to other administrative areas of the country. The other document is an unsigned handwritten plan for prospective development of the yishuv in the political and economic exigencies of the time. This document, dated 1917, in the Weizmann Archives available at Brandeis University, gives an account of the Jewish population as being 100,000 souls, but does not delineate in what specific geographical area.[16] The second document (possibly written by Weizmann himself) may have had a political motivation in showing a large Jewish population, but most importantly, these wartime sources, together with other material, help shift the basic assumptions of the yishuv's weakness and division to one of communal leadership and organization.

There have been some recent attempts to reassess existing population figures for Muslims, Christians, and Jews, taking into account some of the geographic oddities of the Ottoman administrative system, ethnic/religious breakdown of the communities, and wartime exigencies—with each researcher adopting a different line of reasoning. Those who have worked with Palestinian population data have had reservations of one kind or another about the accuracy of the Ottoman or Zionist records, both prewar and during the war. Some demographers have used the 1922 population census—carried out by the British Mandatory government and the first one considered to be substantially reliable—as a base-point from which to work backward in order to "correct" the previously accepted wartime and prewar population figures. This exercise seems questionable, in light of both wartime migrations and difficulties of internal communal organization, neither of which has yet been adequately studied.

Another common practice requiring reassessment is the dividing of the yishuv into "old" and "new" segments. For the most part, the delineation has been that the "old" yishuv lived on charity while the "new" yishuv residents were actively working to build a new society. Those in both the "old" and "new" yishuv, in fact a large percentage of the population, lived on money coming from outside Palestine. Whether it was from charitable or other contributions, the result was the same: neither the elderly nor the new immigrants could stand on their own feet financially.

Beyond this economic differentiation, there is a second, more seriously flawed underlying assumption: that members of the "old" yishuv in the four "holy" towns of Jerusalem, Safed, Tiberias, and Hebron were not involved in any activities of the community, that they had gone to Eretz-Israel only to pray and die, while the new immigrants were the backbone of the revitalization of the community. These traditional terms of *old* and *new* yishuv distort the perspective of the reader and build a false expectation of those who lived in specific areas, visualizing those in the "old" yishuv as elderly, dying people, and those in the "new" yishuv as young, vibrant individuals. This was simply not the case.

Within the documents of the period, divisions within the Jewish community in Eretz-Israel were usually characterized along five main lines: geographic, political, economic, religious, and ethnic—particularly when the writers were referring to progress or to problems within the community. These—rather than "old" or "new" yishuv—were the main reference-points for reports, articles, and speeches. But it appears that the division of "old" and "new" was utilized in order to highlight the progress of part of the community, as well as to emphasize issues of political contention between groups. Terminology became value-laden, maximizing the record of early Zionist achievement. The old-versus-new delineation also created or reinforced a divide between the First and Second aliyot, and between Ashkenazi ultra-Orthodoxy and Sephardi traditional Orthodoxy, on the one hand, and secular, East-European worker immigrants, on the other—emphasizing the positive contribution of this new immigrant blood.

An example of this may be found in the assumptions underlying Ruppin's program for the development and colonization of the yishuv in his book, *Three Decades of Palestine: Speeches and Papers on the Upbuilding of the Jewish National Home*.[17] We need to be aware of these subtle value-laden terms, and strive to use more neutral distinctions to characterize the yishuv's composition and development when discussing its strengths and weaknesses, its leadership and organization, as well as the contentious issues over which its leaders debated.

Another set of often-used terms that needs to be reexamined is that of *Zionist versus non-Zionist* as distinguishing those who supported the "new" yishuv from those who did not. During the war, as well as during the British Mandate, the so-called non-Zionist Jews were the financial backbone of the yishuv. Those who contributed money to their coreligionists did so not as "Zionists" or as "non-Zionists," but rather in answer to the age-old call of helping their fellow Jews, not specifically as Jews living in the Holy Land.[18]

The depiction of the ZO as one single monolithic body during the war is also questionable. In fact, over the duration of the war, the World Zionist Organization was split into four Diaspora centers: (1) Copenhagen, in neutral territory, collected information about the yishuv in Palestine; (2) Berlin, inside "enemy" lines, was the place where the Greater and Smaller Actions committees met and made decisions; (3) America, as the organization's temporary meeting place, was the center of fund-raising, passing information and channeling money to Palestine; while (4) the organization's London office was the center of Chaim Weizmann's activities and a propaganda post. The ZO was not a single entity, nor was Weizmann yet the sole leader, although he was acknowledged as one of the movement's leaders.[19] The organization was geographically dispersed and thus it is possible to view the success of the ZO only within the framework of a well-coordinated network, involving a wide assortment of politically active individuals with an acumen for executing unusually difficult tasks.

The approach of Jewish and Zionist historiography to the yishuv has been that Eretz-Israel is a unique, unifying element of the Jewish people throughout history, and that the yishuv's continued existence during the war was a product of this link through continued aid and support. By focusing on the yishuv through the prism of Jewish-Zionist history alone, the Jewish community becomes cut off from general surrounding events and from the various communities that helped shape the contours of the yishuv's development. Viewing the history of the yishuv as being molded in a vacuum, without direct relevance to its surroundings, is a concept that needs reexamination. Seen in this Jewish-Zionist light, the survival of the Jewish community comes across as a miracle, rather than as a phenomenon subject to the natural laws of cause and effect.

Current historiography regarding the early yishuv has been based upon the alleged divisiveness among groups within the Jewish community in Palestine that made it impossible for any community action or problem-solving leadership to arise. A fresh approach needs to be attempted that would view the community as a unit, searching for points of contact among prewar institutions and bodies that continued to function during the war. This new approach would also focus on the network of leaders who maintained a loose coalition among various groups and committees, and the search for consensus upon which to base decisions allowing the community to survive.

Looking closely at a number of the articles in the edited collections under review and at Efrati's monograph, as well as at additional source material, it appears evident that, although there were factions and divisiveness from within, there was also a mutual goal that overrode all other considerations: the survival and strengthening of the Jewish community. By combining and comparing the contents of a number of articles, a composite picture emerges of a Jewish community in transition and expansion, one able to withstand harsh conditions. A broader scope of source materials—for example, taken from the Nili group, the American Joint Distribution Committee (AJDC) files, and the newspapers of the period—and its integration into the present "traditional" material would offer a more nuanced and layered picture of the Jewish community, one that would yield a variety of comparisons and opinions. This would lead to a deeper understanding of the dissonance, individual dislikes, and decisions rendered within the Jewish community and the external networks that allowed the channeling of money into the yishuv and the transfer of information both ways. For example, the highest figure for funds brought into the yishuv during the First World War, according to published sources read by this author, was approximately $600,000—an amount that turns out, after archival research, to be greatly underestimated.[20] [See Table 1.] Consulting such new sources would allow a different view of the Jewish community to emerge, one that showed the capabilities of the internal Palestinian community leadership for organization and policy-making.

How can we explain the persistence of the "traditional" history of the early yishuv? Part of the answer emerges from Israel Kolatt's introduction to his volume. First, the contributors were requested to offer material that had already been published. Although he claimed that the volume contained new material indicating progress in research, this does not clearly come through in the contributors' pieces. The fact that this was to be an "educational" collection, proposed and funded by the Israel Ministry of Education and Culture, offers a clue as to the intent of the series as a tool for historiographic study. The Kollat and Eliav collections, published in the early 1990s, reflect the same historical perceptions that the two editors published in the 1970s.[21]

While some recent historiography has begun to point backward to yishuv development at the end of the 1920s (e.g., Shapira, "Political History of the Yishuv," pt. 2, chap. 1, in Lissak, Shapira, and Cohen), it is during the war years that the actual framework became more organized with a sense of communal effort. Selected articles in the Eliav collection and in Efrati's book have opened the door to a more serious reassessment of the capabilities of yishuv leadership and to its participation in communal activities during the war years.

The question is not so much, Which is "the" correct view?—but, What part does historical writing play in the education of youth and in framing a national consensus relating to present and future policies and projects? This has resonance as our present frames of reference

Table 1
Joint Distribution Committee Appropriations Sent to Palestine

Date of Appropriation	Voucher Number	Date Sent	Through Whom in America	To whom in Europe as Transfer Agent	Recipient Bank or Committee	Purpose	Amount	Acknowledged by
		Brought forward					$1,256,929.60	
Feb. 10, 1918	1,299	Mar. 1, 1918	Guaranty Trust Co.	Jewish Colonial Trust of London	Anglo-Palestine Co. Jerusalem	Gen.Rel. & Maint. of Soup Kitchens & Health Bureau	100,000.00	Hooflen's Report 4/9/18
" 10, "	1,357	" 5, "	Disb.Clark, State Dept.		Hadassah	Hadassah Medical Unit	100,000.00	
Jan 29, "	1,325	" 7, "	"					
Mar. 25, "	1,378	" 27, "	"	Amer.Charge D'Affair, Cairo		Rel. of Poale Zion	10,000.00	
" 25, "	1,403	April 12, "	"	Spanish Consul, Beyrouth	Spanish Consul,Beyrouth	Rel. of Jewish Amer. Citizens deported in British occupation	1,000.00	
	1,434	" 18, "	"	Diplomatic Agent, Cairo	Jack Mosseri & S.Hooflen	Charitable Inst. in Palestine	100,000.00	Zion Rel.Com. 5/31/18
May 6, "	1,478	May 11, "	"	U.S.Consul, Alexandria		Expense on account of Medical Supplies, S.S.Sterling	161.10	
July 25, "	1,827	July 31, "	"	Diplomatic Agent,Cairo	Jack Mosseri, S.Hooflen & Local Disb.Com.	Gen.Rel. & Maint. of Soup Kitchens	50,000.00	Zion Rel.Com. 5/31/18
Aug. 26, "	1,975	Aug. 26, "	J.D.C.Remittance Bureau	"	Jack Mosseri	"	60,000.00	Zion Rel.Com. 8/31/18
" 26, "	2,055	Sept.11, "	Disb.Clark,State Dept.	State Dept.		Rel.for Rabbis, Hebron Jaffa, Jerusalem	4,896.00	
Oct. 1, "	2,200	Oct. 7, "	Guaranty Trust Co.	Jewish Col.Trust Co.(London)	Zionist Commission	Gen.Rel. & Maint. Soup Kitchens	70,000.00	Zion.Commission Letter 8/24/19
" 1, "	2,248	" 11, "	Zion.Org. of America	"	"	Medical Unit in Palestine	70,000.00	
" 31, "	2,359	Nov. 6, "	Guaranty Trust Co.	"	"	Gen.Rel. & Maint. Soup Kitchens	100,000.00	
Dec. 5, "	2,617	Dec. 27, "	"	"	"	" for December	150,000.00	
" 5, "	2,741	" 30, "	"	"	"	Rel. Strauss & Dryfus Soup Kitchens	100,000.00	
Mar. 18,1919	3,555	Mar. 20,1919	"	"	"	Gen.for March & Apr. 120M Special for Matzoth 30M	32,000.00	
Apr.30, "	3,997	May 1, "	"	"	"	Gen.Rel.Jan.Feb.& May May, June, July & Aug. Straus	150,000.00	
" 30, "	4,103	" 12, "	"	"	"	Soup Kitchen 16 M Dryfus 16 M Health Bureau 8 M	160,000.00	
May 4, "	4,171	" 15, "	"	"	"	Ext.Rel.May 10M.Bedding & Clothing for orphans 60M for girls agricultural work, Jerusalem 5M	40,000.00	"
June 14, "	4,378	June 2, "	"	"	"	Gen.Rel.for June	75,000.00	"
" 9, "	4,857	July 4, "	"	"	"	Gen. Relief for July	70,000.00	"
							70,000.00	"
		Carried forward					$2,789,976.70	

Source: The American Jewish Joint Distribution Committee Archives

are not created in a vacuum but are molded over time, in a continuous process that is passed on through the national education system. The aim of history is to teach, and the role of historians is to frame the parameters of the history that is to be handed down and transferred. As "guardians of cultural heritage, ... [they may] train the mind, enlarge the sympathies and provide a much-needed historical perspective on some of the most pressing problems of our time."[22] This is accomplished through a process of critical assessment and reassessment of material with a willingness to break the barriers of past taboos in order to provide a broader perspective of historiographic material for educational purposes.

The "dual" histories—both traditional-Zionist and revisionist-reassessed—portrayed in these five volumes mark a point of departure and change in the field of yishuv historiography, particularly as new source material is added and as reevaluations of traditional material occurs, and as perceptions of the state, relations with Israel's neighbors, and the idea of Jewish continuity and its ties to the state evolve. There is a small but growing group of historians who understand the need to invigorate traditional history with a wider range of source materials and to sharpen our critical analysis in order to produce a more nuanced, layered, and integrated history. By doing so, historians may inculcate both a deeper self-awareness and an empathy with others, and may help to relate this history more effectively to present-day problems.

Notes

1. The terms *Eretz-Israel* and *Palestine* are used interchangeably as a geographic entity without political overtones.

2. Isaiah Friedman, "The Question of Eretz-Israel during the First World War," in Lissak, ed. *The History of the Jewish Yishuv in Eretz Israel*, chapter 1.

3. Yaakov Markovsky, "Mobilization of the Sons of the Jewish Community to the Turkish Army," ibid., 110; Nathan Efrati, "Eliezer S. Hoofien," ibid., 93; Yaakov Goldstein, "The Organization of ha-Shomer and its Function during World War I," 111–31.

4. Efrati, "Eliezer S. Hoofien," loc. cit.

5. Friedman, "German and American Intervention," ibid., 188.

6. Aaron Rodrigue, *French Jews, Turkish Jews: The Alliance Israelite Universelle and the Politics of Jewish Schooling in Turkey, 1860–1925*

(Bloomington: Indiana University Press, 1990), 32; Avigdor Levy, Introduction: "III. The Structure of the Jewish Community," and "V. Ottoman Jewry in the Modern Era, 1826–1923," in *The Jews of the Ottoman Empire,* ed. Avigdor Levy (Princeton NJ: Darwin Press, 1994), 42, 105.

7. There are some lists that contain names of deceased, but we have no way of knowing how complete they are. Also, it does not appear that birth records were integrated into the census.

8. Davis Trietsch, *Palæstina Handbuch* (Berlin: Judische Verlag, 1911).

9. Even while taking issue with some aspects of Arthur Ruppin's calculations and of the Ottoman records, Uziel Schmeltz nevertheless defends Ruppin's count (based partly on Ottoman census records) as being the closest available one to the truth.

10. Kemal Karpat, "Jewish Population Movements in the Ottoman Empire, 1862–1914," in *The Jews of the Ottoman Empire*, 399–421.

11. Justin McCarthy, "Jewish Population in the Late Ottoman Period," ibid., 375–96.

12. Joan Peters, *From Time Immemorial: The Origins of the Arab-Jewish Conflict over Palestine* (New York: Harper, 1984). For critiques, see Yehoshua Porath, "Mrs. Peters's Palestine," *New York Review of Books*, 16 January 1986, pp. 36–39; and Norman G. Finkelstein, "Disinformation and the Palestine Question: The Not-So-Strange Case of Joan Peters' *From Time Immemorial*," in *Blaming the Victim: Spurious Scholarship and the Palestine Question,* eds. Edward W. Said and Christopher Hitchens (London and New York: Verso, 1988), 33–69.

13. Reports by Albert Lucas in circulars dated 1 and 2 April, 4 May 1917, file 121 ("Synopses of Four Circulars Issued by the Central Evacuation Committee in Judea with Reference to the Evacuations from Jaffa, April 1917"), AJDC 1914–18, American Joint Distribution Committee Archives, New York; Mordechai Ben-Hillel HaCohen, *War of the Nations: An Eretz-Israel Diary, 1914–1918,* new ed. (Jerusalem: Yad Yitzhak Ben-Zvi, 1981), I: 47–53. (Hebrew)

14. Another means of counting the population could have been through a tally of lists drawn up for dividing food among the population, but these lists were not compiled throughout the yishuv.

15. CZA, Yudelowitz Files, A192/1121. This is consistent with the Jerusalem administrative delineation offered by Trietsch in his 1911 population figures.

16. Weizmann Archives, Brandeis University, Reel 21, File 338B.

17. Ruppin, *Three Decades of Palestine: Speeches and Papers on the Upbuilding of the Jewish National Home* (Jerusalem: Schocken, 1936), 35–65 ("A General Colonization Policy"), which emphasizes the need for young blood and financial support.

18. A large portion of financial aid went to the Jewish populations in Russia and Eastern Europe who were devastated and dislocated due to the war.

19. Chaim Weizmann was not formally appointed president of the World Zionist Organization until 1921, after the war. By 1917, he had been "catapulted by events, as well as by his own energy, talent, and ambition, to the position of primus inter pares within the World Zionist Organization's leadership on the continent." Jehuda Reinharz, *Chaim Weizmann: The Making of a Statesman* (New York: Oxford University Press, 1993), 397.

20. According to the papers of S. Hoofien and the AJDC, the sum channeled into the yishuv between 1914 and 1918 was approximately $2.5 million, not counting nearly another $1 million that continued to enter the community in the year immediately following the end of the war.

21. Mordechai Eliav, *Eretz-Israel and Its Yishuv in the 19th Century, 1777–1917* (Jerusalem: Keter, 1978); Israel Kolatt, *International Seminar on the History of Palestine and Its Jewish Settlement During the Ottoman Period:* "The Organization of the Jewish Population of Palestine and the Development of Its Political Consciousness Before World War I" (Jerusalem: Yad Yitzhak Ben-Zvi, 1970). (Both in Hebrew)

22. John Tosh, *The Pursuit of History: Aims, Methods and New Directions in the Study of Modern History* (London: Longman, 1984), 24.

3. The Transition to a Market Economy: The Road Half Taken

Ofira Seliktar

This essay provides a critical examination of Israel's still-unfinished, and still debated, transition from a socialist-Zionist to a market economy, focusing on privatization, government regulation, subsidization, and private investment. The author also analyzes the future of the Histadrut in a market economy and examines the underlying themes of state and statism in Israel. The essay stresses the need for a successful combination of political will, electoral support, and unified government strategy if further progress is to be made along the road to an efficient market economy.

Barkai, Haim, *The Lessons of Israel's Great Inflation*, Westport CT: Praeger, 1995.

Ben-Porat, Amir, *The State and Capitalism in Israel*, Westport, CT: Greenwood, 1993.

Elizur, Yuval, *The Shekel and the Olive Leaf: The Israeli Economy between War and Peace*, Haifa: Gestalit, 1992. (Hebrew)

Grinberg, Lev Louis, *The Histadrut Above All*, Jerusalem: Nevo, 1993. (Hebrew)

The Israeli Economy at the Threshold of the Year 2000. Organization and Efficiency in the Economy and Civil Service, Jerusalem: Jerusalem Center for Public Affairs, 1992. (Hebrew and English)

Kanari, Baruch, *Zionist and Socialist-Zionist Planned Economy*, Ramat Efal: Yad Tabenkin, 1993. (Hebrew)

Plessner, Yakir, *The Political Economy of Israel: From Ideology to Stagnation,* Albany: State University of New York Press, 1994.

Shalev, Michael, *Labor and the Political Economy of Israel,* Oxford: Oxford University Press, 1992.

Since the late 1980s, Israel has been making a slow and halting transition to a market economy. The hallmark of this process is privatization, defined here as a set of policies designed to curtail the size of the state's ownership in the economy by means of selling off publicly owned enterprises. Some, known as SOEs (state-owned enterprises), are owned directly by the government, whereas others are publicly or collectively owned bodies. The Histadrut (Israel's major trade union organization) owns a large number of such enterprises.

The transition to a market economy has generated a fierce public debate and a correspondingly large volume of scholarship. The books considered in this essay offer a wide range of views of the problems that led Israel to embrace market reforms and to analyze the obstacles to their implementation. At the same time, the books both reflect and contribute to the debate that has pitted the advocates of market economy and privatization against the defenders of the mixed-economy model offered by socialist-Zionism.

I

Israel is part of a large group of developing countries in which SOEs have been a dominant factor in the economy. The justification for opting for a strong public sector is based on a concept of development in which economic rationality has been generally subordinated to political needs. The heroic task of creating a Jewish state in Palestine prior to 1948 was seen as superseding economic considerations and, in turn, led to an exalted view of the state as the supreme instrument of political and economic will.

The model of the mixed economy that Israel adopted was based on the assumption that neither free enterprise nor pure socialism could produce a healthy state of economic being. The resulting compromises mandated that the state should, to a large extent, substitute for market mechanisms. Public-sector enterprises were put in control of the "commanding heights" and of other strategic sectors of the economy, in many cases by creating monopolies. An extensive regulatory system helped to correct the effects of market mechanism, enhancing the autonomy of the public sector.

The state improved its capacity to intervene by creating public financing institutions, nourished by the public capital generated through the generous financial support of world Jewry and the United States. Restrictive codes on private foreign investment and various limitations on foreign trade further extended the statist grasp on the economy.

Since its inception in the yishuv (prestate) period, the mixed economy model encountered periodical difficulties, but it was only after the economic slump following the 1973 war that it ran out of steam. Between 1973 and 1991 the economy did not grow and hyperinflation reached three digits in the mid-1980s. The ensuing stabilization program generated a national debate during which the system of public enterprises came under particular indictment. Two major criticisms were leveled against the public sector: that it was inefficient, and that it was not profitable. The case of the Histadrut-owned company Koor, which ran up tremendous deficits in the 1980s, and the near financial collapse of the kibbutzim and moshavim in the same decade were viewed as highly symptomatic in this context. The net transfer of credits from the state to the ailing public sector has been estimated in the billions of dollars, creating huge budgetary deficits. The farm bailout alone cost the state some $6 billion. The bank scandal exposed in the early 1980s, which forced the state to acquire controlling shares of all major banks at a cost of some $7.5 billion, fueled the controversy over the wisdom of the state's intervention in the economy.[1]

Responding to public criticism and to some American pressure, the government announced its plans to privatize the public sector. The program has been conducted at three different levels: privatization of government-owned industries and service companies, the sale of banks, and the sale of enterprises controlled by the Histadrut. Starting in the mid-1980s, the government instituted a number of measures to facilitate the process. It created the Government Companies Authority and appointed a number of American firms, including First Boston Corporation, to oversee the divestiture program.

However, the pace and scope of the privatization effort has been disappointing. Between 1986 and 1992, only about $1.5 billion worth of state-owned companies had been sold. The Labor government of Yitzhak Rabin, which defeated the Likud-led coalition in 1992, promised to accelerate the process and announced that it would sell billions of dollars worth of shares in state-owned companies. In 1993 about $1.3 billion worth of companies were sold, but between 1994 and the end of Labor tenure in mid-1996 privatization contributed only $925 million. Upon his election, Benjamin Netanyahu promised to lead a "Thacherite revolution." The government announced plans to establish a Privatization Trust Fund that would encourage indigenous business investors equity participation in the privatized firms. But the beleaguered Likud government was even less successful than its predecessor.

All in all, between 1985 and 1996, some $3.6 billion worth of companies were sold, only a fraction of state holdings. The majority of the privatized companies are small or middle sized, while most of the large monopolistic corporations—such as the utilities, telecommunication, refineries, Israel Chemicals, the national air carrier El-Al, the state shipping company Zim, and Israel Aircraft Industry—are still awaiting action. Fourteen years since the government effectively acquired control of the major banks, it has yet to sell even minority control in the Ha-Poalim, Leumi, or Discount banks. The sale of some SOEs, notably the Paz Oil company, bought by an Australian businessperson and resold to two defunct Polish financiers, was severely criticized. Even the most optimistic observers find Israel's privatization slow and arduous.[2]

A growing literature has revealed that successful privatization depends on a number of factors: the economic culture of a country, the strength of key economic players, and the "will" of the state.[3] The books reviewed here provide a valuable context in which to examine how each of these factors affects the privatization process in Israel.

Data on Privatization of State-owned Companies 1986–1995/96

Period	Receipts from Privatization (in million dollars)
1986–1990	427.4
1991–1992	1,025.7
1993	1,241.2
1994	207.5
1995	536.0
January–May 1996	181.5
Total	3,619.3

Source: Katz, *Privatization in Israel and the World* (Tel Aviv: Pecker Publishers, 1997), p. 213. (Hebrew)

II

The term *economic culture* is used by economists to describe the way in which societies view their economies. Yakir Plessner defines it as "the complex of attitudes members of a society develop toward the economic environment in which they operate." People acquire the opinions and information to make political and economic choices "through a learning process, which is very much determined by the economic environment in which people grow up," and conditioned by the experience that they encounter (p. 79).

Plessner goes on to describe the Israeli economic environment as "contrived" and "artificial," since the government drives a *wedge* between the "productive sector and the consumer" (p. 127). Plessner, a former deputy director of the Bank of Israel, calls Israel "a laboratory case for the study of inefficient economies" and blames the artificial environment on the contradictory imperatives of socialism and nationalism in the formative years of the state. Socialism was expected to eradicate all national differences, rending a national solution to the Jewish problem all but superfluous (p. 3). At the same time, socialist-Zionist thinkers like Nachman Syrkin, Ber Borochov and A. D. Gordon argued that Jews could not be "redeemed" through socialism until they changed their occupational structure that was top-heavy with small-time commerce and finance. In the view of these socialist-Zionist ideologues, the unhealthy "upside-down" occupational pyramid that developed in the Diaspora could be normalized only in a national setting (pp. 95–97).

According to Plessner, the fusion of nationalism and social redemption through manual labor—a formula widely adopted in the yishuv period—had produced from the very beginning contrived economic behavior. He lists its main characteristics as the primacy of noneconomic consideration, the denial of economic reality, and the inefficient use of economic resources. Plessner charges that, in their pursuit of the Socialist-Zionist agrarian Utopia, the leaders of the yishuv forced a largely urban population into a nonprofitable farm economy. They even pressured the marginally profitable private farmers of the first aliyah to employ Jewish workers instead of Arabs, thus forcing the colonists to behave in an uneconomic fashion (pp. 99, 154).

In offering a scathing description of socialist-Zionism, Plessner follows in the footsteps of other academic and lay critics, notably Baruch Kimmerling, Daniel Doron, Ezra Sohar, and Oded Yinon. In his pioneering study, Kimmerling focused on the "conflict between building a society and what appeared to be rational economic behavior" in Palestine.[4] Doron railed against the utopian nature of the Palestinian economy and called Zionism and socialism a "deadly mix."[5] Sohar and Yinon argued that, early on, the Histadrut developed the theory that conditions in Palestine would be not only inimical to profit-making but would require permanent aid from abroad. From these modest philosophical beginnings, the concept of a "supported deficit economy" became the guiding light of Israeli economic thinking.[6]

Plessner is one of the first critics of socialist-Zionism to demonstrate how this ideology affected the contemporary economic culture. Plessner holds that the "idea that business enterprise should serve as instruments for the attainment of national economic objectives" has continued to guide the economic culture of Israel. The absence of market discipline embedded in such thinking has created a wedge between effort and reward and has encouraged state relief from personal responsibility. The former hurts economic motivation and the latter teaches individuals (and firms) that they would be "bailed out in case of difficulties" arising from their own actions (pp. 80–81, 90–91).

It is easy to see how these deeply held attitudes make the Israeli political culture hostile to privatization. At its core, the market economy rests on a causal relationship between effort and reward and is underpinned by beliefs in personal responsibility. Risks are borne by individuals and firms and the government is not expected to underwrite most types of economic outcomes, even if they fail. The Conference on Privatization, a major effort to analyze the problem of divestiture sponsored by the Jerusalem Center for Public Affairs, deals with these themes. The conference participants emphasize that aversion to risk-taking among wide sections of the society has hurt the process of privatization. In their view, ideological concerns about the alleged evils of a market economy have been even more of a hindrance (*The Israeli Economy*, p. 29, Hebrew text).

But privatization and the promise of a more competitive economy have mobilized others to defend the economic culture of socialist-Zionism. Kanari, the author of a project sponsored by Yad Tabenkin, a research institute of the kibbutz movement, criticizes those who equate socialism with Utopia and is scornful of the claim that the collapse of the Soviet Union discredited the socialist system. He defends the choice of socialism in Palestine as both rational and grounded in the economic praxis of European countries after World War I. According to Kanari, the special character of the Jewish people and the limited absorptive capacity of Palestine made a centrally planned, state-owned economy a necessity. He calls the settlement policy of the yishuv "original and innovative" and points out that, far from being utopian dreamers, Syrkin and other socialist-Zionist leaders engaged in detailed economic calculations of the agricultural and industrial needs for absorbing millions of Jews (pp. 18–19, 55, 117, 124).

Central to Kanari's defense of a statist economy is his assertion that the Jews who arrived in Palestine—even in the mass immigrations of the fourth and fifth aliyot—preferred a noncapitalist environment. By contrast, those who could thrive in a market economy emigrated to the United States or to other Western countries. As a result, all efforts to develop the yishuv in a capitalist fashion failed. In Kanari's view, this process of philosophical self-selection has continued into the period of statehood and has dictated state intervention in the marketplace (p. 15).

Kanari justifies the continuation of a planned socialist economy in Israel in terms of security and absorption needs, including the recent waves of Russian immigrants. Although the author does not discuss market economy per se, his conclusions attest to the fear that market mechanisms will impede the continuous nation-building effort of Zionism. While Kanari's defense of socialism is normative, others have a more empirically grounded belief that Israel is destined to provide shelter for Jews who do not share the capitalist ethos. It is common knowledge that the relatively large Jewish emigration from Israel (estimated at more than half a million since 1948) opted for the relative affluence of Western market economies over a national attachment. While some chose to portray those who stay as "nationalists," it is equally plausible that such Israeli Jews may stay because they are less enamored of market competition.

Significantly, both views of the economic culture of Israel bode ill for the future of the privatization effort. If, as Plessner asserts, Israelis have come to expect the state to shelter them from market risks, public support for privatization will be limited. Similarly, if Kanari's postulate that Israeli Jews are philosophically and psychologically inclined to live a relatively sheltered economic existence is correct, the effect will be the same. Rather than welcoming the opportunities of privatization, they may feel deprived of the benefits of public ownership and state intervention. Either way, the economic culture in Israel is expected to throw considerable political roadblocks in the path of privatization and to legitimize the efforts of those who would like to derail it.

III

Theoretical studies suggest that in order to successfully fight opponents of privatization, governments need to consider what one expert calls "the political logic of privatization." When privatization is large in scope, Mariusz Mark Dobek argues, its execution amounts to promoting collective political action. According to rational-choice theory that deals with collective action, in such situations there is a widespread "free-rider" problem. In a nutshell, rational choice theory postulates that individuals will welcome the long-term benefits of privatization, and especially the higher standards of living associated with Western market economies. However, few are willing to pay the immediate costs of giving up job security and the welfare provisions built into the public-sector economy. Public enterprises normally operate in a noncompetitive environment and, even if they are grossly inefficient, can count on government bailouts to stay afloat. Privatization thus creates an immediate threat to the workers and is opposed by labor unions, which have become the ultimate "free rider."[7]

Breaking the resistance of the labor unions is especially difficult in Israel because of the power of the Histadrut. The Histadrut, the General Organization of Workers in the Land of Israel, was founded in December 1920 and claims some three quarters of all wage earners as members. It is involved in some 85 percent of all labor negotiations. Unlike other trade unions, the Histadrut is also a large-scale public-sector employer. Through its holding company, Hevrat Ovdim, the Histadrut has controlled a large number of public enterprises such as the Koor Group, the Solel Boneh Group, and a large number of financial institutions, including Bank Ha-Poalim, the Ha-Sneh Insurance Corporation, and pension-provident funds. In addition, the Histadrut operates the largest health plan in Israel, the Kupat Holim Klalit.[8]

A number of authors focus on the ability of the Histadrut to dictate economic policies to the government. Lev Louis Grinberg (pp. 13, 20, 30, 61, 221) and Michael Shalev (p. 194) both agree that, unlike in other democracies, the Histadrut in Israel is uniquely powerful. They attribute this power to the role that the Histadrut played in blocking Arab labor from accessing the developing economy of the yishuv. The "Jewish-only" labor union was a convenient way to institutionalize the principle of Hebrew labor (*avoda ivrit*), and as Grinberg put it, "to bring a total separation between Arabs and Jews" (p. 13). A Jewish economy was viewed as essential to the process of nation-building and a framework through which the social redemption of the immigrants could be achieved.

But the Histadrut's contribution to creating an ethnically separate economic entity has come at a price. Grinberg argues that the perceived need to fight Arab-driven market forces enshrined the principle of "centrality of politics over economics" (p. 23). It led to what Shalev describes as a "labor-movement economy," in which market competitiveness is shrouded in a complex system of wage linkages and where indexation protects citizens against inflation (p. 194). What is more, after independence, the trade union came to compete with the state in running the economy in an arrangement that Kanari calls "the equivalency between statism and Histadrut" (p. 128).

Grinberg and Shalev point out that sovereignty unleashed a bitter struggle between the state and the Histadrut elites. According to Grinberg, Israel's first prime minister, David Ben-Gurion, who became convinced in the late 1950s that some economic relaxation was necessary, resented the fact that the Histadrut blocked even modest market reforms. While Ben-Gurion cannot be described as a free-market convert, Grinberg (p. 77) claims that his campaign to promote statism (*mamlachtiut*) was nevertheless a thinly veiled effort to curtail the "Frankenstein-like" power of the trade union. He argues that the prime minister used the infamous "Lavon Affair"—the ill-conceived plan by Israeli intelligence to bomb American and British targets in Egypt in 1954—to settle scores with Pinhas Lavon, the leader of the Histadrut elite. Ben-Gurion apparently knew about the plot in 1954, but waited until 1960 to implicate Lavon, who had been defense minister at the time of the botched plan (pp. 92–94).

Even more important is Grinberg's revelation that in 1964 the government toyed with the idea of mounting a frontal assault on the Histadrut. The option of triggering planned unemployment or of importing foreign workers was discussed at the highest levels. Thus, the 1965-67 recession was either induced or, at the very least, the government refused to end a naturally developing downturn through conventional Keynesian measures. While one can only speculate what the outcome of such a struggle might have been, the Six-Day War of 1967 changed the situation in an unexpected way. Grinberg (p. 209) and Shalev (p. 68) argue that the influx of Arab labor from the territories conquered in 1967 restored a certain amount of market rationality to the Israeli economy; the Arabs worked for very low wages, enabling the Histadrut to protect the overblown salary and benefit structure of the Jewish workers. As

Shalev puts it, in a binational community what normally prevails is "socialism in one nation" (p. 69).

The Six-Day War provided only a temporary relief in the struggle between the state and the Histadrut. The collective bargaining, the economy-wide "framework agreements" (negotiated every two years for each economic sector), and the cost-of-living-allowances (COLAs), a prominent feature of the Israeli economy, have contributed to periodical inflations. However the effects of the 1973 war and the fact that Likud, which came to power in 1977, was even less successful in controlling Histadrut's demands triggered a wave of inflation that plagued Israel for more than a decade. In his detailed study of the "Great Inflation," Haim Barkai (pp. 7, 11) proceeds on the undoubtedly justified assumption that the hyperinflation—which reached three digits in the mid-1980s—was part of a chronic cycle of inflations that had first manifested themselves in pre-1948 Palestine. Inflation was acute in the first years of the state, followed by a relatively stable period from the mid-1950s through the 1960s. Still, between 1949 and 1971 the consumer price index rose by some 560 percent.

While Barkai does not believe that the entire inflationary cycle can be explained in terms of "wage push" factor, he notes that "the wage setting procedures in the highly unionized Israeli labor market and the institutional setup, which involves the government employers and the Histadrut," were a contributing factor, along with two-year contracts and COLAs. He blames these populist "forward-looking" social-policy demands for forcing the government's hand. The ultimate cost of such inflationary pressures is a distorted wage-and-price structure and a "persistent misallocation of labor capital" (pp. 21, 202, 207).

As already noted, the shock of hyperinflation led to a reevaluation of the doctrine of the mixed Israeli economy. A stabilization program was started on 1 July 1985, less than a year after Likud and Labor formed a National Unity government. Yet, as expected, the Histadrut successfully used its considerable power to hinder the divestiture process. From the perspective of the trade union, obstructionism and "free-riding" make perfect sense, not the least because labor costs in Histadrut-owned firms (and the public sector in general) are higher than in the private economy.[9] Since the public-sector unions provide the Histadrut with most of its leverage against the government, the struggle against privatization has become the focal point of its activity.

The Histadrut-led general strike in late December 1996 put the government of Benjamin Netanyahu on notice that his "Thacherite revolution" may be in trouble. The newly invigorated trade union has also tried to undermine some early divestiture efforts: at the privatized Haifa Chemicals, the Histadrut paid the wages of workers striking against a new salary structure.[10] While the Histadrut agreed to sell off some of its troubled Koor companies, it has been fighting a rearguard action to slow down the overall momentum toward privatization. For instance, in July 1997 the trade union backed a strike by 6,000 Bezek workers who were protesting the sale of 12.5% of the company shares to Merrill Lynch. Some 60,000 workers at ten major government-owned companies, including El-Al, the utility company, and defense industries, supported the Bezek employees. The one-day walkout shut down the airport, disrupted telephone services, internet connections, and even curtailed stock exchange trading.

IV

The problem of overcoming strong "free-riding" foes of privatization has been analyzed within the context of theories of state. One popular theory, known as corporatism or neocorporatism, deals with countries where the relations among state, labor unions, and employers are part of a larger social compact. Rather than exposing itself to the vagaries of the market, the corporate or neocorporate state seeks to create a controlled economy as a way to guarantee political stability. P. C. Schmitter, a leading authority on corporatism, developed this model to describe the political economy of Latin America, among others.[11]

Using Schmitter's model, Grinberg[12] and Shalev make a convincing argument that the Israeli state has sacrificed true economic competition on the altar of nation-building and on its relations with the trade unions. But, while this comparison has many merits, it does not explain why Israel could not follow the example of former corporatist and neocorporatist states that have made rather successful transitions to a market economy. Some, like Chile and Argentina, have been hailed as models for such a transformation. To understand Israel's failure to divest its state enterprises, it is necessary to consider what privatization experts call the "will" of the state.

According to traditional theories, what gives the state the ability to implement a policy opposed to the interests of powerful social groups is state autonomy.[13] But the collapse of mixed and socialist economies in the 1980s offers an alternative explanation. For most developing countries a major factor in the decision to sell SOEs was the need to reduce fiscal pressures. To finance the money-losing enterprises, most of the governments had to borrow on the international markets. At the beginning of the 1980s there was a downturn in the terms of trade of most of these states and their indebtedness increased dramatically. Pressed by international lenders and faced with default, governments had to summon the "will" to embrace a more liberal market philosophy.

Scholars note that in order to qualify for loan rolling (a form of loan consolidation) or debt forgiveness, a large number of developing countries had to submit to the stringent market conditions imposed by the International Monetary Fund, the World Bank, and private lenders. It is particularly remarkable that the "will to divest the state in favor of the private sector"—as two observers put it—transpired within a few short years. By the mid-1980s, most of the notoriously debt-ridden economies in Latin America and elsewhere were on the capitalist mend.[14]

Ironically, Israel's relatively easy access to nonmarket types of foreign capital has undermined the state's "will" to adopt market discipline. A number of authors call attention to the fact that, unlike other states, Israel has always enjoyed substantial capital transfers with few strings attached. Yuval Elizur points out that much of this money, known as unilateral transfers, is in the form of American grants and contributions from world Jewry. In the early days, the state's deficit spending was underwritten by reparations payments from Germany. What is more, Elizur decries the fact that these unilateral transfers have enabled the government to increase the public sector at the expense of the private one (p. 31).

Appealing to Jewish businesspeople to invest in Israel is another unorthodox way of attracting capital. Of course, such "charitable investments" have a long history, going back to Baron Edmond de Rothschild's purchase of land for immigrants of the first aliyah at the turn of the century. More contemporary efforts included the Jerusalem Conference in 1968, which sought to capitalize on the wave of Six-Day War enthusiasm to attract Jewish venture capital, or the high-profile dealings of the ill-fated British financier Robert Maxwell. However, as Elizur argues, both unilateral transfers and private, albeit "charitable," investments are highly detrimental to developing a market economy. He quotes a leading Israeli industrialist to the effect that "in order for the private sector to be rich the government needs to be poor" (pp. 14, 21, 45–46).

Plessner (p. 117) charges that these unilateral transfers are a "major anomaly" in the Israeli economy. He maintains that such transfers distort market rationality and contribute to the "contrived" economy of the Jewish state. They enable the government to finance deficits generated by the bloated and inefficient public sector. Barkai (p. 31) and Shalev (p. 309) likewise harshly denounce the impact of such net inflows of funds. The participants of the Privatization Symposium found that, unlike countries in Central and South America and Eastern Europe, Israel has never faced an absolute economic crisis. Hence, "the Israeli government has not decided, on its own accord, to initiate radical change such as reordering priorities and promoting free markets and increasing privatization" (*The Israeli Economy*, p. 63, English text).

Other experts agree with the conclusion that unilateral transfers saved Israel from a real debt crisis and numbed her "will" to privatize. An economist with the U.S. Treasury Department charges that this infusion of capital—running into billions of dollars since 1948—has enabled Israel to indulge "in forty years of perverse economic policies." He argues that the Likud victory in 1977 did not change the habit; rather than instituting market reform promised before the election, the weak Begin government "took the large increase in foreign aid that followed the Camp David agreement and used it to buy political support."[15]

Another critic contends that these timely unilateral transfers—even if they were temporary, like the German reparations—created an impression that every fiscal emergency can be somehow met: "a solution to the ever growing financial problems had almost always appeared in time." Worse, it enabled the government to disregard the dire warning of impending economic disaster and created the impression that the country could proceed as usual. Still, in his opinion, such national bailouts are costly in the sense that they resulted in postponing the solution to the deep structural problems of the economy.[16]

Indeed, according to these and other observers, the transfusion of foreign capital has enabled the Israeli government to sustain the large bureaucracy that runs the public sector. The Privatization Symposium points out that state bureaucrats who do not run businesses as efficiently or profitably as private owners will resist any serious efforts to reform. Many officials oppose privatization because it reduces their authority and opportunities for patronage, a factor that is especially important in Israel's coalition government. For instance, when the small corporation Massof Mitanim was sold, nineteen governmental bodies registered their protest (*The Israeli Economy*, p. 61, English text and p. 29, Hebrew text).

V

The books reviewed here have offered good insights into the complexities of the privatization process in Israel. What makes reform so difficult is the synergistic nature of the three major obstacles—the economic culture, the free-riding of the Histadrut, and the absence of state "will." Since the state is able to finance much of the deficit spending without incurring the type of market discipline faced by other countries, it has no incentive to overcome the resistance of the trade union and other opponents of capitalism. Indirectly, foreign bail-outs have sustained the economic culture that expects the state to shelter the individual from the vagaries of a market economy.

What is more, the issue of whether Israelis should be exposed to market discipline in the first place has been hotly debated. The normative strictures of early Zionism still exert a strong hold on the economic beliefs of the society. While some feel that Jews should continue to strive for socialism on ideological grounds, others fear that patterns of immigration and emigration have left Israel saddled with Jews who do not thrive in a market economy. Ironically, the supply of cheap Arab labor since 1967 has helped Jewish employees to take the sting out of their professed socialist life-style.

An important canon of privatization emphasizes the need to create a momentum in support of divestiture. As the successful British experience shows, such a momentum involves a coherent privatization strategy and a series of carefully timed sales to impress upon the public that the program can work. To overcome the free-rider problem, the government must bypass the labor unions, while offering key groups of potential supporters tangible benefits.[17]

None of the authors is optimistic that such conditions can be created in Israel any time soon. On the contrary, they complain about the piecemeal and haphazard character of the sales and the frequent and confusing changes in the rules. They lament the poor culture of governing and management in the public sector and argue that privatization can only succeed if there is a radical change in these deep-seated habits (*The Israeli Economy*, pp. 2, 111, Hebrew text).

However, those who would like to see the process succeed point out that, in order to compete in the global economy, Israel would be forced ultimately to adopt a market discipline. According to a number of surveys, foreign companies listed Israel's socialist economy as a major deterrent to investment (*The Israeli Economy*, pp. 62–63, English text). International competitiveness through exports has also been spurring market forces. The emerging high-tech sector is, by and large, private and the least likely to be unionized. Ultimately, the growing integration into the global economy may create the momentum that Israel needs in order to travel the full road to privatization.

Notes

1. The bank scandal started when the Histadrut-owned Bank Ha-Poalim inflated the price of its shares by having other Histadrut companies buy them. Soon other banks began coordinating the manipulation of their shares, bidding up prices to highly unrealistic levels. The scheme collapsed on 6 October 1983, when the public tried to redeem their bank stocks. All in all, the holders demanded over $7 billion—a third of all savings in the country. The government was forced to promise to buy back all the bank shares and to redeem them within five years. By 1984 the government acquired controlling shares of most of the country's banks and promised to privatize them soon after. Barry Chamish, *The Fall of Israel* (Edinburgh: Canongate, 1992), 199–203.

2. Shlomo Eckstein, Ben-Zion Zilberfarb, and Shimon Rozwitz, "The Process of Privatization of State-Owned Companies in Israel. A Survey and a Prediction," *Rivaon le-Kalkala* (May 1993), 30–47 (Hebrew); Yitzhak Katz, *Privatization in Israel and the World*, Tel Aviv: Pecker Publishers, 1997. (Hebrew)

3. Mariusz Mark Dobek, *The Political Logic of Privatization. Lessons from Great Britain and Poland* (Westport CT: Praeger, 1993), 1–7; O. Bouin and Ch.-A. Michalet, *Rebalancing the Public and Private Sectors: Developing Country Experience* (Paris: Development Center of the Organization for Economic Co-Operation and Development, 1991), 11–72; Eliot Berg and Mary M. Shirley, *Divestiture in Developing Countries* (Washington DC: World Bank, 1987), 1–20.

4. Baruch Kimmerling, *Zionism and Economy* (Cambridge MA: Schenkman, 1983), 14.

5. Daniel Doron, "Zionism and Socialism: A Deadly Mix," *Moment Magazine,* April 1992, 36–41, 50.

6. Ezra Sohar and Oded Yinon, "Israel's Economy: Legacy of the 1920s," *Midstream*, February–March 1991, 26–29.

7. Dobek, *Political Logic of Privatization*, 4–5, 15.

8. Haim Barkai, "Fifty Years of Labor Economy: Growth, Performance, and the Present Challenge," *Jerusalem Quarterly* 50 (Spring 1989), 81–109.

9. Ibid.

10. Peter Hirschberg, "The Workers Fight Back," *Jerusalem Report*, 6 February 1997, 16–18.

11. Philippe Schmitter, *Interest Conflict and Political Change in Brazil*, (Stanford: Stanford University Press, 1971); and "Still the Century of Corporatism," *The Review of Politics* 39 (1974), 85–131.

12. Lev Louis Grinberg, *Split Corporatism in Israel* (Albany: State University of New York Press, 1991), 19–37.

13. Theda Skocpol, "Bringing the State Back In: Strategies of Analysis in Current Research," in *Bringing the State Back In*, eds. Peter Evans, D. Rueschemeyer, and Theda Skocpol (Cambridge: Cambridge University Press, 1985), 3–27.

14. Bouin and Michalet, *Rebalancing the Public and Private Sectors*, 109–10.

15. Bruce Bartlett, "The Crisis of Socialism in Israel," *Orbis* 35:1 (Winter 1991), 53–68.

16. Rafael N. Rosenzweig, *The Economic Consequences of Zionism* (Leiden: E. J. Brill, 1989), 228.

17. Dobek, *Political Logic of Privatization*, 119.

4. Israel as a Liberal Democracy: Civil Rights in the Jewish State

Ilan Peleg

This essay examines the argument that Israel is a "democratic" regime by focusing on the civil rights of its citizens in four areas: the constitutional question, the Arab question, state-religion issues, and foreign affairs. The author challenges certain axiomatic assumptions by arguing that the label "ethnocentric republican order," rather than "liberal-democratic regime," best describes Israel of the 1990s.

Barak-Erez, Dafna, ed., *A Jewish and Democratic State,* Tel-Aviv University, School of Law, 1996. (Hebrew)

Shapiro, Yonathan, *Politicians as a Hegemonic Class: The Case of Israel,* Tel-Aviv: Sifriat ha-Poalim, 1996. (Hebrew)

Troen, S. Ilan, and Noah Lucas, eds., *Selected Essays from Israel: The First Decade of Statehood,* Albany: State University of New York Press, 1995.

Yiftachel, Oren, *Watching Over the Vineyard: The Example of Majd al-Korum,* Ra'anana: The Institute for Israeli Arab Studies, 1997. (Hebrew)

The nature of Israel's political regime, today and in the formative era, is increasingly debated among scholars. Some observers of Israel's public life *assume* that it is fully democratic. In the opening sentence of the preface to Dafna Barak-Erez's edited book, the late dean of Tel-Aviv University's School of Law, Ariel Rozen-Zvi, states categorically: "The State of Israel is a democratic state." All he offers by way of evidence is his declaration: "This is the way its citizens view it, and this is how it is treated by most of the states of the world" (p. 5). Yet, Avigdor Levontin, one of Israel's senior jurists, argues in the same volume that the gap between Israel's Jewishness and its democracy is unbridgeable (p. 82), while Avigdor Feldman, one of the country's best-known civil rights attorneys, examines that gap against the different rights of Arabs and Jews in Israel. Oren Yiftachel, in *Watching Over the Vineyard: The Example of Majd al-Korum,* substantiates this discrepancy empirically by offering a detailed, microcosmic study of the Arab village of Majd al Korum in the Galilee.

Yonathan Shapiro, in this last book before his recent death, examined Israel's democracy from a broad sociological perspective. He concluded that the country's founding fathers purposefully did not establish a liberal democracy, knowingly ignored the rights of individuals and minorities, and defined the boundaries of the Israeli collectivity along ethnic and religious lines, thus, linking theocentricity with ethnocentricity (p. 59). He believed that Israel's turn to nationalism and to what he calls "populism" was determined by these early actions by the leadership. Although some authors—for instance, Alan Dowty in the volume edited by S. Ilan Troen and Noah Lucas, *Selected Essays from Israel: The First Decade of Statehood*, evaluate the formative era in a positive light, other contributors call attention to long-term damage to the character of Israel's democracy through the "nonadoption" of a constitution (Philippa Strum), Ben-Gurion's aggressive foreign policy (Gabriel Sheffer) and its impact on the emergence of a militaristic spirit in the country (Yona Hadari-Ramage), and the discriminatory policy toward the Arab minority (Ilan Pappé).

The purpose of this essay is to review briefly this new, rich, and challenging literature and to integrate it into a larger picture of Israel's political culture. While none of the issues covered by this diverse literature—Israel's constitutional order, the Arab question, the country's foreign policy, relations between the state and religion, and the status of citizens' rights—can be fully treated here, their general review will enable us to present an overall, integrated view of Israel's democracy.

The importance of Shapiro's thin book lies in shedding new light on Israel's formative era and in emphasizing the critical role played by the leadership of the Mapai party in shaping the character of the state. Using Shapiro's perspective as a starting point, a few general principles may be outlined. First, it seems that certain cultural and political tendencies within the body politic can be reinforced or deemphasized by the elite, seeking to promote its own or the polity's interests:[1] the elite can give the political culture a *direction*. Second, once the general character of the regime has been determined and the overall *trajectory* has been set, it is extremely difficult to change: earlier policies are overwhelmingly important for subsequent options.[2] Third, in assessing elite choices within a given historical context, it is important to reject the assumption of predestination or determinism, as well as that of total freedom of choice, in favor of a *mixed model of decision-making* and, above all, empirical examination of decisions as they were made at particular historical junctures.[3] These conceptual tools are useful in evaluating Israel's constitutional order as it emerged in the formative era and evolved until today.

What was the overall character of the constitutional order established by the Mapai elite under the leadership of David Ben-Gurion? The authors of the various studies are often in sharp disagreement. Thus, Dowty, writing on Israel's first decade under the telling subtitle "Building a Civic State," views the initial statehood period as "a high point of universalist/civil/liberal fulfillment" (Troen and Lucas, p. 36) somewhat of a Golden Age. He, and others with a similarly positive view of the Ben-Gurionist Republic, emphasize its commitment to the notion of *mamlachtiut,* seen as a universalizing device designed to overcome internal division and factionalism within Israel.

Shapiro and some of the contributors to the Troen and Lucas volume, as well as Yiftachel and some of the contributors to the Barak-Erez collection, view the early period much more critically. They emphasize the establishment of a state that is highly ethnocentric and collectivist, with pronounced signs of militarism and increasing religiosity—not a liberal democracy that emphasised equality or civil rights. And, indeed, although it is impossible to identify a coherent philosophy behind all of the actions and decisions taken by the Mapai elite, it seems clear that its goals were invariably ethnocentric, that is, they focused exclusively on the promotion of the interests of Israel's Jewish community (Yiftachel). The *structure* used for the achievement of these goals was the state and its various organs or associated arms such as the Jewish Agency, sanctified through the invented concept of *mamlachtiut* (Eliezer Don-Yehiya, in Troen and Lucas). The *instrument* for the achievement of the goals was more often than not military power and coercion, and (as several of the authors show) theocratic notions were used to *legitimize* the system, its actions, and its boundaries.

Establishing the Israeli polity on these attitudinal pillars—ethnocentrism, statism, militarism, and religiosity—meant a pronounced de-emphasis of a series of alternative values. Thus "constitutionalism" that would have made blatant ethnocentrism impossible was nipped in the bud, making the country's political culture quite unique among Western democracies. The de-emphasis of individual rights, and of the development of a civil society in general, were but the natural result of statism.

This combination of values determined the overall character of the Israeli regime. It emerged, from the very beginning, as an ethnocentric republican order, with heavy theocratic overtones, and clearly not as a Western-style liberal democracy.[4] In this sense, the common depiction of the 1967 war and the resulting occupation of Arab territories as producing a flawed Israeli democracy, a depiction often adopted by those who emphasize the positive in the Ben-Gurionist Republic,[5] is fundamentally wrong. Ethnocentrism was not a post-1967 development, but rather a built-in component of the Israeli polity since 1948.

Moreover, the direction that the Mapai leadership chose and the trajectory established by that choice made changes in the character of the Israeli regime extremely difficult to achieve. The tensions inherent in the system are reflected in almost every chapter of the Barak-Erez collection. As for the formative era, the more moderate, liberal, and peaceful line endorsed by some of the Mapai leaders, in opposition to the more radical, ethnocentric, and belligerent line adopted by Mapai's dominant group, was, by and large, ignored: its promoters, notably Foreign Minister Sharett, were initially marginalized and eventually removed altogether.[6] Similarly, the universalist left (represented by Mapam), while initially a serious contender for power, was quickly brought to its knees: it joined Ben-Gurion's coalition as a minor partner in 1955, and once there, quietly accepted Ben-Gurion's nationalist line (e.g., a line reflected in the 1956 Sinai Campaign).[7]

In assessing Israel's political system in the formative era, one has to take into account the conditions under which the country emerged, not only the inclinations and preferences of its people and its elite. The 1947 Partition Resolution called for the establishment of an Arab and a Jewish state in Mandatory Palestine, allocating 55 percent of the territory to the Jews. As a result of the

1948 war, all of the area allocated to the Arab state was conquered by Jordan, Egypt, and Israel (which ended up with 80 percent of the Mandate area). In the territory under Israeli control, merely 95 out of 447 pre-1948 Arab villages and towns remained.[8]

Two alternative lines could have been adopted after the war by the Mapai leadership: a *conciliatory line*, accommodating at least some Arab demands while rejecting others, or a *confrontational line*, rejecting all Arab demands out of hand and adopting a noncompromising and, on occasion, aggressive policy toward the Arabs. Israel's elite under Ben-Gurion, who was deeply influenced by Moshe Dayan, clearly chose the second option. It then actively cultivated a political culture supporting that option. There is documentary evidence that General Dayan was successful in convincing Ben-Gurion that the 1949 Armistice lines were dangerous for Israel and that they must be erased through an *initiated* war.[9] The reprisals policy and, eventually, the Sinai Campaign were designed to bring about such a change. The political culture was functionally used as a tool to generate, create, and cultivate the type of nation that the leadership wanted and felt it needed for achieving its goals.

In evaluating the essence of Israel's polity in both the formative era and later, it is essential to recognize (as both Shapiro and Yiftachel do) the continuing dominance of the conflict with the Arabs as a determining factor. Although the style and technique of Israeli behavior changed between 1948 and 1967 (when Arab lands were inside the territorial bounds of the State of Israel) and following 1967 (when Arab lands became "occupied territory"), the centrality of the Arab-Jewish conflict over land remained a constant. Gershon Shafir goes even further in arguing that

> there is a need for a theoretical approach that is capable of understanding the continuity between the founding period of the Israeli-Jewish society in Ottoman and Mandatory Palestine and the period of the independent state and the one after the 1967 war and the rise to power of Likud.[10]

For quite some time, analysts of the yishuv and later of Israeli society tended to ignore or underestimate the Arab factor as an all-important determining element, central for the understanding of the overall character of the Israeli society, including its political culture. Thus, there was a tendency among leading Israeli sociologists to equate Israeli society with Israel's *Jewish* society, dealing with the Arabs as a separate, external "minority." Only a focus on the Arab-

Jewish *interaction* can give us a correct reading of Israel's political culture and of its main features. Some of the works reviewed here have begun to adopt such a focus.

When Israel came into being in May 1948, there was an expectation that it would become a liberal democracy, based on full equality for all citizens, a formal and written constitution, and a comprehensive bill of rights. This expectation found expression in such documents as the famous U.N. Partition Resolution and Israel's own Declaration of Independence. Yet, a liberal democracy did not emerge, despite the adoption of such democratic practices as general and free elections. Instead, a particularistic-ethnic regime quickly developed: the principles of universalistic citizenship, based on equal treatment under the law, were never adopted.

While clear differentiation between Arabs and Jews in post-1948 Israel was established in regard to control over the land, as documented by Yiftachel and Pappé, this differentiation was multidimensional, comprehensive, and all-encompassing. Military government was imposed on most of the areas heavily inhabited by Arabs; tellingly, it applied, in practice, only to Arabs (but not to Jews) residing in these areas.[11] The post-1948 era was characterized by the enhancement of physical separation between Jews and Arabs. The weakened Arab community—officially called now the "Arab Sector"—became totally controlled, politically and economically, by the Jewish majority. The cultural separation between the two communities became a fixture and the Arabs were never allowed to become part of the emerging Israeli nation. In the post-1948 Israeli "ethnic democracy," all citizens enjoyed some minimal universal rights (most notably the right to vote and to be elected). Yet, one ethnic group was guaranteed total control over all resources and thus domination over the other ethnic group.

Ethnic separation in Israel has become such an integral part of the political culture that, within the Israeli political culture, the Arab emerged as an entirely unmeltable, unintegratable "other."[12] As a group, the Arab minority was perceived as hostile, a class of citizens whose loyalty to the state cannot be assured and who must be carefully supervised and actively controlled. While the State of Israel recognized the Arabs as a religious, linguistic, and cultural minority—thus assuring their clear separation from the Jewish majority—the Arabs were never recognized as a national minority with political rights, a status that would have allowed them a measure of politico-legal protection. This arrangement, liberal on its face but thoroughly discriminatory in practice, enabled the state to fortify its overall character as an ethnic democracy.

Shapiro and Strum document the all-important debate over the adoption of a constitution in the early formative era. During that debate it became clear that Ben-Gurion wanted to avoid a written document that would give too much power to minorities. And, indeed, the large-scale expropriation of Arab lands following the 1948 war, estimated at 65–75% of the lands owned by Arabs,[13] could have been complicated or even stopped by a liberal constitution.

The ethnic ethos clearly won within the Zionist movement and the establishment of the state of Israel further strengthened, and legally ratified, the result. While Dan Horowitz and Moshe Lissak argue in their important book, *From Yishuv to State*,[14] that the mass *aliyah* (immigration) did not enable the young state to simultaneously achieve social justice and security, it is clear that the commitment to national goals—often expressed as "national security"—won over the commitment to social justice, and did so rather early. Theoretically, one can usefully identify two or more versions of Zionism, as skillfully presented by Horowitz and Lissak in their *Trouble in Utopia: The Overburdened Polity of Israel*.[15] On the one side of the divide, there were within the Zionist movement liberal and even social-democratic forces that emphasized cooperation between Arabs and Jews. On the other side, beginning in the early 1920s, Zionism saw the emergence of a radical right that emphasized the inevitable antagonism between the two nations and that claimed exclusive Jewish control over all of Eretz-Israel. Yet, even though the Labor-Zionist Mapai party emerged as the dominant political force in the Yishuv in the 1920s and 1930s, the confrontational, nationalist line was not defeated. Mapai, simply put, moved rightward as Arab-Jewish relations deteriorated.

The establishment of the State of Israel did not change this trend. Ben-Gurion continued to refer to himself and to his party as "socialist," emphasizing the demand for a model society (*hevra moffet*) and a special or chosen people (*am s'gula*) but in reality he pursued ethnocentric policies, systematically and energetically. If ethnocentrism was the fundamental principle on which Israel's political culture was established and the purpose for which the state was created (as Ben-Gurion stated clearly in the Knesset debates over the Law of Return), the state was perceived as the main institution for guaranteeing this principle. Under the banner of mamlachtiut, the state became the focus of Ben-Gurion's political philosophy.

The notion of *mamlachtiut,* derived from the Hebrew *mamlacha* (kingdom), is often translated into English as "statism." Nevertheless, some analysts argued that Ben-Gurion's mamlachtiut did not mean "statism," since Ben-Gurion did not consider the state an end in itself. According to Medding, Ben-Gurion wanted to instill in Israelis respect for "legitimate state public authority" or a "sense of public responsibility."[16] Whatever Ben-Gurion's ultimate philosophical beliefs, executive state institutions were, in fact, at the center of the political system that he developed, and these institutions were committed, exclusively and openly, to the promotion of the interests of one ethnic group. Ethnocentrism and statism were, thus, intimately linked, inseparable Siamese twins for all intents and purposes.

Some commentators saw the emphasis on the state by Ben-Gurion and others as "universalistic." In some way it was, but not in other ways. Ben-Gurion was committed, in theory, to the elimination of all sectarian organizations within the state, but he never insisted on "the inalienable rights of the individual" or other liberal, universalistic formulas. His state was a collectivist creature, promoting the exclusive interest of one ethnic group. Second, the essence of mamlachtiut demanded that it discriminate, particularistically, against those who did not belong to the majority group. Third, in implementing mamlachtiut, enormous power was given to state organs, without significant checks and balances such as a written constitution, a bill of rights, a watchful public opinion and combative press, or a tradition of human and civil rights. Under these circumstances, undemocratic, capricious, and harmful action against a large number of people occurred (e.g., the military government over the Arab sector from 1948 to 1966).

These general points require elaboration. Although Ben-Gurion's mamlachtiut viewed the promotion of the interests of sectarian groups within Israel's Jewish community as negative, it saw the promotion of the particular interests of that community positively. Thus, within the wider context of Israeli politics, mamlachtiut was a tool for promoting particularity, not universality. Most importantly, Ben-Gurion and the state often deviated from "statist" principles, demonstrating systematically that *ethnocentricity as a goal was superior to the state as an institution.* Examples of deviation from "statism" abound: Orthodoxy was given, in fact, a special status (e.g., deferment of military service to yeshiva students, and special status to religious education), violating the declared statist universalism; Arabs were defined and treated as second-class citizens, harming the civic nature of the state; organizations such as the Histadrut (the General Federation of Jewish Labor) and the Jewish Agency kept their special, for-Jews-only status. All the deviations from "civic" statism were designed for keeping the Jewish public unified by offering concessions to sectarian interests or by offering exclusive services and benefits to members of the Jewish majority. The Israel Defense Forces (IDF), easily the most important state organ, was established on an ethnic basis: those who were not allowed to join it, the Arabs, were thus excluded from the Israeli nation.[17]

The establishment of the state in 1948 made it possible for the Mapai elite to push the new polity in the direction of a liberal democracy, despite the serious constraints imposed by factors such as the war (that ended, however, by early 1949) and the political culture of the Jewish population. Yet, the dominant group within Mapai opted for the creation of an ethnic republic, openly excluding some citizens (Arabs) and treating others unequally (e.g., by institutionalizing the supremacy of Orthodox Judaism). Thus the state, rather than becoming the instrument of universalistic liberalism—by institutionalizing equality for all as its fundamental principle—quickly became the instrument for particularistic ethnocentrism. Thus, while some analysts have argued that it was a synthesis between national particularism and universalism,[18] mamlachtiut was in fact a conceptual tool for the creation of a centralized ethnic state, serving exclusively an ethnic elite and its constituency.[19]

It is important to realize that "statism" was not only an abstract idea but also a political reality. The establishment of the state was accompanied by the creation of a new class. Members of this class included individuals whose status and influence in society depended on the state and who therefore owed their loyalty primarily to the state: military officers, managers of state-owned enterprises, and high-level bureaucrats were among the most prominent members of the new class.

A few analysts interpreted Ben-Gurion's statism as an attempt to create a new focus of loyalty, and thereby to replace traditional foci of loyalty. Noah Lucas, for example, argues that Ben-Gurion realized that there would not be large-scale immigration from the West, and that relations with world Jewry therefore became secondary and the "identification with the state became the crux of the new nationalism" (Troen and Lucas, p. 308). For Don-Yehiya, statism can be seen as an attempt to replace traditional religion (Troen and Lucas, p. 173). Others have also noticed the abandonment of socialism and the search for alternative sources of identification (e.g., Lucas in Troen and Lucas).

In some ways all of these interpretations have a measure of truth to them. Ben-Gurion invented a concept—mamlachtiut—that enabled him and the state to claim and demand the loyalty of all *Jewish* Israelis. For the nonreligious Zionist, mamlachtiut was a secular concept, but full of deep historical connotations, a perfect component within the Ben-Gurionist civil religion. For the religious Jews, mamlachtiut per se was not sacrilegious: it did not negate religion. On the contrary, with its ancient allusion and link to the notion of *"malchut Israel"*—the biblical and religiously sanctioned Kingdom of Israel—mamlachtiut also generated support among religious Jews. Mamlachtiut, thus, was the perfect concept and formula for supporting the ethnocentric agenda of the new state.

※

In the pre-Zionist era, Jews were defined as a religious community, not as a "nation" or "ethnicity." This was also the basis of defining the Jewish community in Palestine under both Ottoman and British rule. When Israel was established, many people expected it to develop into a full-fledged Western, liberal, and secular democracy, a regime that gains its legitimacy from the equality of all of its citizens. To gain legitimacy as a Jewish state, however, Israel decided to rely heavily not only on Judaism in general but on traditional Orthodoxy, a decision reflected in the selection of symbols, the reliance on Orthodox religious institutions (e.g., the chief rabbinate), the character of its governmental coalition (where the National Religious Party [NRP] was permanently present), and a series of legislative decisions.

The 1948 Declaration of Independence promised to protect "freedom of religion and conscience" in Israel. This early commitment was already in contradiction with the 1947 Status Quo Agreement between the Jewish Agency and Agudat Israel, an agreement that offered extensive concessions to the Orthodox public at the expense of the secular majority by giving the rabbinate exclusive control over large segments of people's lives (e.g., matrimonial law). Agreements reached after 1948 created what might be called an expansion of this status quo.

In general, the Ben-Gurionist system reaffirmed the old Ottoman millet system, strengthened it by state sanction, and refused to establish a civil state in which all aspects of life (e.g., marriage) are determined by universalistic and egalitarian arrangements. In this system, all Israeli Jews were defined as members of a religious community, exclusively controlled in certain important aspects by the

Orthodox rabbinate. The establishment of religion in the center of Israel's political life affected numerous aspects:

1. a written constitution (which would have signified the emergence of Israel as a Western, liberal democracy) was never enacted, to some extent due to Orthodox opposition;
2. the religious-nationalists and the Haredi (ultra-Orthodox) communities were allowed to establish their independent school systems, while Labor education (*zerem ha-ovdim*) was eliminated;
3. in the all-important area of defense, it was decided that while Jews would be recruited into the IDF, non-Jews (other than Druze) would not, making religion the criterion for obtaining acceptance and legitimacy;
4. as a coalition-builder, Ben-Gurion preferred the National Religious Party to other partners, thereby legitimizing its power in the state even further.

In addition to these and other policy decisions, which introduced religion and religious affiliation as criteria for determining the personal status of individuals and the overall character of the state, the "declaratory policy" of the state indicated a reliance on religion as a legitimizer of the state. The Declaration of Independence committed the new polity to be a Jewish state, although it also committed Israel to maintain universalistic and civil equality.[20] Ben-Gurion continuously and increasingly used religious terminology and symbolism in his speeches, thus deeply influencing the political culture. Not only was the country, in general, focused on biblical archaeology, but Ben-Gurion personally emphasized the Bible as a source of legitimacy. Amos Oz complained bitterly at the end of Ben-Gurion's era that everything he did "in the last few years [was] based on national religious mythology and concepts" (Shapiro, 60). Many of the country's laws, and primarily the Law of Return, guaranteed that Israel would assume a primordial ethnic character. With time, religious emphasis grew in many areas: state ceremonies, the teaching of "Jewish identity" in schools, and so forth.[21]

Why was the religious component so powerful, despite the fact that Zionism began as a thoroughly secular movement and that most Israelis were nonobservant? The explanation, in my opinion, ought to be functional: it must focus on the role of religion in legitimizing the Ben-Gurionist republic. The Israeli ruling elite faced two specific issues of legitimacy during the formative era: (a) when the elite decided to desert liberal democracy—a move reflected in the decision not to adopt a constitution—it needed an alternative principle to legitimize its rule (Shapiro, pp. 61–62); and (b) the decision to keep the Arabs out of the socio-political boundaries of the new nation-state required powerful "glue," an integrative principle, to keep all *Jewish* groups in Israel together.

Judaism, in its *national, religious, and Zionist version,* served the legitimizing function perfectly, despite the secularism of Ben-Gurion, the elite, and most Israelis. It supplied the state with its symbols and mythology, just as it had contributed these to the Zionist movement in the prior era. Baruch Kimmerling believes that the Jewish religion facilitated a mythical image of the common external enemy, the "Gentiles," and the inclination to divide humanity into Jews versus the rest of the world.[22]

In offering this kind of antagonistic prism—a prism that became even more dominant after 1977—religion in its Orthodox and nationalistic form was more than a common denominator for all immigrants. It was the glue for holding together the main elements of the emerging political culture: ethnocentricity, statism, and militarism. In terms of *ethnicity,* orthodoxy gave the state a definition of Judaism that most Israeli Jews could unify around, despite the violence it did to Jewish pluralism, especially in the Diaspora. In terms of *statism,* as long as the state was willing to be the instrument for carrying out policies based on the Orthodox definition of Jewishness, the alliance between the state and organized religion was natural. The leading nationalistic role of the Military Rabbinate under Gen. Rabbi Shlomo Goren indicates the very close relations between ethnocentric policy, the state, the military, and organized religion. Once again, the post-1967 period is rather instructive in that regard: it reveals, in clearer colors, what was already the situation in the pre-1967 era.

The infusion of religiosity into the nation-building project ought to be understood primarily in political and cultural terms. A country locked into a blood feud with all of its neighbors and a large segment of its own population, one in which the Jewish majority traditionally views the world as a hostile place, could naturally adopt a religious rationale for its predicament. Yet, the adoption of religion as a "glue" made sense not only culturally, but also politically. A traditionally socialist party, Mapai was at a distinct political disadvantage when hundreds of thousands of immigrants started arriving in Israel from Arabic-speaking countries. Mapai's "Great Leap Rightward," toward ethno-nationalism based partially on theological foundations, was possibly the only way it could have sustained its political dominance during the formative years. It was a preemptive strike, dealing simultaneously with potential challenges from the nationalist Herut and from the national-religious Mafdal parties.

When the State of Israel declared itself to be "Jewish," its Jewishness could have been expressed in a number of different ways: a state where the majority of the population is Jewish (the "State of the Jews" model), a state whose symbols are rooted in the Jewish tradition, a state that celebrates Jewish pluralism, and so forth. Yet, the Ben-Gurionist Republic chose to emphasize Orthodoxy as a model for its Jewishness: Orthodox forces were given exclusive power over the rabbinate, the Mapai-NRP alliance guaranteed exclusive power to Orthodox nationalists, Orthodoxy was given exclusive power over separate education, and so forth.

The lack of a liberal tradition among most Israelis, a dominant characteristic of the political culture before and after 1948, enabled the elite to infuse religiosity into the political infrastructure of the country with impunity. While modernization in the Western world was marked by separation between religion and nationality, as well as between religion and state, and while those separations were an integral part of the liberal-democratic model, Israel in its formative years reaffirmed and strengthened the links among all three of these entities: religion, nationality, and the state. In fact, the post-1948 concepts were interpreted in the narrowest possible way: religion was of one type alone (national, Orthodox, and Zionist); nationality was perceived and promoted as fiercely as possible; and the state was dedicated exclusively to what its leaders defined as the national agenda.

The solidification and institutionalization of the link between religion and nationality necessarily violated the first principle of liberal democracy, that of equality of all citizens. It meant that a non-Jew could never be fully an Israeli, although he could hold, formally, Israeli citizenship. Thus, religion became the marker of the boundary to full "Israeli-ness." The religion-nationality mutation was not a natural, organic, or necessary development, especially since most Israeli Jews were secular. It was a solution strongly supported by the national-religious camp and adopted by the dominant secular party, Mapai, as a means for strengthening Israel's ethnic purpose in the formative years and a technique of fortifying its own political position.

The infusion of religion into the system and, in fact, its incorporation as a main infrastructural element meant a permanent distortion of the liberal credo, a fact recognized by several authors (Levontin and Feldman, in Barak-Erez). The religionization of the state prevented the integration of non-Jews and interfered in the rights of nonreligious Jews. The adoption of Judaism, in its religious and orthodox form, also violated the character of what could be called "classical Zionism." It set the Israeli mind back to pre-Zionist, diasporic times. While classical Zionism, in its Herzlian or socialist versions, had a vision of *normalizing* Jewish existence, the new Israeli political culture, and particularly its religious overtones, cherished abnormality, uniqueness, and chosenness. It adopted a decidedly bipolar approach to the world: "us and them," "Jews and Gentiles," "we and others."

The Barak-Erez volume looks at the issue of religion from the perspective of the 1990s. It leaves the reader with the sense that the issues of state-religion relations are truly unsolvable, that the tensions are deep and destructive, and that time does not work in favor of a solution. From the perspective of this essay two points must be emphasized: (a) the problems did not emerge of "themselves"—they were created by decisions taken by the leadership; and (b) the role of religion in Israel has been rather negative when it comes to the civil rights of a large number of people, Arabs and Jews alike.

Israel's political culture in the formative years de-emphasized a series of values and ideals which, in the eyes of the elite, contradicted the country's fundamental goals. Among the neglected values in Israel's political culture we may identify the following:

1. ***Constitutionalism.*** This is the written formulation of rights and liberties in a constitution, a bill of rights, or similar protected document(s).
2. ***Human and civil rights.*** Not only has Israel's collectivist orientation worked against attention to these type of rights—which are often individually based—but the statist approach and the ethnocentric attitude pushed the country in the very same direction.
3. ***Equality before the law.*** From the very beginning, Arabs did not have the same legal status as Jews. Some legislation (e.g., the Law of Return) was openly discriminatory. As Gad Barzilai has shown,[23] even the High Court of Justice decided issues on the basis of ethnicity, and other courts (e.g., those dealing with criminal cases) did the same.

4. *Equal opportunity.* This relationship between ethnic groups and between the genders was also not kept, and the lack of a constitution allowed discriminated groups no redress.[24]

In hindsight, it seems that the decision not to adopt a constitution was critical to all of these deficiencies and lacunae in Israel's political culture. Strum sees the effect of the "nonadoption" as "the absence of civil liberties as a basic element of Israeli political culture" (p. 49). The conflict with the Arabs and the tendencies of both the elite and the general public pushed Israel in the direction of collectivism, statism, and ethnocentrism, and away from an individualistic civil-libertarian perspective.

The political culture of the 1950s provided the foundation of the ethnocentric order established in Israel's formative years. From the very beginning, the elite was determined to promote an "ethnic democracy."[25] Therefore, it was trying to heal the rifts within Israel's Jewish public (the Ashkenazi-Sephardi, the religious-secular, and the ideological rift between the Zionist left and the Zionist right), but emphasized and enhanced the rift between Arabs and Jews. All non-nationalist challenges within Israel's Jewish community—from the Canaanites, the Communists, and Mapam—were politically eliminated by the elite. The result was that by the 1960s the nationalist character of the state was well established.

In the debate over *when* Israel ceased to be a universalistic liberal democracy, I would argue that almost every single move of the Mapai elite in the post-1948 era indicated a desire to establish a nonliberal, particularist, nationalist system, at the expense of the ideals of open, liberal, and egalitarian democracy. While this policy affected most dramatically the status of the Arabs, against whom discrimination was formal and legally enshrined, it also affected the inner workings of the Jewish public (e.g., via religious legislation). So, Israel's "fall from grace" ought not to be seen as occurring in 1967 or 1977, as so many critics seem to suggest, but rather in 1948.

Moreover, the post-1948 policies prepared the groundwork for the further nationalization of the Israeli body politic in 1967 and 1977. They did so by preparing an Israeli Jewish public that saw the world in ethnocentric terms, which was ready to march under a statist banner without a strong "civil" inclination to resist state authority,[26] which allowed the military spirit to control public debate (e.g., the debate over the future of the occupied territories), and that was induced by *religious* fantasies to support a nationalistic foreign policy.[27] The inclination of some analysts to separate the political culture of the formative years from the policies after 1967 is unconvincing. Israel was not reinvented by 1967; it just moved into a new phase.

Notes

1. See Yonathan Shapiro, *Israeli Democracy* (Ramat Gan: Massada, 1977) (Hebrew), in addition to the preface and chapter 1 of the book reviewed here.

2. A number of contributions to the Troen-Lucas volume emphasize the long-term effect of events and trends in the formative era, notably Strum, Sheffer, and Hadari-Ramage.

3. See also Shulamit Carmi and Henry Rosenfeld, "The Emergence of Militaristic Nationalism in Israel," *International Journal of Politics, Culture and Society* 3:1 (1989), 5–49.

4. See, for example, Yoav Peled, "Ethnic Democracy and the Legal Construction of Citizenship: Arab Citizens of the Jewish State," *American Political Science Review* 86:2 (June 1993), 432–33; Peled and Gershon Shafir, "The Roots of Peacemaking: The Dynamics of Citizenship in Israel, 1948–93," *International Journal of Middle East Studies* 28:3 (August 1996), 391–413; and Sammy Smooha, "Minority Status in Ethnic Democracy: The Status of the Arab Minority in Israel," *Ethnic and Racial Studies* 13 (1990), 389–413.

5. For example, Peter Medding, *The Founding of the Israeli Democracy, 1949–1967* (New York: Oxford University Press, 1990).

6. See, particularly, Sheffer, in *Selected Essays from Israel* as well as Benny Morris, *Israel's Border Wars, 1949–1956* (Oxford: Clarendon Press, 1993).

7. See Hadari-Ramage, in *Selected Essays from Israel*.

8. See Avishai Ehrlich, "A Society in War: The National Conflict and Social Structure," in *Israeli Society: Critical Perspectives,* ed. Uri Ram (Tel Aviv: Breirot, 1993), 253–74 (Hebrew); as well as Benny Morris, *The Birth of the Palestinian Refugee Problem, 1947–1949* (Cambridge: Cambridge University Press, 1988).

9. See, for example, Motti Golani, "Did Ben-Gurion Oppose or Support Dayan? Israel on the Road to Preemptive War," *Cathedra* 81 (September 1996), 123–32. (Hebrew)

10. Gershon Shafir, "Land, Labor and Population in Zionist Colonization: General and Particularist Perspectives," in *Israeli Society,* 104–19.

11. See Ian Lustick, *Arabs in the Jewish State* (Austin: University of Texas Press, 1980); Don Peretz, "Early State Policy Towards the Arab Population, 1948–1955" (82–102); and Elie Rekhess, "Initial Israeli Policy Guidelines towards the Arab Minority, 1948–1949" (103–21), both in *New Perspectives on Israeli History: The Early Years of the State,* Laurence Silberstein, ed. (New York: New York University Press, 1991). For an alternative approach, see Natan Yanai, "Ben-Gurion's Concept of *Mamlachtiut* and the Forming Reality of the State of Israel," *Jewish Political Studies Review* 1:1–2 (Spring 1989), 151–177; and Yanai, "The Citizen as Pioneer: Ben-Gurion's Concept of Citizenship," *Israel Studies* 1:1 (Spring 1996), 127–43.

12. On the Arab "Other" in Israeli politics, see Ilan Peleg, "Otherness and Israel's Arab Dilemma," in *The Other in Jewish Thought and History,* eds. Laurence Silberstein and Robert Cohn (New York: New York University Press, 1994), 258–80; and Peleg, "The Arab-Israeli Conflict and the Victory of Otherness," in *Books on Israel, Vol. 3,* eds. Russell Stone and Walter Zenner (Albany: State University of New York Press, 1994), 227–43. In literature and cinema, see Gila Ramras-Rauch, *The Arab in Israeli Literature* (Bloomington: Indiana University Press, 1989); and Ella Shohat, *Israeli Cinema: East/West and the Politics of Representation* (Austin: University of Texas Press, 1989).

13. Lustick, *Arabs in the Jewish State*, 276.

14. Dan Horowitz and Moshe Lissak, *From Yishuv to State* (Tel-Aviv: Am Oved, 1977), 91. (Hebrew)

15. Horowitz and Lissak, *Trouble in Utopia: The Overburdened Polity of Israel* (Tel Aviv: Am Oved, 1990), 160–61. (Hebrew)

16. Medding, *Founding of the Israeli Democracy*, 135.

17. See Uri Ben-Eliezer, *The Making of Israeli Militarism* (Bloomington: Indiana University Press, 1998); and "A Nation in Uniform and War: Israel in its First Years," *Zmanim* 49 (Summer 1994), 51–65. (Hebrew)

18. Eliezer Don-Yehiya, *"Mamlachtiut* and Judaism in Ben-Gurion's Thought and Policy," *ha-Tsiyonut* 14 (1989), 51–88. (Hebrew)

19. Yagil Levy, *The Role of the Military Sphere in the Construction of the Socio-Political Order in Israel,* Doctoral Dissertation, Tel-Aviv University, 1993 (Hebrew); as well as "Military Policy, Ethnic Relations and Internal Expansion of the State: Israel 1948–1956," *Teoria u-Vikoret* 8 (Summer 1996), 203–23.

20. See Erik Cohen, "Israel as a Post-Zionist Society," in *The Shaping of Israeli Identity: Myth, Memory and Trauma,* eds. Robert Wistrich and

David Ohana (London: Frank Cass, 1995), 203–14 (esp. p. 204). [Ed. note: Cf. the article in this volume by David C. Jacobson, 114–116].

21. Horowitz and Lissak, *Trouble in Utopia*, 187–88.

22. See Baruch Kimmerling, "Militarism in Israeli Society," *Teoria u-Vikoret* 4 (1993), 123–40 (Hebrew); and "Religion, Nationalism and Democracy in Israel," *Zmanim* 50–51(Winter 1994), 116–31. (Hebrew)

23. Gad Barzilai, "Political Institutions and Conflict Resolution: The Israeli Supreme Court and the Peace Process," in *The Middle East Peace Process: Interdisciplinary Perspectives*, ed. Ilan Peleg (Albany: State University of New York Press, 1997), 87–105.

24. See Horowitz and Lissak, *Trouble in Utopia*, 187–88.

25. Smooha, "Minority Status in Ethnic Democracy."

26. Only during the 1982 Lebanon War do we see the first strong signs of antistatism.

27. Witness the religious language used after 1967, not only by religious people but also by secular public figures such as Moshe Dayan.

5. "Normal" or "Special"? Israel's Relationships with America and Germany in Historical Perspective

David Rodman

This essay challenges the dichotomy between "special" and "normal" relationships usually made in terms of the relative weight of ideological considerations (which are commonly associated with "special" relationships) and unsentimental "national interests" (which generally characterize "normal" relationships). By taking an historical perspective, the author reveals both "normal" and "special" characteristics of the Israeli-American and Israeli-German relationships and focuses on the strains and changes that have taken place since 1948.

Feldman, Shai, *The Future of US-Israel Strategic Cooperation*, Washington DC: Washington Institute for Near East Policy, 1996.

Lavy, George, *Germany and Israel: Moral Debt and National Interest*, London: Frank Cass, 1996.

Reich, Bernard, *Securing the Covenant: United States-Israel Relations after the Cold War*, Westport CT: Praeger, 1995.

Sheffer, Gabriel, ed., *U.S.-Israeli Relations at the Crossroads*, London: Frank Cass, 1997.

Wolffsohn, Michael, *Eternal Guilt?: Forty Years of German-Jewish-Israeli Relations*, New York: Columbia University Press, 1993.

Diplomats, academics, and journalists often speak of a "special relationship" between states. The Anglo-American partnership of the immediate post-World War II decades is perhaps the most frequently cited example of a special relationship. Many others can be identified without too much difficulty. The current American-Canadian and Franco-German relationships, to mention only two, are routinely referred to as special.

Just what is a special relationship? While this concept has rarely been defined with any precision, it has had a generally accepted meaning. International relations observers suggest that the bond between states in a special relationship is broader and stronger than the bond between states in a "normal relationship." The bond between states in a special relationship is not confined to a handful of narrow issues, like agricultural trade or arms sales, but rather consists of a large and complex array of diplomatic, military, economic, and cultural ties. This bond is also able to survive crises between states, to outlast even the most serious disagreements. International relations theorists further suggest that a special relationship is based on powerful ideological currents and potent transnational forces. In contrast to a normal relationship, national interests are not of overriding importance in this type of relationship.

Most scholars of the American-Israeli and German-Israeli relationships think of them as special. To support their position, these observers point to the extensive and intricate web of diplomatic, military, economic, and cultural ties that have developed over the years between the United States and Germany (West Germany before reunification), on the one hand, and Israel, on the other hand. Moreover, this school of thought maintains, explicitly or implicitly, that the evolutionary paths taken by the relationships have been dictated principally—some would say exclusively—by ideological currents (e.g., common value systems, common political systems, and common historical experiences) and by transnational forces (e.g., ethnic and political interest groups). The national interests of the three states, accordingly, have been of much less, or no, importance in shaping the paths of these relationships.

To a greater or lesser extent, the volumes produced by Shai Feldman, Bernard Reich, Gabriel Sheffer, George Lavy, and Michael Wolffsohn reflect this perspective. Feldman, formerly a researcher at Harvard's Kennedy School of Government who has written widely about nuclear weapons in the Middle East, examines one particular component of the American-Israeli relationship—strategic cooperation. He defines this cooperation as those measures—including intelligence-sharing, military maneuvers, defense-industrial collaboration, and diplomatic coordination—that the United States and Israel have taken in the past or could take in the future to counter the plans of their mutual adversaries: formerly, the Soviet Union and its radical Arab allies and, today, the remaining radical Arab states and Iran. Reich, a political science professor at George Washington University who has published numerous books and articles on the American-Israeli relationship, adopts a very different approach to this relationship. Instead of focusing exhaustively on one of its components, he provides a general overview; and, contrary to what the title of his work implies, he is far more interested in probing the past than in predicting the future. Sheffer, a political science professor at Hebrew University and another veteran observer of the American-Israeli relationship, has collected a series of articles by well-known international relations and Middle East experts that assess this relationship in the context of the Cold War and post-Cold War worlds. Lavy, a longtime lecturer at a British university, has produced a dispassionate introductory text on the German-Israeli relationship, tracing its ups and downs over the past half century. In contrast, Wolffsohn—an Israeli-born academic now residing permanently in Germany—brings a much more personal point of view to bear on this relationship. He writes about what he calls the "German-Jewish-Israeli" triangle not as a detached chronicler of history, but instead as an active participant in an ongoing drama. Consequently, he mixes freely fact and opinion, an intellectual recipe that results in a decidedly idiosyncratic account of the German-Jewish-Israeli encounter.

Collectively, these volumes furnish solid summaries of the American-Israeli and German-Israeli relationships. Their analyses of the relationships, however, are somewhat less impressive. To varying degrees, these analyses fall into precisely the same trap as most earlier interpretations of the American-Israeli and German-Israeli relationships—they do not distinguish carefully enough between motives and substance. To put it another way, they tend to assume that the driving forces behind the relationships have largely been special because the relationships themselves have been special at times.

Although his insightful contribution to Sheffer's volume covers only the American-Israeli relationship, Charles Lipson ("American Support for Israel: History, Sources, Limits," in Sheffer) discerns the basic problem with this line of reasoning as it pertains to both relationships: it simply cannot account for the historical shifts that have occurred in the relationships over the last fifty years. As all of the volumes illustrate in some detail, American-Israeli and German-Israeli diplomatic, military, economic, and cultural ties have *changed* drastically since 1948; but the ideological currents and transnational forces that have ostensibly propelled both relationships have remained remarkably *stable* over the same decades. Constants, of course, cannot explain variables. Unlike ideological currents and transnational forces, though, perceptions of American, German, and Israeli national interests have *changed* dramatically over time. And variables, of course, can explain variables.

U.S.-Israeli Relations until the 1960s

The American-Israeli relationship from the late 1940s to the early 1960s, as Reich and Sheffer's volumes demonstrate, is best described as strained. To be sure, the Truman administration recognized Israel's independence; and both it and the successive Eisenhower administration provided some economic assistance to the new state. During the same years, however, the United States enforced a strict arms embargo against Israel. Indeed, during its 1948–49 War of Independence, the Jewish state obtained the arms that ensured its immediate survival—and later triumph—from the former Soviet Union (via Czechoslovakia). The Truman and Eisenhower administrations also generally favored Arab positions on such contentious issues as border clashes and water allocation. In addition, the Eisenhower administration threatened to impose crippling diplomatic and economic sanctions on Israel if it did not withdraw from the Sinai and Gaza Strip in the wake of its successful 1956 assault on Egypt. Finally, neither the Truman nor Eisenhower administrations gave any serious thought to the possibility of incorporating Israel into the West's Middle Eastern defense plans.

For its part, Israel refrained from siding openly with the United States in the latter's anti-Soviet crusade until the mid-1950s. It did not consult America about its decision to join France and Great Britain in the 1956 war, and its policies on issues like border clashes and water allocation were not particularly responsive to American wishes. While Israel did expend considerable energy in attempts to upgrade its ties to the United States, it concentrated much of its diplomatic effort until the early 1960s on nurturing and maintaining close ties to France and Germany. Only in the realm of culture—for example, scientific and educational cooperation—could American-Israeli ties be described as close from 1948 onward.

This period of the American-Israeli relationship presents the greatest challenge to those who argue that the relationship has been shaped mainly or solely by ideological currents and transnational forces. The United States and Israel, after all, have always shared Western, Judeo-Christian values and have always had democratic political systems. Furthermore, influential interest groups in both states began to press for a special relationship between the two early on. In the United States, the American Jewish community and, to a lesser extent, authoritative members of Congress promoted the idea almost from the moment of Israel's birth. In the Jewish state, powerful elements of the political elite in the late 1940s and 1950s desired close ties. The mass publics in both states appeared receptive to the idea of a special relationship, too.

Why a special relationship nevertheless failed to emerge in this period becomes clear by examining American and Israeli perceptions of their national interests. Steven David's contribution to Sheffer's volume rightly emphasizes the immense importance of Middle Eastern oil to the West. He notes that, in the mid-1990s, "[t]he United States imports half of its petroleum needs. American allies are even worse off, with foreign oil accounting for more than 60 percent of West European requirements and almost all of Japan's needs" (David, "The Continuing Importance of American Interests in the Middle East after the Cold War," in Sheffer, p. 98). Indeed, American leaders have considered a secure supply of oil so crucial to the West that their principal goal in the Middle East since World War II has been to guarantee unimpeded access to this resource. Until the downfall of the Soviet Union in 1991, they believed that safeguarding the West's oil supply was dependent on minimizing the Kremlin's influence in the region. From the late 1940s to the early 1960s they concluded that, as part of their strategy to protect this oil supply, the United States should try to curry favor with the Arab world, if need be at Israel's expense. That these leaders also judged the Jewish state to be a militarily weak state unable to promote United States Middle Eastern interests made it that much easier to maintain a distance from it.

Israel's main goal has been much more basic: survival is about as fundamental a state goal as could be imagined. Israeli leaders initially thought that close ties to the United States could help to secure this goal. But they eventually came to the conclusion that, as the price of a close relationship, America intended for Israel to make concessions that (they believed) would imperil its existence. Thus, they turned to France and Germany—states that were not demanding similar concessions as the price of close ties. In retrospect, neither the United States nor Israel was especially interested in actually forging a close relationship with the other from the late 1940s to the early 1960s because both felt that the potential costs of such an arrangement would outweigh the potential benefits.

German-Israeli Relations until the 1960s

While the German-Israeli relationship did not become special overnight, as Lavy and Wolffsohn's accounts reveal, it did get off to a more promising start than the American-Israeli relationship. In 1952, Germany and the Jewish state signed the Luxembourg Agreement. Under its terms, Germany agreed to give Israel large-scale economic assistance. As a result of this and subsequent economic agreements, the Jewish state would for a long time occupy a preferential place in German aid programs. During the late 1950s, Germany also began a covert supply of arms. In return, Israel supported Germany with intelligence information about Soviet activities in Europe. At about the same time, the two states inaugurated substantial scientific and educational exchange programs. On the other side of the ledger, Germany and Israel failed to establish formal diplomatic ties throughout the 1950s and early 1960s. At first, the Jewish state balked at taking this step. Later it was Germany that displayed a reluctance to recognize Israel formally. As Lavy points out, "[j]ust at the moment . . . when the Israeli government had overcome its inhibitions towards the Germans and declared its willingness to establish normal diplomatic relations with the Federal Republic, the West German government held back" (p. 29), in deference to Arab sensibilities. Despite this gap in ties, the German-Israeli relationship was still broad enough and strong enough by 1960 to be considered special.

The shared historical experience of the Holocaust, as Lavy and Wolffsohn's volumes correctly contend, had a significant impact on the course of the German-Israeli relationship in its early years. German guilt and Israeli anger over the destruction of European Jewry certainly affected every sphere of the relationship, from political negotiations to cultural contacts. Israeli leaders, according to Lavy, originally resisted establishing formal diplomatic ties with Germany because its Nazi past was too fresh in their minds. German leaders, Wolffsohn writes, encouraged meaningful scientific and educational cooperation in order to atone in some small way for the harm done to European Jewry.

But, as both volumes also correctly assert, pragmatic considerations of German and Israeli national interests were at least as crucial in molding the development of ties. German leaders faced a dilemma. On the one hand, they wanted to restore their state's legitimacy in the eyes of the world community. To accomplish this goal, it was necessary for them to earn and sustain Israeli goodwill, hence, their decisions to provide overt economic and covert military assistance. On the other hand, they wanted to protect Germany's traditionally privileged position in the Arab world. Not only would close ties to Arab states assist in Germany's postwar economic recovery, but they would also help to ensure that those states did not recognize East Germany, which would advance the West German leadership's policy of national reunification. They therefore decided to put off, for much of the 1950s and early 1960s, establishing formal diplomatic ties with Israel.

Israeli leaders, too, faced a dilemma. On the one hand, German economic and military assistance would be of tremendous value to Israel's struggle for survival, especially in light of Soviet hostility and American aloofness. On the other hand, accepting this assistance might be interpreted by both Germany and the international community as a sign that the Jewish people had forgiven the former's past sins. Like their German counterparts, Israeli leaders ultimately opted for compromise. They took the assistance, but refused (especially in public) to absolve Germany of responsibility for Nazi crimes.

U.S.-Israeli Relations during the 1960s

The German-Israeli relationship would continue to be very important to Israel after 1960, but it would gradually be superseded in significance by the American-Israeli relationship. The Kennedy administration's rise to power, as Reich and Sheffer's volumes show, heralded a shift in American-Israeli ties. While this administration continued to court the Arab world at Israel's expense, it did so with less enthusiasm than the Truman and Eisenhower administrations. More importantly, it ended the arms embargo against Israel. The Johnson administration amplified these trends. It sold more military equipment to Israel and manifested even less eagerness to woo Arab states. Israel responded to this new regional orientation by displaying more sensitivity to America's policies. For example, it did not object as strenuously as it had in the past to American arms sales to

Arab states. Similarly, on the eve of the 1967 Six-Day War, it refrained from going to war for several weeks in order to give the United States every chance to end the latest Middle Eastern crisis peacefully. In short, the seeds of the future special relationship were planted in the early 1960s.

This improvement in the American-Israeli relationship cannot be attributed to ideological currents or to transnational forces. Each state's value system had been rooted in Western, Judeo-Christian ethics and each state's political system had been rooted in democratic principles well before the positive trends of the 1960s. American Jewry's political influence had not suddenly swelled in the early years of that decade, nor had the warm feelings toward Israel expressed by Congress and the mass public. Likewise, influential elements of the political elite and the mass public in Israel had been fond of the United States well before the 1960s.

Rather, this improvement can be attributed to changing perceptions of American and Israeli national interests. First, American leaders had watched with increasing dismay as Soviet influence throughout the Arab world grew in the 1950s, despite American efforts to keep Israel at arm's length. During the early 1960s, they came to the conclusion that enhanced American-Israeli ties would not do additional great harm to American-Arab ties. Those Arab states that were still friendly to the United States, particularly Saudi Arabia, Jordan, and Kuwait, were not going to move into the former Soviet Union's orbit, complain as they might about the expanding American-Israeli relationship. Second, American leaders realized that Israel had evolved into the most formidable Middle Eastern power by the early 1960s—a power that was on the verge of acquiring nuclear weapons and whose conventional military forces, as evidenced by their outstanding performance in the 1956 war, were capable of operating deep inside Arab territory. Americans reckoned that a state with such capabilities could be both a potential asset and a potential liability to the United States. On the one hand, a strong Jewish state could serve as a convenient deterrent to military adventurism on the part of pro-Soviet, radical Arab states. On the other hand, a powerful Israel could also flex its military muscle in ways that could harm America's Middle Eastern interests. By tightening the American-Israeli relationship, however, such negative developments could be avoided. The United States, American leaders astutely concluded, would gain substantial influence over Israeli foreign policy if it moved closer to Israel. For a number of reasons, then, the Jewish state became an attractive client during the early 1960s.

From the Israeli leadership's perspective, the United States became an attractive patron during the same years. For starters, neither the Kennedy nor Johnson administrations demanded massive Israeli concessions to the Arabs in return for closer ties. Moreover, France—Israel's patron since the mid-1950s—was beginning to distance itself. After the end of the Algerian War in 1962, Franco-Arab ties began to warm up quickly—a trend that France expected to encourage by cooling its relationship with Israel, which it no longer needed as a counterweight to Arab states and nationalist movements. Israeli leaders realized that the Jewish state required a new benefactor, one that could provide it with the diplomatic and military support that France was steadily withdrawing. The United States fit the bill.

German-Israeli Relations during the 1960s

While the American-Israeli relationship was heating up in the early 1960s, the German-Israeli relationship peaked, as Lavy and Wolffsohn's volumes suggest. Germany continued to provide large-scale economic assistance to Israel. It has been estimated that this economic assistance amounted to a significant percentage of the Jewish state's gross national product during these years. Germany also continued to furnish arms, with the silent approval of the United States. In return, Israel continued to supply ample amounts of very useful intelligence data to Germany. Scientific and educational exchanges expanded in scope. German tourism to Israel, Wolffsohn writes, began to pick up. Finally, Germany and Israel established formal diplomatic ties in 1965. Further testifying to the strength of the German-Israeli relationship in this period, Lavy notes, was its ability to weather the diplomatic storm created by Germany's unwillingness to take serious action against ex-Nazi scientists helping Egypt to acquire ballistic missiles and weapons of mass destruction for possible use against Israel.

Memories of the Holocaust, as Lavy and Wolffsohn sensibly assert, still played a role in determining the course of German-Israeli ties. But the national interests of both states had more of an impact on how these ties unfolded in the early 1960s. From the perspective of German leaders, assisting Israel aided Germany's ongoing quest for international legitimacy. That this policy also pleased Germany's chief ally, the United States, was yet another incentive to continue it. From the perspective of Israeli leaders, German economic and military assistance was still considered critical to the state's well-being and thus accepted: lingering anger over Germany's Nazi past was not permitted to stand in the way of pragmatic self-interest.

The circumstances under which Germany and Israel established formal diplomatic ties clearly illustrate the greater importance of national interests in this period. When the covert supply of arms to Israel became public knowledge, German leaders decided that it would have to come to an end. They feared that Germany's privileged position in the Arab world would be undermined if they did not sever the military connection with Israel. As in the past, they were especially concerned about the fact that Arab states would grant de jure recognition to East Germany, thereby harming Germany's prospects for eventual reunification with the East. At the same time, though, they acknowledged that Germany's stature in the international community, not to mention its relationship with the United States, would be damaged if they did not offer Israel some type of compensation for lost arms. Therefore, they consented to establishing official diplomatic ties. If their foreign policy toward Israel had been driven largely by memories of the Holocaust, would Germany's leaders have been so concerned about Arab reactions to the German-Israeli arms connection? The answer must be no. For their part, Israeli leaders prudently welcomed the diplomatic recognition, looking elsewhere for a supply of military necessities.

U.S.-Israeli Relations since 1967

The cessation of the German-Israeli arms connection was followed in just a few years by the Six-Day War of June 1967. Israel's spectacular victory in the war would have profound effects on both the American-Israeli and German-Israeli relationships. Reich and Sheffer's volumes point out that the former has become much more intimate over the last three decades. Since the 1967 war, the United States has provided Israel with extremely generous amounts of military and economic assistance. Despite heated disputes with its client, particularly over the Jewish state's policies in the administered territories, it has also extended considerable diplomatic support, especially in international forums, such as the United Nations. In return, Israel has stepped up its military and intelligence cooperation with the United States, cooperation that had been quite limited during the 1950s and early 1960s. Partly in recognition of the military and intelligence benefits derived from its ties to the Jewish state, Feldman indicates, America has substantially expanded its level of strategic cooperation with its client since the early 1980s. According to him, "[t]he advent of the Reagan administration in early 1981 dramatically altered Washington's view of Israel's possible role in U.S. designs for the security of the Middle East" (p. 10). Of greater significance to the United States, the Jewish state has been willing at crucial moments over the last thirty years to subordinate its foreign policy to America's. Business, scientific, and educational ties between the states have exploded since the Six-Day War, too. Over the last three decades, in short, the United States and Israel have been partners in a special relationship.

Like the pre-1967 changes in American-Israeli ties, the post-1967 shift cannot be attributed to either ideology or transnational penetration. Neither America nor Israel's basic ethical and political systems have changed in the post-1967 period. Support for Israel among the American Jewish community was not markedly less enthusiastic before the 1967 war. Although support in Congress and among the general public may have grown somewhat, particularly right after that war, it bears repeating that these groups have always favored Israel over the Arab world. The rise of a sophisticated pro-Israel lobby also fails to explain this shift in the American-Israeli relationship. Even the most strident critics of AIPAC (American-Israel Public Affairs Committee), the chief pro-Israel organization, contend that its alleged influence on the relationship began only during the mid-to-late 1970s—that is, only well after the present pattern of American-Israeli ties had come into existence. Similarly, neither the political elite nor the mass public in Israel developed a newfound fondness for the United States. Pro-American sentiment was a feature of Israeli political life long before the Six-Day War.

Again, the explanation for the shift in the American-Israeli relationship is to be found in American and Israeli perceptions of their national interests. Contrary to what Edward Luttwak's essay ("Strategic Aspects of U.S.-Israeli Relations," in Sheffer) implies about the attitudes of American leaders, the United States has opted for an intimate relationship with Israel since 1967 in part because these leaders have perceived that state to be a "strategic asset" in their quest to advance America's Middle Eastern and global interests, for several reasons. Israel has supplied the United States with valuable intelligence information about the Middle East, Africa, and Eastern Europe. It has handed over key technical information about—and even many samples of—Soviet arms; and it has furnished copious data about the Israel Defense Forces' combat tactics, which have been put to use effectively by American military forces in Vietnam, Grenada, Panama, and the Persian Gulf. It has quietly agreed to host American forces on its soil should an emergency arise in which those forces are denied access to other local facilities. It has acted as a "sword bearer" for the United States, especially in Latin America and Africa, by assisting states and nonstate movements that America could not openly support. Finally, it has acted as a substitute for American muscle in the Middle East, most notably during the September 1970 Jordanian civil war, when it deterred a Soviet-backed Syria from aiding the Palestine Liberation Organization (PLO) in that movement's unsuccessful attempt to overthrow King Hussein's pro-American regime. Steven David and Charles Lipson argue that Israel's role in that crisis was crucial in promoting its image as a strategic asset to the United States. Lipson, in fact, claims that its role in the "Black September" crisis "[led] to a reevaluation of [its] importance as a regional ally" ("American Support for Israel," in Sheffer, p. 141).

The story does not end here, however. American leaders have also tightened America's ties to Israel in order to retain a substantial measure of control over Israeli foreign policy. They have deliberately employed diplomatic, military, and economic assistance to manipulate the Jewish state's wartime policies in ways that have promoted America's Middle Eastern interests. In the 1969–70 Egypt-Israel War of Attrition, American leaders first pressured Israel to end its "deep-penetration" air campaign and later pressured it to abide by a cease-fire agreement that Egypt and its Soviet patron had flagrantly violated. They forced restraint upon their client in order to weaken Soviet influence in Egypt and to foster pro-American feelings among Egyptian leaders. In the 1973 Yom Kippur War, American leaders first encouraged the Jewish state to forgo a preemptive strike against Arab armies massed along its frontiers and later compelled it to spare Egypt's Third Army from total defeat. They did these things in order to lure Arab states, especially Egypt, out of the Soviet camp and into the American camp. They believed that another crushing Israeli victory would make it impossible to conduct postwar peace negotiations, which they hoped to manipulate to America's advantage. In the 1982 Lebanon War, American leaders initially consented to an Israeli operation against the PLO in southern Lebanon because they thought that such a move would reduce Soviet influence in the Middle East. They later forced Israel to end the war when the fighting threatened to damage American-Arab ties rather than Soviet-Arab ones. And, during the 1991 Gulf War, American leaders pressured the Jewish state to stay out of the conflict, despite repeated ballistic missile attacks against Tel Aviv and other population centers, in order to facilitate their goal of maintaining a Western-Arab coalition under whose umbrella America could liberate Kuwait and smash Iraq's armed forces.

The motives of Israeli leaders have been much simpler. They have allowed the United States to manipulate their state's behavior, even though this manipulation has been very costly to the state at times, because they have astutely perceived that the American-Israeli special relationship has been much more beneficial than harmful to the state's long-term interests. Besides, what real alternative have they had? For most of the post-1967 period, Israel has been a pariah state in the world community. It simply has not had genuine opportunities to turn to other states to seek better arrangements.

German-Israeli Relations since 1967

While the American-Israeli relationship has become more intimate over the last thirty years, the German-Israeli relationship has deteriorated in significant respects, as both Lavy and Wolffsohn's volumes make clear. Indeed, it is doubtful that the post-1967 relationship deserves to be called special. Unquestionably, economic ties between the two states have remained close. Each state, for instance, has invested heavily in the other's economy. Scientific, educational, youth, and tourist ties, all of which receive generous attention from Wolffsohn, have steadily expanded as well. Nevertheless, Germany and Israel have been at odds for much of the last three decades. With the exception of the Gulf War, Germany has provided only token military assistance. Furthermore, it has generally gone along with the European Community's pro-Arab line for a solution to the Arab-Israeli conflict, albeit with less enthusiasm than some states, particularly France. In fact, the only real diplomatic service that Germany has rendered to Israel since the Six-Day War occurred during the 1973 Yom Kippur War, when it looked the other way (until the war was just about over) as the United States used German airfields and ports to supply the Jewish state with arms. In response to German ambivalence, Israel has essentially abandoned the notion of a close German-Israeli partnership. Israelis have apparently shown little interest in trying to renew the previous military connection. Nor has Israel done more in the diplomatic arena than occasionally ask Germany to use its influence within the European Community to blunt the policies of the community's more pro-Arab members.

Memories of the Holocaust may have had some effect on the German-Israeli relationship since the Six-Day War. Perhaps German leaders decided to facilitate the American arms airlift to Israel in 1973 in part because they felt Germany still owed a debt to the Jewish people. Perhaps they approved of the dispatch of military equipment to Israel during the Gulf War in part for the same reason. Perhaps Israel's declining emphasis on Germany as a diplomatic-military partner can be partially explained by the instinctive distrust and hostility toward Germans felt by Likud leaders (and by Holocaust survivors), like Menachem Begin and Yitzhak Shamir. But such memories of the past do not seem to have been a major influence on the German-Israeli relationship in the years since 1967.

The post-1967 change in the German-Israeli relationship has been determined primarily by the perceived national interests of both states. Germany's closer alignment with the Arab world has been dictated mainly by the latter's ability to employ its oil resources to achieve diplomatic ends and to derive vast wealth. Like their counterparts in the rest of Europe, German leaders have adopted a pro-Arab stance in order to secure a plentiful supply of cheap oil and to pave the way for lucrative business deals. Even in those instances when German leaders have taken steps to assist Israel, they have done so principally because it was in Germany's interest to do so. During the Yom Kippur War, German leaders looked the other way primarily to avoid angering Germany's most important partner, the United States. During the Gulf War, which brought Iraqi missile strikes against Israel, Germany cooperated with the Allied coalition against Iraq primarily to deflect criticism over Germany's role in having helped Iraq to prepare for the war. German industry had, after all, played a massive role in helping Iraq to build ballistic missiles and weapons of mass destruction. German leaders, in other words, assisted Israel primarily to protect their state's international reputation.

For their part, Israeli leaders have not been unduly concerned by the post-1967 decline in the German-Israeli relationship because of Israel's special relationship with the United States. They have been cognizant of the fact that Germany has not had the capability, let alone the inclination, to offer the Jewish state a better deal than America. That is the major reason why they have not vigorously pursued a diplomatic and military partnership with Germany since the Six-Day War.

Conclusion

The American-Israeli and German-Israeli relationships have been *special* for portions of their histories in one sense. Feldman, Reich, and Sheffer's volumes correctly point out that the United States and Israel have treated each other preferentially in diplomatic, military, economic, and cultural affairs at various times during the last half century. Lavy and Wolffsohn's volumes accurately identify the same pattern in German-Israeli ties. The American-Israeli and German-Israeli relationships have been, however, essentially *normal* in another important sense. Although ideological currents and transnational forces have contributed to the development of special relationships, especially in the German-Israeli case, they have been of much less importance than perceptions of national interests, which are the hallmark of "normal" relationships. While all of the volumes under review do acknowledge the fact that national self-interests have played a role in shaping the American-Israeli and German-Israeli relationships, they all exaggerate (Lavy and Wolffsohn's works less so than the others) the extent to which ideological currents and transnational forces have affected the development of these relationships.

Part II

Society and Culture

6. Mythmaking and Commemoration in Israeli Culture

David C. Jacobson

This essay is primarily concerned with the phenomenon of the simultaneous appearance of these studies in the contemporary context of the cultural and scholarly trend generally known as post-Zionism, which has so forcefully questioned the established cultural and political myths of Israel. The author situates the current challenges to established myths as the latest in a series of challenges that began in 1948 and that gained strength as a result of the Sinai campaign, the June 1967 war, the 1982 invasion of Lebanon, and the Palestinian Intifada. He considers the different methodologies of the writers under review, and the impact of current academic trends in literary criticism, history, and anthropology on their studies of Israel's myths.

Ben-Yehuda, Nachman, *The Masada Myth: Collective Memory and Mythmaking in Israel*, Madison: University of Wisconsin Press, 1995.

Gertz, Nurith, *Captives of a Dream: National Myths in Israeli Culture*, Tel Aviv: Am Oved, 1995. (Hebrew)

Wistrich, Robert, and David Ohana, eds., *The Shaping of Israeli Identity: Myth, Memory and Trauma*, London: Frank Cass, 1995.

Zerubavel, Yael, *Recovered Roots: Collective Memory and the Making of Israeli National Tradition,* Chicago: University of Chicago Press, 1995.

It can hardly be a coincidence that in 1995 four scholarly works dealing with issues of mythmaking and commemoration in Israeli culture were published. These works are clearly an outgrowth of the "post-Zionist" cultural climate in Israel, in which, as Robert Wistrich and David Ohana put it in the introduction to their collection of essays, "there are no great causes left [and] debunking the founding fathers and myths of Israel has become a national sport" (p. viii). In such a climate, the scholarly studies in these works were written not so much to debunk Israeli myths as to seek to better understand the processes by which the founding myths of Israel were established, the causes for their weakening impact on Israeli culture, and the ongoing creation in Israel of new myths to commemorate the past.

The monographs by Nachman Ben-Yehuda, Nurith Gertz, and Yael Zerubavel differ in a number of ways. Ben-Yehuda and Zerubavel are primarily interested in tracing the ways in which historical events have been mythologized as part of the process of the development of Jewish identity in the Land of Israel before and after the establishment of the state. Ben-Yehuda focuses on the mythologizing of the fall of Masada (73 C.E.), whereas Zerubavel compares the mythologizing of three events: the fall of Masada, the Bar Kokhba rebellion (132–35 C.E.), and the failed defense of the Zionist settlement Tel Hai (1920). Gertz organizes her study differently. She traces mythic themes that have played a central role in Jewish culture in the Land of Israel: the struggles of the few against the many and the children of light against the children of darkness, the conflict between East and West, the perception of the Jews as an isolated people as opposed to the perception of the Jews as a people belonging to the community of nations, and the tension between the individual and the collective.

Reflecting the current trend in literary studies to broaden the definition of text, Gertz states in her introduction that the sources of her study include not only works of literature, but other texts, including political expressions (speeches by leaders, posters, and election advertisements); the communications media (newspaper articles, television reports, and advertisements); film; and even public posters and graffiti. Her assumption is that each text includes an ideologically based mythic narrative that is not expressed directly but can be discerned as a subtext. She sees the expression of these mythic narratives in these texts as playing an important political role in society, for in each case she believes the purpose of these narratives is to shape the worldview of the society and to lead to certain action. These mythic narratives have such political power because what they do, in effect, is to present historical realities as eternal phenomena, thereby transforming history into myth. Thus, for example, the Arab-Israeli conflict has often been presented as part of the eternal Jewish historical experience of the few threatened by the many, thereby insuring that Israeli Jews will always see themselves as being at a disadvantage in this conflict.

Mythic narratives in Jewish culture of the Land of Israel, Gertz argues, have undergone periods of greater or lesser influence, some dominating at certain times and others dominating at other times. In order to trace this process, she focuses on key periods of ideological change, most of which occurred in times of violent conflict: the period of Arab violence against Jews in the 1930s, the 1948 war, the 1967 war, the Lebanon War, the Intifada, the Gulf War, as well as the rise of the Likud to power in 1977. It is significant that the myths on which Gertz chooses to focus all have to do with relationships, and in most cases relationships of conflict, either between opposing Jewish cultural and political camps or between the Jewish people and the world. There is much validity to this approach, since so much of personal and national identity is defined by how one views one's relationship to "the other."

Gertz is particularly preoccupied with the role of mythic narratives in the ongoing struggle between the political left and right that dates back to the emergence of the conflict between Labor Zionism and Revisionism in the early twentieth century. In chapter 1, for example, she explores the myth of the few against the many embodied in manifestos, speeches, and literary works of the 1930s. She notes the degree to which both Labor Zionists and Revisionists tended to see themselves as the few struggling with the many political parties opposed to them, but nevertheless as the true representatives of the national interest. Each side drew on narratives of the few against the many in the biblical, postbiblical, and modern periods to reassure itself and its followers that it will ultimately triumph as the dominant Zionist ideology.

Gertz is also concerned with the ways in which these mythic narratives have defined the relationship of Jews in the Land of Israel to Arabs, to Jews of the Diaspora, and to the nations of the world. In chapter 1, for example, she traces the extent to which political manifestos, polemical essays, and many literary works of the prestate period ignore the historical causes of the Arab-Jewish conflict. The conflict tends to appear in these texts as an absolute, universal situation with no causes or reasons, while the Arabs come across as a destructive force operating in an arbitrary manner. The result of this portrayal of the Arab-Jewish conflict is the transformation of historical understanding into mythic perception.

In chapter 2, Gertz examines journalistic reports of the first three months of the 1948 war and works of literature of the war period. As has so often been characteristic of mythmaking in the Land of Israel, these journalistic reports make connections between the 1948 war and earlier historical periods (the conquest of Canaan by Joshua, the Maccabees, the early period of Zionist settlement, and the fight against the British Mandate), thereby affirming the notion that the Jews of the Land of Israel can affect history, and that the present will end in victory as did past national efforts.

She notes that in the journalistic reports of 1948 the narrative of the few against the many did not play a central role. Perhaps, she speculates, this was because journalists felt that Israel's position in the early months of the war was so vulnerable that they did not wish to undermine national morale by emphasizing Jewish weakness. What journalists did do was to locate the 1948 war in the context of a mythic narrative of the ongoing struggle between the forces of enlightenment represented by Europe (the Jews) and the uncivilized forces of the primitive East (the Arabs). This had the advantage, she notes, of linking the 1948 war with the recent victory of the Western Allies in World War II against the barbarism of the Axis powers, thereby emphasizing the identification of the newly established State of Israel with the "good guys" who had triumphed in 1945.

Gertz observes that this mythic narrative represented an interesting paradigm shift in Zionist thinking. Early Zionist settlers had often viewed Eastern culture as more vital than that of Europe and the Arabs as a cultural model for how to transform the weak Jewish people of the Diaspora into a nation reborn in its ancient homeland in the Middle East. This change in the perception of Arabs, as Gertz comments, did not begin abruptly in 1948: it can be traced to the increase in violent Arab opposition to Zionism in the 1920s and 1930s that transformed the Arabs in the consciousness of the Jews from an admired model to an implacable enemy.

In some sections of her study, Gertz makes a point of noting the degree to which certain works of literature (often those that have come to be part of the central canon of modern Hebrew literature) undermine the national certitude embodied in the mythic narratives of other political and literary texts. In the case of the 1948 war, while journalistic reports and works of literature and speeches of the period all shared a sense of connection to history based on the ideology of the secular Jew who controls history, some works of literature expressed doubts about the ability to control history and conveyed a strong sense of existential angst accompanying such doubts. As powerful representatives of this trend she cites Nathan Alterman's poem *"Magash ha-Kesef"* (The Silver Platter, 1947) which laments the deaths of the youthful defenders of Israel in the war, and S. Yizhar's stories *"Ha-Shavuy"* (The Prisoner, 1948) and *"Hirbet Hizeh"* (1949), which takes as its title the name of a fictional Arab village. All of these pieces raise serious moral questions about the abuse of power by Israel in its struggle to defend itself against the onslaught of its Arab enemies.

Gertz shifts in the next three chapters to consider the dominant mythic narratives of the period in which the Likud rose to power in the late 1970s and early 1980s. Of particular interest in her analysis is her claim that the mythic narratives of this period presented a synthesis of right-wing ideological positions with myths of the traditional Jewish worldview that had been rejected by classical Zionism. Classical Zionism, she maintains, had fought against the traditional notion that the Jewish people had a unique history that moved it through cataclysmial periods of destruction and redemption beyond human control. Instead, the basic assumption of Zionists was that the Jews were like any other nation, and that therefore their fate would be determined by normal historical actions by human beings.

One example of the right-wing reappropriation of traditional mythic narratives is the image portrayed of Likud prime ministerial candidates Menachem Begin (in 1977 and 1981) and Yitzhak Shamir (in 1984). They were presented in political advertisements as father figures who had the power to redeem the people. Gertz sees this as similar to the very tendency of traditional Jews to passively wait for redemption—a passivity that classical Zionism rejected. Political rhetoric of this period tended to take an ahistorical approach, suggesting, in effect, that the past and future were not relevant, but rather that Israelis lived in an eternal, mythic present that kept repeating itself. In effect, according to this rhetoric, the Jewish people had been caught in a cyclic historical pattern of being the unjustified victims of other evil nations (the Arabs, as well as a largely unsympathetic world community of nations). Therefore, the argument went, only some kind of miraculous event—such as a grand military victory—would rescue Israel from this fate. As Gertz sees it, it was this mode of thinking that fueled Israel's ill-fated invasion of Lebanon in 1982. Although she tends to associate such rhetoric primarily with the Likud, Gertz does note that one can see the seeds of this approach already in the statist positions of Ben-Gurion in the 1950s and in the revival of religious consciousness after the victory in 1967. Furthermore, as Gertz points out, a whole range of parties began imitating this rhetoric after Begin's successful elections in 1977 and 1981.

This dominance of mythic narratives drawing on right-wing and traditional Jewish worldviews did not go unchallenged in Israeli culture. As was true in her analysis of the 1948 war period, Gertz sees in a number of Israeli literary works a critical view of these later mythic narratives. She makes the significant point that, already in the early 1960s, even before the outbreak of the 1967 war, the early fiction of A. B. Yehoshua (including such stories as *"Masa ha-Erev shel Yatir"* (The Yatir Evening Express, 1959) and *"Mul ha-Ya'arot"* (Facing the Forests, 1963) discerns the dangers inherent in what was already developing as an underlying Israeli feeling of being alone in the world and on the verge of imminent destruction. In these stories by Yehoshua, as well as in Amos Kenan's later work *Shoah 2*, she asserts, the right-wing mythic narrative of miraculous triumph over the problematic fate of Israel as "a nation that dwells alone" was portrayed as dangerously self-destructive.

In her study, Gertz suggests that when, in the aftermath of the Lebanon War and the Intifada, Israelis became increasingly disillusioned with the effectiveness of military power to produce the kind of miraculous redemption promised by right-wing mythic narratives, they increasingly challenged these narratives. This was particularly true in the aftermath of the Gulf War. In his public statements about the war, Prime Minister Yitzhak Shamir played down the immediate cause of the war, Iraq's invasion of Kuwait. He focused instead on Iraq's missile attacks on Israel as illustrations of Israel being part of the narrative of the few against the many and as the children of light against the children of darkness, declaring that the war would eventually end in the defeat of the enemy, thereby redeeming Israel from danger. In his speeches, furthermore, he would associate the Gulf War with the mythic events associated with such holidays of redemption as Passover, Purim, and Hanukkah.

Unfortunately, Gertz observes, Shamir's political rhetoric did not fit historical reality. In fact, Israeli policy during the Gulf War, she notes, more closely resembled that of the Labor Zionist approach of self-restraint of the prestate period than the Revisionists' more rhetorically fiery approach of armed battle conveyed in Shamir's mythic narratives. While Shamir's rhetoric foresaw a miraculous redemptive victory against a world that has always hated the Jews, his policy of acceding to American wishes that Israel not retaliate against Iraq was more in keeping with what she sees as the classical Zionist position that the Jewish people have a normal history and must relate to its historical challenges in a rational, pragmatic fashion. In effect, Gertz claims, the 1967 war and the rise of Likud to power in 1977 opened the way for the dominance of right-wing mythic narratives in Israel, but subsequently the Lebanon War, the Intifada, and the Gulf War contributed to the reappropriation of the rival Labor-Zionist myth that contributed in part to the return of Labor to power in 1992 and to the opening up of the peace process initiated by Yitzhak Rabin and Shimon Peres.

Yael Zerubavel draws on a variety of sources to trace the role of the mythologizing of the fall of Masada, the Bar Kokhba revolt, and the failed defense of Tel Hai in Israeli culture, including public-school textbooks, educational brochures produced by Jewish youth movements, educational publications by the Israel Defense Forces (IDF), newspaper articles, television and radio programs, popular songs, jokes, children's literature, as well as poems, plays, and works of fiction. Zerubavel includes in her study interviews she conducted with children ages twelve to fourteen and their parents from which she sought to determine how the popular Israeli imagination perceives these three historic events. She is particularly interested in how the development of national narrative and ritual has provided Jews before and after the establishment of the state with commemorative frameworks within which to understand their identities. Like Gertz, Zerubavel insists that mythic narratives do not maintain a static existence in culture, and so in her study she traces the ongoing political and intellectual debates about the cultural significance of the commemoration of each of these events.

Zerubavel's choice of these three events was not arbitrary. She sees the mythic commemorative approaches to these events as central to the emergence of Zionism as an ideological alternative to traditional Judaism. As she notes, Jewish tradition saw the key historical turning point in antiquity to be the destruction of the Second Temple in 70 C.E. It largely ignored Masada and had an ambivalent attitude toward the Bar Kokhba revolt. Zionist culture in the yishuv (prestate) period elevated Masada and the Bar Kokhba revolt into central turning points in ancient times. In so doing, Zionists interpreted both events as examples of Jews taking their fate into their hands that would be inspiring for modern immigrant settlers. The 1920 defense of Tel Hai against Arab forces came, in turn, to be seen in prestate Zionist culture as a turning point illustrating how, in the early days of Zionist settlement, Jews once again acted in the fighting spirit of Masada and the Bar Kokhba revolt.

Zerubavel devotes much of her study of the commemoration of these three events to outlining the ways in which each of them became the kernels of national myths. Of the three events, Tel Hai was unique because it was the only one to take place in the modern period. It emerged as a national myth based on a number of elements: a compelling story that concluded with the dramatic words of the fallen leader of Tel Hai, Yosef Trumpeldor, usually rendered "It is good to die for our country"; a sacred site at the cemetery where the fallen defenders of Tel Hai were buried, on which was constructed an impressive sculpture of a lion; and the establishment of the day of the fall of Tel Hai (the eleventh of Adar in the Hebrew calendar) as a national memorial day. Trumpeldor was an attractive mythic hero because, although he grew up in Russia, his life-style as an assimilated Jew who had lost his arm fighting in the czar's army fit well with the Zionist desire to transform the weakened Diaspora Jew into a new fighting Hebrew. The Tel Hai commemorative narrative of a small group of Jewish settlers fighting Arab attackers, Zerubavel notes, became an important paradigm for the mythic narrative of the few against the many which, as Gertz wrote, has long played a central role in Israeli culture. Over time the Tel Hai site, which now includes a youth hostel and a museum, became institutionalized as a place to commemorate the origins of the State of Israel. The mythic status of Tel Hai was reinforced in versions of the story told in children's literature taught in yishuv schools in the early part of the twentieth century, which would often link Trumpeldor directly with ancient Jewish heroes.

The Bar Kokhba revolt emerged as the basis for a national myth, according to Zerubavel, because it was seen as the Jewish nation's last fight for its freedom in antiquity, a fight that Zionism was taking up once again after almost two thousand years. A curious aspect of this mythologization of the revolt is the transformation by the Zionist mythic narrative of what turned out to be a *failed* revolt into a symbol of the successful expression of *national power*. In commemorating this event, the defeat of Bar Kokhba came to play less of a role than the image of taking up arms for the sake of national freedom. In addition, while Jewish tradition had marked the end of the revolt on the ninth of Av (which also commemorated the destruction

The Roaring Lion at Tel Hai. Courtesy the Haganah Archives, photo 8583.

of the Second Temple), the yishuv came to commemorate the revolt on Lag Ba-Omer, which is associated in Jewish tradition with the period when the revolt was still viable. As was the case with Yosef Trumpeldor, children's literature in the yishuv schools celebrated Bar Kokhba as a legendary hero. A central feature of this literature was a tale of Bar Kokhba overcoming a lion, thereby associating him with a variety of ancient heroes, such as Samson and David, who had to overcome such challenges before they could emerge as true heroes. The continued existence of the Bar Kokhba revolt as a national myth was reinforced in the 1960s with the excavation of the Bar Kokhba caves, which provided a tangible connection between the present and the ancient past.

The story of the fall of Masada had played even less of a role in traditional Jewish collective memory than that of the Bar Kokhba revolt. For centuries its memory was preserved for Jews primarily in the Hebrew version of Josephus' *Wars of the Jews*, known as Jossipon. With the publication of a modern Hebrew translation of Josephus in 1923 and of the immensely popular Hebrew poem "Masada" written by Yitzhak Lamdan in 1927, Masada assumed a more central place in the consciousness of Zionist settlers. A tradition of youth pilgrimages to the impressive site developed in the prestate period. These pilgrimages involved physically challenging walks through the desert culminating with a climb to the top of Masada. Zerubavel believes that these field trips to Masada constituted powerful ritual reenactments of the ancient Israelites' travels through the desert following the Exodus, as well as the ascent to the Temple Mount on pilgrimage holidays in biblical times. Masada also became a location for army induction ceremonies. Awareness of Masada expanded as a result of its excavation in the 1950s and 1960s. Eventually it emerged as a major tourist site. As was the case with the Bar Kokhba revolt, the mythic narrative of Masada had to be adjusted for it to serve as a paradigm of a heroic defense of freedom. After all, according to Josephus the Jews at Masada did not fight their Roman enemies heroically to the end, but rather committed mass suicide in anticipation of a Roman victory. The distinction between this suicidal end of the Masada fighters and the notion of fighting to the end was therefore often blurred in the mythic commemoration of Masada.

The final section of Zerubavel's study is devoted to the ways in which each of these national myths has become, over time, a source of controversy within Israeli culture. She cites the ongoing debate in the 1930s and 1940s between Labor Zionists and Revisionists over who was the true inheritor of the spirit of Tel Hai. Revisionists saw in the heroic defenders of Tel Hai support for their call for armed resistance against the British and the Arabs. Labor Zionists, on the other hand, emphasized the Tel Hai defenders' commitment to working the land, which they saw as supporting the priority they put on settling the land and exercising restraint in the use of arms.

The debate over Tel Hai was reawakened in the late 1970s at the time of the Camp David Agreement with Egypt, with the emerging controversy over what to do with the territories Israel had captured in 1967. Both those favoring territorial compromise with the Arabs and those opposed to such compromise interpreted the events of Tel Hai as justifying their position. At this time a strong challenge to the Tel Hai myth was issued by the Israeli journalist Nakdimon Rogel, who developed a series of radio and television programs and a book—*Tel Hai: Hazit le-lo Oref* (Tel Hai: A Front Without a Rear), 1979—based on his study of the defense of Tel Hai. In his study Rogel raised serious questions about the way in which the myth of Tel Hai encouraged the notion that Jews must always be devoted to sacrificing their lives to hold onto territory in the Land of Israel. Historically, he argued, this was not really what happened at Tel Hai: the defenders of Tel Hai had in fact retreated, and yet in the end the part of the Galilee that they were defending did become part of the State of Israel.

The words attributed to Yosef Trumpeldor just before his death— "It is good to die for our country"—became harder to sustain as a national slogan as Israelis became increasingly disillusioned after 1967 with the seemingly endless Arab-Israeli conflict and the painful events of the 1969-70 War of Attrition, the 1973 Yom Kippur War, and the 1982 Lebanon War. As Zerubavel notes, one of the most powerful expressions of that challenge to the heroic figure of Trumpeldor came in the Israeli film *Late Summer Blues*, in which high school seniors about to be drafted into the War of Attrition in 1970 plan a graduation ceremony skit mocking his dying words. A wave of sometimes grotesque jokes about Trumpeldor swept across Israel in the 1970s and 1980s, focusing in particular on the fact that his arm had been amputated. Such mockery can be seen perhaps as an expression of anger at the elevation of self-sacrifice as a principle by those who were being asked to risk their lives in the ongoing conflict with the Arabs.

The most forceful dissent from the Bar Kokhba myth was issued by the late Yehoshafat Harkabi, a former hawkish chief of military intelligence who became dovish in his later years as a scholar of international relations. In a series of publications in the early 1980s, Harkabi critiqued the glorification of the revolt that was central to the mythic narrative accepted by Israelis. The revolt, he argued, was a misguided act of national suicide, since it had no chance of succeeding. Behind Harkabi's attack on the Bar Kokhba myth was a warning to his fellow Israelis to avoid the dangers of what he saw as the Likud's policy of uncompromising attitudes toward territorial compromise with the Arabs that might end up to be self-defeating. Partly out of a wish to defend Bar Kokhba and Likud policy against Harkabi's attack, Prime Minister Menachem Begin arranged a state funeral in 1982 for bodily remains that had been found two decades earlier in the area where letters of the Bar Kokhba revolt had been discovered. Based on the assumption that these remains were those of the Bar Kokhba freedom fighters, the funeral was held on Lag Ba-Omer with the clear expression of a symbolic link between those ancient warriors and the contemporary military defenders of Israel.

Scholars and other writers outside of Israel, and to a lesser extent inside Israel, have attacked the Masada myth as the basis for a dangerous tendency in the Israeli psyche to ignore political realities and to put itself into a situation that could lead to national suicide. One of the most prominent examples of such an attack came from the American journalist Stewart Alsop, who criticized Israel under the leadership of Prime Minister Golda Meir in the early 1970s as burdened by what he called a "Masada complex" that was leading it to uncompromising positions in the Arab-Israeli conflict that would ultimately destroy it.

In his study of the Masada myth, Nachman Ben-Yehuda is primarily concerned with determining how during the period of the yishuv and since the establishment of the state the mythic narrative of Masada has developed. On the basis of existing historical documents (youth-group publications, textbooks, newspapers, etc.) and interviews of Israelis, he examines the actual content of how the story of Masada has been told in Jewish culture in the Land of Israel, as well as the individuals and social institutions that shaped the telling of that story as part of a larger agenda to forge a new Jewish identity. Although the accuracy of Josephus' account of Masada has often been challenged, Ben-Yehuda decides to use it as the closest approximation of the historical reality available. This account then serves as the benchmark against which he measures deviations by the various forms of the mythic narrative that contributed so powerfully to the shaping of Israeli identity.

As Zerubavel has noted in her study, the story of Masada presented problems for Zionist ideologues who sought to use it to inspire Jews to fight for the establishment and defense of Israel. The most obvious difficulty, as we have seen, was the fact that the fighters committed suicide, an act that would not seem to have been compatible with the ethos of modern Zionism. As he examines the Josephus narrative, Ben-Yehuda notes a number of other elements that make the story problematic. According to Josephus, the people who died on Masada were members of the Sicarii sect, who were extremist Jewish fighters who did not shrink even from assassinating fellow Jews. In fact, according to Josephus, they went to Masada because, even before the end of the revolt against Rome, they had been driven out of Jerusalem by their fellow Jews, who could not tolerate their extremism. While at Masada they raided surrounding settlements for food and even engaged in a massacre of Jews at Ein Gedi. Furthermore, there is no record in Josephus of any battles that the Sicarii of Masada fought with the Romans who besieged them.

Mythic narratives of Masada could function effectively only if the Josephus narrative was significantly modified. The versions of the Masada saga that Ben-Yehuda examines tended to eliminate the identification of the Masada fighters as Sicarii and to identify them instead with the Zealot party of the time. Furthermore, the impression was often given in these mythic narratives that the fighters at Masada fled Jerusalem only after its destruction in 70 C.E., rather than being expelled by their fellow Jews before the end of the revolt against Rome, and that they therefore deserve credit for pursuing the central goals of the revolt against Rome for an additional three years. Mythic narratives of Masada eliminate reference to the Jews of Masada raiding surrounding settlements, and these narratives include references to battles between the Jews on Masada and the Romans. The suicide was portrayed as the last heroic act of those who, having fought till the bitter end, would rather die as dignified free men than submit to the degradation of Roman enslavement.

How did the myth of Masada become so widespread in Jewish culture in the Land of Israel? Ben-Yehuda argues that the two individuals who had the greatest impact on the development of the Masada myth were the Labor-Zionist activist Shmaria Guttman and the general and archaeologist Yigael Yadin. Both played the role of what he calls "moral entrepreneurs" who effectively formed and transmitted the Masada mythical narrative to Jews. Guttman, as Ben-Yehuda presents it, provided the main inspiration for the emergence of Masada as a place of ritual pilgrimage for Zionist youth groups in the years leading up to the establishment of the state. If Guttman's impact was largely on Jewish culture of the yishuv, Yadin's was of greater scope. His excavation of Masada in the 1960s and the public role that he played as an interpreter of the significance of Masada gave that site world renown. While Ben-Yehuda accepts the professional integrity of Yadin as an archaeologist who never falsified the data, he makes it clear that Yadin's presentation of the Masada story to the public deviated from the Josephus story in the same ways as the heroic version of the Masada mythic narrative that was central to Israeli culture.

As a sociologist, Ben-Yehuda is particularly interested in examining the social institutions that reinforced and transmitted the Masada myth. He discusses the role of the trek to Masada as a socializing ritual in Zionist youth groups and its status as the location of the swearing in of the IDF armored units for many decades. These ritual pilgrimages to Masada were clearly in the spirit of the Masada myth that saw the fighters of Masada as heroic models.

Ben-Yehuda turns to textual sources as well. He demonstrates that the way in which Israeli high school history textbooks, some dating back to the prestate period, have told the story of Masada has been very much in keeping with the mythic narrative of Masada. Other texts that he sees as disseminators of the Masada myth are Israeli newspaper accounts of the Yadin excavations in the 1960s and guidebooks for tourists. In addition, Ben-Yehuda observed a number of guides leading tours at Masada, only to discover that their accounts were largely in the spirit of the Masada myth as it has been developed over the decades.

The authors of these three monographs have engaged in a thorough examination of a variety of sources to trace the processes of myth-making and commemoration in the Land of Israel. At the same time, one can discern in the scholarship of each of these Israeli-born academics the pursuit of a "personal agenda." While Gertz is less explicit than Ben-Yehuda and Zerubavel in stating her personal agenda, one senses a clear bias on her part against the dominance of mythic narratives favored by the political right, which she sees as blinding Jews to historical reality. Such mythic narratives include the notion that the Arabs are a manifestation of the eternal existence of enemies of the Jews. She believes that it was the synthesis of such right-wing and traditional religious mythic narratives in the late 1970s and 1980s that led to the disaster of the Lebanon War. One can almost hear, in her description of the undermining of the right-wing mythic narratives in the aftermath of the Gulf War, a sigh of relief that in the swing of the pendulum of dominant myths Israel had been (at least at the time of publication of the book in 1995) saved from misguided legends and was once again basing its policies on reason.

Zerubavel and Ben-Yehuda share a somewhat different personal preoccupation. For both, the motivation to study myth and commemoration in Israeli society stemmed from their discovery that historical memory as it had been presented to them growing up in Israel was actually socially constructed. This then led to their interest in examining the methods by which that construction was achieved. In the preface to her book, Zerubavel states that the idea for her study was the result of a greater self-consciousness about the nature of Israeli identity that she developed after emigrating to the United States in the 1970s. It was when she began to observe how different from American Jewish culture was the secular Israeli culture in which she was raised in Israel that she became curious to explore how that secular Israeli culture came about.

While Zerubavel writes as one who gained new perspective on her culture by emigrating away from it, Ben-Yehuda writes as an Israeli still living in Israel who is angry that the artificial construction of the past has been foisted on generations of Jews in the Land of Israel, including his own. When he first discovered that the way in which the Masada narrative had been taught to him departed so significantly from Josephus' account, he writes, he "felt cheated and manipulated" (p. 5). He was particularly perturbed because, for him and his fellow Jewish Israelis, Masada was

> not just a story. Masada provided, certainly for my generation of Jewish Israelis, an important ingredient in the very definition of our Jewish and Israeli identity. Now what was I supposed to do when it turned out that such a major element of my identity was based on falsehood, on a deviant belief? (p. 5)

Even with all of his indignation, Ben-Yehuda apparently felt conflicted about uncovering the truth about the Masada myth. Interviews he conducted with Shmaria Guttman were an important source for his understanding of how the myth was formed and transmitted. At the end of the first interview with Guttman, Ben-Yehuda reports, the elderly Zionist leader put his arm around him and asked, "You are not going to do bad, Dr. Ben-Yehuda, are you?" "No," Ben-Yehuda replied, "that is not my intention" (p. 82). This interchange apparently raised a serious, perhaps subconscious, challenge to Ben-Yehuda: if he pursued his study and revealed the historical distortions of Zionist mythmaking, he would be engaged in an inappropriate revolt against the cultural hegemony of his parents' generation. This subconscious challenge seems to have been formidable, for as Ben-Yehuda informs us, he actually put off the study for almost a year and a half, and even after completing it, he writes that he thought and hoped "that in publishing this book [he was] not doing something 'bad'" (ibid).

We turn, finally, to the collection of essays edited by Robert Wistrich and David Ohana, which first appeared in the spring 1995 issue of the London-based journal *Israel Affairs*. The editors subsequently published a Hebrew volume,[1] not considered in this essay, which includes some of the essays in the English volume and several others. It is beyond the scope of this essay to consider the wide-ranging concerns of all of the historians, social scientists, and literary scholars who contributed to the collection. Most relevant to the monographs we have been considering are those essays that specifically address the process of Israeli mythmaking and commemoration.

In his article, "Ben-Gurion's Mythopoetics," Ze'ev Tzahor views Israel's first prime minister as a "mythopoetic leader" (p. 63) who knew how to use myths to serve his ideological goal of transforming Diaspora Jews into a reborn Israeli people. His frequent associations between the biblical period (especially the period of the conquest of Canaan) and contemporary Israel were part of his attempt to play the role of national educator. His declared insistence that not all of the descendants of Jacob left Canaan to go into slavery in Egypt is a prime example of how he manipulated the past in order to assert his belief that "the exilic condition is not an inherent aspect of the Jewish people, but a deviation from their true nature" (p. 68).

The Ben-Gurion era can be seen as the final flowering of the classical Zionist myth of the transformation of the Diaspora Jew into a new secular Hebrew. Yet even in Ben-Gurion's day that myth came to be undermined. In his essay, "Political Dimensions of Holocaust Memory in Israel During the 1950s," Yechiam Weitz cites Eliezer Don-Yehiya's observation that the Eichmann trial, which was so directly orchestrated by Ben-Gurion, can be seen as a retreat from the extreme negation of the Diaspora that was at the heart of Ben-Gurion's mythic understanding of Jewish history. The testimony of Holocaust survivors at the trial granted a greater role than had been possible before for the voice of the weakened Diaspora Jew to participate in Israel's commemoration of its past.

The national institutionalized ways of commemorating the Holocaust in Israel, such as the Yad Vashem museum and the annual observance of Yom ha-Shoah, are well-known. Nevertheless, it is not only the political and cultural elite that have engaged in the construction of mythic patterns of commemoration. In her essay, "'In Everlasting Memory': Individual and Communal Holocaust Commemoration in Israel," Judith Tydor Baumel explores the ways in which Israeli Holocaust survivors, without the direct sanction of the government, have found their own ways to commemorate the Holocaust. These acts often reflect a mythic understanding of the past that is very different from the Zionist myth that Ben-Gurion had sought to perpetuate in the early years of the state. These grass-roots forms of commemoration have included Yizkor (memorial) books commemorating Jewish communities in Europe destroyed in the Shoah, communal tombstones marking ashes transported to Israel from concentration camps, and memorial panels in synagogues. These commemorative expressions tend to depart from classical Zionist myth in that they do not generally celebrate Jewish acts of physical heroism in the Shoah that were so emphasized in the official commemoration of the Holocaust in the early years of the state. They also pay close attention to lovingly remembering the life of these Diaspora communities, thereby challenging the standard Zionist negation of the Diaspora. These memorials depart from Israeli mythic self-understanding in another significant way, as well: while the standard Israeli mythic narrative finds comfort after the Shoah in the establishment of the State of Israel, the pain of the survivors who created these memorials was apparently too great to tell their story as if it could come to a comforting conclusion in 1948.

Holocaust survivors may be seen as representing one of the first grass-roots challenges to the myths of Zionism. As Erik Cohen discusses in his essay, "Israel as a Post-Zionist Society," with the gradual breakdown of the Zionist consensus in Israel of the past few decades, many ideological alternatives have been "vying for hegemony" in Israeli culture. Classical Zionism assumed that the Jewish society that would be established in the sovereign Jewish state in the Land of Israel would be secular. Two essays in this collection examine the emergence of religious communities as contributors to the mosaic of cultural myths that has come to characterize Israeli society. In his essay, "Paradigms Sometimes Fit: The Haredi Response to the Yom Kippur War," Charles Liebman examines the mythic patterns that governed the response of ultra-Orthodox Jews in Israel, particularly as represented by the Agudat Israel party, to the 1967 and 1973 wars. His study of the coverage of these wars in the ultra-Orthodox press reveals a mythic understanding that would be foreign to early Zionists: wars come about as punishment for sin, particularly for the sin of pride that Israeli Jews had committed by believing they could rely only on their own power to save them, and while Israeli Jews had to fight bravely to defend themselves, victory came ultimately as a divine miracle. This ultra-Orthodox approach also assumes that there is the possibility of exploiting the sense of miraculous victory experienced by secular Israelis to influence them to return to the ways of tradition.

Another voice in Israel's mosaic of cultural myths is that of Mizrahi popular religion. Yoram Bilu and Eyal Ben-Ari explore one example of the popular traditions imported by the Jews of the Middle East and North Africa in "Modernity and Charisma in Contemporary Israel: The Case of Baba Sali and Baba Baruch." The emergence of the ascetic, otherworldly Baba Sali as a revered saint in the Jewish community of Moroccan origin represents a significant attempt on the part of Moroccan Jews to import their religious worldview into the primarily secular Israeli culture. Even more fascinating is the way in which, after the death of Baba Sali, his son, who is now known as Baba Baruch, was able to construct a mythic narrative that preserved the memory of his father and elevated Baruch himself (despite his questionable moral past) to be his father's spiritual heir. As he now functions in this role, Bilu and Ben-Ari point out, Baba Baruch reflects a distinctly Israeli version of sainthood characterized by materialism and involvement in the affairs of the world that clearly departs from the more traditional Moroccan-Jewish sainted, ascetic and otherworldly life-style of his father.

The current drive to shatter Israel's cultural myths that has been so prominent in scholarly and popular forums seems at times to be accompanied by an attack on the validity of mythmaking itself. It is as if those who attack Israel's mythic narratives are saying that their great accomplishment has been to remove the wool that was pulled over the eyes of the Israeli public by its political and cultural elite for too long. In the introduction to their collection of essays, Wistrich and Ohana argue that myths do not have to be seen merely as deceptive manipulations of the truth:

> Above all, most myths are to some degree narratives which seek to anchor the present in the past—and the Zionist "myths" under attack today do not differ from this pattern. Myths seen in this light, as a special kind of narrative, as symbolic statements or frames of reference which give meaning to the past, are not necessarily false or harmful examples of pseudo-history. (p. ix)

As the editors argue, the main purpose of studying myths need not be to attack the mythmakers, but rather to gain from such a study a greater understanding of the nature of Israeli culture: "The . . . true significance [of myths] more often lies in what they can tell us about the ways in which a particular nation, social group, or set of individuals seek to organize its collective memory and to establish a distinctive identity" (p. ix). These four scholarly studies of mythmaking and commemoration in Israel do indeed provide many illuminating insights into cultural trends that have shaped, and will continue to shape, the ongoing formation of Israeli identity.

Note

1. *Myth and Memory: The Transformation of Israeli Identity*, eds. Robert Wistrich and David Ohana (Tel Aviv: Van Leer Jerusalem Institute and ha-Kibbutz ha-Meuchad, 1996). (Hebrew)

7. Prophecy of Wrath: Israeli Society as Reflected in Satires for Children

Yaakova Sacerdoti

This essay explains how popular satirists have developed a unique political and social whip, using simple language, humor, and fantasy, combined with complex literary structures, to address adult audiences through their children. The author shows how, in the highly charged and polarized atmosphere of Israeli society, satirists use a down-to-earth approach to attack the rising power of religious institutions at the expense of the secular, corrupt leaders and foolish citizens, and the absurdity of the Arab-Israeli conflict.

Sidon, Efraim, *Baldy Heights,* Tel-Aviv: Am-Oved, 1995. (Hebrew)

———, *A Strange and Amazing Story about a Small Island Named Logic*, Jerusalem: Keter, 1993. (Hebrew)

———, *Uzo and Muzo from the Village Kakaruzo*, Jerusalem: Keter, 1993. (Hebrew)

Shalev, Meir, *How the Neanderthal Man Incidentally Invented the Rumanian Kabob*, Tel-Aviv: Am-Oved, 1993. (Hebrew)

———, *Nechama the Louse*, Tel-Aviv: Am-Oved, 1995. (Hebrew)

I

Israel is a unique ethnic, religious, and cultural patchwork. For Jews, it is the land of Abraham, Isaac, and Jacob. From all over the world, Jews gather to find in this petite Promised Land a shelter from persecutions, and a solution to their religious and national identity. Ashkenazi, Sephardi, ultra-Orthodox, and secular Jews live side by side trying to find their place inside this bubbling melting pot. For Christians and Muslims, it is also a Holy Land, the scene of their religious development. The Arab-Israeli conflict, rooted in ancient times, is an infected birthmark, scarring this beautiful country of desert and green mountains with blood and hostility. Sadly, many Israelis have become used to the conflict with the Arab world.

The 1990s found Israeli society in a phase of quasi eruption, with some people talking of civil war. Many agree that it all began during the mid-1982 Lebanon War that divided the country into two hostile camps—right and left. *"Shalom ha-Galil"* (Peace for the Galilee), a war that was supposed to bring peace and quiet to the northern part of Israel, became an Israeli Vietnam. Soldiers went to the front not as messengers of hope and heroism but rather to carry the burden of a split society. The Intifada (Palestinian uprising) which erupted in December 1987 widened the gap. Citizens and soldiers were pounded by daily confrontations in the Gaza Strip and the West Bank, which became an issue of deep domestic disagreement. Some waved the flag of Jewish supremacy over the land, while others flooded the streets to demonstrate against the government's policy in the name of morality. There seemed to be an erosion of unity of purpose as a growing number of Israelis started to doubt whether they were indeed struggling for survival, or whether David had become Goliath.

The lava continued to bubble under the surface when the 1993 Oslo agreement was signed. Opponents decried the sale of Israel's birthright for a "mess of lentils," waving the flag of nationalism and religious rights to the land. Urban plazas were packed with demonstrators carrying signs depicting the prime minister, Yitzhak Rabin, as Hitler or as an SS officer, some calling for his death. Rabin's supporters, on the other hand, were delighted by the course of events set in motion in Oslo, and regarded these rallies as a passing phenomenon. No one could believe that words of hate would soon become bullets of death.

The November 1995 assassination of Yitzhak Rabin by a religiously motivated young Jew shook the country as never before, and with bitter irony people were saying: "Now we are a nation like all the nations." Israeli society entered a labyrinth of groups and subgroups: Israelis against Palestinians, and among Israelis, right versus left, religious versus secular, Ashkenazim versus Sephardim, and "native" Israelis against Russian and Ethiopian immigrants.

II

In this state of chaos, criticism, and hostility, all sides mobilized their forces. Politicians and political activists were echoed by the media. Newspaper articles and TV programs became harsh; nothing was sacred, no one was secure, and satire flourished. Comedians who had once attacked cultural and linguistic taboos switched to satire that targeted political issues and actors. *"Zehu-Zeh"* (That's it!), once an entertaining TV program for children, became a satirical show for adults. *"Hartzufim,"*[1] a new satiric show, swept the country with its vulgar, straightforward, and cynical skits. The attacks came from every corner, including the area of children's literature.

Efraim Sidon, a well-known Israeli satirist and left-wing activist, embraced children's literature as one of his political and social whips. Influenced by the works of Jonathan Swift, Lewis Carroll, Dr. Seuss, and others, he chose children's literature as the looking glass for Israeli society. Using simple language, humor, and fantasy as well as complex literary structures, he addresses his adult audience through its children, thus rejuvenating his well-known positions and keeping them at the forefront of public attention. The targets are clear and defined. In *A Strange and Amazing Story about a Small Island Named Logic*, it is the dominance of religious institutions and the impotence of the secular sector. In *Baldy Heights*, it is corrupted leaders and foolish citizens. In *Uzo and Muzo from the Village Kakaruzo*, it is the absurdity of the Arab-Israeli conflict. By forcing their readers to look in a distorted mirror and to confront the faults of Israeli society, these texts reflect the present while predicting the future.

III

Uzo and Muzo is the story of two brothers who loved each other dearly until a question is raised: "When a man or a woman wants to sit on a chair and cross one foot over the other, which leg goes on top and which underneath?" (p. 5). Uzo thinks the right leg, while Muzo favors the left. A terrible fight breaks out that ends with them building a wall that divides the house and the family. Now separated by the wall, the brothers plant hatred and fear in the coming generations with inflated legends about a terrifying monster living on the other side of the wall. One day a small child named Uzo overcomes his fears and hesitation and decides to climb the wall in order to see the monster. On the other side he meets a girl named Muza. Finally their belief in humanity, together with pure common sense, persuades them to introduce their families and to get married.

Uzo and Muzo focuses on the tension between initiator and victim within the Arab-Israeli conflict, either of whom can be, as described by David Alexander, "[t]he simple citizen . . . a naïve and embarrassed victim. A silly individual maintained by clichés, one that cultivates slogans, gradually becoming a war fan."[2] Uzo and Muzo, as archetypes of the Arab and the Israeli leaders' faults, represent war and separation between the two nations.[3] Absurd and groundless hatred, fanatically transmitted from generation to generation, is the text's main theme. The theme is supported and heightened by a reservoir of allusions to the stories of hatred between brothers in Genesis and the metaphorical image of the wall.

The story of Cain and Abel was the precursor of endless conflicts within human history. The jealousy of the one and God's preference of the other result in murder: "And when they were in the field, Cain rose up against his brother Abel, and killed him" (Gen. 4:8). The story of Isaac and Ishmael continues this motif, planting the seeds of hostility between two nations-to-come. Two brothers are destined to hate without cause even before they are born, as demonstrated by God's promise to Abraham: "And I will give to you, and to your offspring after you, the land where you are now an alien, all the land of Canaan, for a perpetual holding; and I will be their God" (Gen. 17:8). This promise would require the two brothers, despite their mothers' jealousy and animosity, to share one country.

The allusion to Isaac and Ishmael clearly emerges from the text: "Uzo brought him a wife from the city . . . also Muzo brought himself a wife from far away" (pp. 10–11). In the Bible, Hagar got Ishmael a wife from the land of Egypt, while Abraham asks his servant to get Isaac a wife not from the Canaanites among whom he lives but rather from his faraway country. (Gen. 21:21, 24:4) Jacob and Esau's relations are doomed already in their mother's womb: "And the LORD said to her: 'Two nations are in your womb, and two people born of you shall be divided.'. . ."(Gen. 25:23). The saga of Joseph and his brothers is another brick in the wall of separation. Jacob's favoritism toward the son of his beloved wife, Rachel, and Joseph's prophetic powers give birth to unmitigated sibling hatred. Although no murder is committed and the story has a happy ending, this hate would give birth to slavery and suffering.

Sidon's text departs from the biblical examples to emphasize the wrongdoings of the modern successors to the patriarchs. Uzo and Muzo, as the founders of Western civilization, sow the seeds of hate and hostility. Their successors, the Arab and Israeli leaders and peoples, are the brainwashed victims. They are like a horse with blinders that can only go straight ahead and is incapable of looking to the side:

> And generation after generation, it was impossible to stop the story of the Satan behind the wall. And the strange thing was no one remembered by then, why the wall had been built or when. (p. 14)

The hostility is mutual, the coin has two sides, and no one is better than the other. Both sides share the same fears and the same demonic stereotypes and the wall built by ethnocentric rulers is a symbol of self-destruction for both nations.

This text calls upon its adult readers to follow four steps. First, they must neutralize their egocentric views. Second, they have to distinguish between the rivals and identify with one of them. Third, they are asked to see themselves through their rival's eyes and understand that the other sees them as the enemy. The open ending of the story, a basic break of children's-literature conventions, is the fourth and the most difficult step to take. The reader is called upon to get up and act.

The Arab-Israeli conflict is only one of a series of conflicts that confront Israeli society. Perhaps the most dangerous one is the cultural war between secular and religious Israelis. In his book, *In the Land of Israel*, Amos Oz writes:

> In a conversation twenty years ago, my teacher Dov Sadan said that Zionism was nothing more than a passing episode, a temporary mundane phenomenon of history and politics, but that Orthodox Judaism would re-emerge, would swallow Zionism and digest it.[4]

Now, thirty-five years later, Sadan's prophecy is rejuvenated and comes to life in children's literature, a literary mode that never before dealt with this controversial issue. Efraim Sidon writes:

The difference between those called "adults" and "children" is only in the number of centimeters. The adults are in fact infantile a little bit longer. Therefore, . . . we stand in the middle of a cultural war witnessing the shift of the religious sector from defense to offense, . . . In 1993 I published a children's book named *A Strange and Amazing Story about a Small Island Named Logic*. Back then it was an apocalyptic prophecy, far and unreal. Today it has become almost a daily report. Facing the angry silence of the secular sector and the religious press that started to move, let me tell you what happened on a small island, the island named Logic.[5]

A Small Island Named Logic is a dystopia predicting the takeover of Israeli society by the ultra-Orthodox. This prophecy of wrath is told as a fantastic story about a happy and somewhat dull majority on the island named Logic, and an isolated minority distinguished in appearance, customs, and beliefs. One Sunday morning the island's minority asks the island's council to adopt one of its customs: to eat without a spoon. At first, everyone opposes the proposal, loudly defending the majority's rights and freedom. The stormy argument, however, was in vain because the majority decides, as an act of goodwill, to accept the proposal. One proposal follows another and the minority accomplishes its carefully conceived strategic plan, to have the majority looking and behaving exactly like them. Only one delegate, firm in his position, refuses to give in to the minority.

The theme behind this satire, which shows up in the book's title, is crystal-clear. The title has a double meaning deriving from the polisemy of the Hebrew word *ei*—a noun meaning an "island," and a prefix denoting the negation "non." The title can be read as both *A Strange and Amazing Story about a Small* **Island** *Named Logic* and: *A Strange and Amazing Story about* **Nonsense** (Illogic). The text's notions are laid bare, confronting the reader through clear and unmistakable references to Israeli society in the 1990s. The secular majority is presented in its daily rituals:

> They hung their laundry on the balcony, waved flags and took out the garbage. Their children, the boys and the girls, went to the army and helped the elderly. When they grew up they got married in a splendid hall with a small orchestra and dough filled with meat. Immediately after, the young couple searched for a house . . . got into debt and got pregnant. (p. 5)

The minority's description is a tailor-made portrait of the ultra-Orthodox community. Vegetables replace the *shtreiml*, the *kipa*, and the beard: shallots in the nose, spinach leaves in the ears, a pea in the mouth, and a small radish in the anus (pp. 6–7). Yellow robes and different dress codes replace the *kapote:* undershirt over the shirt and underwear over the pants. Religious rituals and rites are also caricatured. The ultra-Orthodox custom of shaving the bride's hair on her wedding day becomes the tradition of replacing her teeth with dentures. The ban on eating pork is exchanged for a prohibition against eating cabbage and therefore everything starting with the letter *C*. The ban on marrying a non-Jew or a secular Jew is replaced with the prohibition against marrying "a donkey, a potato, or a cloth" (p. 9).

The island's council is a distorted mirror of the Israeli Knesset[6] and its impotent members who are willing to sacrifice the people's freedom on the altar of political gain, with obvious references to the political power that the religious parties have over the ruling parties, whether Labor or Likud. Both play into the hands of the ultra-Orthodox who fan the flames. The demands of the island's minority are a grotesque reflection of ultra-Orthodox legislative demands, such as the enforced observance of the Shabbat, the ban on eating or selling pork, abortion legislation, and the controversy over "Who is a Jew?" The text not only targets the leaders but also the island's citizens—the Israelis. The text despises the citizens who kneel and accept absurd orders that will turn their life upside down by forcing them to live a life-style that is not theirs. They suffer and complain but they do not rebel.

The citizens, a herd fooled and confused by their corrupt and selfish shepherds, are the focus of another satire, *Baldy Heights*. In a city named Baldy Heights there live bald citizens who choose their mayor by the perfection of his bald head. One morning the mayor discovers that a hair has grown on his head. As the hours pass by, the hair grows longer and longer. After consulting with his counselors, he decides to hide the hair under a huge hat. He then faces a public that is already suspicious. While appearing in public, the mayor's shame is exposed. The people angrily call for his resignation and escort him into exile, but, on his way out, his disgrace becomes a lifesaver. The mayor uses his hair to save two children who were kidnapped by a big bird, to rescue some people from a burning building, and as a string to stitch the guards' pants. Shamed by their behavior, the people of Baldy Heights ask for forgiveness and beg the mayor to return to his position. Feeling secure in his position, the now-proud and pompous mayor decides that his place is among hairy people. He leaves his city for "Curly Hills" where at the gate he is stopped by a guard who dismisses him with shouts of "Go away baldy head" (p. 26).

Baldy Heights is a text dealing with conformity and nonconformity. The mayor is not elected in democratic elections and the ballot is not an indication of popular support. The mayor is elected on the basis of the attributes of his baldness: how it can light a haystack, its sparkle, and its smoothness (p. 3). The absurd competitions are a caricature of election campaigns in the democratic world where rivals try to "enlighten" voters, who are no more than "haystacks," with empty slogans. The people, for their part, vote for sly[7] and superficial candidates, attractive on the surface but empty within.

The hair that suddenly grows on the mayor's head stands for all the minor and major deeds that can stain a leader's reputation; secret bank accounts, lovers who suddenly pop up, and suspicions of fraud. Voters love to trash their leaders' personal and public lives, turning molehills into mountains. As rumors and journalists take over the situation, all attempts to cover or dismiss any allegations of wrongdoing are in vain: "Some said: 'the man is drunk. . . .' Others said: 'he stole the money and he is hiding now.' Some said 'he lost his mind' and others claimed the mayor is pregnant" (p. 6). The citizens, even though they declare their blind support for a leader, are willing to turn their backs on him. Yet, as soon as he becomes useful again, they reverse themselves with no remorse and support him. However, in doing this, the people now create an "arrogant, proud and boastful" clod (p. 24), who will take control over them, his creators.

IV

Sidon's satires are a satiric cannon, a visible, noisy, and destructive weapon. His writings dominate the satiric arena in children's literature, but they are not the only ones. Meir Shalev is another author who decided to draft children's literature into the political battle. His satiric criticism is a landmine, pointed but hidden. If you step on it, it explodes and hurts you; if you miss it, you survive. Two of his texts, *Nechama the Louse* and *How the Neanderthal Man Incidentally Invented the Rumanian Kabob*, are such satiric landmines.

Nechama the Louse tells the adventure story of a small louse named Nechama. Though born on a child's head and a new member to a well-established community of lice, Nechama decides to leave her home in search of adventure. Her journey takes her to foreign and interesting heads. With a soldier in the Israeli reserve force, she is drafted into military service. With a flight attendant, she travels around the world. With a minister, she joins the government. With a talk show host, she runs a popular TV show called "Between the Hair."[8] Her growing popularity among the lice communities does not bring her happiness and she is looking for peace and quiet on a loving scalp. Her wish finally comes true, as she becomes a lovable pet on a bald man's head.

This story with a happy ending is actually a sharp and sarcastic satire targeting Israeli society and its leaders. Since it is published as a children's book, the satire is hidden under humorous expressions taken from colloquial as well as from biblical Hebrew. The heroine's name is Nechama, an archaic name meaning "consolation." It is a name that in the Israeli culture is associated with elderly women (Grandma Nechama). In the subtext, Nechama represents the older generation, the one that carried the Zionist dream and ideology. The adult-reader will recognize in the name "Nechama" the allusion to Efraim Kishon's skit, "*Shir ha-Emek*."[9] While rehearsing a typical kibbutz song, a choir and its conductor, who is flirting with one of the singers (named Nechama), expose the decline of the pioneers' dream. In Shalev's satire, Nechama is the trickster exposing the mediocrity of the Israelis in their earthly and materialistic desires. These are presented, in verbal anecdotes, with an extramarital affair,[10] the chauvinistic, arrogant, and useless Israeli male,[11] and the Israelis' obsession with traveling abroad.[12]

Shalev, like Sidon, is fed up not only with the Israelis but also with their leaders. In his book *The Bible Now,* Shalev writes:

> Stupid, smart, able and weak-minded people populate and cross all the age boundaries in our country. There is no need or right to interfere in their personal affairs. However, in those cases where they reach a governmental position—let me quote the book of Ecclesiastes: "O land, when your king is a servant." . . . Anyone who reads today the fable of Yotam[13] and looks around cannot escape the thought that bramble-bushes are spread throughout our country, and it should not be hard to find them. In the Bible the bramble is mentioned

only in the fable of Yotam, but today it exists everywhere in our political life.[14]

Nechama the louse, as the author's textual representative, expresses Shalev's thesis. While sitting on a minister's head Nechama

> made decisions, was engaged in meetings, participated in election rallies, heard secrets, and appeared in city squares. One day, at one meeting, the minister raised his hand (only to scratch his head) and that's how the budget proposal was passed, by one vote. (p. 16)

Living on a minister's head is not one of Nechama's high moments as she wonders: "How long can I sit on a minister's head? A head on which nothing happens? One can die of boredom" (p. 16). With Nechama's thoughts in the background, the text describes a televised interview with the minister: "They dressed him, powdered his face and wrote for him all the answers. . . . The minister talked about the existing circumstances, the great hopes, the mistakes of the past, and the plans for tomorrow" (p. 17). The bombastic use of hollow words reflects the minister's impotence as well as the emptiness and worthlessness of his declarations. The people and its leaders really deserve one another. Both are partners in a long and hopeless chase after earthly and egotistical gain, while leaving behind the dreams of Israel's pioneers.

The attack on the worldly obsessions of Israelis takes a more philosophical turn in *The Rumanian Kabob*. It is an adventure story about a Neanderthal man's obsessive culinary hunt for the perfect Rumanian kabob. The Neanderthal man with his egotistic craving is a social misfit. While his neighbors are engaged in modernizing their lives,[15] he stays behind dreaming about satisfying his appetite. It seems, at first, that the text prefers the society that places the public interest as a top priority ahead of the Neanderthal man who places his private interests first and foremost. This preference is a temporary and ironic one, since at the end of the story the reader discovers that the culinary modernization wins over the technological one and becomes a daily ritual:

> All of a sudden the smell spread. Oh the smell. . . . A smell nobody smelled before. Everybody smiled and asked; what is this great smell? What is this wonderful aroma? The Neanderthal man said: "This is my kabob, guys, the kabob that I

was looking for since I was a young man." . . . Immediately everyone came shouting "Kabob now," and "Bless the Lord," and "Give us kabob to eat, now." They lit a fire and barbecued all day, as grandma's brother does in his backyard. But no kabob, I mean no kabob, was ever as delicious as that first one. (pp. 22–23)

The story of the Rumanian kabob is a satire on the hedonistic Israeli chasing materialism while living his life in a boring and dull routine. The Neanderthal man's daily routine is brought to light in the description of his pre-kabob meals:

The Neanderthal man didn't have anything to do, so he ate all kinds of stuff. In the morning he ate the root mush. For lunch he ate lizard soup. On Saturday he ate thorn pudding. Finally he jumped and announced: "I'm sick and tired of all this rubbish!" (p. 4)

Every day resembles the next and the desire to break the oppressive routine results in looking for something abstract. The Neanderthal man, as an archetype of the typical Israeli, will do everything to fulfill his earthly desires. Both are impotent and when they reach their goal it has no meaning or value:

All of a sudden, one day, as if by a miracle, the kabob was invented. Someone accidentally dropped some meat with garlic on the ground, and totally by mistake an onion was rolling nearby. Plus, by chance, somebody kneeled down and some parsley jumped from her basket. Then, by error, a mammoth passed by and with its huge foot stepped on it and from everything made a meatball. Unexpectedly a storm began and one bolt of lightning accidentally hit the tree that by chance grew near the cave and a burning branch happened to fall on the meatball. All of a sudden the smell spread. Oh the smell. . . . A smell nobody smelled before (pp. 18–21)

The Rumanian Kabob is a textual allusion to the biblical incident of the "fleshpots." In this incident, the Israelites complain to Moses and Aaron: "If only we had died by the hand of the LORD in the land of Egypt, when we sat by the fleshpots and ate our fill of bread; for you have brought us out into this wilderness to kill this whole assembly with hunger" (Exod. 16:3). The Neanderthal man, the Israelites, and the Israelis are variants of the same primitive and base whim, as the meat is a metaphor for human hedonism and for the yearning for an unreachable and abstract state. In *The Rumanian Kabob,* the storyteller notes that the Neanderthal man "didn't even know what a kabob was. He didn't even know what it should look like" (p. 6). This commentary turns the Neanderthal man's statement into irony: "I know exactly what I want. I want a Rumanian Kabob" (ibid.). For the Neanderthal man, the Israelites, and the Israelis, the goal justifies the means. For a full stomach, one is willing to abandon one's family, return to slavery, betray one's leader, and sacrifice one's beliefs. Even after thousands of years, the goal is the same, but the means change.

V

On the operating table lies a sick and distorted society, exposing its faults and wrongdoings. However, it does not just lay there bare for everyone to pick at; rather, the surgeon digs inside and removes its malignant tumors for everyone to see. Is the surgeon here to operate and heal, or to sign a death certificate? The answer is a complex one.

One can argue that satires do not attack in order to destroy, but rather to expose defects and to offer some correcting norms. From this point of view, good and bad are distinguished. Fools and dictators are punished for their actions and are judged according to undeniable principles offered by the texts' narrators and some of their textual allies.[16] This view might instill within the reader a sense that life has a clear and direct moral meaning. On the other hand, satires express a pessimistic view suggesting that nothing can change what is already rotten. At this level, satires can leave the reader in a blind alley.

In *Baldy Heights,* the reader's feeling of hope and catharsis is based on the fact that the pompous mayor is punished. "Time betrays and hangs the thief," we say, and the mayor is his own executioner. However, he is not the only one punished; the people of Baldy Heights are punished too. They raised and nourished a monster named "The Mayor." Tricky actions and appearances captivated them and therefore they are left without a leader, without an idol to admire. "What will happen now?" the reader will ask. Will the mayor come back and mend his ways? And, if he does, will they be so stupid as to take him back? The text does not offer clear answers, but the way in which things are presented one can assume that the people of Baldy Heights, that is, the Israelis, will look to foster another hollow leader. The absurd competition will be held again. Worthless slogans and false promises will again charm the people and the only hope is that the next mayor will not grow hair.

An Island Named Logic does not have a happy ending, since the extremists rule the island, enslaving the majority to their doctrines. Are they the only ones to blame? No, since they used a democratic system to reach their goal. The majority deserves the punishment and humiliation, since they failed to protect and stand up for their rights. As one of the minority's delegates says: "Ladies and gentlemen, . . . you are stupid and pitiful jackasses. You are dummy potatoes. People who can't keep their rights and don't fight for their beliefs, people who give up all just for the sake of it, are worthy of the title "dumb public" (p. 33). The light at the end of the tunnel might come from the author's hope found at the end of the story: "This is just an imaginary tale, and a stupid majority that surrenders to the minority does not exist, does not exist" (p. 31). This is a sarcastic and ironic ending, since a majority exists in Israel that does surrender to the minority. The irony is a slap on the face that he hopes will wake up an Israeli society that refuses to arouse itself from a deep coma. The real hope, if there is one in the text, comes from the presence of one member of the majority.[17] He is the only sane figure in the text who refuses to give up, and who openly declares that "I won't stick shallots in my nose! . . . And all this is an absurd situation and wrongdoing" (p. 27). His textual presence is the author's tribute to a left-wing political group, Meretz, which stands firm and refuses to give in to ultra-Orthodox manipulation.

The family saga in *Uzo and Muzo*, unlike its biblical and more recent parallel versions, ends in a different tone: "Far, far away behind the mountain, in the village Kakaruzo near the river, a young couple bought a small and clean house. Who is the couple? Muza is the name of the bride. . . . Uzo is the name of the groom" (p. 29). A happy ending—the rivals are united again, but the unification is not achieved thanks to the older generation, or to God's guidance. The older generation is only an obstacle: "How stupid we were, how stupid. Why did we believe? Why did we not question? Why did we not check the facts? Why did we not ask? Why did we accept all those fairy tales?" (p. 31). The younger generation is the leading force, the voice of common sense and morality, challenging their elders' words: "Oh well . . . that's the way things are. If our neighbors are unknown, instead of investing some effort in understanding and reaching them, it's much easier to determine they are monsters and not human" (p. 13). In their marriage, Uzo and Muza do not mark the end of the conflict, not even the beginning of the end, but rather the end of the beginning. Their parents' meeting and the scene where they sit together drinking coffee is just a tiny accomplishment, since after the ideal ending the author adds: "Uzo and Muza are a great couple. If nothing has happened between the two, if no strange argument has erupted, then they are living in a peaceful routine, till this day at quarter to seven" (p. 32). This addition questions the existence of the ideal, as is the case with many satires on the Arab-Israeli conflict. David Alexander points out:

> The satirist who takes a strong anti-nationalist position does not stand outside the camp. He is not an objective guard watching from the top of a detached position. The satirist is the youngest son who rebels from within. As an inseparable part of the fight, he is part of the new myth created after the end of one battle that will become the walking miracle anticipating the next. . . . That is the sharp sensation erupting from the awareness that the situation is permanent, with no solution. . . . The satires about the Israeli-Arab conflict . . . are a cease-fire . . . in a succession of continuous wars.[18]

In the character of the Neanderthal man and his deeds, Meir Shalev visualizes his philosophical view that man is divided into two. This philosophy is rooted in the author's analysis of the two versions of the creation of the world in Genesis. Shalev divides men and women into two distinct characters: the person in version A was commanded by God to control all the creatures and did not know Heaven; the person in version B was created out of loneliness and knew the favor of God's presence.[19] Both characters were united in *The Rumanian Kabob*. The Neanderthal person, "social, active, working on his earthly life and its improvement,"[20] is the one who considers his existence the crown of creation. The second one is the ironic storyteller, "the one who knows that no technological progress, no military victory, or no materialistic gain will bring him the Lost Paradise and the touch of God's hands."[21] Shalev reveals his reference to Israeli society saying:

> That is the Israeli society we live in. A society that at the same time has the vigor for power, ruling and supremacy and the old and good doubt. Here is a society . . . that sees in

every action a fulfillment of God's will . . . and at the same time has the wisdom that, like the First Man, we are not perfect. The wheel will not reverse its course and the future does not prepare us for anything remotely similar to paradise.[22]

VI

The satires of Sidon and Shalev have a high level of personal involvement. They are direct and painful, and their cynical and bitter tone reflects the authors' participation in the frustrating experience of attempting to enlighten their fellow Israelis. The satires are not based on abstract ideas and they are not necessarily an ideological attack. They are rooted in the surrounding reality experienced by the authors and their narrators. They have practical and earthly goals: to attack their readers from a different corner, to expose them again to the ugliness and absurdity of their existence, and to warn them about the terrible consequences of their apathy.

The satires written in the late 1980s and early 1990s are more relevant to the current state of the Israeli society than ever before. To those who read them when they were first published, they seem to be a prophecy of wrath that came true. To those reading them for the first time today, they seem to be a copy of Israeli society, an imaginary one but nevertheless all too real.

Notes

1. *"Hartzufim"* is a combination of two Hebrew words: *hara* (shit), and *partzuf* (face). This show is based on "The Muppet Show." Every character is a distorted puppet of a known political figure. In a survey done at the beginning of 1997, Israelis said that the most beloved puppet was that of Yasir Arafat, characterized as a stupid and harmless figure.

2. David Alexander, *The Court Clown and the Ruler: Political Satire in Israel 1948–1984* (Tel-Aviv: Sifriat ha-Poalim, 1985), 143. (Hebrew)

3. The childish reason for the quarrel between the brothers brings to mind the play *The Bathtub Queen*, by Hanoch Levin. When first put on stage, this play stirred up a huge public debate that caused it to close after several performances. The play discusses the Arab-Israeli conflict and the Six-Day War. It shows the victory that stretched Israel's borders and that

released sacred places as a childish struggle between five family members on the right to control the bathroom. When their wish is fulfilled, they prevent their cousin, a subtenant, from using the bathroom.

4. Amos Oz, *In the Land of Israel* (New York: Harcourt, 1983), 9.

5. Efraim Sidon, "A Strange and Amazing Story about a Small Island Named Logic," *Maariv*, November 1996.

6. Twenty honorable elderly members that get together every Sunday to legislate new laws textually represent the Israeli Knesset with its one hundred twenty delegates.

7. In the third competition, a dwarf is asked to slide on the competitors' heads and decide which is the best slide. The Hebrew word to slide—*le-ahalik*—brings to the reader's mind two adjectives: *halak,* meaning "smooth," which functions in the literal level of the text, and *halaklak,* meaning "sly," which refers to the satiric level of the text.

8. Nechama's TV show is a parody on a famous Israeli talk show of the early 1990s, "Between the Chairs."

9. This skit is a satire on the kibbutz. The choirs in the kibbutzim (the most famous one, the "Gevatron," from Kibbutz Geva) used to sing about the pioneers who work the land and about kibbutz life. In this skit, the conductor tries to teach his choir an absurd parody of a repetitive song. But he doesn't care about his choir's performance, since he is busy flirting with one of the singers, addressing her as "Great Nechama" and flattering her on her singing. The conductor's flirtation emphasizes the sad but realistic fact that the outside world invaded the Israeli kibbutz with its materialism and sexism.

10. In a day-care Nechama jumps from one child to another and from one child's mom to another child's dad (p. 8). The intimacy of the two adults, hidden from the text's young addressee, is evidence to the adult of an extramarital affair.

11. With Uncle Rafi, Nechama goes to the army. There she finds out that "the soldiers have small heads" (p. 10). This means that the Israeli man, although proud in his military service, is no more then a small and useless screw in a huge mechanism.

12. With Rina, the flight attendant, Nechama visits the duty-free store to buy "a new shampoo and some hair color" (p. 15) and fulfills every Israeli's desire to "have a free air ticket," "to see the world," and to "have fun" (p. 13).

13. Judges: 9.

14. Meir Shalev, *The Bible Now* (Tel-Aviv: Schocken, 1995), 130, 155. (Hebrew)

15. The Neanderthal man's family argues that while he is looking for culinary satisfaction, "[a]ll the neighbors already make stone tools, cut wood and manufacture furs . . . in the cave on the mountain, they have domesticated the dog by now and in the cave located in the valley they have a bow and a spear by this time" (pp. 12, 15).

16. Among the narrators' textual allies are Nechama the louse, Grandpa Yakir, the storyteller in *The Rumanian Kabob*, young Uzo, the guard of "Curly Hills," and the one delegate who refuses to surrender to the minority's demands in *An Island Named Logic*.

17. A caricature of Yossi Sarid, a member of Meretz, a left-liberal party.

18. Alexander, *Court Clown and the Ruler*, 145.

19. Shalev, *Bible Now*, 31–38.

20. Ibid., 37.

21. Ibid.

22. Ibid., 38.

8. Women's Issues in the Literary Marketplace: Anthologies of Israeli Women Writers

Hanita Brand

This essay brings to light the correlation between the appearance of Israeli women's writings in anthologies and the general status of women's issues in Israel. Taking an historical perspective to include early women's writing in the pre-1948 yishuv, the author examines a phenomenon which she calls the "double hurdle" faced by Israeli women writers: getting published in Israel, and getting translated and known abroad.

Diament, Carol, and Lily Rattok, eds. *Ribcage: Israeli Women's Fiction*, New York: Hadassah, 1994.

Domb, Risa, ed., *New Women's Writing from Israel*, London: Vallentine Mitchell, 1996.

It is a truism to say that decisions involved in teaching a course in Hebrew literature in translation depend first and foremost on available and accessible translated works, rather than on choices regarding their topics. No matter how original and interesting a topic may be, it will only lead to a dull and bland course if the primary sources pertaining to it are out of reach. But even with this knowledge in mind, one is bound to recognize that the scarcity of accessible women's literature is not yet another technical problem, as it exceeds the range of general difficulties in getting hold of quality translated material for teaching Hebrew literature. This is definitely a substantive issue, being a result and a manifestation of a certain situation pertaining to women in Israeli society. Thus, the very difficulty of accessing such material is in itself part of the content of any given course that is designed to include it.

This is why the recent appearance of two anthologies of translated short stories by Israeli women writers is a veritable cause for celebration. When Carol Diament and Lily Rattok's anthology, *Ribcage: Israeli Women's Fiction*, came out, I welcomed it as a much-needed addition to my courses. Hardly two years have passed, and before news of this book reached all those who teach Hebrew literature, a second anthology has appeared, Risa Domb's *New Women's Writing from Israel*.[1] It is indeed evidence that times are changing. On this happy occasion I propose to sketch out Israeli women writers' publication and translation patterns as they pertain to existing anthologies, and then situate these two important additions within the overall picture of writing by women in Israel.

This essay is limited in scope. It is not designed to provide an in-depth analysis of the translated stories appearing in the new anthologies; there will be other opportunities to assess the value and contribution of these, once the books are sufficiently used in both general and class situations. Nor is it intended as an all-inclusive history of Israeli women's writing in Israel and abroad. Rather, its aim is to locate the meeting point between the general picture and these two particular books, and to give as much material as needed to create a background for appraising the contribution of the books to the field of women's literature.

As far as translated short fiction is concerned, the voice of Israeli women was muted for a long time. Until two years ago, the best way to search for such literature would have been to survey byways, such as periodicals, since the highways were almost totally male dominated. It is true that a few collections of well-known female writers, such as Dvorah Baron, Leah Goldberg and, in later years, Shulamith Hareven, did make it to the English book market, but these were rare occurrences. The majority of women writers, particularly new emerging talents, were invisible to the English reading public. For these female authors, the possibility of coming out with their own collections of short stories was (and still is) highly unlikely. It is here that anthologies are most beneficial, providing a much-needed venue for a variety of voices to be heard. Yet a look at some of the general translated anthologies that were widely used in the last forty years will reveal the extent to which women writers have been excluded.

Of the six anthologies I examined,[2] only two included women writers among their selected authors. Table 1 is a breakdown of the six books.

Table 1
General Translated Anthologies of Modern Israeli Stories

Editor's Name	Year of Publication	Number of Stories	Number of Authors	Number of Women
Kahn	1957	15	14[3]	0
Blocker	1962	9	8[4]	0
Michener	1973	15	15	1[5]
Tammuz & Yudkin	1973	7	7	1[6]
Alter	1975	18	13[7]	0
Lelchuk & Shaked	1983	8	8	0

The numbers in this table speak for themselves.[8] Women writers' representation "peaked" in 1973 at the total of one per anthology. In all other years, *no* women-writers appeared, even in cases where editors found room from more than one piece by certain prominent male authors. The year 1973 is significant, as is the number 1, as we shall see in the next section.

But before turning to these, let me add a few important observations. Special emphasis should be placed on the fact that all six anthologies were *general*, that is, supposed to give a general taste of what the Israeli short story is about. But one would expect from anthologies that are general in nature—whether dedicated to the short story, poetry, or the essay—to be more representative collections, even as allowances are made for the editors' personal tastes and interests, or for their gender (which was male in all cases).

Another problematic issue is the matter of correlation, or lack thereof, between the reality of women's literature in Israel and its representation in these anthologies. To be sure, the pattern and numbers regarding the appearance of publications by women writers in Israel, including those in the genre of short fiction, clearly suggest, at best, a lack of encouragement and a general patronizing attitude and, at worst, downright rejection. Still, the realities are a far cry from the dismal picture arising from the translated anthologies. There are several reasons for this discrepancy, the most obvious of which is the limited range of the collections. One can hardly do justice to Israeli literature in its entirety in a selection comprising eight short stories.

Yet a more fundamental reason is what I term the *double hurdle* faced by Israeli women writers on their road to establishing a name for themselves: first, getting published in Israel and, second, getting translated and known abroad. This has to do with socialization factors going beyond questions of literary merit, and of necessity leads to a feeble participation of women writers in translations. As many women writers are blocked at the first hurdle, there are few who remain to compete at the second.

This point can be seen by turning our attention to a sample of Hebrew anthologies from Israel.[9] Table 2 conveys a different overall picture than did table 1. Even though women writers' representation is extremely limited, one can still detect some progress in the percentage of women representation (with the exception of 1966). In addition, the sheer volume of the collections allows for more women to be included; therefore the number 0 does not appear here, as it did in table 1. This is the manifestation of only the first hurdle. As mentioned earlier, publication and translation patterns are not only about literary merit. They also involve personal acquaintance and social contacts with editors, magazines, scholars, and critics, as well as everything that goes into public exposure and fame. These are all assets to a writer, and authors both famous and unknown try their best to cultivate them. In Israel (as elsewhere), writers are also associated with specific circles, which serve as support networks. They frequently meet, or sit at designated cafés, where strangers are hardly welcome. In such gatherings, the presence of women is felt more as an audience than as participants. For many years, women writers were mostly excluded from such circles, and the reality of their creative life was lonely and powerless. It is to their credit that they were active enough in writing and publishing to be included in collections and anthologies at all.

Table 2
General Hebrew Anthologies of Modern Hebrew Stories

Editor's Name	Year of Publication	Number of Stories	Number of Authors	Number of Women
Lichtenbom	1960	112	113[10]	16
Rapoport	1966	45	29	1[11]
Barzel	1972	16	6	1[12]
Stavi	1993	30	30	8

The double hurdle means that whatever is already difficult in Israel will be even more so abroad. A woman writer who finds it hard to be associated with a specific circle or literary magazine stands very little chance of having her works translated abroad. This is, after all, a further step down the road of public exposure. In most cases, decisions regarding translations involve a broader network of people: editors, translators, scholars, or even fellow writers. Foreign editors know little about the intricacies of Israeli literature. To make up their mind about the possibility of a translation, they turn to people who are in the know for advice. If they were to ask the advice of editors from Israeli publishing houses or from literary magazines, they would be given names of prominent figures with whom these editors are in touch. Thus, the double hurdle also means that what is done in Israel is held up as some kind of model for translations abroad, albeit a model yet to undergo a process of reduction. In short, here and there gender discrimination is at work, yet its added effect is felt more strongly at the end of the translation chain.

Despite differences in the two tables, one aspect is uncannily similar: the number 1, which reappears in both tables. All in all, in the ten anthologies surveyed this number appears *four* times regarding women's participation. It could be argued that its appearance in table 1 is modeled after the pattern of table 2. In table 1 it features in the two anthologies dating from 1973. If the 1973 editors were to look for a model, the most recent Israeli anthologies available at the time (i.e., the ones from 1966 and 1972) were indeed patterned after the "one-woman" model. And even if the specific anthologies were not the direct source of inspiration for the 1973 ventures, the reality that gave rise to this pattern might have been. Still, this does not explain why other models were not as influential, and—more importantly—why the increasing percentage of women writers participating in the Israeli anthologies was not reflected in a similar (or even smaller) increase in the translated ones. But not every pattern is copied. As we can see in table 1, after 1973 the English anthologies go in the opposite direction, reverting back to excluding women writers altogether. What, then, could be the reason for the apparent strength and recurrence of the one-woman pattern?

Any attempt to locate the reason for the predominance of the one-woman pattern has to take into account other fields of women's participation in Israel, since, strangely enough, it also tends to appear outside literature. As a matter of fact, this number appears in almost all spheres of the public domain, representing a phenomenon I refer to—somewhat sarcastically but not inadequately—as *the Golda Meir syndrome*.[13] The term is not meant to reflect on the *intrinsic* value of the women who have been active in any specific area of Israeli public life, nor on the women whose attempts to enter it have been thwarted, as each case has to be weighed on its own merits. Rather, it characterizes the way in which Israelis view these women. This syndrome is a manifestation of an Israeli tendency to divert attention away from the majority of women, or from women's issues in general, by focusing the public gaze on one particular successful female figure at the expense of all others. Thus, the glorified presence of one acts as a fig leaf, covering up the discrimination and rejection that are the everyday experience of most women inside and outside the public arena. The Golda Meir syndrome allows a country that is not progressive in the area of gender equity to *appear* so—achieving a self-image of being just and equitable—and thereby to feel purged of any discrimination.

As the term obviously suggests (and as indeed was the case with the late prime minister), the one woman positioned at the top achieves a superstatus, complete with halo and legendary proportions, with devout disciples and staunch enemies. Even though the hyperbole surrounding Golda Meir contains a degree of resentment, criticism, or even mockery, popular views describe her as not merely situated at the top, but as an absolute ruler, and during her "reign" she indeed seemed invincible. There are myths woven around her and her kitchen cabinet,[14] or her description as "the only real man in the government." These myths regarding Mrs. Meir did not die out even after her forced resignation. Such a woman channels all the frustration of inequality toward that one glorious position.

Another example of the same phenomenon was the figure of Leah Goldberg. The same absolute power and same legendary proportions, albeit in the fields of poetry and poetics, were attributed to Goldberg, who was not only the unofficial poetess-laureate of Israel throughout her life,[15] but also a powerful, ostensibly tyrannical head of the Department of Comparative Literature at Hebrew University in Jerusalem. In 1952 she was given the task of organizing the department, and then went on to chair it until her death in 1970. Her case clearly manifests symptoms of the Golda Meir syndrome: people feared her, revered her, or hated her, but none succeeded in opposing her, at least not on her own turf. In fact, the birth of the Department for World Literature in Tel Aviv University in the late 1960s is attributed to the rebellious flight of her assistants from the Hebrew University and from her tyrannical rule. But to this day few would deny her great talent as a poetess and scholar, and for a good reason. It should be added that, like Golda Meir, she too was not considered an outsider in male-dominated society: she was a member of a very prominent literary circle, that of the poet Avraham Shlonski.

Other cases of the Golda Meir syndrome were perhaps not as dramatic and did not evoke as many emotional reactions, but they too served their purpose in the same way. The woman who occupied the number-one position in women's Hebrew prose writing throughout most of the first half of the century was Dvorah Baron. She provided her own powerful myth, since she spent the last twenty years of her life, until her death in 1956, in utter seclusion, not unlike the famous American poetess Emily Dickinson. Baron appears in table 2 as a single woman writer in an otherwise totally male anthology (1966). In the 1970s Amalia Kahana-Carmon emerged as the one and only woman prose writer. She appears twice, in both tables 1 and 2 (1973 and 1972, respectively), as the sole woman writer.

Let me stress here again the fact that scrutinizing these cases is by no means intended as a reflection on the real talent of these women. Baron and Kahana-Carmon reached such elevated positions because they deserved them. Baron's memorable family sagas still fire the imagination to this day, and Kahana-Carmon is a uniquely gifted writer with her own inimitable style of writing. The expression "Golda Meir syndrome" and the scrutiny of those few women who benefited from it point to the tendency in Israel (and not only there) to use the woman who made it to the top as a way to justify or ignore an otherwise grim situation pertaining to women's equality.

To prove this point, one needs only to look at eras or areas where there was little consensus over *who* that one woman might be. What these cases reveal is that the tendency to crown one woman still remains, even when there is no obvious name upon which all critics and experts would agree. In other words, the tendency exists even where there is no clear candidate for the position. This can be detected in table 1: the 1973 anthology includes as its only woman writer Hedda Bosem, who is not known so much as a literary writer. Her (deserved) fame comes from her excellent work as a columnist. The one-woman model, combined with the double hurdle, can also account for the zero participation of women writers in four out of the six translated anthologies. With a process of reduction occurring in translated collections, there is not much leeway to go down from one: zero is the next option.

Thus, the two new anthologies edited by Diament and Rattok and by Domb add a bounty of translated material where there was none. Side by side one might find the old and the new, the established, and the less known. Amalia Kahana-Carmon and Shulamith Hareven (who appear in both books) and Dvorah Baron (who is found in *Ribcage*) are joined by Ruth Almog, Yehudit Hendel, Savyon Liebrecht, and Haya Esther, and even by younger talents such as Orly Castel-Bloom,[16] all of whom appear in both anthologies. Readers will find it hard to choose between the two anthologies, whether for personal reading or as a primary source for a course, as some of the more unique women writers of today appear only in one of the books. Thus, one of Dahlia Ravikovitch's takes on prose writing, "A Slight Delay,"[17] or a sample of the unique style of Dorit Peleg can be found only in *Ribcage*, while the seductive writing of Hannah Bat-Shahar appears only in *New Women's Writing*.

Another reason that may make it difficult to choose only one of the two books relates to the category of stories centered around women figures who are Holocaust survivors. If you decide on Michal Govrin's quiet yet charged "La Promenade, Triptych" (*Ribcage*), you will miss out on two spell-binding stories from *New Writing*: "Twilight" by Shulamith Hareven and "Until the Entire Guard has Passed" by a very sensitive and original young author, Leah Aini. All three represent a recent trend in writing Holocaust literature, as their treatment of their main topic is somewhat tight-lipped. Rather than dealing with the Holocaust atrocities overtly, they focus more on their aftermath, in the struggle their protagonists have with an unwritten taboo that does not allow them to speak openly about their experience. While they themselves seem mute in this respect, the story leads us to certain moments where the unmistakable odor of the suppressed horror leaks out, permeating and suffusing "normal" everyday reality. Suddenly, what could look like a spring vacation in Europe, a pregnancy in a working-class Israeli neighborhood, or a sunny morning in a Jerusalemite family assumes the air of living an unimaginable and unmentionable nightmare, one from which the subjects can never wake. The stories show how difficult a task everyday living is for Holocaust survivors.

In addition to the subject of the Holocaust, the anthologies provide a broad representation of the topics and motifs prevalent in current mainstream women's literature in Israel. The two books share some common themes, such as motherhood, childhood, infidelity, sexual abuse, death, women's life in a religious community, and Arab-Jewish relations. However, the treatment of these themes is not always parallel. Though neither book can be defined as "feminist," and although one cannot speak in general of feminist writing in today's Israeli mainstream literature, of the two books *Ribcage* leans more in that direction, while *New Writing* is more conservative. Thus, mothers and wives tend to be represented as not powerful enough in *Ribcage*, and—on the whole—too overbearing or uncaring in *New Writing*. Spousal infidelity is mostly male in the former and mostly female in the latter. As for young girls, they appear to be seduced and threatened in *New Writing*, while in *Ribcage* they are the seducers, as in what is perhaps the best-known short story by a woman writer in Israel, Amalia Kahana-Carmon's "N'ima Sassoon Writes Poems."

In their darker stories, both books present a picture of social degradation in which, in an Israeli twist on the famous feminist dogma of the personal being political, the harsh political reality in Israel infiltrates the personal fabric of life, descending on the family unit with its increased violence, harshness, lack of sensitivity, or total alienation. One of the darkest stories is Orly Castel-Bloom's portrayal of Israeli *yordim* (Israeli emigrants living abroad) in *New Writing*, "The Mystery of the Pigs' Heads." Savyon Liebrecht's "Room on the Roof," which tackles Arab-Jewish relations, is the only story appearing in both anthologies. *Ribcage* contains another story on this subject, the cryptic "Ummi fi Shurl" by Orly Castel-Bloom. Both suggest possibilities of mutual understanding on a human and humane basis. *Ribcage* also offers stories about the consequences of war: war widows, a recurring motif in Israeli literature and film; and sexual abuse in the army, a topic that has gained relevance in both the United States and Israel today. These are Yehudit Hendel's "Apples in Honey" and Dahlia Ravikovitch's "Slight Delay," respectively—the latter having been published originally in 1965.

Haya Esther, a very interesting writer who is a well-known portrayer of religious women's lives in Israel today, has a story in each anthology. Both stories happen in a place that is alien and exotic for most Israeli women: the *mikve,* or ritual bath, where according to religious law a married woman has to take a ritual bath after menstruation and before sexual intercourse with her husband is allowed. In the life of secular women (the overriding majority of women in Israel), the only time this place plays a part is before their marriage, as Israeli law does not permit civil marriage, and under religious laws a ritual bath is also required before a wedding. There are many tales, some funny, some scary, told by brides about this one time (or about how they used bribery to avoid this custom). It might explain the fascination with Haya Esther's stories. Here too, *Ribcage*'s choice ("Liar") is more critical of the treatment of women in religious communities (as is another story included, by Savyon Liebrecht), while *New Writing* chooses a sweeter version, "Nechama-Gittel."

One difference worth noting is the general orientation of the books: while *New Writing* was conceived as a standard anthology, *Ribcage*, which was published by Hadassah's Department of Jewish Education, is intended to be used for Jewish educational purposes, and therefore includes extensive prefaces, background material, and suggestions for analysis and discussion.

The difference in the editorial preferences of the two anthologies is not necessarily rooted in ideological considerations, but rather in the different approaches to the selection process. Since no book can be all-inclusive, choices have to be made. In this case, while *Ribcage*'s choice was to present a longitudinal section of Israeli women's literature, *New Writing* went for a contemporary cross-section. The reason for these choices may have more to do with the order of the books' appearance than with ideological inclinations. To explain how chronology can have such an impact on the selections, the two books need to be situated in one more general setting: that of women's anthologies inside Israel. Their peculiar publication pattern reveals the dire results of the Golda Meir syndrome regarding at least one important period, and may explain the difference between the two books in hand.

Ribcage and *New Writing* join a handful of similar Hebrew anthologies, almost all of which came out only in the last decade.[18] One would have to cast a long and hard look to find any previous endeavor of this nature: rarely did mainstream all-women books appear inside Israel.[19] And without such books women writers who did not make it to the top of the traditionally male list of authors could be easily omitted from Israeli history, as they frequently were. Women's anthologies were needed to preserve female heritage and achievements for future generations, once original books and publications were no longer available. In their absence, male dominance was insured, as in each generation Israeli women had to start all over again, weakened and unsure, considering themselves aberrant. No wonder Lily Rattok titled the first section in both her afterword to *ha-Kol ha-Aher* and her introduction to *Ribcage* "The Missing Profile," referring to the missing "Portrait of Women as Israeli Writers." This also contributed to their feeling of alienation and isolation from their own gender.

The most obvious omission was that regarding women writers at the turn of the century and within the early Zionist yishuv. Yaffa Berlovitz set out to rectify the situation in 1984, with a collection of their writing. When Berlovitz's anthology *Sipurei Nashim Bnot ha-Aliyah ha-Rishona* appeared in 1984,[20] it came as a surprise. The majority of the Israeli reading public encountered the stories contained in this slim book for the first time. Yet the stories were written—and had been widely read—almost eighty years earlier. They had appeared in both books and magazines. What, then, happened to them and to their writers in the interim? Several reasons explain why this literature was forgotten, not all of which have to do with gender discrimination; ideological, political, and historical factors also played a part. The early Zionist settlement, inadequately "shrunk" by historians into the years 1882-1904 under the term "first aliyah," was not necessarily that unified among its constituent parts, but is nevertheless considered to be generally centrist or right-leaning. It is the next wave of immigrants—known as the "second aliyah" (1904–14)—which gave the whole yishuv and the subsequent state its socialist, labor, or left-of-center character.

Since socialist-Zionist ideology later won the day, one may suspect a bias towards literary enterprises from the second aliyah at the expense of earlier writers, especially since the most prominent writers of the time still lived in Europe. Yet, it is important to note that the era of the early Zionist settlement *has* been studied in schools, and some of its male writers' names, such as Yechi'el Michal Pinnes (pre-first aliyah), Moshe Smilansky (first aliyah), or Simcha Ben-Zion (early second aliyah) are still known. It seems that only the women's share has disappeared.[21] Thus, in what seems like an anomalous publication pattern, these women's stories actually had two lives: first they had a brief literary career at the beginning of the century, then they were forgotten, and some eighty years later they resurfaced as something new. This was achieved through the efforts of a unique scholar, Yaffa Berlovitz, and a unique publishing house: not a regular commercial publisher, but the literary publishing arm of the Israel Defense Forces, Tarmil.

As the literary marketplace is connected to women's issues in general, this pattern, whether anomalous or not, does reflect social realities. In fact, if one were to represent every single aspect of Israeli women's history, from politics to the arts, by a separate curve, one would come up with almost overlapping curves in all but the very recent era. Starting from the pre-1948 yishuv, the early eras would show first a slightly more pronounced female presence (both relative to women's status in other areas at the time and in relation to subsequent eras in Israel), and then a major continuous decline until and beyond the middle of the century. The late 1960s would start a slight progress, which would culminate in the 1970s with the inception of the feminist movement. Only from the 1980s on would the curves diverge: those of women's prominence in politics and social life as well as women's status in general would decline, while the ones representing women's place in literature and the arts would shoot up. In between the two would be the professional and financial curves, going up only modestly.

In this general picture, 1973 would indeed seem to be an important year. It yielded the first fruits of the recently initiated feminist movement, and brought the only feminist representative to the Knesset (Marcia Freedman). The feminist enterprise, which came at the time marginal voices such as those of immigrants, religious and Oriental Jews, Holocaust survivors, and Arabs were heard for the first time inside Israel's mainstream, achieved only a small political success. But, from the 1970s on, women began to be active on the cultural, artistic, and literary scenes. In more than one aspect, Berlovitz's anthology sits well within the era of the rising cultural curve. It both continued a 1970s trend started by the feminist movement of revisiting women's history, and ushered in a new era in women's literature in the 1980s and 1990s. It started a chain, being the first in a series of women's anthologies. Indeed, it is mentioned in all the later collections. From the stories featured in it, both *ha-Kol ha-Aher* and *Ribcage* took "Aphia's Plight" by Nechama Puchachevski, and *Ribcage* added "Votes for Women" by Hannah Trager. Even the latest Hebrew anthology, *Ezrat Nashim*, which is mostly contemporary, included one of its stories, "Mother and Daughter" by Hanna Bolotin (Luntz). Of course, the diachronic collections included—in addition to these—other early stories, written by women writers who were "number one" in their time.

In this chain, the order of the books' appearance is significant, as each book facilitated the agenda of the next. Berlovitz's *Sipurei Nashim* filled a vacuum by providing a missing historical layer, thus enabling the next book, *ha-Kol ha-Aher*, to present a more extensive diachronic collection. And once a longitudinal selection, that is, of women's writing over time, was on the market, one could come up with a contemporary cross-section, such as *Ezrat Nashim*, which has only one early story.[22] A similar chain in the translated anthologies explains their choice of material: *Ribcage*, the first to appear, is based on the Hebrew *ha-Kol ha-Aher*—indeed, Lily Rattok edited the Hebrew volume book and is coeditor of the anthology under review. Being the first, it too was published not by a regular commercial publisher, but by Hadassah's Department of Jewish Education. And, here too, once the historical selection was on the market, the next anthology, Domb's *New Writing*, could afford to present a contemporary cross-section.[23] Even their different choices regarding recent stories can be understood in this connection. An historical approach is affected by the earlier subjects, as it links the old with the new,[24] and stories shared by the different generations tend to include those dealing with women's struggles. On the other hand, a collection not bound by the historical dimension can reflect more accurately the present-day picture, which is, as mentioned earlier, less feminist in its leanings.[25]

The two new anthologies reviewed here deserve an enthusiastic welcome from both the general readership and from instructors and students in courses of Hebrew literature in translation. One can only hope that they do not fall victim to the omission patterns just described, which constitute something of a literary abyss for the outstanding work of so many Israeli women writers.

Notes

1. Risa Domb mentions another anthology, *Stories from Women Writers of Israel* (New Delhi: Star, 1995).

2. *A Whole Loaf: Stories from Israel,* ed. Sholom J. Kahn (New York: Vanguard Press, 1957); *Israeli Stories: A Selection of the Best Contemporary Hebrew Writing,* ed. Joel Blocker (New York: Schocken, 1962); *First Fruits: A Harvest of 25 Years of Israeli Writing,* ed. James A. Michener (Philadelphia: Jewish Publication Society of America, 1973); *Meetings with the Angel: Seven Stories from Israel,* eds. Benjamin Tammuz and Leon Yudkin (Plymouth UK: Clarke, Doble and Brendon, 1973); *Modern Hebrew Literature,* ed. Robert Alter (West Orange NJ: Behrman House, 1975); *Eight Great Hebrew Short Novels,* eds. Alan Lelchuk and Gershon Shaked (New York: New American Library, Meridian, 1983).

3. S. Y. Agnon was represented twice.

4. Here too, Agnon was represented twice.

5. Hedda Bosem.

6. Amalia Kahana-Carmon, considered the foremost woman writer in Israel.

7. H. N. Bialik and H. Hazaz had each two pieces; Agnon had four.

8. The numbers also explain why I did not use a curve to represent this grave situation: the number 0 cannot be represented in diagrams or curves.

9. It is difficult to find an exact parallel to Table 1 inside Israel in terms of the years of publication or the range of stories (which tends to be broader in Israel). One has to bear in mind the different needs for anthologies in these two different settings. The Israeli reading public is not generally thought of as needing "a taste of what the Israeli short story is about." Israelis are more likely to embrace anthologies that are restricted in topic (e.g., love stories) or eras (as the 1948 generation), and so forth. However, some general anthologies do appear from time to time, and I have chosen four that seem to be the least limited in their collections. They are: *The Hebrew Story*, ed. Yosef Lichtenbom (Tel Aviv: N. Tverski, 1960) (Hebrew); *Hebrew Writers*, ed. Yosef Rapoport (Jerusalem: M. Newman, 1966) (Hebrew); *Six Writers*, ed. Hillel Barzel (Tel Aviv: Yachdav, 1972) (Hebrew); and *Thirty Years, Thirty Stories,* ed. Zisi Stavi (Tel Aviv: Sifrei Yediot Ahronot, 1993) (Hebrew).

10. One of the stories was written by two writers (Yonat and Alexander Sened), who are a married couple and habitually write their works jointly.

11. Dvorah Baron.

12. Amalia Kahana-Carmon.

13. Golda Meir served as Israel's prime minister from 1969 to 1974. She was forced to resign after protests regarding the government's handling of intelligence information prior to and during the Yom Kippur War of 1973.

14. This refers to rumors that she used her kitchen to hold meetings with her most trusted cabinet members. Even as this was probably true, similar domestic myths regarding other prime ministers and their coteries were less circulated in the general public. They might surface in memoirs and books, but they did not cling so persistently to male figures during their lifetime, and were not quoted as often.

15. She was awarded the Israel Prize only posthumously.

16. Orly Castel-Bloom is the most famous of the new female voices in Israeli literature today.

17. Dahlia Ravikovitch, winner of the 1998 Israel Prize for poetry, was regarded as one of the top women poets in Israel in the 1960s.

18. I could come up with only three similar anthologies that are both mainstream and readily available. In fact, one of these (the third) is somewhat narrower in its theme, which focuses on relationships between women, and includes three stories written by men on that topic. The books are *Stories of the Women of the First Aliya*; in Hebrew: *Sipurei Nashim Bnot ha-Aliya ha-Rishona*, ed. Yaffa Berlovitz (Tel Aviv: Sifriyat Tarmil, 1984); *The Other Voice: Women's Fiction in Hebrew*; in Hebrew: *ha-Kol ha-Aher: Siporet Nashim Ivrit*, ed. Lily Rattok (Tel Aviv: ha-Sifriya ha-Hadasha, ha-Kibbutz ha-Meuchad, 1994); and *Women's Section: Hebrew Stories about Love, Hate and Hope*, ed. Hannah Naveh; in Hebrew: *Ezrat Nashim: Sipurim Ivriyim al Ahava, Eiva ve-Tikva bein Nashim* (Ramat Gan, Israel: Poetika, Tobi Sofer, 1996).

19. There is one early book, often mentioned by scholars, which holds a collection of diaries, memoirs, and some literary texts. It is *Women Workers Speak*, ed. Rachel Katzenelson-Rubashow (Tel Aviv: Moetzet ha-Poalot, 1930). (Hebrew). It is very hard to come by today, but was apparently popular at the time, because it was translated first to Yiddish and later to English in 1932 through the efforts of the Pioneer Women's Organization, under the title *The Plough Woman: Records of the Pioneer Women in Palestine* (Westport CT: Hyperion Press reprint, 1976).

20. Berlovitz, *Stories of the Women of the First Aliyah*.

21. A detailed discussion of the reasons and circumstances of the brief success and subsequent disappearance of these women writers exceeds the scope of this short essay.

22. In describing such a chain I do not mean to imply a historical necessity regarding the order of appearance. Of course, the contemporary collection could have been attempted first. But, in this case, each book clearly paved the road for the appearance of the next, making its publication more plausible.

23. In her introduction, Domb mentions all the previous anthologies, including *Ribcage*.

24. In fact, Rattok arranged her Hebrew book according to subjects, rather than eras, and even as the English language *Ribcage* is arranged more or less chronologically, connections and links between the stories are made in the prefaces and adjoining material.

25. This fact is acknowledged by both Domb, in her introduction to *New Writing*, and Barbara B. Spack in an afterword to *Ribcage*. The latter says: "Interestingly, many of the authors would hardly describe themselves as feminists nor their works as supportive of feminist issues" (p. 278).

9. Yemenite Jews on the Zionist Altar

Nitza Druyan

This essay highlights the steadfast resistance of the Yemenite community to the integrationist pressures of Israeli society. Departing from the standard approach that focuses on the absorption and amalgamation processes at work among Yemenite Jews in Israel, the author focuses on the literature and cultural dynamics of the segregationist forces that maintain the uniqueness of an ethnic community which, five decades after the mass immigration of 1949 and a century after the early pioneers, has not relinquished its traditional culture in spite of tremendous social pressures to assimilate.

Dachoch-HaLevi, Yosef, ed., *Afikim Springs, Studies in Literature, Language, Traditional Law and Custom, Education, Society and History of Yemenite Jews*, Tel Aviv: Afikim, 1995. (Hebrew)

Nini, Yehuda, *Kinneret's Yemenites: Their Settlement and Removal from the Land: 1912–1930*, Tel Aviv: Am Oved, 1996. (Hebrew)

Parfitt, Tudor, *The Road to Redemption: The Jews of the Yemen 1900–1950*, Leiden/New York: E. J. Brill, 1996.

Introduction

The Jews of Yemen were about fifty thousand at the turn of the twentieth century and by 1950 the overwhelming majority had made Israel their home, bringing the Yemenite Jewish population there to about one hundred thousand. In spite of their geographic and topographic remoteness for hundreds of years in the southwestern corner of the Arabian Peninsula, they were not isolated from the Jewish world. Through the centuries they received all the major news and Jewish religious literature, while developing a distinctive folklore due to their unique surroundings. Although the population of the Jews of Yemen was always a minute percentage of the Jewish people, their religious and folkloric ways were not hidden from their coreligionists worldwide, especially in the twentieth century.

The first significant wave of Yemeni Jewish immigration to Palestine (Eretz-Israel) was made in 1882, coinciding with the East European "First Aliyah" of Zionist historiography. Additional waves of immigrants arrived in the early 1890s and 1900s. By the year 1914, fully one-tenth of the Jewish population of Yemen had made aliyah, an extraordinary proportion in comparison with other diasporas.[1] The Yemenites' unique cultural legacy was brought to Israel by the early settlers as well as by the waves of immigration that continued into the British Mandate period. At first, most immigrants tended to resist any change in religious ritual or social practices. They held tenaciously to their customs and generally did not deviate from age-old traditions ingrained in their culture. However, this steadfastness gradually eroded. Eventually, some particularly Yemenite cultural traits (e.g., dance steps, silverwork, embroidery, and music) influenced the evolving Israeli-Jewish cultural identity.

In the research literature about the Jews of Yemen, two major approaches can be discerned. One approach examines the history, literature, and cultural traditions independently, while the other considers them in comparison to parallel investigations about other Jewish communities. The three volumes under review here all fall under the first approach. Yet, a major question that occupies modern historians regarding Yemenite Jews in the last two decades is: what was the relationship of Yemenite Jews to the Zionist movement and to the Jewish yishuv in Eretz Israel? This question is the common thread that joins the three books reviewed here.

The Road to Redemption

Tudor Parfitt's book, *The Road to Redemption: The Jews of the Yemen 1900–1950*, is a comprehensive history of the Jews of Yemen in those years. The book expertly describes most political, social, and economic aspects of Yemenite Jewish life, including the mass emigration to Israel in 1949–50. The reader is provided with a portrait of Yemenite Jews in the twentieth century based on the author's original research as well as previously published accounts. The first two chapters offer historical background, expertly summarizing the circumstances of Jews from their early settlements in the area to the eve of the twentieth century. Parfitt cites the accepted estimates of about fifty thousand Jews dispersed in more than a thousand villages and towns of Yemen, for many generations until the mass evacuation in the mid-twentieth century. Many villages contained only a few Jewish families, some towns with a few tens of families, but Sanaa held a large concentration of a few thousand Jews and was a center of commercial and economic activity, as well as the seat of a recognized and authoritative rabbinic leadership.

What were the basic circumstances of Yemenite Jewish life? Parfitt agrees with the accepted historical analysis that the two main forces that affected the Jews of Yemen in the twentieth century were (a) the policies of the Imam and (b) the penetration of developments from the modern world. He describes in detail the legal limitations imposed on the Jews by Muslim *shari'a* law. Regulations that were intended to oppress the Jews and to keep their status as an inferior minority in Islamic societies, in general, were often tightened and given a harsher practical interpretation in Yemen. For example, Jews were not allowed to raise their voices against a Muslim, construct houses higher than those of Muslims, brush against Muslims in the street, engage in the same commerce as Muslims, find any fault in Islamic law, insult the Prophets, discuss religion with a Muslim, ride animals using a normal saddle, wink when observing the nakedness of a Muslim, raise their voices during prayers, blow the shofar (ram's horn) too loudly, or lend money at interest. Furthermore, Jews were obliged to get to their feet before Muslims (pp. 41–42).

However, the author acknowledges that the reality of Jewish life in Yemen, as well as in other Muslim countries, was vastly more complex than living under these difficult restrictions. It was often the socioeconomic day-to-day interaction between Jews and Muslims that determined the nature of their relationship in any given locality. Parfitt thus devotes quite a few pages to this interesting and multilevel association between the Jews, mainly as artisans and traders, and their Muslim neighbors, who were often in agriculture.

Although the author does not spare relevant details, his writing artistry moves the reader along in a flowing manner. Both the expert and the nonprofessional audience will be captivated by the intriguing account. In his introduction, Parfitt presents himself as an outsider:

> Historians now concede that the selection and deployment of their facts and the way they see the past are a consequence of their own past and upbringing. Jewish and Yemenite Jewish scholars, as well as a number of Arab Muslim scholars, will have brought their own historical experience to bear on this subject. As a British Protestant, I have inevitably brought mine. Nonetheless, I am somewhat outside the arena and can only hope that this work will be embellished by its relative detachment. (p. 1)

However, with respect to his immersion and grounding in the subject, Parfitt is hardly an outsider. He has carefully incorporated into his extensive documentation and footnotes pertinent previously published material on the Jews of Yemen, and his meticulous archival searches have yielded voluminous citations.[2] He has traveled extensively in Yemen, collected oral documentation, and is quite familiar with the issues of the Yemenite Jewish community in Israel. As such, his tone is sympathetic, particularly when describing hardships and tribulations. In this regard, Parfitt's book is similar to works by other non-Yemenite scholars,[3] writers and travelers in the nineteenth and twentieth centuries who were inspired by this exotic, remote Jewish community and who provided admirable studies and descriptions that have served the scholarly community until today.

In the bulk of the book, the author traces the trials and tribulations of the Jews of Yemen in their efforts to emigrate from their land of origin through Aden to Eretz-Israel during both the British Mandate period and the early years of the State of Israel. There are those who paint the tiresome journey from Yemen to Palestine as a colorful picture of exotic camel caravans crossing the desert. But Parfitt's account, fully grounded in historical fact, reveals that the road to redemption was full of hardships and dangers:

> [A]ccounts of the journey paint a depressing picture. As people tried to leave the Yemen, they arrived in Qataba. If they had money, they rented rooms. Otherwise, they lived in makeshift tents or in nearby caves for years on end. Some of them were killed by wild animals, others suc-

cumbed to starvation. Perhaps as many as a third of the people who left at this time died on the way to and/or around Qataba. Not only Arabs but also Adeni Jews tried to cheat them and take what little money they had left. But by distributing bribes, sometimes by dressing up in Arab clothes and shaving off their sidelocks, they managed to get into Aden. (pp. 146–47)

Readers will be especially touched by the vivid description of the aliyah camp in Aden and by the credible and dramatic tale of conditions there. The administration was faced with an extremely difficult task of caring for thousands of refugees who arrived on the verge of total exhaustion and starvation, with many diseases caused by their long and difficult trek. The camps were large, crowded quarters with minimal hygienic conditions and replete with social friction. They served as a temporary shelter to weary families, usually for several months and sometimes for years. The camp medical and other workers, who were mostly non-Yemenite, took it upon themselves to transform the newcomers into "Westernized" people, at least in their external appearance. Of all the descriptions this reviewer has read, this is the most inclusive and objective.

Parfitt is very critical of both the camp staff as well as those who sent them in the early days. He summarizes an unpublished confidential memorandum sent by Joan Comay, who visited Aden in September 1949:

On the Way. Courtesy the Central Zionist Archives.

> She contrasted the absolute lack of facilities for the Yemenites with the utility room for the doctors and nurses "with a table and chairs and the continuous flow of iced beer and lemonade. . . ." She also made some trenchant comparisons between the rations and organization of food for the refugees and those for the workers. Joseph Simon, who had lamented that he had no staff to prepare powdered milk for the children, joined them for dinner at the camp . . . "a five-course meal served beautifully. . . ." [T]he refugees first had to wait in line between eight and twelve hours and were then served "a loaf of bread per person, two radishes and a handful of dates, handed out in lumps by a guard, while another marked off the ration card. Guards with sticks kept them in line as they neared their turn. . . . They have sticks which seem to be their insignia of authority and which they don't hesitate to use . . . many [immigrants] have running sores or trachoma. . . . There is an average of four deaths daily." She noted the overcrowded and unsanitary conditions of the camp hospital but the under-used and over-staffed Joint-financed hospital in Aden to which the Yemenites were not taken. (pp. 220–21)

However, the Hashed Camp changed completely with the appointment of Max Lapides as camp director in November 1949. Parfitt describes in detail Lapides's able leadership and his devotion to the Yemenite immigrants. Lapides, an American Jew with a Yale legal background, developed very warm and honest feelings for his charges, an ethnic group that was until then totally unknown to him.

> Quite unlike his predecessors, Lapides was a kind and sympathetic man and had considerable management skills. . . . He surrounded himself with an unlikely group of people, many of whom succumbed to his charm. With the Yemenites and Adenites, Muslim and Jew alike, his easy, physical manner, his ability to hug and embrace, stood him in good stead. On the other hand, his impressive service record enabled him to hold his own over drinks with British officers and colonial administrators. If anyone was equipped to ensure both the co-operation of the Yemenite refugees and continuing British co-operation it was Lapides. He managed to get the best out of his staff, some of them volunteers. (pp. 229–30)

Everything improved: living quarters, the distribution of food, and medical services for adults and children. In addition, the special amicable relations between Lapides and the Israeli-Yemenite Yosef Zadok (the Israeli emissary responsible for the Yemenite aliyah) also contributed to significant betterment of the whole operation.

The last chapters of Parfitt's book are devoted to the description of the elimination of the Yemenite Diaspora, from the acceleration of the departures from villages and towns to the boarding of the aircraft. Both Zadok and Lapides were determined to bring out every last Jew from Yemen. Parfitt, however, documents the many obstacles that impeded the exodus from Yemen as well as from Aden. Nevertheless, by September 1950, 49,637 Jews (mostly Yemenites, but including 1770 Adenites) left for Israel. The overwhelming majority of Jews in those diasporas had fulfilled their age-old dream: they had been finally redeemed.

But, in his evaluation of "Operation Magic Carpet," the author takes issue with those who have overemphasized the religious, messianic sentiments of the Yemenites' motivation for aliyah. Their mass response "was rooted in sound common sense, in full awareness of what was happening in Eretz Yisrael and was undertaken with considerable circumspection" (pp. 284–85). Just like other Jewish immigrants, they too aspired to become partners in the national revival of Eretz-Yisrael and in the building of the Jewish state.[4] Yet, there is no question that this exodus and settlement in Israel could hardly be described as an effortless, unperturbed venture, as implied by the code name "Magic Carpet." In his consistently sincere tone, Parfitt does not omit mentioning the crimes committed against the Yemenite immigrants. He relates the early patronizing and abusive Israeli attitudes and, most importantly, the disappearance and theft of both private and community property. Invaluable ancient Hebrew manuscripts were taken from Yemenite Jews, never to be recovered by them. Their jewels, silver works, gold, and other objets d'art could never be retrieved. Indeed, this unjustifiable sacrifice on the Zionist altar left an open wound in their hearts for many years to come.[5]

Parfitt's book is compulsory reading for anyone seriously interested in the Jews of Yemen in the twentieth century. It is definitely an asset to scholars and students of the period, but with its maps, plates, high-quality photos, comprehensive good bibliography, and index, it can certainly serve as an introduction to the saga of this community for the more casual reader as well.[6]

Pioneers in Israel: Kinneret's Yemenites

Who were the Yemenite families of Kinneret and what was their saga? More than one Yemenite group arrived in the settlement of Kinneret, on the shores of the beautiful northern lake of the same name, in the years immediately preceding World War I. However, it is a specific group of ten families that Yehuda Nini sets out to describe. The group arrived in the beginning of the winter of 1912 with the distinct intention of settling there and with the pioneering spirit of those days: a willingness to endure the ordeal of building the Jewish homeland.

Their story is drawn out in a long, cumbersome narrative[7] in Nini's interesting and sad book. The author relies on archival documents, interviews, newspaper articles, as well as previously published material. Nini specifically identifies these people by their names and their family affiliation (p. 90), since it seems that his most important purpose in writing the book was to document their meaningful contribution to the settlement of the area. Members of these ten families remained in Kinneret for eighteen years. They labored under unimaginable hardships to bring forth produce from the soil, barely able to hold on and cultivate the small plots of land allotted to them. They toiled at clearing stones from the rocky land, removing thorny wild shrubs and bushes from the countryside, preparing the soil for planting, and manually irrigating the fields. In addition, Nini also relates their cooperation in performing any other task or service that was required for Kinneret's agricultural settlement.

The author describes the Yemenites' living conditions in explicit detail. They were very crowded and lacked even minimal hygienic facilities. Their quarters were close to the swamps, thus exposing the families to epidemics of malaria and other sicknesses. No wonder their mortality rate reached alarming proportions, and every family suffered tragic losses. Nini, mourning the absence of a memorial to those Yemenites who succumbed to untimely deaths (in clear contrast to the monuments erected for Eastern European victims/ heroes in the area), names them again, adults and children alike, as his own special testimonial.

Throughout the book, Nini is consistent in describing the settlers' difficulties, which he documents well. Although he is certainly not the first researcher to write about the early twentieth-century Yemenite agricultural settlements, his is the first published book devoted to the plight of the Yemenites of Kinneret.[8] His main argument

In the courtyard of Kinneret. Courtesy the Central Zionist Archives.

is that, although these ten families were among the first settlers of Kinneret, in 1930 the Zionist authorities chose them for expulsion and relocation, as opposed to more recent European immigrants. Even the Yemenites' vocal opposition to the directive and their affiliation with the Labor movement (well documented by Nini) did not shield them from this forced relocation. The authorities, both in

Kinneret and in the Zionist offices in Jerusalem and Tel Aviv, rationalized the expulsion by claiming that the scarcity of good agricultural land did not allow a tolerable level of subsistence for the many inhabitants who were already in the area. This claim, as Nini argues repeatedly, could not justify the expulsion of the veteran Yemenites, rather than newcomers to the area. Moreover, the injustice was so much worse because Kinneret was not a settlement of privately owned land, but rather nationally owned property, for decades financially dependent on national institutions. Decisions regarding the settlers, financial support, and assistance for infrastructure were made by the Zionist authorities of Eretz-Israel, as was the determination to force the ten Yemenite families out of the area and to resettle them in Kfar Marmorek near Rehovot, leaving Kinneret to other non-Yemenite settlers.

One would have expected the Yemenites' pioneering efforts and productive agricultural activities between 1912 and 1930 to be perceived with the same approbation and acclaim as that accorded other pioneers of those years, lauded in Zionist historiography for providing the absolutely necessary basis for the rebirth of productive Jewish life in Eretz-Israel. Israeli history has always hailed and put on a pedestal the image of Jewish pioneers, especially from pre-World War I days, who were prepared to sacrifice everything they owned and even lost their lives in the hardships of settlement all over Israel. But, as Nini complains, the Yemenites' exemplary pioneering contribution was minimized and they were deliberately ignored, even though their story logically belongs to the legendary "second aliyah." The author's complaint, echoed through many chapters of the book, has been raised many times before, both with regard to Yemenite Jews and with regard to other immigrants from Muslim countries.[9] Nini concludes that the expulsion of the Yemenites from Kinneret, the absence of a memorial for those who died there, and their exclusion from the annals of Zionist history all reflect ingrained attitudes of ethnic-cultural discrimination, an unfortunate attitude displayed by the Zionist-Israeli leadership and the Labor movement, both of which were dominated by Eastern European Jews (p. 313).

It is precisely this conclusion that relegates the book to the genre of publications by other Yemenite Jews trumpeting the discrimination against their ethnic group throughout the twentieth century.[10] Beyond expressing the feeling of ethno-cultural discrimination, Nini offers no further explanation of the injustice. Yet Nini's pleading the case for recognizing Yemenite Jewry as full partners in the Zionist project and in Israeli society relates well to my own experience and views, which have been shaped by long-standing involvement in studying the Yemenite Jewish community in Israel. I recall many occasions when I lectured about the plight of the early Yemenite settlers, based on my research into their extreme hardships in the urban centers of Jerusalem and Jaffa and also in the agricultural settlements.[11] Almost always, I encountered an immediate apologetic response that can be paraphrased as: "But did not all the pioneers suffer in the early years? Were they not all in a state of continuous crisis, on the verge of starvation and/or dying from malaria?" My answer has been: "Yes, the suffering of the early pioneers was universal, but the Yemenites' troubles were singular, magnified in their severity and, most importantly, notable because of the general apathy toward them as contributors to the Zionist enterprise." Zionist visionaries and pioneers could often endure the rigors of their situation sensing that they would one day bathe in the glory and recognition of the importance of their sacrifices on behalf of the Jewish people. The Yemenites, on the other hand, were denied even this consoling privilege.

For a long time there has been some discomfort, especially among the old leadership, but also within the rank and file of the early pioneers, associated with the treatment of Yemenite Jews within Zionist and Israeli settlements. This has prompted denials of mistreatment, or unconvincing appeals to "understand" it in the context of the general conditions of those years. An outright rejection of both of these positions would require a drastic critique of the Zionist fathers and of their moral judgments. This is a direction that neither Nini nor many other scholars seem prepared to take. Who is to blame for ignoring the Yemenites' contribution to the early settlement of the area? Who is to blame for the injustice of the forced relocation of these veteran settlers of Kinneret in 1930? Nini invented a concept called "Prince of History," which allows him to see the phenomenon as something that was inevitable, albeit deplorable but unintentional. According to this view, it was an unfortunate misunderstanding (chaps. 22–23).

The reader learns much from this book about the early Kinneret settlers, Yemenites, and others, the pioneers of the 1910s and the 1920s in the Galilee, labor leaders, the Zionist authorities, and their plans and activities. As much as we learn about this history, we also learn about the author, Yehuda Nini, professor of history at Tel Aviv University, son of Yemenites, and his feelings, thoughts, and sensitivities. The reader finds an Israeli Jew torn between his loyalty to the legacy, ideology, and prestige of the Labor movement, on the one hand, and his compassion and inevitable identification with his scarred Yemenite brethren, on the other.

Afikim Springs

Afikim is a cultural organization that publishes a periodical by the same name devoted to Yemenite Jewish life in Israel, stressing the cultural traditions of the community. Since its inception *Afikim* (the periodical) has also included many articles on general social and cultural issues of Israeli society. It particularly emphasizes themes concerning Israelis whose ethnic origin is from the Muslim world. *Afikim Springs* is a collection of articles in a "Jubilee Volume" published to mark the occasion of the hundredth issue of the periodical and the completion of thirty years of activity. The subtitle, *Studies in Literature, Language, Traditional Law and Custom, Education, Society and History of Yemenite Jews,* testifies to the wide scope of subjects referenced.

The opening article by Shimon Avizemer makes a courageous attempt to consolidate a description of Yemenite contributions to the Israeli cultural scene in music, dance, arts, literature, and history. He enumerates scores of personalities in the arts and entertainment arena, as well as in the academic and scholarly world. He reviews the accomplishments of famous singers such as Bracha Tzfira and Shoshana Damari; recognized authors such as Mordechai Tabib, Aharon Almog, Nissim Benyamin Gamlieli, and Tuvia Sulami; the dance choreographer, Sarah Levi-Tanai; actors such as Sa'adia Damari and others; painters such as Avshalom Okashi, and Itamar Siani; as well as more than a dozen university scholars (including Yehuda Nini and the author of this review).[12] His unequivocal conclusion is that the creativity of Yemenite Jews in Israel, derived mainly from, or influenced mainly by, their unique ethnic heritage, has enjoyed a universal appeal in the arts and entertainment arenas.

Yosef Dachoch-HaLevi, founding editor of *Afikim* and editor of *Afikim Springs,* is the undisputed source of inspiration behind this plethora of cultural productivity. Not in vain is the name of the organization *Afikim li-T'hiya Ruhanit ve-Hevratit*—"Pathways to spiritual and social rejuvenation." He has a distinct vision of what should be the components of Israeli cultural identity, as he explains in his eloquent article, "National Revival and National Identity." His thesis is that the essential criterion for Israeli-Jewish national independence is the development of a singular cultural identity. In this context he ascribes much importance to the Hebrew language. Indeed, all those familiar with his speeches and writings can testify that his pronunciation, grammar, vocabulary, and syntax are extraordinarily flawless. Just like Ahad ha-Am, he sees Eretz-Israel not only as a socioeconomic haven for Jews, but rather as a homeland that once again places Jews and their unique Hebrew cultural identity as a distinct and separate nation on the international stage. It is in this framework that a special task is assigned for Yemenite Jews and their particular preservation of the Hebrew language. Dachoch-HaLevi's vision is not necessarily shared by many in Israel who do not consider such insularity of their society among the nations of the world as desirable. The editor, who is not politically naive, would be the first to admit the existence of such prevailing attitudes; but, as a classic idealist, he refuses to give in to them and tirelessly promotes what he believes to be most appropriate.

The literary section includes poetry, prose, and literary analysis. Particularly noteworthy is Yosef HaLevi's[13] examination of Mordechai Tabib's previously unknown poems. Tabib's prose has been well publicized in Israel, and HaLevi found it interesting and illuminating to look into his 1938–44 poems that did not meet with popular acclaim at the time. In his comprehensive chapter, HaLevi applies rigorous criteria to an analysis of the poems and concludes that they ought to be recognized as an essential introduction to Tabib's more mature and significant later stories. Other interesting themes covered in this literary section include a glimpse into the world of Yemenite women through their popular poems (e.g., Yehuda Ratzhabi), a sampling from Shalom Shabazzi, the seventeenth-century Yemenite Tzadik (Ratzon HaLevi), and a chapter from an autobiographical novel, *Aluf Teman*, by Nissim Benyamin Gamlieli.

Yemenite Jewish culture is heavily connected to religious observance. This was perhaps the most serious obstacle to its being embraced by the wider secular Israeli society. In the growth of Zionism in Eretz-Israel, there was indeed a general desire to abandon the Diaspora Jewish character with its traditional religious emphasis in favor of creating a new national identity. Many Yemenites were thereby alienated from the mainstream, while the mainstream remained largely ignorant of the Yemenites' cultural heritage, even to the extent of denying that the culture existed. Afikim's mission has always been to redress this imbalance.

Among the articles on traditional law and custom, two essays are particularly noteworthy. Aharon Gimani describes the Jewish religious leadership in Yemen and its hierarchy, and investigates to what extent Yemenite Jews observed Jewish law according to the *Shulhan Arukh* of Rabbi Yosef Caro. The reader should find his discussion about the blessing over bread—and whether the most senior person performs the blessing for all present, or whether each person should make his own private blessing over the bread—fascinating and most relevant to contemporary Jewish banquets. Gimani concludes in a sophisticated manner that the complexity of *halakhic* (religious legal) decisions precludes an unequivocal inference. Ha-Rav Ratzon Arusi skillfully integrates a practical rabbinic decision for our times into his legal treatise about the chanting of the Aramaic translations of the Torah and Haftorah readings on the Sabbath. He cites numerous precedents to conclude that Jews of Yemenite descent, even in our days, are not exempt from this part of their religious heritage, even if it makes the service cumbersome and is not always pragmatic. A scholar, a pulpit rabbi, and the head of a cultural religious organization, Halikhot Israel, he combines two spheres of erudition, religious law and custom.

In "Women and Allowances for Ritual Slaughter," Yosef Tzurieli describes a select cadre of women who were given permission to work as ritual slaughterers, an amazing incursion into a traditionally male pursuit. Bat-Zion Eraqi Klorman writes, in the historical section, about twelfth-century messianism in Yemen, well publicized because of Maimonides' famous *Epistle to Yemen*. Klorman, who has written extensively on Yemenite messianism, sees a strong correlation between the phenomenon and its counterpart in the local Muslim society. The list of topics also extends to sociocultural aspects of Yemenite Jews in Israel. Yael Shai describes wedding customs, Nissim Rejwan discusses the role of Middle Eastern culture in the developing Israeli identity, and Yosef Meir laments the shortcomings of the educational system.

Any collection of such a great number of essays is bound to include several that do not excel in the novelty of their ideas and/or in their analyses.[14] *Afikim Springs* nonetheless shows the intensity of the interest of Yemenite Jews (and a few non-Yemenites) in delving into their traditions. The breadth of the volume testifies to their devotion and perseverance in their scholarly pursuit of Yemenite Jewish culture. Regrettably, their literary traditions, as well as most historical aspects, are mostly unknown to the wider Jewish society in Israel and elsewhere.

The prevailing attitude behind all of Afikim's efforts reflects many Yemenites' frustration with, and alienation from, modern Israeli culture, whose school curricula and informal educational programs have largely ignored the rich Yemenite cultural heritage. It did not escape their attention that historical and literary references were made to other Diaspora cultures, especially from Europe. For example, one could justifiably ask why Galut Mawza (the devastating exile of Sanaa Jews in the eighteenth century) should not be studied with as much fervor as other tragedies in the Jewish experience. Jews from Yemen (and from other Muslim countries) have felt victimized by this trend and were offended that their poetry, prose, and philosophy were overlooked in reestablishing the intellectual roots of Israeli identity. In fact, all too often only the folkloric aspects (food, dance, embroidery, and music), representing only the outward trappings of a rich culture, have received wide attention.

Since cultural diversity was not encouraged in Israel for the first three decades, many Yemenites felt that they had to preserve and promote their own traditions for their progeny, while hoping that they could also educate others in their multidimensional culture. *Afikim Springs* indeed provides the Hebrew reader with a wellspring of information covering a wide scope of Yemenite Jewish heritage. The implied message is a hope that this heritage will one day be accepted as a worthy component of the traditional-historical roots of an emerging overall Israeli-Jewish identity.

Conclusion

Since the turn of the twentieth century, what were the Yemenites' relationships with the Zionist movement? From the outset, they harnessed themselves to the mission of aliyah and settlement in Eretz-Israel and their trials and tribulations were part of the continuous sacrifice for the rebuilding of the Jewish homeland. But their sacrifices were presented upon an ungrateful Zionist altar. Only seldom were their contributions, even when primary and original, recognized as meaningful and substantial, and only rarely were they mentioned in Zionist-Israeli historiography as equal partners to the rejuvenation of the Jewish nation in its ancient land.

The Yemenites' physical destiny was all too often in the hands of others. They had no influence over immigration certificates to Palestine during the Mandate period, no control over the logistics of transport to Israel in 1949–50, nor any say in the budgets earmarked for settlement activities. Thus, Zionist-Israeli history and historiography tended to ignore them because they were not leaders in positions of authority or part of the decision-making cadre. Both Parfitt and Nini, each in his own way, remind us of the Yemenites' difficult years in immigration and settlement. But their physical efforts during the elimination of their Diaspora community and the years of settlement in Eretz-Israel were not the only tragedy this community faced. Many Yemenite Jews have also sacrificed their cultural heritage on this Zionist-Israeli altar. The Yemenites' religious traditions and their very distinct customs were initially perceived as an obstacle to their integration into the evolving Israeli society. They were led to believe that by adopting the ideologies and identity of the Zionist enterprise (which bore the imprint of the secular, Labor-dominated leadership), they would facilitate their entry into the mainstream. On the other hand, manifestations of their culture often appeared too exotic to become part of the mainstream Israeli identity. All too often, there was no real attempt to penetrate the depths or to consider the breadth of Yemenite culture. Rather, people contented themselves with only a superficial appreciation of some folkloric aspects of Yemenite culture.[15]

Many Yemenite Jews assimilated themselves gradually into the newly formed secular Zionist culture, while others resisted the pressures for such "Israeli" acculturation. Those who resisted held fast to the reins of control over their spiritual legacy, nurturing it throughout the intervening decades and bringing it into the modern Israeli landscape of organizational activities that proudly promote a broad spectrum of the Yemenite Jews' rich cultural, literary, and religious heritage.[16] *Afikim Springs* is a recent manifestation of this unique and multifaceted traditional legacy. This legacy should be recognized not only by Jewish writers of Yemenite background, but by the larger community in Israel. Optimists among us would conclude that perhaps it will, one day, constitute a meaningful contribution to the evolving Israeli cultural identity.

The Zionist vision and the Israeli experience in the twentieth century demanded many sacrifices from all Jews who emigrated from their diasporas and joined together to fulfill the ancient dream: the ingathering of the exiles. These three new books remind us again of the Yemenites' eager response to this call. It is lamentable, however, that in the process of building the homeland and its new society, the Yemenites were forced into unnecessary and most agonizing sacrifices on the altar of Zionism.

Notes

1. On the eve of the First World War, Yemenite Jews numbered about 5,000 in Eretz-Israel. Of these, some 3,000 lived in Jerusalem, another 1,100 in agricultural settlements and about 900 in Jaffa. In 1914, Yemenite Jews

were about 6 percent of the Jewish population in Palestine, while in the Jewish world, they were less than one-half of 1 percent. For more details, see Nitza Druyan, *Without a Magic Carpet: Yemenite Jews in Israel 1882–1914*, Jerusalem: The Hebrew University of Jerusalem and Yad Yitzhak Ben-Zvi, 1981.

2. Parfitt consistently relegates to his footnotes most of the documentation and discussion concerning conflicting testimonies or contradictions. The narrative is thus not overburdened with the author's presence and opinions.

3. See, for example, writings by S. D. Goitein and E. Brauer.

4. See also my conclusions in *Without a Magic Carpet*, 157–60.

5. The most tragic of all such losses was the kidnapping of infant children in the early years of the state. Parents were told that they died, only to discover the lie years later, exacerbating their loss and creating bitterness among the Yemenite community in Israel—a scar that has yet to heal, even half a century later.

6. The book costs over a hundred dollars and was not available for purchase in New York. The publisher should take steps to increase its availability, in a less costly paperback edition.

7. The narrative would have been more fluent and easier to read had Nini relegated his frequent arguments and debates to footnotes or endnotes.

8. See, for instance, Dina Greitzer, *Yemenite Settlement in Kfar Marmorek*, MA Dissertation, Hebrew University of Jerusalem, 1986, and "The Settlement of Yemenite Immigrants at Kfar Marmorek: Between Separation and Integration," *Cathedra* 14 (January 1980), 121–52. (both in Hebrew)

9. Nini regrettably ignores some previously well-documented published material on this subject, especially with regard to the Yemenites' image as natural laborers and to their complex relationship with their Eastern European counterparts. His citations are often superficial and taken out of context (e.g., pp. 46–49); relevant and legitimate historical analyses that do not serve his immediate mission are minimized or simply overlooked. Academic correctness is no mere formality, and is sorely missing in this book.

10. In the context of Nini's research, publications, and public statements during the last three decades, it is indeed astonishing to find this explicit conclusion in his book, identifying him, publicly and unequivocally, as bemoaning the fate of the Yemenite pioneers from his own ethnic group. Still, in his introduction and elsewhere, Nini also identifies himself as an old-time member of the Labor movement who still believes in its ideology and worships its early "giants" who eventually became Israel's political leaders. Understandably, his pain over the Yemenites' fate is thus magnified.

11. See, for example, *Without a Magic Carpet: Pioneers of the Yemenite Immigration,* ed. N. Druyan (Jerusalem: Jewish Historical Sources no. 8, Zalman Shazar Center/Israel Historical Society, 1982) (Hebrew); "Ha-Chacham, Dr. Moshe Gaster and the Yemenite Jewish Community in Jerusalem," *Cathedra* 6 (1978), 168–75 (Hebrew); "The Efforts of the American Zionist Community on Behalf of Yemenite Jews in Eretz Yisrael in the Years 1912–1914," *American Jewish History* 69 (1979), 92–99; "The Immigration and Integration of Yemenite Jews in the First Aliyah," in *The Jerusalem Cathedra,* ed. L. Levine (Jerusalem and Detroit: Yad Yitzhak Ben-Zvi and Wayne University Press, 1983), 193–211; "The Natural Laborers: Yemenite Immigrants in the Agricultural Settlements," in *Sei Yonah: Yemenite Jews in Israel,* ed. S. Seri (Tel Aviv: Israel Ministry of Defense, 1983), 195–210 (Hebrew); "Self-image and Image of the Other: the Yemenite Jews," *Les Nouveaux Cahiers,* 85 (1986), 54–58 (French); "Yemenite Jews in Israel: Studies of a Community in Transition," *Jewish Folklore and Ethnology Review* 11 (1989), 32–35; and "Yemenite Jewish Women: Between Tradition and Change," in *Pioneers and Homemakers, Women in Pre-State Israel,* ed. D. Bernstein (Albany: State University of New York Press, 1992), 75–87.

12. *Afikim,* pp. 23–31. It is of course not possible to list here all of the personalities and their contributions that Avizemer is careful to mention. He also includes the categories of politics, the military, folk crafts, music, education, and so forth.

13. Yosef HaLevi, senior lecturer of Hebrew Literature at Bar-Ilan University, one of the pioneering scholars researching Yemenite Jewish writing in Eretz-Israel, passed away in 1997, before his time.

14. A number of articles do not make reference to any body of scholarship, even when relevant. This lack of citation may have been unintentional, or may reflect a petty avoidance of giving proper credit where it is due, a regrettable editorial lapse.

15. See Nitza Druyan, "The Outsiders: On the Cultural Dimension of Ethnic Diversity in Israel," *Zionist Ideas* 18 (1990), 83–92; and "Yemenites in Israel: In Search of a Cultural Identity," *Hebrew Annual Review* 14 (1994), 43–54.

16. The activities of contemporary Yemenite cultural organizations in Israel were described and analyzed in my lecture, "The Yemenites of Israel: a Quest for Cultural Separatism?" The Twelfth World Congress of Jewish Studies, Jerusalem, 29 July–5 August 1997. Thanks to Margolit Shilo and Shlomo Deshen, with whom I discussed the concept of the "Zionist altar." In addition to Afikim and Halkhot Israel, another noteworthy popular and successful Yemenite cultural organization is ha-Agudah le-Tipuah Hevra ve-Tarbut.

Part III

※

Israel in the Region

10. Policy Transformation in the Middle East: Arms Control Regimes and National Security Reconciled

Hemda Ben-Yehuda

> *This essay examines the debates over what regional changes will follow the end of the Cold War and the establishment of a new world order with the approach of the twenty-first century. While contributors to the volume under review may be divided into "realists" who emphasize the need for states to maintain full military capability and "liberals" who believe that norms of decision-making should constrain short-term power maximization, the author focuses on a neglected but crucial element in policy-making: elite attitudinal change, which she illustrates with examples from her original research into Yitzhak Rabin's evolving policy toward the Palestinians.*

Inbar, Efraim, and Shmuel Sandler, eds., *Middle Eastern Security: Prospects for an Arms Control Regime*, A BESA Study in Middle East Security, London: Frank Cass, 1995.

The collection of essays, *Middle Eastern Security: Prospects for an Arms Control Regime*, by Efraim Inbar and Shmuel Sandler is the product of a November 1993 international conference on

"Arms Control in the Middle East" held at Bar-Ilan University, integrating research by scholars from Europe, Israel, and the United States. This diversity adds to the scope of issues addressed in the book and makes it a valuable source for those who seek to understand the dynamics and prospects of conflict and cooperation in today's Middle East.

The studies in this anthology bring together two concepts: security and regimes. These are core issues in international relations (IR) literature, and are not, in and of themselves, specific to this volume. *Security* can be defined as a situation of "self-preservation, obtained by ensuring that the territorial and political boundaries of the homeland and 'vital' territory cannot be changed by others."[1] This concept derives from the "realist" school in international relations literature, which suggests that the best way to safeguard security is to maintain a powerful military capability, thereby ensuring that the threat posed by others is minimal.

Regimes, the second concept, comes from the "liberal" school in IR literature, and is commonly defined as "principles, norms, rules and decision-making procedures around which actor expectations converge in a given issue-area" that serve to "constrain immediate, short-term power maximization."[2] When viewed together, both concepts form a "security regime," that is, "those principles, rules and norms that permit nations to be restrained in their behavior in the belief that others will reciprocate. The concept implies . . . a form of cooperation that is more than the following of short-term interests."[3] Moreover, a security regime is characterized by an acceptance of limitations on the use of military force, and includes agreements on arms control, Confidence and Security Building Measures (CSBMs), and a certain level of institutionalization.

Security and regimes are hard to reconcile, since the former emphasizes self- and short-term interests while the latter are based on collective, long-term cooperative arrangements. One of the strengths of the Inbar and Sandler volume is that it covers a wide range of thinking on the realism-versus-liberalism debate, including both studies that advocate the merits of reaching a security regime in the Middle East and those that support the virtues of preserving a traditional military balance of power in the region.

Security and regimes not only provide fodder for theoretical debate, but also bear policy implications for those leaders involved in the ongoing negotiation process. Since the October 1991 Madrid conference, Israel and a number of Arab countries have participated in multilateral negotiations on Arms Control and Regional Security

(ACRS). During the biannual plenaries and frequent workshops conducted within this framework, participants address a wide range of issues, including CSBMs and verification for conventional as well as for nonconventional weapons (e.g., Steinberg, pp. 80–81).

The different studies in the Inbar and Sandler anthology share many common assumptions, and the core topics linked to the problem of arms proliferation and disarmament in the Middle East are similar. Even the conclusions of most of the essays are identical: namely, that an arms control regime in the Middle East could be very helpful, is desirable, and is even supported by some of the leading states in the area—but nevertheless seems unlikely to emerge in the near future.[4] First, the authors agree that for various reasons the United States, Russia, and the European states are unlikely to play a decisive and positive role in regime creation in the Middle East (see, in particular, Lieber, p. 12; Klein, pp. 45–46; and Brzoska, p. 20). Second, Israel, with its reputed nuclear capability, would support such a regime only under specific conditions and providing that the agreement would be "far more robust than what current Non-Proliferation Treaty [NPT] procedures can guarantee" (Solingen, pp. 144–45). And third, traditional modes of security are most likely to endure, but the need to restrain nonconventional weapons proliferation may also promote an agreement on conventional weapons (Zanders, p. 105).

With the exception of Jean-Pascal Zanders's study on chemical warfare weapons proliferation, the Inbar and Sandler essays are mainly empirical. The focus is on both states (Israel, Egypt, Syria, Iran, Iraq, and Libya, as well as the superpowers and major European powers), and on processes, such as the Arab-Israel and Palestinian-Israeli conflicts, the Camp David accords, the Iran-Iraq War, the Gulf War, the Oslo breakthrough, and Israeli-Palestinian rapprochement. Common to all the essays is an assumption that the new global world order and the fading of Cold War realities must leave their imprint on regional politics (see, e.g., Lieber, pp. 1-4; Brzoska, pp. 28-29; Karp, pp. 125, 127; Solingen, p. 141; and Inbar and Sandler, p. 179). Most studies point to the fact that regimes and regional arrangements are a product of interstate interaction patterns, of conflict and its resolution, at both the global and regional levels. At the same time, many of the contributors also note the importance of domestic inputs to the arms-control debate. To illustrate the dual purpose of arms in the region, Aaron Karp asserts that by acquiring strategic ballistic missiles, countries in the region serve both "their orthodox role deterring adversaries in war-time . . .

[and] domestic political power in peace-time" (p. 115; see also, Zanders, p. 101 and Solingen, pp. 131-32).

Moreover, a spillover effect exists, according to some essays, among domestic, regional, and global developments. These linkages make the decision-makers' task of shifting from traditional forms of defense based upon self-reliance to those of collective security difficult and uncertain. Avner Cohen points to this uncertainty and interconnection when he analyzes the impact of Iran's pursuit of a nuclear option on long-range stability in the region:

> The fate of Iranian aspirations for hegemonic dominance in the Middle East depends, to a large extent, on whether a new regional order of peace succeeds or fails. If Arab-Israeli reconciliation succeeds, the Iranian ideological cause weakens, and vice versa. In return, if Iran is getting closer to the bomb, this could radicalize the Middle East and harm the cause of Arab-Israeli peace. (p. 53; see also, Steinberg, pp. 80–81)

The first section of the book deals with superpower and European Union contributions to regional security in the Middle East. The second part addresses the topics of nuclear and nonconventional weapons proliferation and their impact on the emerging order in the area. The third section considers the effects of context—both regional and domestic—on the process of attaining an arms-control regime and stability in the Middle East. The discussion of past trends and continuing processes serves as a basis for the volume's concluding exploration of scenarios most likely to unfold in the coming decade. Although many of the conclusions are necessarily speculative, this volume is a rigorous analysis of nearly half a century of conflict, armament, escalation, and conflict-management efforts between adversaries. As such, it contributes much to our understanding of protracted turmoil and to the prospects of reaching a stable order in the coming decade.

For a reader who is interested in the evolution of arms control in the Middle East, but is unfamiliar with the theoretical concepts related to the debate, a good starting point may be the two last essays of the collection. Yair Evron's study, as well as the concluding section written by Efraim Inbar and Shmuel Sandler, present a concise and clear conceptual overview of the core topics of security, regimes, arms control, and CSBMs. The authors base their conceptual approach on global deterrence theory and draw as well on research on arms proliferation, arms control, and their impact on national security and stability. All these are applied very successfully and with caution to the study of security, regimes, and stability in the Middle East (see, e.g., Cohen, p. 49; Zanders, p. 85; Karp, pp. 111–13; Solingen, pp. 130–31; and Evron, p. 159).

The Middle East, traditionally regarded as a zone of turmoil, crises, and war, is engulfed in two levels of conflict: interstate and intercommunal. The first identifies the core rivalry between Israel and the Arab states. The second describes the substate elements of the conflict going back to the confrontation between Jewish and Arab communities during the British Mandate, and also reflects the Palestinian and Muslim-fundamentalist struggle against Zionism and Jews in Israel.

In reality, both levels of rivalry overlap, thereby making the overall conflict exceedingly difficult to resolve. Evidently, the complexity of levels (interstate and intercommunal); issues (territory, security, regime heterogeneity, economics, natural resources, religion, and culture); and actors (Arab states and Israel, as well as nonstate actors such as the PLO and the Islamic fundamentalists), makes it impossible to envision a sudden shift from total conflict to a Utopia of real and lasting peace. Yet current manifestations of rapprochement—the 1979 peace treaty between Israel and Egypt; the 1991 Madrid peace conference and subsequent bilateral and multilateral talks; the 1993 Oslo Declaration of Principles (DOP) between Israel and the PLO and the follow-up 1994 Cairo Agreement and 1995 Oslo II Accord; and the 1994 peace treaty between Israel and Jordan—are significant enough to raise two questions: (1) Why now? and (2) What are the sources promoting such a change in regional politics?

These questions form a research agenda relevant to all of the essays in the book, but I will argue in this review that there is one vital element missing in the Inbar and Sandler collection: namely, the study of elite attitude change. A proper understanding of the change from realist-embedded security to liberal regimes and to a new regional order cannot be had without a rigorous consideration of evolving political attitudes. In the following pages, I will attempt to fill the void in the Inbar and Sandler volume by offering an analysis of shifts in decision-makers' attitudes over time, revealing the process of change in elite perceptions taking place—a prerequisite for foreign-policy transformation to follow. More specifically, we will see that willingness to forsake short-term security requirements in pursuit of an unfamiliar regime (which might be more secure in the long run) requires that leaders change their belief systems and demonstrate a personal willingness to confront the domestic constraints associated with a major change in foreign policy.

Case Study: Yitzhak Rabin

Yitzhak Rabin makes an especially interesting subject for research on attitudes and policy since he was not only involved in formulating Israeli policy over an extended period in multiple roles, both military and political in nature, but also served in several governments, some where the Labor party was a leading factor and others (e.g., the 1984 national unity government) where the Likud party was the core constituent in formulating Israel's foreign policy. Within the Labor party, Rabin represented the more hawkish strand that emphasized the overwhelming importance of the security dimension in shaping Israeli foreign policy, and therefore hesitated to take the risks entailed in territorial compromise with longtime adversaries. This was particularly true with respect to dealing with the PLO, which Rabin and his like-minded colleagues regarded as a terrorist organization, with an unreliable leadership unable to deliver its commitments. As defense minister in the 1984 National-Unity government led by Likud's Yitzhak Shamir, Rabin worked on a daily basis to shape Israel's Palestinian policy during the outbreak and escalation of the Palestinian civil uprising known as the Intifada. Therefore, the shift from his advocating an "iron fist" policy toward the PLO and its Palestinian supporters in early 1988, to recognizing the PLO and accepting the Oslo 1993 DOP cannot be attributed solely to a shift in position from opposition to power.

How can one account for this apparently massive change in position on the Palestinian issue? The following is an analysis of Rabin's attitudes and preferred policy during three periods: the 1967-87 period, before the outbreak of the 1987 Intifada; the years from 1988 to September 1993, which were somewhat of a transition period, dominated by the Intifada but also witnessing the beginning of direct and semiformal negotiations between Israel and the PLO, culminating in the September 1993 DOP; and the October 1993–November 1995 period, during which Palestinian and Israeli negotiators began translating the abstract DOP principles into practical measures for the transfer of powers to the Palestinian Authority. Changes in political and economic domains were agreed upon and formalized in subsequent agreements of May 1994 and September 1995.

Elsewhere, I have analyzed Rabin's attitudes toward the Palestinian issue, demonstrating that changes in a leader's perceptions of security have a crucial impact on policy formulation.[5] Once Rabin accepted Israel's inability to overcome the PLO by military means, the path to a diplomatic negotiation process opened. Rabin's prolonged preoccupation with the Intifada led him to view the Palestinian uprising as a reflection of genuine Palestinian national aspirations. Accepting the constraints of power politics in the Palestinian camp, Rabin came to believe that seeking a Palestinian negotiation partner other than the PLO was futile. Though territorial compromise with Jordan was still his most preferable option for peace, Rabin was frustrated with King Hussein's hesitation and by his mid-1988 administrative and legal disengagement from the West Bank. Rabin came to believe that a new partner had to be found because future escalation of the conflict might endanger Israeli security. Compromise with the Palestinians, he hoped, could lead to the evolution of security regimes and to a new order in the region.

Phase 1: Existence Conflict, 1967–1987

Yitzhak Rabin's position changed dramatically between 1967 and 1995, from a long-standing interest in reaching a territorial compromise with Jordan, to recognizing and implementing interim agreements with the PLO for a transfer of powers and for a stable five-year transitional period during which negotiations on a plan for permanent separation and a peace would take place.

This shift in Rabin's political preferences and plans vis-à-vis the Palestinians, from total conflict to gradual accommodation, was a result of change in four major elements in his approach to the Palestinian issue:

1. his motivation and perceived need to find a settlement to the ongoing rivalry;
2. his overall view of the protracted Arab-Israel conflict and the role of the Palestinian feud within it;
3. his definition of preferable and available partners;
4. his characterization of an acceptable agreement.

Attitude change of such magnitude also reflected the impact of major political events in the global and regional scenes in which Rabin participated.

From the start of his military and political career, predating Israel's 1947–49 struggle for independence, Rabin was a strict adherent of political realism. He viewed the world through a state-centric lense and placed emphasis on the security needs of his country and on the military means to promote them. Accordingly, for Rabin, the Palestinian problem was only a minor issue in the protracted Arab-Israel conflict. He saw the Arab states, rather than the PLO, as threatening opponents to either confront in war or to encounter at the negotiation table.

During the 1967–73 period, the 1967 Six-Day War, the 1969–70 War of Attrition with Egypt, and the 1970 PLO-Jordan crisis ("Black September") shaped Rabin's approach to the Palestinian conflict. With Israel's new sense of enhanced security, based on its superior military power and on self-reliance, Rabin felt no need to hasten the diplomatic process and therefore sought no alternatives to comprehensive peace with Jordan. The 1973 war triggered a new power configuration among the participants in the conflict. Israel suffered a major surprise attack and a gradual shift in regional hierarchy occurred, with the PLO gaining legitimacy at the expense of the Hashemite Kingdom. The disengagement agreements with Egypt and Syria in 1974 and 1975 emerged as a possible model for a solution on the eastern front as well. Slowly a step-by-step strategy replaced the traditional search for a comprehensive peace. Rabin's motivation for reaching a compromise agreement increased, but his preferred partner was still Jordan.

Egyptian president Sadat's historic visit to Jerusalem in November 1977 and the signing of the 1978 Camp David Accords between Israel and Egypt represented a significant breakthrough in Israel's relations with Egypt, the most important Arab state. Rabin thought that peace with Egypt would lead to agreements with other Arab states, starting with Jordan. The idea of a regime-based security arrangement seemed less a Utopia and more a realistic long-term political goal. Rabin supported autonomy for the Palestinians in the West Bank and Gaza as part of the overall Camp David agreements, seeing it as an interim arrangement that would allow Israel and Jordan to jointly administer the territories. Although the Camp David autonomy never materialized, Israel and Jordan engaged in prolonged secret discussions. By 1985, after constant Jordanian pressure, Rabin was also willing to accept some form of Palestinian participation in future peace dialogues. Rabin's new position, however, did not reflect respect for the PLO or support for Palestinian claims to statehood, but rather a desire to satisfy Jordanian sensibilities and to facilitate Jordan's decision to come to the negotiation table.

Throughout the first period, Rabin shared the general Israeli perception of the PLO as a terrorist organization committed to the destruction of the State of Israel. He viewed all interim PLO goals as part of a "program of stages" designed to establish a Palestinian state that would eventually replace Israel. Rabin regarded the PLO as an extremely hostile enemy with politicidal aspirations and, when referring to its terrorist acts, he departed from his usual restrained style and used harsh terms such as "organization of murderers" and "assassins' organization."[6] However, Rabin maintained a more forthcoming attitude toward the Palestinian population. He viewed the Palestinians living in the territories as members of a social community with the right to live in peace and prosperity. Rabin was therefore ready to grant them all the conditions necessary to advance their standard of living and well-being in the economic domain, but with no spillover to the political sphere.

The 1982 Lebanon War made the Palestinian issue the focus of Israeli and world attention. Although the PLO suffered a severe blow and was forced to leave Lebanon, political proposals such as the 1982 Reagan Plan and the Fez Arab Summit Resolution transformed its military defeat into a political success. In both the Middle East and the international arena, the PLO's legitimacy and the Palestinian people's right to an independent state gained widespread approval. Rabin gradually accepted the fact that Israel's significant military power had its limits. Hence, in conjunction with his support for a persistent military struggle against the PLO, Rabin opted for a political solution with the Palestinians that would accommodate Israel's security needs. Security based on self-reliance seemed to need the supportive elements of a consolidation of regional arrangements that the creation of a security regime might provide.

When Rabin became defense minister in 1984, the Palestinian issue fell once again under his direct authority. His main objective then was to drive a wedge between the PLO and the local inhabitants through a "carrot-and-stick" policy. The stick, in the form of a harsh IDF stance, was applied to the PLO and to its supporters whereas the carrot, in the form of participation in negotiations, was offered to those Palestinians who rejected PLO directives. This position reflected Rabin's willingness to promote genuine and effective local Palestinian representation but at the same time to rule out the participation of official PLO leaders. Yet this new outlook did not replace his core belief that an agreement with Jordan was the best long-term diplomatic solution that justified compromise and promised stability and peace.

Phase 2: From Iron Fist to Handshake, December 1987–September 1993

During the second phase under study, the seeds of transition from existence conflict to coexistence became visible. The breakup of the Soviet Union and the 1990–91 Gulf crisis and war reshaped the basic political order of the Middle East, inducing Israel and the Arab world to reassess their positions in their protracted conflict. Rabin often pointed to evolving global trends, claiming that Israel too should "join the campaign of peace, reconciliation and international cooperation that is currently engulfing the entire globe, lest we miss the train and be left alone at the station."[7]

Although Rabin maintained a hostile posture to the PLO throughout most of 1988–93, he reintroduced his dual policy: an iron-fist response toward the Palestinian Intifada, accompanied by political negotiations with moderate Palestinians. Rabin challenged leaders along the spectrum of Palestinian politics: "Are any of you, any group among you, prepared to say that you, you the residents of the territories, are willing to be our partner in a political settlement?"[8] However, all attempts to find authentic non-PLO Palestinian partners failed, and several rounds of Israeli-Palestinian talks in Washington under the Madrid process ended in deadlock. Rabin eventually realized that only the Tunis-PLO leadership had real decisional power and gave his reluctant approval to the opening of the Oslo back-channel. Afterward, Rabin explained his conclusion: "This may not be pleasant, but it is a fact," elaborating: "peace is not made with friends, peace is made with enemies."[9]

Highly skeptical of the Oslo negotiations, Rabin still spoke of the PLO, Hamas, and Islamic Jihad as terrorist organizations that were waging "a total war over our existence" and whose goal was to destroy the State of Israel and "to foil all the chances for peace."[10] Throughout this second period, Rabin railed against the PLO and its insistence on the "right of return" that he regarded as one of the gravest dangers to the State of Israel: "if we accept [this demand] it would be tantamount to committing national suicide."[11] However, unlike the 1967–87 years, Rabin now grouped the Palestinian population with the PLO in one antagonist camp.

The change reflected his perception of the Intifada: "for the first time since 15 May 1948 we witnessed a struggle waged by the Palestinian inhabitants," an uprising with profound political implications. Rabin declared: "This is a clash between two national entities waged through violence by civilians wishing to attain the same goals they could not achieve through terrorism and war."[12] In a detailed description of the PLO and Hamas roles in the Intifada, Rabin explained: "This is a confrontation between two different entities—different theologically and politically—and we could say nationally. . . . Let us be candid: the majority of the Palestinian public identify with these organizations and with their objectives."[13] Yet, even in the midst of the Intifada, Rabin preserved a moderate stance toward the Palestinian population detected in the pre-1987 years, still supporting talks with non-PLO Palestinians designed to "dampen the flame of hatred between the Palestinians and the state of Israel."[14]

Eventually, the Palestinian uprising led Rabin to depart from his earlier conception of the Arab-Israel conflict as an interstate affair, convincing him that a more difficult situation existed in which many nonstate elements played crucial roles. Adjusting to this new perception of reality, Rabin proclaimed:

> I would like to dwell on the complexity of this confrontation. . . . It does not resemble the wars that Israel waged against the armies of Arab countries. Those were wars between armies with clear boundaries, with weapons used in accordance with internationally acknowledged rules. . . . [T]he boundaries are unclear in this [present] case.[15]

Rabin's acceptance of autonomy as the only viable solution for the short run also reflected a significant change in his attitudes. His earlier reluctant support for the 1978-79 Camp David autonomy plan derived from the hope that it would pave the way for renewed Jordanian participation in the peace process; in January 1989 Rabin introduced his own phased plan for Palestinian autonomy, as a solution in and of itself. Though the internal political realities of the National Unity government made Prime Minister Shamir's parallel plan the only official Israeli policy, Rabin's proposal was an embryonic prototype for the post-Oslo arrangements for a transfer of powers to the Palestinians.

The Rabin plan of January 1989 included four stages: (1) a cooling-off period, (2) elections, (3) a transitional period, and (4) a permanent settlement. Rabin explained that the logic behind this plan was the link between its stages:

> We are talking right now of calm. It is inconceivable that elections will be held while violence is raging. Second, representatives of the territories will be elected by the inhabitants of the territories. They will elect not a municipal council but a political representation to stand for the 1.5 million Palestinians residing in the territories, on the conditions that its goals are to reach negotiations. Thus that representation will ultimately serve as the nucleus for the self-rule authority once expanded autonomy is established or once any other interim agreement takes effect. That representation, together with Jordan, will constitute our partner to negotiations for peace along our eastern borders.[16]

Rabin hoped that transitional-phase dynamics would "create through an interim agreement . . . a new reality which may bring about a change in positions. We hope this change occurs on their side, but they have the right to hope the change occurs on our side. This is the logic and I think also the wisdom of dividing progress toward peace into stages."[17]

Separation of populations was an additional aspect that emerged in Rabin's political approach to the Palestinian issue. It originated in the short-term closures that Israel repeatedly imposed upon the territories after terror attacks within Israel. Over time, Rabin came to regard separation as more than a temporary tactical measure, although in this period he was loathe to prescribe it as a permanent political solution.[18] Though Rabin never regarded terror as an existential threat, he did not underestimate the impact it had on personal security and on daily life in Israel.[19] Even before Oslo, Rabin foresaw the dangers of Israelis and Palestinians intermingling and warned that "without separation there will be no personal security."[20] Whereas the Begin government had proposed autonomy in an effort to erase the green line and to ensure that Judea and Samaria remained part of greater Israel, Rabin's separation concept constituted a redrawing of a modified green line.

On the whole, this second phase was marked by change rather than by preservation of old attitudes. Rabin now viewed the conflict as a complex process in which states and nonstate actors were engaged in both violent confrontations and regional peace negotiations. He recognized that King Hussein had ruled out the "Jordanian option." The most significant change at the close of this period resulted from Rabin's failure to find genuine, non-PLO, Palestinian leaders with whom to negotiate his autonomy plan. This led him to the realization that only the PLO leadership in Tunis was capable of implementing decisions. This change was the precondition to the Oslo breakthrough.

Phase 3: Step-by-step Reconciliation, October 1993–November 1995

The post-September 1993 period of implementing the DOP was dominated by Rabin's recent departure from a state-centric view of the Arab-Israel conflict to one that recognized the importance of multiple nonstate actors such as the PLO, Hamas and Islamic Jihad, and their supporters outside Israel. After signing the DOP, Rabin frequently referred to the spillover effects between the interstate and the substate elements that could, in his eyes, work either for or against further agreements and stability. Rabin particularly cared about the relationship between Israel and Jordan. Though *de facto* peace had characterized the situation along Israel's border with Jordan, the Oslo process and the rapprochement with the PLO bore fruit in the form of the long-sought-after formal peace treaty between Israel and its Hashemite neighbor in October 1994.[21]

With the Jordanian treaty secured, Rabin's endeavors with the PLO now focused primarily on the Palestinian issue. After suffering through the handshake and witnessing Arafat's signature on the unprecedented political documents, Rabin threw his whole weight behind the Oslo process and the fact that a new and improved PLO had emerged. When he presented the Oslo accords to the Knesset, Rabin pointed out to his fellow parliamentarians that he believed the Israelis and the Palestinians were "destined to live together, on the same soil in the same land."[22] Rabin admitted that the Palestinian issue was most important, recognized the Palestinians as a political entity, comprehended the fact that both Israelis and Palestinians were linked to the same contested territory, and accepted the PLO as the representative of the Palestinians. The DOP marked, according to Rabin, a turning point in the goals and policy of the PLO. Rabin accepted the fact that the former terrorist organization was now willing to coexist in peace with Israel and to resolve the conflict through negotiations; he now argued that, since the signing of the

DOP, Arafat's supporters had refrained from the use of terror as a means in its political struggle.[23]

Rabin replaced his hostility to the PLO with a sense of partnership in a joint venture toward rapprochement. Although he still viewed the PLO leaders as "those who held knives . . . [and] pulled the trigger," he concluded that "we cannot choose our neighbors, or our enemies."[24] Interestingly, Rabin never hid his personal antipathy toward Arafat, and confided that he had actually felt sick at the prospect of shaking his hand at the DOP signing ceremony.[25] But, in this third phase, he responded to a question as to whether he disliked Arafat by replying in a very neutral mode: "Personal feelings are irrelevant to diplomatic relations. Mr. Arafat is at the head of the Palestinian Authority. We agreed to consider him our partner in this strategic plan."[26] At the signing of the 1995 interim agreement, Rabin observed that hearts no longer quivered at the sight of Israeli and Palestinian partnership and cooperation, and described the long road that he and Chairman Arafat had traveled to reach the present stage: "We began to get used to each other, we're like old acquaintances."[27]

Rabin's state-centric view of the Arab-Israeli conflict broadened to encompass a multidimensional view in which the Palestinian conflict played a core part. According to his new perspective, in the interim period preceding a permanent solution Israel should provide the population in the territories with the conditions that would assure them a proper standard of living, while maintaining the law and order that Israel's security in the area demanded. The policy changes that Rabin advocated accorded with his January 1989 four-phase plan. The negotiations he supported between Israel and the Palestinians proposed a two-stage formula: five-year interim self-government arrangements, to be followed by negotiations on the permanent-status issues. Rabin declared that the long-term goal of the negotiations and interim agreements was to "reach peace with a Palestinian entity in Judea, Samaria and the Gaza Strip."[28] This formulation indicated movement beyond the autonomy idea toward genuine rapprochement.

The proposal for a separation between Israel and the Palestinians that emerged in the second period further crystallized during this third stage and acquired a territorial dimension for a long-term solution. While the early idea of separation had resulted from Israel's closures of the territories in order to curb the rising tide of Islamic terror, it gradually emerged as Rabin's plan for future coexistence between two units: Israel, and a Palestinian entity under a Palestinian Authority "that is not a state."[29] This plan effectively constituted a new version of Rabin's territorial compromise idea, but with the PLO as partner instead of Jordan. Rabin reached the conclusion that there would neither be a solution to the conflict and an end to terrorism, nor security, well-being, and peace, "without long-term separation between Israel—albeit not in the 1967 borders—and a Palestinian entity existing by its side."[30] Although separation had territorial implications that almost certainly meant the establishment of a Palestinian state, Rabin was not willing to go so far as to voice support for Palestinian sovereignty.

Conclusion

More than any of the factors measured and analyzed in the Inbar and Sandler collection, it was Rabin's evolving policy of reconciliation, his willingness to accept Palestinian autonomy combined with some element of territorial compromise, and his embrace of a separation of populations that enabled the Israeli side to negotiate an Israeli-Palestinian rapprochement in Oslo. An analysis of three different periods—1967–87, 1988–93, and 1993–95—reveals significant shifts in Israeli attitudes and policy toward the Palestinian issue. The changes in Yitzhak Rabin's political preferences and plans, from total conflict to gradual accommodation, necessitated transformations in four different aspects of his approach to the Palestinian problem:

1. a new urgency to find a settlement to the ongoing rivalry;
2. a new appreciation for the centrality of the Palestinian factor in the protracted interstate Arab-Israel conflict;
3. a redefinition of the PLO as a viable peace partner;
4. the acceptance of autonomy and separation as satisfactory interim agreements.

Major political events in the regional and global arenas, such as the 1982 Lebanon War, the Intifada, and the collapse of the USSR, played a major role in shepherding Rabin along his personal path of psychological and political transformation. The policy of rapprochement that Rabin came to prescribe for Israeli-Palestinian relations reflected the evolution in his own thinking and, by extrapolation, the conclusion that security and regimes can indeed be reconciled. The post-Oslo relationship between Israel and the Palestinian Authority constitutes a new political-security regime. If it succeeds, it is likely to trigger and facilitate the achievement of arms-control regimes between Israel and the Arab states. If it fails, Israel must continue to endure the high cost of relying solely upon its own military and intelligence resources to maintain its security within a region of increasing instability.

During the process of creating an arms-control regime and a broader security regime, states vacillate between their traditional preference for self-reliance and an interest in new forms of regional cooperation and interstate defense systems. The two modes of securing a state's defense may seem contradictory since they are based on opposing elements: self or collective. Each of these has its merits, and leaders can find ways to bridge them in order to draw on their respective strengths. Once a relatively stable regime emerges on any front, decision-makers can learn that state security and regional cooperation via the adoption of regimes do not contradict but rather support and complement one another.

The Camp David Accords, with the security arrangements they included for the demilitarization of the Sinai Peninsula, serve as an illustration. Presenting other leaders with evidence that peace and mutual security arrangements can be attained without forsaking one's own defense needs, these accords initiated an admittedly slow spillover process in that they functioned as a model that the Rabin government could draw upon in drafting the DOP and the Israel-Jordan peace treaty, fourteen and fifteen years later, respectively.

Most authors in the Inbar and Sandler volume agree that the Middle East is still a long way from adopting a security regime. Yet a preliminary academic discussion on the topic may serve to help Israeli and Arab decision-makers along the path toward establishing such a regime. The major contribution of these studies, and the source of the book's importance, lies in its in-depth analysis of diverse aspects related to the creation of an arms-control regime in the Middle East. However, both the more technical arms-control agreements and a comprehensive security pact cannot take place without a conceptual shift on the part of the decision-makers. The emergence of regimes as a form of providing for state security means that leaders must compare the benefits of economic and military power based on self-reliance with the advantages of a power-structure based on mutual agreements. While the former do not safeguard states from the hazards of violence and war, the latter seek to:

1. establish procedures for conflict regulation or resolution;
2. define limitations on arms acquisitions;

3. create institutions to maintain a stable balance of power;
4. enforce sanctions against states which do not comply with the agreed regulations.

A shift from self-reliance to mutual agreements, in an area where conflict is a core attribute of interstate political interactions and war is a frequent phenomenon, requires not only persistent effort by decision-makers but also genuine change in elite beliefs and in the popular atmosphere that would spill over to encompass all of the major participants of the area. Those leaders who are the early supporters of a security regime are the actors that might induce such a positive spillover process. Yitzhak Rabin played a crucial role in the post-1993 period by shaping and implementing four important accords with the PLO and its successor PA, thereby moving toward more comprehensive regional security arrangements. Despite its antipathy to the Oslo process, the Likud-led government elected in mid-1996 has, reluctantly, maintained these agreements as the basis for its policy toward the PLO and other Arab states. A case in point is the January 1997 Israeli withdrawal agreement from Hebron which, although behind schedule, adhered to the Oslo stipulations.

The main subject of the study under review is regional change in the Middle East, involving a shift from a realist security arrangement based on state interests and power politics to a liberal order that envisions the emergence of security regimes. Both the book and this review address the sources that explain such a change, ranging from domestic constraints on the actors involved to the impact of changes in the global system that affect the region. This review, however, highlights a vital and missing element in the Inbar and Sandler volume—the impact of leaders' attitudes—and applies it to the analysis of change in Rabin's attitudes and in the accompanying transformation in Israel's Palestinian policy. Parallel research into attitudinal change among Arab leaders will provide an even more complete picture of the possible evolution of a regime-based security structure for the Middle East.

Notes

1. Scott D. Bennett, "Security, Bargaining and the End of Interstate Rivalry," *International Studies Quarterly* 40:2 (1996), 163.

2. *International Regimes,* ed. Stephen D. Krasner (Ithaca NY: Cornell University Press, 1983), 1, 3.

3. Robert Jervis, "Security Regimes," *International Organization* 36 (1982), 357–78.

4. See, for example, in the Inbar and Sandler collection, the essays by Lieber (p. 12), Brzoska (p. 30), Klein (pp. 45–46), Cohen (p. 67), Steinberg (p. 81), Karp (pp. 127–28), Solingen (pp. 144–45), Evron (pp. 168–69), as well as Inbar and Sandler (pp. 182–83). Some scholars are more pessimistic in their assessment of the consolidation of a security regime ever taking place (e.g., Lieber and Klein), while others seem slightly more optimistic about long-term developments (e.g., Zanders, Karp, and Evron). A third group attempts to stay neutral but points to the merits of raising an academic and public discussion on the topic of arms control and security regimes, even though steps toward their establishment are premature (e.g., Cohen and Steinberg).

5. H. Ben-Yehuda, "Attitude Change and Policy Transformation: Yitzhak Rabin and the Palestinian Question, 1967–95," *Israel Affairs* 2: 3–4 (Spring–Summer, 1997), 201–24 (special issue, "From Rabin to Netanyahu: Israel's Troubled Agenda," ed. Efraim Karsh).

6. Y. Auerbach and H. Ben-Yehuda, "Attitudes to an Existence Conflict: Rabin and Sharon on the Palestinian Issue 1967–87," in *Conflict and Social Psychology,* ed. K. S. Larsen (Oslo: International Peace Research Institute and London: Sage Publications, 1993), 154.

7. *Divrei ha-Knesset* (Knesset Records; hereafter DK), 13 July 1992: 8–9; cf. English text in *The Israel-Arab Reader: A Documentary History of the Middle East Conflict,* 5th rev. and updated ed., eds. Walter Laqueur and Barry Rubin (New York: Penguin, 1995), 590.

8. JDTV (Jerusalem Domestic TV), 14 January 1988, Foreign Broadcast Information Service, Daily Report (hereafter FBIS).

9. FBIS, 30 August 1993; and IDF Radio, 3 September 1993.

10. FBIS, JDR (Jerusalem Domestic Radio), 25 October 1993, and IDF Radio, 7 March 1988, respectively. See also, JDTV, 14 December 1992, JDR, 22 February 1993, and DK, 26 October 1992: 4, 20 January 1993: 2724, 3 February 1993: 3078, and 28 July 1993: 6948.

11. FBIS, JDTV, 8 December 1988.

12. FBIS, *Davar,* 12 February 1988: 16; and *Davar,* 24 February 1988: 1–2, respectively.

13. FBIS, JDTV Chanel 2, 22 March 1993.

14. DK, 13 July 1992: 9 and 26 October 1992: 4.

15. FBIS, JDTV Chanel 2, 22 March 1993 (from the Knesset).

16. FBIS, JDTV, 20 January 1989, JDR, 31 January 1989, London–BBC, 28 February 1989.

17. FBIS, IDF Radio, 18 May 1989.

18. FBIS, *Davar,* 12 March 1993.

19. FBIS, *Jerusalem Post,* 20 February 1989: 10; JDTV, 4 September 1992.

20. FBIS, JDR, 8 April 1993.

21. DK, 15 May 1995: 53 (unpublished stenographic protocol). Cf. Laura Zittrain Eisenberg and Neil Caplan, *Negotiating Arab-Israeli Peace: Patterns, Problems, Possibilities* (Bloomington: Indiana University Press, 1998), Chapter 5.

22. DK, 21 September 1993: 7680; cf. translation of speech in Laqueur and Rubin, *Israel-Arab Reader,* 615–20.

23. DK, 21 September 1993: 7680; 3 October 1994: 4; and 15 May 1995: 46 (unpublished stenographic protocol).

24. DK, 21 September 1993: 7679, 7680, 7682; cf. Laqueur and Rubin, *Israel-Arab Reader,* 615–620.

25. R. Slater, *Rabin of Israel* (London: Robson Books, 1996), 583, 586.

26. FBIS, Paris, *al-Watan al-Arabi,* 6 January 1995: 15–19.

27. Israel Ministry of Foreign Affairs Website (www.israel-mfa.gov.il) or (www.israel.org/peace), speeches at the signing ceremony of the Israeli-Palestinian Interim Agreement, 28 September 1995.

28. DK, 15 May 1995: 45 (unpublished stenographic protocol).

29. FBIS, JDTV, 24 March 1995; see also, JDTV, 23 January 1995; IDF Radio, 24 January 1995; and JDTV, 27 February 1995.

30. FBIS, JDTV Chanel 3, from the Knesset, 28 February 1995.

11. Palestinian Sovereignty and Israeli Security: Dilemmas of the Permanent-Status Negotiations

Naomi Weinberger

This essay examines Palestinian and Israeli negotiating strategies in the current transitional and approaching "permanent-status" stages of the peace process in terms of the two parties' divergent goals: achieving Palestinian sovereignty, and guaranteeing Israeli security, respectively. In covering the immediate issues of Jewish settlements, border adjustments, redeployment of the Israel Defense Forces, and the establishment of Palestinian security forces along with the broader questions of Jerusalem, the return of refugees and sharing of water resources, the author examines the impact of asymmetries in the two parties' power and status, a timetable governed by conditionality and reciprocity, public opinion, and external constraints posed by regional actors and great powers.

Alpher, Joseph, *Settlements and Borders*, Final Status Issues Series: Israel-Palestinians, no.3, Tel Aviv: Jaffee Center for Strategic Studies, Tel Aviv University, 1994.

Aronson, Geoffrey, *Settlements and the Israel-Palestinian Negotiations*, Final Status Issue Paper, Washington DC: Institute for Palestine Studies, 1996.

Boutwell, Jeffrey, and Everett Mendelsohn, *Israeli-Palestinian Security: Issues in the Permanent Status Negotiations,* Cambridge MA: Report of a Study Group of the American Academy of Arts and Sciences, 1995.

Elmusa, Sharif, *Negotiating Water: Israel and the Palestinians*, Final Status Issue Paper, Washington DC: Institute for Palestine Studies, 1996.

Gazit, Shlomo, *The Palestinian Refugee Problem*, Final Status Issues Series: Israel-Palestinians, no. 2, Tel Aviv: Jaffee Center for Strategic Studies, Tel Aviv University, 1995.

Gold, Dore, *Jerusalem,* Final Status Issues Series: Israel-Palestinians, no. 7. Tel Aviv: Jaffee Center for Strategic Studies, Tel Aviv University, 1995.

Heller, Mark, "Towards a Palestinian State," *Survival* (Summer 1997), 5–22.

———, *The Israel-PLO Agreement: What If It Fails? How Will We Know?* Final Status Issues Series: Israel-Palestinians, no. 1, Tel Aviv: Jaffee Center for Strategic Studies, Tel Aviv University, 1994.

Inbar, Efraim, and Shmuel Sandler, *The Risks of Palestinian Statehood,* Mideast Security and Policy Studies, no. 33, BESA Center for Strategic Studies, Ramat Gan, Israel: Bar Ilan University, 1997.

Khalidi, Ahmad, *A Palestinian Settlement: Towards a Palestinian Doctrine of National Security,* Israeli-Palestinian Peace Research Project Working Paper Series, Jerusalem and Rome: Arab Studies Society, Harry S. Truman Research Institute for the Advancement of Peace, and the Institute for International Affairs, 1992.

Sayigh, Yezid, "Redefining the Basics: Sovereignty and Security in the Palestinian State," *Journal of Palestine Studies* 24:4 (Summer 1995), 5–19.

Shalev, Aryeh, *Options for Security Arrangements*, Final Status Issues Series: Israel-Palestinians, no. 4, Tel Aviv: Jaffee Center for Strategic Studies, Tel Aviv University, 1995. (Hebrew)

Shikaki, Khalil, *Transition to Democracy in Palestine: The Peace Process, National Reconstruction, and Elections.* Department of Politics and Government, Nablus: Center for Palestine Research and Studies, 1996.

———, "Israeli Security, Hegemony and the Political Negotiations," *Palestinian Politics* I:1–2 (Winter-Spring 1994), 40-48. (Arabic)

Tamari, Salim, *Palestinian Refugee Negotiations: From Madrid to Oslo II,* Final Status Issue Paper. Washington DC: Institute for Palestine Studies, 1996.

The Negotiating Framework

Since the signing of the September 1993 Israeli-Palestinian accords, analysts have speculated on whether further negotiations would indeed resolve the "permanent status" of the West Bank and Gaza. Will there be a Palestinian state? Will Israelis, Palestinians, and the region as a whole achieve greater security? Despite occasional notes of optimism, sober assessments prevail.

Intermittent publications by Middle East research institutes delve into the issues that must be resolved in permanent-status negotiations. Monographs by Israeli scholars (at the Jaffee and BESA centers) and Palestinian scholars (at the Institute for Palestine Studies [IPS] and the Center for Palestine Research and Studies [CPRS]), alongside the more comprehensive report on *Israeli-Palestinian Security* by a study group of the American Academy of Arts and Sciences,[1] reveal substantial discrepancies between the positions of the relevant parties. Nonetheless, the voices of leading academic thinkers yield valuable insights that may enlighten negotiators if diplomatic prospects improve.

Palestinian analysts agree that the goal of negotiations must be sovereignty, but disagree over whether the "Oslo process"[2] can deliver. Should a Palestinian state come into being, virtually all Israeli analysts express reservations about its potential to contribute to regional stability. Some argue, however, that Palestinian sovereignty may be sufficiently constrained so as to reduce potential risks to Israeli security. But even these seasoned and sophisticated Palestinian and Israeli observers seem to speak past each other, in that efforts to accommodate the other side's internal constraints and sensitivities fall short of what may be minimally acceptable.

The range of divergent perspectives becomes apparent when one asks what the peace process has accomplished thus far. What tangible changes have occurred in the post-1967 status quo of Israeli occupation of the West Bank and Gaza? Are these changes enduring or reversible? In short, is the peace process leading toward Palestinian sovereignty? Is Israel becoming more or less secure?

An Israeli analyst who has given sustained attention to the prospects of Palestinian statehood over the years is Mark A. Heller of the Jaffee Center for Strategic Studies at Tel Aviv University.[3] In his recent writing, Heller observes that

> the argument about whether a Palestinian state should or should not exist is anachronistic; the semi-independent Palestinian state already exists.... [T]he real Israeli-Palestinian agenda now focuses on the borders of that state—a variant of the territorial disputes with which the traditional study of international relations is replete—and on its authority—a central issue in the emerging study of trans-national, supra-national, and post-national regional and international institutions. ("Towards a Palestinian State," p. 9)

Heller argues that a Palestinian "semistate" came into being following the reluctant acceptance of the principle of partition by both Israelis and Palestinians. A Palestinian political entity began to emerge once Israeli withdrew from Gaza and Jericho in June 1994, and then redeployed its forces away from major West Bank towns in 1995. The Palestinian entity is already endowed with many "substantive manifestations of statehood," including

1. effective control of territory (about 1,800 square kilometers) and people (almost all of the approximately 2.4 million Palestinians in the West Bank and Gaza);
2. functioning executive, legislature, judicial, and security structures;
3. widespread international recognition and representation in many international institutions and organizations;
4. governmental legitimization through relatively free elections.

Although setbacks in negotiations have raised doubts about prospects for a permanent-status agreement, the prognosis remains that "no settlement will be possible unless it incorporates some kind of Palestinian state." Therefore, unless the peace process unravels completely and Israel reoccupies the territories from which it has withdrawn, the Palestinian "semistate" will continue to exist. Indeed, Heller believes that it is in Israel's best interests to recognize an independent Palestinian state, with specified limitations on its authority (pp. 5–9).

A more pessimistic assessment of the feasibility of reconciling Palestinian sovereignty and Israeli security is offered by Efraim Inbar and Shmuel Sandler of Bar Ilan University. They point out that the "strategic environment in which a Palestinian state might emerge is riddled with security threats" and that "the peace process could collapse" (pp. 25, 26). At present, "[t]he PA [Palestinian Authority] has not yet passed the main criterion for being a state—exercising a monopoly of coercive power—and the Lebanonisation of a future Palestinian state cannot be excluded." Nonetheless, Inbar and Sandler conclude that "establishing a Palestinian state . . . seems to be only a question of time." Indeed, these scholars are convinced that "the status quo is not tenable in the long-run" and that "a Palestinian state is inevitable." One means of reducing the potential damage to Israel was to extend the timetable of negotiations, rather than being bound by the May 1999 date initially agreed upon for the conclusion of a permanent status agreement (ibid., pp. 23, 28, 34–35).

Still another cautionary voice about the pacing of the negotiating process is that of Aryeh Shalev of Tel Aviv's Jaffee Center. He argues that even once a permanent-status agreement is reached, implementation will involve delays in accordance with set "stages in the implementation of the agreement, which will be spread out over [a number of] years." His longer-term prediction is, however, relatively optimistic. Although "the Israeli-Palestinian permanent status agreement is likely to be fragile and unstable in the initial stages of its realization," Shalev believes that "as time passes and the agreement is indeed implemented, the risks will be gradually reduced. . . . It is therefore appropriate that security arrangements should not be uniform throughout the permanent status period, but should rather be much more stringent in the beginning, and then be gradually relaxed" (pp. 2–3).

From a Palestinian perspective, by contrast, there is a sense of urgency about achieving sovereignty.[4] According to Yezid Sayigh of the University of Cambridge, there is an "imperative need for an independent state. Until this state comes into existence, the Palestinian people remain under one degree or another of Israeli military occupation" or in a precarious state of exile (p. 8). Even if negotiations do lead to statehood, "[f]lawed sovereignty and structural weakness will be intrinsic features of any Palestinian state." In effect, a Palestinian state may be created "because the external powers that count most—Israel, followed by the U.S. and Jordan—come to the conclusion that there will be little real difference between Palestinian autonomy and nominal sovereignty" (pp. 6–7).

In the meanwhile, however, an assessment of Palestinian circumstances yields a discouraging view about how much has actually changed in the status quo. Geoffrey Aronson, in a contribution to the Final Status Issues Series published by the Institute for Palestine Studies in Washington, DC, indicates that "[a] close reading of the

September 1995 ["Oslo II"] accord shows that the occupation has not ended" and that the PLO was "not really assuming sovereign power. The military government [was] not being abolished. . . . Israel remain[ed], with Arafat's consent as well as according to international law, the *de facto* sovereign of the areas that the PLO will now administer under contract with Israel" (p. 36). Indeed, the Oslo accords have perversely transformed Israel's "belligerent" rule over Palestinians into "a partnership operating with Palestinian consent," technically transforming Israel's occupation army into a "guest army" (pp. 31, 33).[5]

Palestinian-Israeli Asymmetries

The deep uncertainty about the future reflects, in part, the specific circumstances in which the Camp David and subsequent Oslo accords evolved. The long-standing insistence by Israel on keeping the final status of the West Bank and Gaza open-ended led to a distinction between transitional and final status negotiations, which is highly unusual in international diplomacy. Both sides are keenly aware of the fact, however, that transitional security arrangements decisively predispose the outcome of permanent status negotiations.

The timetable of negotiations is governed by the principle of conditionality designated by Israel to determine whether the Palestinian Authority established in territories yielded by Israel has lived up to prior commitments before moving to the next stage of negotiations. As Heller explains: "The DOP [Declaration of Principles, i.e., first Oslo Accord of September 1993] is not a peace agreement. It is, at most, an agreement to enter into an open-ended, multistaged process leading to a peace agreement." This diplomatic mechanism intentionally "does not provide for automatic transition from one phase to the next." As a result, "whether or not any transition takes place depends . . . on Israel's assessment of the experience of the previous phase" (*Israel-PLO Agreement,* pp. 1–2).

There are two "performance criteria" by which Israel will judge the outcome of the Oslo peace process. One is the "peace dividend," a positive measure of improved relations with Arab states. The second, more immediate, criterion for judging Palestinian compliance is security. As Heller explains, "security is essentially a negative objective: the reduction . . . and ultimate elimination of threats or damage to life and property stemming . . . from acts of terrorism." If the Palestinian Authority is unable or unwilling to curb terrorism, Israel would have several options. It could *"freeze* the process, either formally (by suspending negotiations), or informally (by purposefully engaging in inconclusive negotiations) . . . thus prolonging the political *status quo.*" Even more drastically, Israel could decide "to *regress,* i.e., move back to a previous stage." Regression might entail "reoccupation of any areas previously evacuated, followed by a brutal and uncompromising repression" (emphasis added, pp. 6, 15–17).

In essence, Heller asserts that Israel regarded the Oslo process as "an ongoing experiment" or as "a test, of which Israel itself will be the judge" (pp. 1–2). Why does Israel get to be the judge? Palestinian sources consistently emphasize the asymmetries of power and status between the PLO and Israel as factors that undermine the Palestinian negotiating position. Such asymmetries derive, first, from the *status* of Israel as a state and the Palestinians as a non-state actor. Secondly, there is a great disparity between Israel's *capabilities* as a major military power in the Middle East and the Palestinians' lack of military assets. Third, the status quo favors Israel, in that Israel holds the territory to which the Palestinians lay claim, and therefore has substantial capacity for unilateral actions that damage Palestinian interests (see Boutwell and Mendelsohn, pp. 15–18).

Yezid Sayigh remarks on the "vast asymmetry . . . in terms of military capability between Israel and the Palestinians, and indeed in almost every other respect; the only equivalence is the equal need of both peoples for lasting peace and security" (p. 11). Sayigh calls attention to the frequently overlooked reality that Palestinians, and not just Israelis, have compelling security needs. He highlights the fundamental vulnerability of the Palestinian population, both under Israeli military occupation and in the Palestinian "Diaspora." Sayigh suggests that instead of thinking of security in the narrow sense of "military defense against direct, physical threats," it would be beneficial for Israelis and Palestinians alike to reflect on an alternative conception. In the broader sense, security means "the ability to protect 'national values,' identified broadly as safeguarding the political and territorial integrity of the state, ensuring the physical wellbeing and survival of the population, promoting economic welfare, and preserving social harmony" (p. 6).

A more pessimistic voice, raising doubts about Palestinian prospects for a secure and independent future, is that of Khalil Shikaki, a scholar at the Center for Palestine Research and Studies in Nablus. Shikaki believes that Israel's objective in negotiations is to perpetuate its security hegemony in the West Bank and Gaza. He views the relationship between Israel and the Palestinians as one of "supremacy and subordination," for which the asymmetrical distribution of military power is a critical determinant. Any concessions that Israel may make in turning over security responsibilities to the Palestinians will, in his view, "only occur within the framework of its hegemony."

Shikaki is especially troubled by the implications of emerging security arrangements for the prospects of democratic change within Palestinian society. He believes that a "solid wall of security exigencies" that Israel will insist upon as a condition for surrendering control "will constrain the Palestinian Authority and make it vulnerable," thereby exposing it to "internal ridicule and external schemes." The result may be increased polarization in Palestinian society, which could lead to "bloody conflict," giving Israel a justification to resume direct military control. Shikaki's pessimistic assessment calls attention to the precariousness of the peace process for residents of the West Bank and Gaza ("Israeli Security Hegemony," pp. 40–48).

Security Issues

Divergent priorities of Palestinians and Israelis—in terms of the primacy of sovereignty or security—define strategies at every stage of transitional and final status negotiations over the future of the West Bank and Gaza. Dividing the issues on the table between those with direct security implications (including internal security, demilitarization, borders, and settlements) and those nonsecurity issues (including Jerusalem, water, and refugees) can be deceptive. Sometimes security requirements are cited to mask ideological imperatives. Conversely, "nonsecurity" issues can have significant impact on the territorial outcomes of negotiations, and hence serious implications for the security of Palestinians and Israelis.

The principal reason cited by Israeli analysts for limiting Palestinian sovereignty is the need to safeguard Israeli security. Since Israel gained control of the West Bank in 1967, the territory's significance as a strategic buffer has frequently been cited.[6] By contrast, the strategic significance of Gaza is discounted by most analysts (Boutwell and Mendelsohn, pp. 50–51). Because of dangers that might emanate from a Palestinian state under hostile leadership, or one unable to control the use of its territory by others, Israel seeks both territorial and functional limitations on Palestinian sovereignty.

In addressing Israel's security imperatives in the permanent-status negotiations, analysts frequently distinguish between *internal*, or current security—that is, security against the ongoing threat of terrorism—and *external*, or interstate security—that is, security against attack by other regional actors (see Shalev). Whereas the threat posed by terrorist acts is very distressing to Israelis in their daily lives,[7] terrorism is not seen as an existential threat—that is, one that could jeopardize the country's existence.

Internal Security

Deterrence of terrorism was a major focus of attention in the negotiation of Israeli-Palestinian agreements on the transitional period of Palestinian self-rule. During the transitional period, responsibility for internal security has been entrusted to the Palestinian police in those areas falling under exclusive Palestinian jurisdiction.[8] The inability or unwillingness of the Palestinian Authority to curb terrorism has provided the most compelling justification for Israel's delaying permanent-status negotiations and for the redeployment of forces. Israeli authorities have charged that "terrorist organizations . . . have acquired greater freedom of action under the PA than under Israeli military occupation" (Inbar and Sandler, pp. 33–34).

Internal security remains a focus of concern for permanent status negotiations, with potential threats to Palestinian as well as to Israeli security even after the achievement of statehood. Yezid Sayigh explains that "potential threats to Palestinian security include possible resort to covert operations by Palestinian individuals or groups opposed to the peace with Israel." In response, the Israeli government might "overreact to the action of *agent provocateurs*. It might then launch military operations against the Palestinian state, in keeping with the emphasis in Israeli military doctrine on preventive and preemptive strikes" (p. 9). Inbar and Sandler concur that "[t]errorist activities from the territories under Palestinian control are likely to trigger an Israeli military response against the Palestinian state. . . . This development could lead to further regional escalation and threaten regional stability" (pp. 33–34).

Ultimately, however, deterrence of terrorism can only be effectively achieved by Palestinian authorities. As Heller argues,

> [s]ecurity against terrorism . . . [can] stem . . . only from Palestinian determination not to allow terrorists the free-

dom to operate lest Israeli retaliation inflict an unacceptable cost.... The PA's ability to act against terrorists undoubtedly exceeds Israel's, and its willingness to do so has been—and will continue to be—a function of its broad calculus of interests, one element of which is undoubtedly its assessment of Israeli reactions in the event that it falls short. ("Towards a Palestinian State," p. 14)

External Security: Demilitarization and Borders

The strategic significance of the West Bank explains why the stakes are so high for its territorial disposition as well as for the residual deployment of Israeli forces. In assessing potential external security threats, Inbar and Sandler maintain that the geographic location of a future Palestinian state, "combined with instability and an uncertain foreign orientation, may make it a potential existential threat to Israel, given its proximity to Israel's heartland." The Palestinian state would be within artillery and rifle range of the Jerusalem-Tel Aviv-Haifa triangle, which contains 75% of Israel's population and 80% of its economic infrastructure (p. 31; see also Boutwell and Mendelsohn, pp. 51–54).

What types of security guarantees would adequately reassure Israel, permitting the relinquishment of sovereign control over the West Bank? Israeli analysts have called for demilitarization of the Palestinian state—entailing *functional* limitations on its sovereignty, as well as Israeli control of the strategically vital Jordan Valley—possibly requiring *territorial* limits on Palestinian authority.

The need for Palestinian demilitarization evokes a consensus among Israeli analysts. Heller explains that Palestinian military forces must be restricted to internal security functions, with no offensive weaponry that would enable them to act beyond Palestinian borders. Nor should Palestinian forces have the wherewithal "to disrupt the eastward movement of Israeli forces if this became necessary to meet or anticipate an emerging threat from other quarters" ("Towards a Palestinian State," p. 15).

Nonetheless, functional limitations will be difficult to enforce once Palestine achieves sovereignty. It may be relatively easy to evade demilitarization clauses, especially once a Palestinian port and airfield offer possibilities for the smuggling of heavy weapons or troops. Moreover, "a violation of demilitarization would pose a real dilemma for Israel.... Failing to respond would encourage salami tactics, while a strong military riposte would trigger an escalation that may lead to international opprobrium" (Inbar and Sandler, pp. 36–37).

The suggested remedy is to negotiate an effective verification regime. Israel would prefer that its own personnel participate in a monitoring system of Palestinian border-crossing points and air and seaports, but may be obliged "to minimise the provocation to Palestinian sensitivities by cloaking . . . [monitoring arrangements] in multilateral garb." Another means of making functional constraints on Palestinian sovereignty more palatable is mutuality—as in a mutual nonaggression pact and joint commitments not to introduce foreign forces (Heller, "Towards a Palestinian State," p. 15).[9]

There is more of a debate among Israeli analysts about what territorial limitations, if any, must be imposed on a Palestinian state in order to meet Israeli security requirements. Such limitations would be primarily intended to deter interstate war with other Arab states, rather than offensives stemming from Palestine itself. In the traditional view of Israeli strategists, "[i]f the Jordan Rift Valley—the area along the River Jordan—is . . . ceded to Palestine, . . . the West Bank could become the springboard for a potential eastern front—a military coalition encompassing Iraq, Jordan, Saudi Arabia and Syria—[in an] effort to cut Israel in two" (Inbar and Sandler, p. 31).

Israel might therefore insist on retaining sovereignty over the Jordan Valley or, alternatively, agree to less stringent arrangements that would intrude less on Palestinian sovereignty. Joseph Alpher, editor of the Jaffee Center series, outlines three possible strategies intended to preserve for Israel, "for years to come, the capacity to move defensive forces to the Jordan River in real time." One strategy would be to annex the entire Jordan Valley, as prescribed by the Allon Plan of July 1967. Second, Israel might annex territory only on the fringes of the Jordan Valley, where Israeli forces would be permanently deployed, so as to retain unfettered access to staging areas along the Jordan River. Third, Israel might preserve a military presence along the Jordan River, but without annexing territory (pp. 25–26). Still another suggestion for retaining the Jordan Valley as a "forward-defense line" would be for Israel to draw up long-term lease arrangements with the Palestinian state, subject to periodic review (Heller, "Towards a Palestinian State," pp. 14–15).

As for Palestinian responses, Ahmad Khalidi of Oxford University contends that one essential component of a Palestinian national security doctrine is a capacity for self-defense. He advocates the creation of a Palestinian Self-Defense Force once a state is established, while accepting the inevitability of quantitative and qualitative limits on the capabilities at its disposal. Second, Khalidi argues that "external reinforcement," through the introduction of international peacekeeping forces, may compensate for Israel's preponderant military assets. Finally, "regional linkage" through close security bonds with other Arab states is the third element of the Palestinian security doctrine. For Khalidi, the overriding goal is "the establishment of a national entity on Palestinian soil as an irreversible reality" (p. 4).[10]

Sayigh believes that instead of seeking to match Israel's military capabilities, Palestinians should consciously opt for a trade-off, "exchang[ing] the demand for a military capability that cannot serve its stated purpose for real political and territorial gains." In light of the Palestinian people's lengthy experience of vulnerability, it has become apparent that "the military dimension is only one component of security, and not always the most important one." Sayigh believes that a future Palestinian state is most likely to face threats to its political, rather than to its physical, security. Due to the precariousness of the Palestinian national enterprise, and lingering challenges to its legitimacy by elements within Israel, the international community must uphold its sovereignty and territorial integrity (pp. 10–11; see also Boutwell and Mendelsohn, pp. 54–60).

Curiously, there is limited discussion in both Palestinian and Israeli sources of the role of Jordan or the implications of the Israeli-Jordanian Treaty of 1994 for security arrangements. The treaty commits Israel and Jordan to make sure their territories are not used for attacks against each other. Neither country may join alliances aimed against the other, nor may they allow other parties to enter, station forces, or operate in circumstances prejudicial to the other party.[11] Since the treaty with Jordan reduces military threats to Israel from the east, Israel may be able to afford to reduce its deployment of military forces in the West Bank more readily. Jeffrey Boutwell and Everett Mendelsohn go so far as to claim that "Israel's 'security border' with potential Arab enemies has moved hundreds of miles to the east, to the Jordanian-Iraqi border" (pp. 24–25).[12]

For some Israeli analysts, latent challenges to the legitimacy of the Hashemite monarchy arouse alarmist conclusions, undermining the long-term benefits of the Jordanian-Israeli accords. Inbar and Sandler project that "[a] Palestinian state would galvanize nationalistic feelings among Palestinians in Jordan . . . [and] . . . could threaten Jordan's sovereignty. . . . The Hashemite regime's fall would probably result in the Palestinian state expanding eastwards towards Iraq. . . . This growth could open the possibility of an 'eastern front' against Israel with territorial contiguity from the Mediterranean to the Persian Gulf—including Palestine, Iraq, and Iran" (p. 33).

Although the foregoing assessment of risks is probably overstated, the Jordanian-Palestinian relationship is indeed precarious. Jordanians harbor concerns that "Palestinians in Jordan and the West Bank could combine to undermine the Hashemite monarchy." Palestinians recall their troubled relationship with Jordan before 1967, when the West Bank was under Jordanian control, and in the 1970 "Black September" confrontation in the streets of Amman, Irbid, and elsewhere. Both parties are therefore likely to tread lightly in considering a proposal for confederation between a future Palestinian state and Jordan (Boutwell and Mendelsohn, pp. 24–26).

The ramifications of Israeli-Jordanian-Palestinian cooperation for regional security could be far-reaching. Sayigh raises the prospect of a "Tripartite Open Zone" among the three countries, portrayed as "a special structure designed to enhance mutual security and economic development . . . reminiscent of the Benelux model." One advantage of the "open zone" would be to "widen the geographical scope of security arrangements throughout the zone and so reduce the intrusion experienced by each member state" (pp. 14–15).[13] For example, in the context of cooperative mechanisms among Israel, Palestine, and Jordan, joint committees might coordinate the sharing of information on military maneuvers and other peacetime operations, as well as intelligence needed to prevent terrorist acts and other violence within and across the three communities (Boutwell and Mendelsohn, p. 99).

In such far-sighted arrangements, Jordan might "help restructure the asymmetries in the Israeli-Palestinian relationship, and provide a key link between the Israeli-Palestinian peace process and the broader process of Arab-Israeli reconciliation" (p. 24). Yet the highly speculative character of predictions about Jordan is symptomatic of the uncertainties plaguing the Israeli-Palestinian peace process. The fallout of positive or negative developments between Israel and Jordan affect the Palestinian track and vice versa. An unraveling of progress in the Israeli-Palestinian track would jeopardize peace with Jordan—as well as prospects for normalization with other Arab states.

Settlements

There are over 130,000 Jews living in about 120 settlements beyond the Green Line (i.e., the pre-June 1967 boundaries) in the West Bank and Gaza, not including Jerusalem. The continuing presence of Jewish settlements is deemed by virtually all Palestinian authors to be incompatible with the realization of Palestinian sovereignty. Yet even relatively dovish Israeli analysts anticipate incorporating major settlement blocs into Israel, requiring significant border adjustments as a condition of Palestinian sovereignty (See Boutwell and Mendelsohn, pp. 39–42, 64–71).

Debate over the future of the settlements and Jerusalem show that territorial limitations on Palestinian sovereignty will not be governed by Israeli security imperatives alone, but also by ideological imperatives. Heller acknowledges that the settlements issue "derives from Israeli domestic political needs and material interests and these—perhaps ironically [rather than the strictly security concerns] are much more relevant to the territorial dimensions of a Palestinian state. . . . No agreement that forcibly uprooted these people [the settlers] or brought them under Palestinian jurisdiction would be tolerated by the Israeli public, and no government that endorsed such an agreement would survive" ("Towards a Palestinian State," pp. 15–16).

Although construction of Jewish settlements began soon after the 1967 war, when Israel was governed by the Labor Alignment, settlement policy was qualitatively transformed under the Likud party after 1977. For the first time, Israel authorized settlement construction in the heartland of the West Bank, close to Palestinian population centers. Geoffrey Aronson alleges that Likud's policy was intended "to disrupt the territorial continuity of Palestinian communities and thereby preempt the possibility of Palestinian self-determination" by making "any territorial division of the West Bank a practical impossibility" (pp. 6–12, 31).

The Israeli analysts under review consider three options for the disposition of settlements. Proposals for leaving all existing settlements in place are generally dismissed, as in Heller's comment that "[n]o agreement that attached all the settlements to Israel, especially the more isolated and remote ones, would permit the practical assertion of Palestinian administration; such a mixture of jurisdictions . . . would fail the . . . test of reasonableness." ("Towards a Palestinian State," pp. 15–16). Sayigh concurs that a Palestinian state would be critically impaired by "severely reduced territory that may also be fragmented into noncontiguous pockets," and that "the possibility of residual intermeshing of Israeli [settler] and Palestinian population concentrations" would lead to "administrative, security, and political complications" (p. 6).

A second option would be dismantling a select group of isolated settlements that would be particularly vulnerable once a Palestinian state arises, and therefore a security liability for Israel. Inbar and Sandler contend that "[c]lear ethnic boundaries reduce violence" and that it is therefore desirable to promote the goal of "clearer separation between Israelis and Palestinians." They therefore advocate "[r]emoving several Jewish settlements situated inside Palestinian population centers." This roughly corresponds to the proposal floated in early 1997 by Prime Minister Benjamin Netanyahu, which was dubbed "Allon-Plus" (p. 35; Alpher, pp. 27–28).[14]

A third option is dismantling *all* of the geographically isolated Jewish settlements, permitting the emergence of a geographically compact Palestinian state in most of the West Bank. This approach reaches more emphatic conclusions about the perils to Israel inherent in the defense of such settlements. Alpher goes so far as to say that "the mixing of populations—Israeli and Palestinian—is the single factor that most disrupts attempts . . . to achieve security. . . . Hence any solution that leaves enclaves of Israeli settlements in the heart of Palestinian territory is liable to constitute a source of friction and a liability for current security." Alpher's solution is for Israel to annex approximately 12% of the West Bank and Gaza, including the bulk of Israeli settlements that are clustered just over the Green Line—around Jerusalem, in the Jerusalem corridor and in the Samarian foothills. This compromise would take demographic considerations into account, since the areas incorporated into Israel would encompass about 70% of the settlers. Alpher argues that his proposal is politically feasible because of divisions between the two major groups of Jewish settlers in the West Bank. Approximately 60% are "economic" settlers, who were attracted to the communities near the Green Line by generous government offers to purchase spacious homes on liberal terms of financing. By contrast, about 40% of settlers profess "heritage" links with the Land of Israel, often identifying with the ideological movement known as Gush Emunim. This group seeks "to establish a national-political presence in places of religious-historic importance . . . [in] the Judean and Samarian heartland." Alpher believes that "a territorial compromise wherein a significant portion of the settlements were annexed to Israel—and a minority were abandoned—would drive a wedge into the settler camp, and would considerably reduce the strength of their lobby, their solidarity, and the intensity of their protest" (pp. 15–17, 27).

Alpher concedes that "[i]n reaching agreement on these issues, . . . Israel could undergo a serious trauma internally." Nonetheless, he assumes that "the dynamic created by a successful Palestinian interim autonomy regime will . . . cause many settlers to reassess their options." If given a choice between staying where they are and coming under Palestinian jurisdiction, or relocating to Israel, "the vast majority of Israeli settlers would not wish to live permanently within the Palestinian entity." Many economic settlers acknowledge that they will not violently oppose a partition agreement that calls for their removal, as long as they receive generous compensation. By contrast, an "overtly violent minority" of the ideological settlers may be expected to use violence "against Arabs, and even against fellow Jews, in order to prevent withdrawal" (pp. 1–3, 16). Alpher's argument is corroborated by a June 1997 poll of West Bank settlers jointly conducted by Bar Ilan's BESA Center and the CPRS, which showed that only 17% of the settlers said they would be willing to live under Palestinian sovereignty, 13% would consider using force to resist a government decision to evacuate settlements, but only 2% advocated active confrontation with the Israeli Army to resist evacuation.[15]

In counterdistinction to the broad Israeli consensus in favor of leaving at least some of the settlements in place, Aronson advises Palestinian negotiators "not to be drawn into extended debate on evacuation of marginal outposts," but to remain firm in their insistence that all settlements must go. His reasoning is that

> [p]ermitting any settlements to remain in final status would obstruct Palestinian achievement of any credible degree of sovereignty . . . not necessarily because of the settlements *per se,* . . . but because of the extensive security measures required to insure their existence, including the permanent presence of the IDF [Israel Defense Forces] in the territories.

In a view shared by most Palestinian analysts, he advocates total Israeli evacuation of Jewish settlements in the context of a permanent status agreement (pp. 63–64).

"Non-Security" Issues

Jerusalem

The issues of Jerusalem, water, and refugees share a common status in that none is valued primarily in terms of its security significance. On the surface, the future of Jerusalem is furthest removed from the debate over security requirements. As Dore Gold points out in his Jaffee Center monograph, "Jerusalem is not a strategic issue. For Israel, the Palestinian Arabs, and the Arab/Islamic world, it is a national-religious question . . . [and] a central value in its own right" (p. 3).

Yet on closer scrutiny, the status of Jerusalem is indeed closely linked to the issues of settlements and borders. This is because the enlargement of Jerusalem's municipal boundaries in the wake of the June 1967 war encroached substantially on the city's West Bank hinterland. On 27 June 1967 Knesset legislation authorized the government to extend Israeli law in the eastern part of the city, including in the enlarged municipal boundaries a segment of the West Bank considerably larger than the Jordanian municipality (Aronson p. 17; Boutwell and Mendelsohn, pp. 44–45, 81–83).[16] As a result, the future of "Greater Jerusalem" has profound implications for the territorial disposition of the West Bank, and the prospects for territorial contiguity within a Palestinian state.

Second, Israel has sponsored the creation of Jewish neighborhoods in the environs of Jerusalem, in which approximately 180,000 Jews reside. As Aronson observes, Israelis long ago ceased to regard their new neighborhoods in East Jerusalem as settlements. Initially, Israeli planners preserved the separation of national and religious groups, and saw to it that "[n]ew Israeli suburbs . . . encircled rather than penetrated existing blocs of Arab habitation." Under the Likud administration, however, Jews were encouraged to take up residence within Jerusalem's Old City, among its Palestinian residents (pp. 18–20, 27). This policy makes it harder to envisage a negotiated solution involving separation between the different demographic groups in the city.

Since the unification of Jerusalem, a wide variety of proposals has been advanced for negotiated solutions. Gold categorizes these proposals into three groups: religious, municipal, and territorial. The Israeli government has consistently advocated a religious solution, recognizing the legitimate international demand for a special status for the Holy places, since Jerusalem is a city holy to several major faiths. Israel has indicated its willingness to place the international administration of the Holy places in the hands of the respective religious leaders.

Implementing a religious solution would require, in the case of Christian interests, the conclusion of appropriate arrangements with the churches representing each denomination. Representation of Islamic interests is intrinsically more difficult since "Israel must negotiate with various state bodies that claim to represent Islamic interests." Israel initially left the functions of religious affairs in the hands of the East Jerusalem religious endowment *(waqf)* associated with the Jordanian administration. Since the signing of the Oslo accords, however, Israel has conveyed contradictory commitments to the PLO and Jordan, assuring first one and then the other of its position as primary interlocutor with regard to the Muslim Holy places in Jerusalem. Obviously, this contradiction will have to be resolved in permanent status negotiations (Gold, pp. 8, 13–17, 30).

Municipal solutions have been suggested as compromise measures by several Israeli politicians, including Teddy Kollek, former mayor of Jerusalem. He advocated creating a network of boroughs, each of which would have its own budget and considerable independence, along the lines of the municipalities of London. Municipal solutions bear some resemblance to the overall concept of autonomy for the transitional period of Palestinian self-rule, with the associated merits and drawbacks. Proponents argue that a municipal arrangement would look "like a united city to Israel, but provide the Palestinians a municipal district that gave them the sense that they had their own separate jurisdiction." Critics see shortcomings for Israelis and Palestinians alike. Israeli critics worry that the Palestinians would seek control of zoning and housing permits, potentially disrupting the demographic balance in the city (pp. 3, 32–33). Palestinian critics consider municipal solutions unworthy of consideration, especially at this stage of the diplomatic game, since they fall far short of sovereignty.

Palestinian spokespeople have long endorsed a *territorial* solution for the future of Jerusalem. Accordingly, the PLO claims that the eastern part of Jerusalem should become the political capital of a future Palestinian state. Since the largest single concentration of Palestinians in the eastern half of Jerusalem is located within the walls of the Old City, Palestinians naturally wish to bring that area under their sovereign control. For their part, Israeli governments have repeatedly asserted Israel's intention and right to retain united Jerusalem as Israel's "eternal and exclusive capital." Knesset resolutions, as interpreted by Gold, have "clearly precluded the idea of making Jerusalem a dual capital, both of Israel and of another political entity" (pp. 16–17, 26–28). One variant of territorial solution endorses a partial Israeli withdrawal from East Jerusalem, creating on the periphery of the city a Palestinian zone, which would serve as the Palestinian capital, while leaving the Old City under Israeli sovereignty.[17] As with other attempted compromises, serious questions remain as to whether a popular and elite consensus could be built around this effort to split the difference on a particularly thorny and emotionally-charged issue.

Water

Due to the scarcity of water in the Middle East, control of hydrologic resources has become increasingly salient as an issue with security as well as economic implications crucial to a state's well-being. Since Israeli control of the West Bank and Gaza has given it access to the water resources therein at the expense of the indigenous population, this issue has become another example of Israeli-Palestinian asymmetry. Moreover, the resolution of disputed claims to water will have significant territorial implications, in view of the location of major water aquifers that Israel may seek to annex in western Samaria.[18]

In comparison to other issues on the table for permanent status talks, negotiations over water as well as over the status of Palestinian refugees have been relegated to secondary status by Israeli authorities. Since the Madrid Peace Conference of 1991, these two are among the five issues subject to discussions in multilateral negotiations, the others being the environment, economic development, and disarmament. Salim Tamari of Beir Zeit University has noted that

> [i]t was assumed that the multilaterals would create avenues toward regional cooperation that would improve the atmosphere of negotiations and facilitate bilateral agreements.... The Palestinians, as the weaker party, viewed this distinction differently. They saw in the multilaterals an arena where they could compensate for their limited options in bilateral negotiations with Israel by seeking alliances in the region and Europe. (pp. 2–3, 43)

In explaining Israel's position in negotiations, Alpher asserts Israel's right to maintain access to water sources in the West Bank over the long term. Indeed, Israel drew from aquifers located underneath the West Bank even before the establishment of the state. Alpher maintains that "[a]bandonment by Israel of its control over West Bank water resources would be disastrous for the country's economy, agriculture, and ecology," in view of the fact that Israel depends on these sources for a significant proportion of its water supply (p. 28).

Palestinian analysts, however, charge Israel with discrimination in allocating water and water rights. According to Sharif Elmusa of the Institute for Palestine Studies, Israel is "firmly in control of the disputed water resources," and there is "a wide gap between the two sides in access to these resources."

In the interim-status negotiations, the Palestinian side achieved limited gains in promoting two principles intended to rectify these asymmetries. The question is, to what extent the principles will be applied in the permanent-status negotiations? The first principle embraced by Palestinians is that "equitable utilization of water rights ... should address the problem of disparity of water extraction and use." Elmusa explains that, as a result of Israeli control, the present allocations of water are heavily tilted in Israel's favor. The Palestinian water supply in the West Bank and Gaza has remained substandard and intermittent. As a result, a "stark water gap" arose between Israelis (including settlers) and Palestinians in all sectors: household, crop irrigation, and industry. In the Oslo II agreement of September 1995, the two sides recognized the necessity of producing extra water, and shortly thereafter concluded a trilateral pact with Jordan designed to increase the water supply. Augmentation of the water supply is predicated on the anticipated inadequacy of fixed, natural freshwater resources in the face of population growth and urbanization. The allocation of "additional water" to the Palestinians as part of Oslo II falls short of even the lowest Palestinian expert demand projections (pp. 31, 53, 63).

The second principle is joint management of water resources. Oslo II granted the Palestinians a role in the management of the water sector in the West Bank, serving on a Joint Water Committee made up of equal members of both sides. However, the scope of the committee's authority is confined to the Palestinian sector only. Furthermore, its decisions must be reached by consensus, giving Israel veto power over the Palestinians' ability to alter the unfavorable status quo. As Elmusa emphasizes, these "provisions must be changed in a final status agreement, because, as they stand, they would impinge heavily on Palestinian sovereignty" (pp. 53–54).

Alpher presents the Israeli counterpoint, arguing that although Israel depends on West Bank sources for a significant proportion of its water supply, adequate supervision and control arrangements through the establishment of a joint water regime would guarantee Israel's rights of usage without annexation. Nonetheless, "exclusive physical control over water resources is safer for Israel than a joint water sharing regime" (p. 28).

Refugees

Negotiations over the status of Palestinian refugees are multifaceted in their implications. Like the issue of Jerusalem, the refugee issue is rife with normative significance for Palestinians and Israelis. As with water, the status of refugees has clear economic repercussions. While Israeli analysts are mindful of the security implications of the refugee issue, their Palestinian counterparts discount the security factor. Finally, as with water, negotiations over refugees have been relegated to secondary status by Israeli authorities. Tamari warns that "the issue of refugees . . . will be further marginalized and neglected by Israeli negotiators, until . . . it becomes an explosive and destabilizing issue in relations between Israel and the Palestinians" (p. 58).[19]

For Israelis, there is fundamental ambivalence about accepting moral responsibility for the refugees' status. Shlomo Gazit of the Jaffee Center suggests that as part of a permanent status agreement, Israel must acknowledge the need "to provide moral-psychological compensation to the Palestinians" by issuing a statement recognizing "the great suffering of the Palestinians who were displaced from their homes" and the need to compensate them for property left behind. Nevertheless, Gazit is at pains to point out that Israel should "not insinuate any Israeli responsibility for this suffering" (p. 26). Tamari concedes that this is a painful issue for Israelis, since "even minor concessions with regard to refugee claims would lead to a general questioning of Jewish rights in Eretz-Yisrael . . . [and open] a Pandora's box of historic claims and rights" (p. 58).

These sensitivities are manifest with respect to Palestinian demands that Israel recognize their "right of return." Tamari (pp. 45–46) cites a proposal by Rashid Khalidi that if Israel accepts, in principle, the right of Palestinians and their descendants to return to their homes, Palestinians would acknowledge that this right cannot be exercised inside the 1948 boundaries, but only in the state of Palestine.[20] Gazit emphasizes the fact that the Palestinian leadership must "announce to its own people, and to the refugees in particular, that it had agreed to a solution to the refugee problem not based on their 'return' to Israel" (p. 26).

There are two major economic dimensions to resolving the refugee issue. With respect to the compensation of refugees, Tamari refers to two separate forms of reparations. The first is *collective* compensation, on behalf of Palestinian refugees in general, which would go toward consolidating the infrastructure of the Palestinian state. The second is *individual* claims to be negotiated between Israel and representatives of the refugees (p. 46). Gazit accepts individual and collective compensation, and suggests that the necessary funding would be provided by an international authority for the rehabilitation of Palestinian refugees. Israel would be one of its contributing members (pp. 27–30).

Another issue affecting the status of refugees is uncertainty over the economic health of the fledgling Palestinian state. Tamari points out that not all Palestinian refugees will choose to relocate to Palestine. The factors determining how many will return include the absorptive capacity of the Palestinian economy, agreed-upon quotas, and "attractiveness of the new regime compared to the relative security or insecurity of Palestinians in their current host countries." Moreover, Tamari cautions that Israeli authorities may obstruct the return of refugees if the returnees threaten to destabilize the PA economically, or to create a large pool of illegal laborers infiltrating into Israel (pp. 44–46).

As for security implications, Gazit asserts that returning displaced persons should not concentrate in the proximity of the Green Line, forming a "negative irredentist-security threat." He cautions that the permanent-status agreement should "offer a clear plan that prevents the refugees from becoming an irredentist element, endangering both Israel and the peace agreement" (pp. 24, 33). But Tamari argues that Israelis use security as a pretext for restricting the relocation of Palestinians to Palestine. He charges that "return of Palestinian refugees is now being portrayed as a security issue within Israel, and as a prelude to a subtle scheme for undermining the Jewish character of the state." In this context, he urges that "[d]emographic arguments in the guise of security concerns should not be acceptable" (pp. 2, 52–53).

Leadership Options

This review of the issues on the table for permanent-status negotiations reveals that even the categorization of the issues and the stakes involved for each side is a highly subjective exercise. Ostensibly security-driven issues often mask ideological commitments, whereas economic or religious imperatives behind the "non-security" issues are often laden with heavy security implications.

Substantial differences have been noted between the positions of Palestinian and Israeli scholars on the full range of issues surveyed.

Nonetheless, the security analysts whose writings are reviewed here share a common arena of discourse. Their independent monographs, as well as the joint monograph of the American Academy study group, reveal substantial room for compromise. Internal constraints upon the leadership in each community, far more than security imperatives or external pressures, account for the difficulty in reaching negotiated agreements. Indeed, there is remarkably little discussion in either Israeli or Palestinian sources of any external influences by regional or Great Powers over their negotiating options.

Palestinian and Israeli leaders are reluctant to make concessions to each other that may exceed the popular consensus. Excessive compromises may provoke a backlash in the form of electoral defeat, assassination, popular uprising, or even civil war.[21] Israeli leaders are more directly responsive to electoral consequences than their Palestinian counterparts, but in fact public opinion is a major determinant of both parties' negotiating behavior. Yet data on public opinion by Israeli and Palestinian research institutes reveals that leaders really do have considerable diplomatic room for maneuver. A September 1997 poll conducted in the West Bank and Gaza indicated that 59% of the public supported the Oslo peace process, although 36% supported suicide bombings against Israelis and 58% said that they could not criticize the Palestinian authority without fear. In Israel, a poll conducted in February-March 1997 indicated 70% support for the Oslo process, with 51% of the public favoring the establishment of a Palestinian state and 77% believing that a Palestinian state would be created within the next ten years.[22]

As Heller argues, Israel's "interest in a stable post-settlement environment impels it to minimise the grounds for Palestinian rejection or subsequent revisionism, by maximizing the settlement's legitimacy in the eyes of the Palestinians themselves, implying 'generosity' in the extent to which it responds to Palestinian territorial and functional demands." Yet Israel retains serious doubts about the reliability of the PLO as "an authoritative interlocutor, in terms of its ability to enforce its own preferences and commit itself or its possible successors" to implementing a negotiated settlement ("Towards a Palestinian State," p. 12; and *Israel-PLO Agreement*, p. 7). Other Israeli analysts are even more pessimistic. Inbar and Sandler believe that "[t]he evolving Palestinian polity will most probably be a dissatisfied entity; . . irredentist sentiments seem guaranteed." If Arafat's regime loses control, "a takeover by an Islamic revolutionary counter-elite is not impossible" and "[a] future Islamic regime will probably renege on the agreements with Israel" (pp. 26–28). It is noteworthy that (with the exception of Khalil Shikaki's *Transition to Democracy*), the monographs cited in this essay barely touch on the progress toward democracy and human rights in the Palestinian entity. Literature on this subject is just beginning to appear.[23]

For its part, the Israeli public is deeply ambivalent about offering further concessions to the PLO which, if deemed excessive, may "provoke a backlash that could delegitimize the government, the peace agreement—or both." ("Towards a Palestinian State," p. 12–13; Alpher, p. 3). Yet the backlash that brought Benjamin Netanyahu to power as prime minister did not easily undo what the Oslo process had already accomplished. For, as Heller points out,

> [o]nce in government, ... Likud soon discovered that its opposition to a Palestinian state could not easily be reconciled with its declared commitment to the Oslo agreements or with the emerging reality since the DOP. Having failed to resolve this conundrum, it has been increasingly preoccupied with the problem of imagining some construct that might satisfy the technical requirements of Palestinian statehood while avoiding its terminological specifications. ... (p. 7).

What is most troubling is that the persistent asymmetries in the circumstances of Palestinians and Israelis mean that the longer diplomatic stalemate prevails, the more likely previous accomplishments are to unravel. In the absence of progress, the least likely outcome is a stable status quo. Instead, one may anticipate further weakening in the position of the Palestinian Authority and its decreasing capacity to keep a lid on violent opposition and terrorism. On Israel's side, unilateral actions transforming the territorial status quo in Jerusalem and the rest of the West Bank will leave less to compromise over. Time is not on the side of peace. Based on the experience of the years since the signing of the Declaration of Principles, one would have to be foolish to believe that the peace process is irreversible.

Notes

1. This study group, assembled in 1992–94, included many authors whose writings are reviewed in this essay. Israeli participants were Joseph Alpher, Shlomo Gazit, and Zeev Schiff; Palestinian participants were

Ahmad Khalidi, Khalil Shikaki, Yezid Sayigh, and Nizar Amar; American participants were Jeffrey Boutwell, Everett Mendelsohn, Shibley Telhami, and Naomi Weinberger.

2. The Oslo accords include a set of agreements on transitional self-government for the West Bank and Gaza initially negotiated with Norwegian assistance. Oslo I, or the Declaration of Principles (DOP), was signed by Israel and the PLO on 13 September 1993. A follow-up agreement for preliminary Israeli withdrawal from Gaza and Jericho, dubbed the "Cairo Agreement," was signed in 1994. "Oslo II," signed in Washington in September 1995, set out a plan for Israeli redeployment from major Palestinian cities in the West Bank prior to the holding of Palestinian elections. According to Oslo I, negotiations on the permanent status of the West Bank and Gaza were to commence no later than May 1996 and to be completed by May 1999. For an overview, with selected documents, see Laura Zittrain Eisenberg and Neil Caplan, *Negotiating Arab-Israeli Peace: Patterns, Problems, Possibilities* (Bloomington: Indiana University Press, 1998), 103–26, 210–16, 231–32.

3. See Mark A. Heller, *A Palestinian State: The Implications for Israel*, (Cambridge: Harvard University Press, 1983); and Heller and Sari Nusseibeh, *No Trumpets, No Drums: A Two-State Settlement of the Israeli-Palestinian Conflict*, (New York: Hill and Wang, 1991).

4. For some early indications, see Walid Khalidi, "Thinking the Unthinkable," *Foreign Affairs* 56:4 (July 1978), 695–703; and Heller and Nusseibeh, *No Trumpets*.

5. See also Jerome Segal, "Does the State of Palestine Exist?" *Journal of Palestine Studies* 19:1 (Autumn 1989), 14–31; and John W. Whitbeck, "Now, Drop the Veil: The Palestinian State Exists," *Middle East International* 546 (21 March 1997), 18–19.

6. See *Can Israel Survive a Palestinian State?* ed. Michael Wildansky (Jerusalem: Institute for Advanced Strategic and Political Studies, 1990).

7. In a poll conducted in 1997, 77% of Israelis surveyed said they were "worried" or "very worried" about their personal safety. See Asher Arian, *Israeli Public Opinion on National Security, 1997*, Jaffee Center for Strategic Studies, Memorandum no. 47 (Tel Aviv: Jaffee Center, 1997).

8. See Naomi Weinberger, "The Palestinian National Security Debate," *Journal of Palestine Studies* 24:3 (Spring 1995), 16–30; and Ahmad S. Khalidi and Hussein J. Agha, *Common Ground on Redeployment of Israeli Forces in the West Bank*, The Initiative Papers, no. 3 (Washington DC: Search for Common Ground, 1994).

9. See also Weinberger, "An Israeli-Palestinian Security Regime: The Role of Peacekeeping Forces," in *Israel at the Crossroads*, eds. Efraim Karsh

and Gregory Mahler (London: I. B. Tauris, 1994), 104–21; and Boutwell and Mendelsohn, 45–49.

10. See also Ahmad S. Khalidi, "Security in a Final Middle East Settlement: Some Components of Palestinian National Security," *International Affairs* 71:1 (1995), 1–18.

11. For a discussion of the treaty and its text, see Eisenberg and Caplan, *Negotiating Arab-Israeli Peace*, 90–102, 217–28.

12. See also Joseph Alpher, "Israel's Security Concerns in the Peace Process," *International Affairs* 70:2 (1994), 229–41.

13. See also Institute for Social and Economic Policy in the Middle East, Jordan, Technology Group, Truman Institute, and PCG, *Towards Free Trade in the Middle East: The Triad and Beyond, A Report by a Team of Israeli, Jordanian and Palestinian Experts: Short Version* (Cambridge MA: Harvard University Press, 1995).

14. For a discussion of the Allon-Plus plan, see Zeev Schiff, "Netanyahu Proposal for Final Settlement: 40% of West Bank to Palestinians," *ha-Aretz* 29 May 1997, Internet edition (www3.haaretz.co.il/eng).

15. "Settlers Poll #2: The Future of Israeli Settlement in the West Bank," June 1997, available on request from CPRS.

16. See also Ian S. Lustick, "The Fetish of Jerusalem: A Hegemonic Analysis," in *Israel in Comparative Perspective,* ed. Michael N. Barnett (Albany: State University of New York Press, 1996), 143–72.

17. For a discussion of the Beilin-Abu Mazen proposal on Jerusalem, see Heller, "Towards a Palestinian State"; and the survey by Jerome Segal, paper presented at the 13th annual meeting of the Association for Israel Studies, Altanta, June 1997.

18. See the very revealing maps in Chayim Gwertzman, *Maps of Israeli Interests in Judea and Samaria,* Surveys in National Security (BESA Institute, Bar Ilan University, 1997) (Hebrew). For a general discussion of the water issue, see Boutwell and Mendelsohn, 79–81, and *Water, Peace and the Middle East*, ed. J. A. Allan (London: Tauris Academic Studies, 1996). [Ed. note: cf. the essay by Jeffrey Sosland in this volume, 221–38].

19. See also Boutwell and Mendelsohn, pp. 71–75; and Elia Zuriek, *Palestinian Refugees and the Peace Process,* Final Status Issue Paper (Washington DC: Institute for Palestine Studies, 1996).

20. Rashid Khalidi, "Toward a Solution," in *Palestinian Refugees: Their Problem and Future,* (Washington DC: Center for Policy Analysis on Palestine, October 1994), 24–25.

21. For a discussion of the prospects of civil conflict in Israel, see Ian S. Lustick, "The Political Legacy of De Facto Annexation: Rabin, the Territories and the Regime Crisis in Israel," in *Israel at the Crossroads*, 87–103.

22. CPRS (note 15) and Arian (note 7) polls.

23. See Efraim Kam, *The Political Framework of the Palestinian Entity*, Final Status Issues Series: Israel-Palestinians, no. 5 (Tel Aviv: Jaffee Center for Strategic Studies, Tel Aviv University, 1995) (Hebrew); Gregory S. Mahler, *Constitutionalism and Palestinian Constitutional Development* (Jerusalem: Palestinian Academic Society for the Study of International Affairs, 1996); and Glenn E. Robinson, "The Growing Authoritarianism of the Arafat Regime," *Survival* 39:2 (Summer 1997), 42–56.

12. The Domestic-International Confluence: The Challenge of Israel's Water Problems

༺❀༻

Jeffrey Sosland

This essay examines the role of water in the peace process and the debate between pessimists, who emphasize water shortages and zero-sum conflict, and optimists, who welcome the recent paradigm shift from conflict to cooperation and who envisage water-sharing and win-win scenarios. The author argues that international institutions and agreements will have an increasing influence on the making of Israel's regional water policy and in reaching a peaceful resolution to disputes over allocation and use of the Jordan waters.

Lonergan, Stephen C., and David B. Brooks, *Watershed: The Role of Fresh Water in the Israeli-Palestinian Conflict*, Ottawa: International Development Research Centre, 1994.

Lowi, Miriam R., *Water and Power: The Politics of a Scarce Resource in the Jordan River Basin,* Cambridge: Cambridge University Press, 1993, 1995.

Wolf, Aaron T., *Hydropolitics along the Jordan River: Scarce Water and Its Impact on the Arab- Israeli Conflict,* New York: United Nations University Press, 1995.

Israel's water problem is easily understood—demand far outweighs existing supply. Without cheap electrical power for Mediterranean seawater desalination, Israel will continue to face difficult water scarcity issues. Understanding that water is a vital and shared regional resource, state leaders must apply the combined forces of international and domestic politics to decrease the water scarcity problem. To a limited extent, funding organizations like the World Bank use international aid to influence domestic policy. Yet domestic and international issues in riparian treaty negotiations have been kept separate. For example, domestic water efficiency requirement issues and international river water allocations are not discussed together. However, during treaty negotiations, state elites could manipulate both domestic and international questions simultaneously to achieve the state and regional objective of reducing water scarcity.

Even before Israeli-Arab talks on water begin, some difficult questions ought to be addressed to better understand Israel's water position. On the domestic level, the importance of farming to Israeli society and to the economy must be assessed. As in most countries, agriculture is the primary consumer of water, and in Israel the farming sector consumes 60 to 70% of Israel's water supply. Agriculture has played a pivotal role in the state's social, cultural, economic, and military history. Nevertheless, in the post-Zionist, postindustrial era, Israeli agricultural policy should reflect real needs rather than a romanticization of the past. On the international level, Israel must determine what role its water resources should play in the peace process. Should "water-for-peace" parallel "land-for-peace" as a negotiable issue, as with the 1994 Jordan-Israel Treaty, or be simply considered a nonnegotiable issue? Specifically, what form should Israeli-Palestinian joint management of shared aquifers on the West Bank assume? Is water "separation" or water interdependence advantageous for the West Bank and Golan? How important is agriculture to Palestinian political and economic development? Finally, what role will Jordan, Syria, and Turkey play in Israel's water future? Israel, like the other Jordan River riparians, has a complex set of national and international interests of which water is only one. Even so, the water challenge is important and must be analyzed critically.

Recent literature on the Jordan River basin has focused on whether water scarcity will lead to the next regional war. The literature also examines what policies should be pursued first—a resolution of the protracted Arab-Israeli conflict, or cooperation on functional issues like water that might lead to a resolution of the larger conflict. Within theoretical and academic circles over the past half century, pessimists (of the realist school)—who warn of conflict over water as a zero-sum game—have dominated the water debate. The advent of a peace process in the Middle East in the early 1990s and initial indications of a regional paradigm shift from conflict to cooperation have allowed optimists (of the liberal camp) to reassert their perspective on water, with their mutually beneficial or win-win scenarios. This essay analyzes the most recent round of literature and seeks to determine whether it contains useful policy recommendations for Israel's water problems.

The Jordan River literature encompasses diverse fields including political science, geography, history, economics, and hydrology. The geographer, Aaron T. Wolf in *Hydropolitics along the Jordan River: Scarce Water and Its Impact on the Arab-Israeli Conflict*, argues that "the inextricable link between water and politics can be harnessed to help induce ever-increasing cooperation in or projects between otherwise hostile riparians, in essence 'leading' to regional peace talks" (p. 3). Representing the optimist school, Wolf supports the view that functional water-related cooperation will not only reduce Israel's water problems, but will also move the Middle East peace process forward.

By contrast, Miriam B. Lowi, a political realist, represents the pessimist camp. In *Water and Power: The Policies of a Scarce Resource in the Jordan River Basin*, she maintains that regional water cooperation cannot proceed until the riparians resolve their political differences (p. 9). Her primary argument is that cooperation over international rivers depends on which state is strong and located upstream, and which riparian is weak and situated downstream. In other words, power politics are preeminent in understanding water politics.

The book *Watershed: The Role of Fresh Water in the Israeli-Palestinian Conflict*, on the other hand, assumes that the protracted conflict between Israelis and Palestinians is over and focuses on practical ways of addressing the problem of water scarcity in the Jordan River basin. Stephen C. Lonergan, a geographer, and David B. Brooks, an environmentalist, provide an overview of the economic, ecological, and geopolitical water crises, and offer immediate, and predominantly nonpolitical solutions to the water problems in Israel, Gaza, and the West Bank.

All three books are well researched and skillfully written. The authors focus our attention on the Jordan River basin and thus enhance our understanding of the role of water in Middle East politics and in the peace process. There are numerous books on water in the Middle East that include material on the Jordan River.[1] While some of these books are noteworthy, they fail to equal the depth of research and analysis on the Jordan River found in the books under review. This essay begins with a brief discussion of why regional water wars have not occurred, despite the severe shortage of that precious resource. Next, it describes Israel's three main water-related problems: sharing West Bank water with the Palestinians, sharing Upper Jordan River water with the Syrians, and decreasing water consumption by Israel's agricultural sector. After analyzing the arguments of the books being reviewed as they apply to these problems, I shall argue that, with the Oslo breakthrough, state-elites on both sides of the table would do well to negotiate international issues such as water allocation and water projects, as well as related domestic issues like water pricing, water efficiency, and conservation in tandem with political issues.

The Water-Wars Cliché

Every state is responsible for securing adequate water supplies for its people. The main problem in the Jordan River basin is one of rainfall distribution. Precipitation in the region is concentrated in the north (Syria and Lebanon), with the remainder of the region (Israel, Jordan, and the Palestinians) dependent on the river systems and underground aquifers for their water supplies. In most of the basin the climate is arid or semiarid. Water is truly scarce in the sense that there is far less available than people would like to consume.

Water: Availability and Withdrawal for Jordan River Riparians[2]

	Renewable Resources Per Capita	Share of Withdrawals (%)		
		Domestic	Industry	Agriculture
Israel	368	27	6	67
Jordan	225	21	4	75
Lebanon	1,407	11	4	85
Syria	439	7	10	83
West Bank	116	30	–	70
Gaza Strip	123	28	–	72

The lack of sufficient quantities has led to the perception that water is a potential source of conflict in the region. Some observers suggest that Jordan, Syria, Lebanon, the Palestinians, and Israel may *never* be able to agree on a peaceful division of shared water resources.[3] Still, the popular assumption that these countries will fight the next regional war over water rather than oil has so far not stood up to close examination. Besides benefiting from improvements in water-management techniques, the riparians have increasingly indicated their awareness of the potential for acute conflict. Leaders seem to agree that war cannot solve the long-term problems inherent in regional water allocation.

However, the water-scarcity issue does generate tensions that have other indirect effects. For example, Syria has increased its support for Kurdish guerrilla movements to exert pressure on Turkey; in fact, Damascus has tacitly linked Ankara's release of Euphrates water to Syria with the halting of Syrian support for the Kurds. Water scarcity has also provoked "saber-rattling" statements in the past even from politicians as "gentlemanly" as King Hussein. Still, rather than seeking to increase their water supply through warfare, Jordan River basin governments have instead tried to manage water scarcity better, despite the political challenges they face. Indeed, some have gone from threatening a conflict over water issues to international cooperation facilitated by cross-border flows. For example, despite the public war of words between Israel and Jordan over the Yarmouk River before their October 1994 treaty, technical experts from both sides held secret meetings to measure and to distribute water allocations for fifteen years during their protracted conflict.[4]

Israel's Domestic Water Politics

While an outbreak of war over Jordan River water is unlikely, Israel still faces some formidable water challenges. The three primary concerns are (a) Israel's domestic water politics, (b) Israel's shared groundwater with the Palestinians, and (c) competing Israeli and Syrian claims on the Upper Jordan River and Golan water resources.

Like many countries, Israel has an agricultural sector whose power is politically disproportionate to its share of the population and to its economic contribution to the gross domestic product (GDP). In the 1950s farming accounted for more than 20% of Israel's

GDP. By the 1990s, agriculture was only 2.5% of the GDP of a much larger economy. In addition, farming jobs make up only 2.5% of the work force, a 35% drop between 1980 and 1990 alone.[5] In the past, as a result of the agriculture lobby's efforts, Israel has developed irrigation policies that are largely unsound, whether economically or environmentally. The primary policy impact is that there has been significant subsidized water available to the country's farmers and too much of Israel's water budget is still allocated to agriculture.

Politicians and the urban population have tolerated this situation because agriculture has been viewed as integral to the fabric of Israeli society. As Lowi states, "water was important insofar as it was part of the 'ideology of agriculture' in Zionist thought" (p. 51). During the first half of this century, agriculture provided an opportunity for Diaspora Jews to return to the land and to abandon traditional urban occupations often associated with European anti-Semitism. Much of Israel's territory was developed through farming and agricultural settlements, a critical defense strategy in the prestate and early days of the state. Small farming outposts often provided the initial means for defending the dispersed population and the new border. In the early years, the government did not question the priority of agricultural development with regard to water. Agricultural interests also were well integrated into Mapai (Labor), the largest and most powerful political party until 1977.

By 1990, after a multiyear drought and a scathing State Comptroller's Report deploring past water policy,[6] agriculture lost much of its remaining political power. Administrative edicts and more judicious crop selections ameliorated the immediate water crisis. The abundant rainfall in late 1991 and early 1992 filled surface reservoirs and did much to replenish groundwater sources. Political changes triggered by the water emergency had more lasting implications for agriculture. The government decreased water price subsidies and allocations to the farm sector. In reaction to the water crisis and to the State Comptroller's Report, Water Commissioner Tzemach Ishai was pressured to resign, and was replaced by Prof. Dan Zaslavsky, who was not considered overly sympathetic to the farm lobby. According to the *Israel Yearbook and Almanac*, "agriculture lost its primacy as a trademark of Zionism and Israel. It had become merely one interest group among many, and its prerogatives came under attack."[7] Additionally, certain agricultural sectors experienced serious fiscal problems, which weakened them politically. The government, in containing privileges for the agricultural sector, reduced subsidies for water, cut price supports, and eliminated or modified regulations that supported agriculture monopolies in the domestic marketplace. However, when Labor returned to power in mid-1992, the agriculture lobby did have enough clout to oust Zaslavsky, the water commissioner who had reduced their water allocations during the drought. There was also a move to restore pre-drought agriculture water allocations. Since Israel joined the World Trade Organization (formerly known as the General Agreement on Tariffs and Trade, or GATT) and lowered trade barriers in April 1995, increased marketplace competition has made agricultural production more efficient.

Nonetheless, with greater international competition, Israeli farmers still demand from the government more subsidized water to stay competitive. In Israel, interest group politics is basic to the political system. Unless Israeli policymakers are able to overcome agriculture's narrow interests, the state's water problem will be exacerbated. It should be noted that all of the other Jordan River parties also have politically strong agricultural sectors and face similar if not greater obstacles in developing new policies regarding water use.

The West Bank

In the 1967 war Israel captured the West Bank of the Jordan River from the Hashemite Kingdom of Jordan. In addition to securing control of the inhabitants and the territory, Israel also gained control of the rich water resources underneath the surface. Rain falls on its hills and percolates down into its aquifers, with water flowing naturally westward toward the coastal plain and north to the Galilee. A third aquifer flows east, away from Israel, toward the Jordan River and the Dead Sea. Since the days of the prestate yishuv, Jewish farmers and city dwellers have been using groundwater originating in the West Bank.

Even before 1967 Israel depended on West Bank groundwater for almost a third of its total supply. When Jordan controlled the West Bank, it did little to develop this groundwater source for the inhabitants and, thus, the lion's share flowed naturally into Israel. After 1967, Israel had direct control of the groundwater sources and established strict drilling and pumping regulations for the Palestinian population so that Israel's groundwater supply would not decrease. Even though the Palestinian population has increased, Israel maintained water allocations to Palestinian West Bank agriculture at the 1967 levels. This was done, in principle, to protect Israel's domestic water supply. The Israel-Palestinian Interim Agreement (Oslo II) of September 1995 describes the "existing extractions and estimated potential of West Bank aquifers."[8]

A major aspect of the Oslo II agreement was that the Palestinian Authority was to take full control of the main West Bank urban cen-

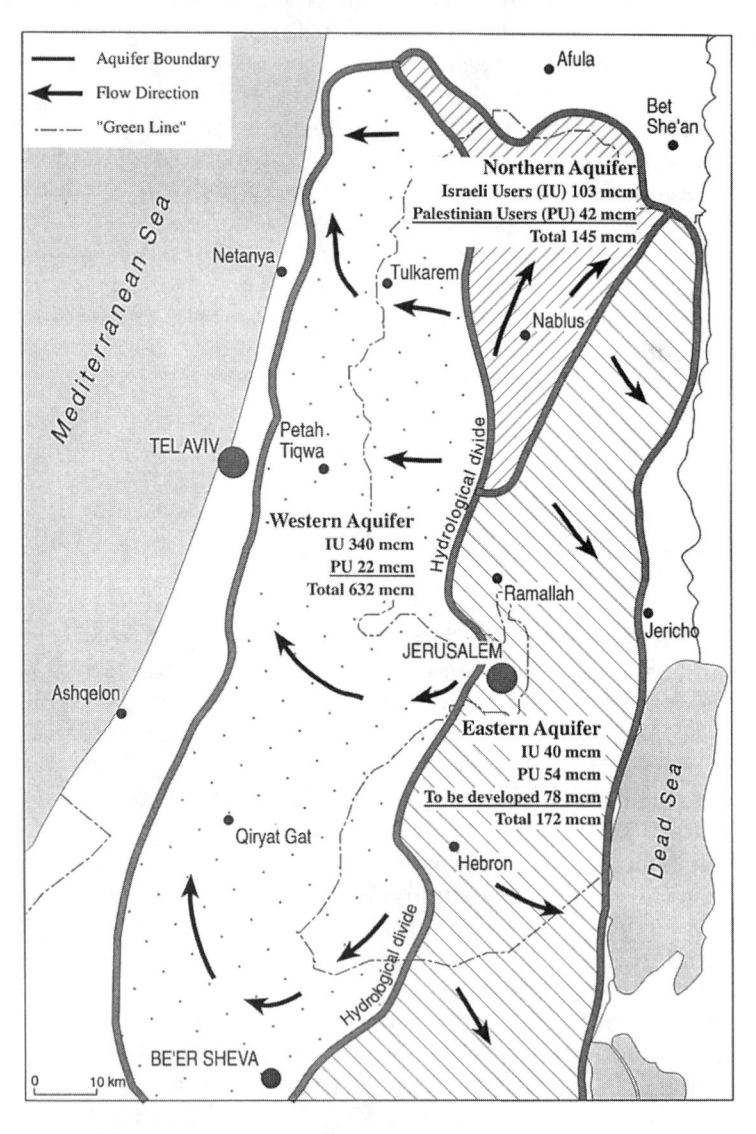

Oslo II: The Shared Palestinian—Israeli Mountain Aquifers

ters. The Palestinians presumed that they would control not only the territory evacuated by Israel but also the water underneath the autonomous Palestinian territory. In particular, Tulkarm, Kalkilya, and the population centers in close proximity sit on top of the Western aquifer. The Palestinians wanted the right to pump underneath their land.

Israel consumes approximately 1.5 billion cubic meters of water, or six times the quantity consumed by Gaza and West Bank Palestinians. According to the Palestinian Water Resources Action Program (WRAP), the per capita Israeli consumption is 375 cubic meters, in contrast to 116 cm for Palestinians in the West Bank. During the Oslo II negotiations, the Palestinians argued that the agreement had to increase their water allocation dramatically and to recognize their water rights. They added that only with access to the western and northern aquifers could their economy improve and peace succeed.

Israel and the West Bank share a critical water source. Israel's West Bank water challenge is to find a way to increase Palestinian water allocations without dramatically decreasing Israel's supply and injuring its economy. Its policymakers must decide whether they wish, jointly with Palestinians, to manage the shared western and northern West Bank aquifers; or whether they want to establish a system of minimal interdependence (e.g., Israel would be solely responsible for the western aquifer while the Palestinians would control the northern and eastern aquifers).

Another critical issue is groundwater quality protection. Aquifers are highly susceptible to pollution, be it urban sewage, agricultural insecticides and fertilizers, or industrial chemicals and heavy metals. Now that the Palestinians control most of the heavily-populated areas above the groundwater, it is up to them to regulate activity so as not to damage the jointly-shared groundwater.

Finally, if West Bank groundwater is overutilized, the aquifer level will decrease to a point where salty water will intrude from other sources and pollute the fresh water supply. This has already occurred on parts of Israel's coastal aquifer. Thus, if Palestinians and/or Israelis take more than the aquifer's safe yield, Mother Nature will punish all consumers with a drastic reduction in usable water.

The Golan Heights and the Upper Jordan River

With its capture of the Golan Heights from Syria in the June war of 1967, Israel increased its control over the tributaries of the Jordan

River. By occupying this territory Israel also gained control of the source of the water runoff from the Golan Heights into Lake Tiberias. Six hundred million cubic meters (mcm), or one-third of Israel's water, comes from the Golan region. Almost 500 mcm flows from the upper Jordan tributaries to Israel.[9] The remaining 110 mcm either flows as springs (60 mcm) to the Lake Kinneret or is used by Golan settlements from wells or artificial reservoirs, on the heights (35 mcm) or at Hamat Gader (15 mcm). Israel's water difficulties on the Golan Heights resemble its West-Bank groundwater problem in that Israel is downstream and dealing with a resource shared with a hostile neighbor. Future Syrian industrial or urban development upstream, including on the Golan, will mean less water for Israel and could pollute an important water source that runs off into Israel's primary reservoir, Lake Tiberias. However, unlike the West Bank, the Syrians do not depend on the Golan for water to the extent that the Palestinians rely on West Bank groundwater for their allocation of water. Syria utilizes the mighty Euphrates that has a total discharge thirty times that of the Jordan.

According to Israeli water analysts, if Israel withdraws from the Golan, and if Syria builds reservoirs for rainwater and drains water from the Banias River for Damascus, the potential water loss to Israel could be 200 mcm per year. This, however, would entail the building of large and expensive water work projects by the Syrians. On the other hand, Syria could use some 100 mcm per year from the existing Israeli infrastructure without much effort or investment.

The Arguments

Within this context of Israel's recent water challenges, we now turn to the central arguments of the books under review, looking for potential solutions for the future. Lowi uses a "classical realist" approach (p. 8) for water politics in the Jordan River basin and is thus pessimistic about the chances for cooperation. She argues that the most powerful riparian decides when and how cooperation will occur. Israel, as the party with the greatest capabilities, would be the one to initiate and maintain cooperation on water issues in the basin.

According to realists and neorealists, a state's power and capabilities are critical to maintaining its position in the international system. If a state's relative power decreases, its security may become more vulnerable. This is in part due to the lack of a Hobbesian "Leviathan" to enforce international agreements and assure states their security.[10] In water-poor regions, countries often view this scarce resource as a national-security issue vital to their relative power. Consequently, Lowi and other realists take a pessimistic position as to whether Israel would make concessions on important sources for water such as the Golan Heights and the West Bank, as may be demanded as part of a political settlement. In addition, Lowi and company strongly advocate separation, believing that the fewer points of interdependence among long-standing enemies, the fewer areas of potential friction and conflict. On numerous occasions Lowi draws a parallel between the Indus River case and the Jordan. In the Indus River case, dividing the river between the riparians resolved the Pakistan-India Indus water conflict in 1960.

However, according to Wolf's functionalist approach, water cooperation can spill over into the political realm and lead to more cooperation in other issue-areas. Wolf calls for the interested parties to focus on promoting water cooperation, which might eventually bring a broader settlement of political problems. The functionalist school emerged in the post-World War II era. In the early years of the European Common Market, many theorists and policymakers believed in organizing international cooperation in specific functional areas such as science, trade, and other economic activities—arguing that, if states could successfully cooperate in these issue-areas, it would bring former adversaries closer together and foster peaceful relationships. Genuine success would see governments prepared to delegate increased authority over functional issues to international organizations, leading ultimately to wider political understanding.

Wolf, as a functionalist, argues that if Israel cooperates with its Arab neighbors on the water issue, it will gain both politically and hydrologically, albeit slowly and in stages. The benefits derived from the water issue-area would encourage riparians to continue cooperative efforts and to move them further away from protracted conflict. Lowi, on the other hand, argues from an antifunctionalist position. Water relations in the Jordan River basin, she argues, have been tied historically to the larger political conflict, and regional cooperation cannot proceed before riparians resolve their political conflict (p. 9).[11] Lowi reminds us that functionalism and neofunctionalism emphasize regional cooperation, and assume that ideologies and external constraints have little impact on cooperation—when in fact they both do. In *Water and Power*, she asserts that even limited cooperation between Jordan and Israel over a period of many years (pp. 164–66) has had "no implications for the end to political conflict. . . . These highly delimited, highly specific arrangements have no conflict resolution potential" (p. 200).

Yet Lowi's conclusions are belied by the Israeli-Jordanian secret cooperation over Yarmouk water, which can be seen to have had a positive impact on the political relationship between the two states. This cooperation, dating back to 1979, led to reduced tensions on the volatile water-scarcity issue and built confidence between water experts and between state elites. Israel and Jordan's common interests maintained the cooperative framework and when they finally sat down to negotiate a peace treaty in 1994, it became much easier because of their history of fifteen years of face-to-face secret water talks and cooperation.[12] Because the parties had long discussed many important and difficult issues, each state came to understand the water needs and to earn the trust of the other. Wolf's approach seems admirably validated by the Jordanian-Israeli peace, reaping benefits beyond what many functionalists might have hoped for or predicted.

But politics still took precedence over functional issues with regard to the timing of the 1994 Jordan-Israel Peace Treaty. It is no coincidence that King Hussein waited for an Israel-Palestinian breakthrough at Oslo before agreeing to a treaty with Israel. Jordan had always made it clear that it would not establish a formal, open relationship with Israel until the latter adequately addressed the Palestinian issue. Even so, state elites on both sides had long recognized that it would have been a serious error of policy for Jordan and Israel not to have engaged in secret water talks prior to the political breakthrough.

Lowi's neorealist approach may well prove to be more accurate for the Israeli-Syrian case, while Wolf's functionalism may prove itself to be more appropriate for the Palestinian-Israeli competition for West Bank water. This prediction is primarily based on the variable of mixed-interests. The Palestinians, like the Jordanians, have so many common water interests with Israel that water cooperation is viable and probable. Syria, on the other hand, has shared few common interests with Israel since 1967, and is thus likely to resolve the water issue only after the resolution of the wider protracted conflict.

The debate between Lowi and Wolf over the role of water and politics is helpful in understanding Israel's international water challenges. Lonergan and Brooks, however, focus on the more practical aspects of water scarcity, which provide an understanding of the domestic water challenges faced by Israel, Gaza, and the West Bank. The authors concede from the outset that "our recommendation bears most heavily on Israel" (p. 252). This is because Israel is stronger and more developed than the Palestinian entity or any other state in the region. Lonergan and Brooks emphasize the need for correcting the economic, environmental, political, and institutional inefficiencies, initially in-house and then regionally. According to the authors, the first priority for addressing the water problem is to moderate water demand by instituting policies and programs for promoting greater efficiency in water use. This includes formal regulations, improved technologies, and public education.

Lonergan and Brooks also emphasize the importance of higher water prices for agriculture and a pricing system that provides incentives for conservation, but without built-in subsidies. Other priorities recommended are improved water institutions, especially strong local and national water planning to moderate water demand and to augment water supply. The system should not be too centralized but instead should allow for local input. The authors also call for augmenting the local water supply by developing alternative sources of water, including rainwater harvesting, desalinating salty water, and using recycled water to fill certain needs. Other recommendations include creating regional water institutions to help states manage shared supplies, to create markets to buy and sell water, and to protect water quality. Finally, Lonergan and Brooks discuss augmenting the regional water supply through capital-intensive mega-projects such as large-scale desalination, multibillion dollar interstate canals, or international pipeline systems. It is better first to focus "on options that are small in scale and locale-specific" (p. 254) and then to move onto more politically and economically complex projects.

These recommendations are useful, insightful, and similar to those under discussion in the Madrid peace process multilateral Working Group on Water. But, like other topics relegated to the mulitlateral track, functional regional water cooperation can also become the hostage of international politics. More importantly to our discussion, Lonergan and Brooks do not indicate how state policymakers can overcome narrow agriculture interest-group politics to realize the controversial, yet important, domestic water policies just described.

Suggestions

How should state elites address Israel's international and domestic water challenges? Effective rules and agreements are critical to solving the region-wide elements of Israel's water problem. Once states begin negotiating, as they did during the Madrid peace process, the insights of liberal institutionalism are useful. According to this approach (an alternative international relations theory to realism and a descendant liberal theory of functionalism), the principal obstacle to cooperation among states with mutual interests is the threat that the other state will not uphold an agreement—in other words, cheat. Thus, neoliberals concentrate on showing how agreements can be made to work to counter the cheating problem.[13] States establish rules and procedures to moderate the effects of anarchy—the lack of an international Leviathan—in order to realize their goals through cooperation. "Regimes [rules of the game] provide information, reduce transaction costs, make commitments more credible, establish focal points for coordination, and in general facilitate the operation of reciprocity."[14] Neoliberal institutionalism does not argue that states cooperate because of purely nominal agreements or vague legal principles that have little or no behavioral implication in promoting cooperation. States cooperate because the underlying configuration of power and interests supports such action.

Like neorealists, neoliberal institutionalists assume that states (a) operate in an environment that lacks a supranational power and (b) act in their own self-interest. Additionally, for neoliberals, agreements are deliberate efforts by states to manage international affairs by capturing joint gains or by preventing common losses. Neorealism neglects or rejects the ability of agreements or institutions to influence independently how states interpret their interests and goals. Furthermore, neoliberals are much more inclined to examine the domestic forces involved in international relations.[15] Neoliberals argue that "international politics is about changing interests of the inhabitants of states (or other entities) and that the underlying forces of change are creating opportunities for increased cooperation."[16]

In fact, treaty negotiations can also be utilized to resolve domestic water problems, as in this example. In negotiations, state elites "are trying to do two things at once—that is, they seek to manipulate domestic and international politics simultaneously. Diplomatic strategies and tactics are constrained both by what other states will accept and by what domestic constituencies will ratify."[17] Middle East water negotiations have been primarily over water allocations and water works. While these are important issues, state elites should also work for consensus on the whole range of controversial domestic water issues that would be binding for all and that would mitigate not only an individual state's water problem, but that of the region as well. For example, states could institute a domestic water pricing system that more accurately reflects the true cost of water.[18] Currently water is not distributed effectively because heavily subsidized water for agriculture skews the market. Water is relatively cheap for farmers so they use it in ways that would not make sense if the water's real cost were reflected in its price. For example, both Jordan and the Palestinians do not yet use water efficiently and much is wasted or lost. It is in Israel's interest to change this situation because Jordan and the Palestinians will come to Israel first when their water situation becomes a crisis, and Israel will then be under great pressure to make further water concessions to them.

According to a recent government-sponsored report, Israel could also use its water more efficiently.[19] If water subsidies are reduced or removed in a wise manner and if the price of water is determined in accordance with the cost of pumping and transporting, low-profit crops requiring large quantities of water will no longer be economically viable. In turn, farmers will grow more profitable crops and will use less water more efficiently. Government leaders argue against removing water subsidies because it would cost jobs in the agricultural sector or might jeopardize a state's food security policy. While jobs and food security are immediate state interests, states must realize that properly managing water scarcity is a critical long-term interest that may require short-term sacrifices. Fair-priced water will make the choice between these interests more rational and based less on emotion.

However, the Jordan River riparians have failed to examine water pricing, for the most part, because the agricultural sector adamantly opposes it. Outside the agriculture lobby, water pricing is recognized as beneficial to the state because it promotes efficiency, thus creating more water and reducing expensive subsidies. If state elites were to negotiate a binding water-pricing system that benefited all Jordan River riparians, negotiators then might be able to convince their domestic constituencies that water pricing is not only beneficial to their state, but is required by negotiators as a prerequisite to achieving important international agreements or to winning international aid. The same method could be used to increase or improve water management, efficiency, and conservation. In municipal and agricultural water systems in the Jordan River basin, a large percentage of water is lost or stolen. Because of poor or old pipes and pumps, some cities and towns, especially in Jordan and the West Bank, lose over 60 percent of their water. Improved delivery systems would decrease the water-scarcity problem for the whole region. Again, if all sides at the international negotiating tables set this as a priority, there would be a much better chance of realizing it domestically. Using this two-level approach, state leaders could achieve many other important but controversial regional and state water projects in the spirit of Lonergan and Brooks' recommendations.

Notes

1. See Daniel Hillel, *Rivers of Eden: The Struggle for Water and the Quest for Peace in the Middle East* (New York: Oxford University Press, 1994); Natasha Beschorner, *Water and Instability in the Middle East* (London: International Institute for Strategic Studies, 1992), Adelphi Paper no. 273; Nurit Kliot, *Water Resources and Conflict in the Middle East* (London: Routledge, 1994); Arnon Soffer, *Rivers of Fire: The Conflict over Water in the Middle East* (Lanham MD: Rowman & Littlefield Publishers, 1997); and *Water in the Middle East: Conflict or Cooperation?* eds. Thomas Naff and Ruth Matson (Boulder CO: Westview Press, 1984). See also multibook reviews by Ofira Seliktar, "Water in the Arab-Israeli Struggle: Conflict or Cooperation?" in *Critical Essays on Israeli Society, Religion, and Government: Books on Israel*, vol. IV, eds. Kevin Avruch and Walter P. Zenner (Albany: State University of New York Press, 1997), 9–29; and Adam Garfinkle, "Hung Out to Dry or All Wet? Water in the Jordan Valley," *Orbis* 29:1 (Winter 1995), 129–38.

2. Data from Israel's Central Bureau of Statistics, Jordan's Ministry of Irrigation, the World Bank, and *The Middle East Economic Digest*, 24 January 1997, p. 8. Domestic and industry shares are combined for the West Bank and Gaza.

3. See, for example, John Bullock and Adel Darwish, *Water Wars: Coming Conflict in the Middle East* (London: Victor Gollancz, 1993).

4. Jeffrey Sosland, *Cooperating Rivals: The Politics of Scarcity in the Jordan River Basin*, Doctoral Dissertation, Georgetown University, 1998.

5. Total agricultural production in 1995 was over $35 billion, including $730 million in exports. See "Seed Money," *Jerusalem Report*, 12 June 1997, p. 37.

6. State Comptroller of Israel, "Management of Water Resources in Israel (Special Report, December 1990)," *Annual and Special Reports: Selected Chapters*, Jerusalem: State Comptroller, 1992.

7. *Israel Yearbook and Almanac 1991/1992*, vol. 46 (Jerusalem: IBRT Translations, 1992), 107.

8. See schedule 10 of the agreement.

9. Dan River 250 mcm, Banias 120 mcm, and Hasbani 120 mcm.

10. See, for example, Robert Gilpin, *War and Change in World Politics* (Cambridge: Cambridge University Press, 1981); Kenneth Waltz, *Theory of International Politics* (Reading MA: Addison-Wesley, 1979); Joseph Grieco, *Cooperation among Nations* (Ithaca NY: Cornell University Press, 1990); and *The Perils of Anarchy: Contemporary Realism and International Security*, eds. Michael Brown, Sean Lynn-Jones, and Steven Miller (Cambridge MA: MIT Press, 1995).

11. Lowi makes the same argument in more recent articles, such as "Bridging the Divide: Transboundary Resource Disputes and the Case of West Bank Water," *International Security* 18:1 (Summer 1993), 113–38; and "Rivers of Conflict, Rivers of Peace," *Journal of International Affairs* 49:1 (Summer 1995), 123–44.

12. See Laura Zittrain Eisenberg and Neil Caplan, *Negotiating Arab-Israeli Peace: Patterns, Problems, Possibilities* (Bloomington: Indiana University Press, 1998), chaps. 3, 5, and appendix 14.

13. See, for example, Robert Axelrod, *The Evolution of Cooperation* (New York: Basic, 1984); Axelrod and Robert Keohane, "Achieving Cooperation Under Anarchy: Strategies and Institutions," in *Cooperation Under Anarchy*, ed. Kenneth Oye (Princeton: Princeton University Press, 1986), 1–24; Keohane, *After Hegemony* (Princeton: Princeton University Press, 1984); *International Regimes* ed. Stephen Krasner (Ithaca NY: Cornell University Press, 1983); *Regime Theory and International Relations*, ed. Volker Rittberger (New York: Oxford University Press, 1995); and *Neorealism and Neoliberalism: The Contemporary Debate*, ed. David Baldwin (New York: Columbia University Press, 1993).

14. Robert Keohane and Lisa Martin, "The Promise of Institutionalist Theory," *International Security* 20:1 (Summer 1995), 42.

15. *Double-Edged Diplomacy*, eds. Peter Evans, Harold Jacobson, and Robert Putnam (Berkeley: University of California Press, 1993); Robert Putnam, "Diplomacy and Domestic Politics: The Logic of Two-Level Games," *International Organization* 42:3 (Summer 1988), 427–60.

16. Mark Zacher and Richard Matthew, "Liberal International Theory: Common Threads, Divergent Strands," in *Controversies in International Relations Theory: Realism and the Neoliberal Challenge*, ed. Charles Kegley (New York: St. Martin's, 1995), 140.

17. Andrew Moravcsik, "Introduction: Integrating International and Domestic Theories of International Bargaining," in *Double-Edged Diplomacy*, 15.

18. Stanley M. Fisher of the MIT Economics Department leads the Harvard Middle East Water Project. Fisher's model, while insightful on an economic level, lacks important political variables.

19. "Water Commission: Demand for Water could be reduced by 15–20 percent," *ha-Aretz*, 16 April 1997, website at www3.haaretz.co.il/eng.

Part IV

Views of Israel from the Arab World

13. On Opposite Sides of the Hill: Syrian and Israeli Perspectives

Eyal Zisser

This essay analyzes Israeli and Syrian mutual perceptions and policy-making in the context of Syria's failed quest to achieve "strategic parity" with Israel and the new regional realities following the collapse of the former Soviet Union. The author highlights each party's continued perception of the other as a hostile enemy bent on regional hegemony and exposes a gap between the parties that is still deep despite the current adoption of the "peace process" as the strategic option of choice by both countries.

al-'Abdallah, Hamidi, *Asad's Strategy, A Comparative Study of Strategic Parity between Syria and Israel*, Beirut: Sharikat al-Haqiqa lil-Sahafa wal-I'lam, 1995. (Arabic)

Hafiz, 'Adil, *Hafiz al-Asad: a Leader and a Nation*, Damascus: al-Markaz al-Dawli lil-Nashr wal-I'lam, 1993. (Arabic)

Ma'oz, Moshe, *Israel and Syria: End of the Conflict?!*, Tel Aviv: Ma'ariv, 1996. (Hebrew)

Yaniv, Avner, Moshe Ma'oz, and Avi Kober, eds., *Syria and Israel's National Security*, Tel Aviv: Ma'arachot, 1990. (Hebrew)

Introduction

The year 1996 will be remembered in the annals of Israel's history, and those of the Arab world surrounding it, as a year of upheaval. First and foremost it saw not only a dramatic political turnaround in Israel, but also, and possibly to no small measure as a result of this, a reversal of the course of history in the entire region. In the early part of the year there were expectations of a breakthrough in the peace negotiations between Israel and Syria. These expectations were based on media reports, as well as on expressions of optimism by official spokespersons and even leaders on both sides. An example of this was a declaration published in January 1996 in the official Syrian organ *Tishrin:* "Next year will be a year of peace."[1] Only a month previously *Tishrin* had granted the then-prime minister of Israel, Shimon Peres, the title of "man of peace."[2]

These expectations, however, never materialized. The peace process soon after reached an impasse, and toward the end of 1996 relations between the two countries had deteriorated to the brink of a possible outbreak of hostilities.[3] The election of a new government in Israel ostensibly caused this downward spiral in Israeli-Syrian relations. Instead of the far-reaching readiness on the part of the Labor government, initially led by the late Yitzhak Rabin and subsequently by Shimon Peres, for full Israeli withdrawal from the Golan Heights, the new Likud government under Benjamin Netanyahu adopted a stand stating Israel's intention to retain the Golan Heights, even within the framework of a peace agreement. The Syrians were quick to declare that they would not negotiate with Israel until the Likud government announced its commitment to the agreement they claimed to have reached with the Labor government, according to which Israel would withdraw completely from the Heights to the 4 June 1967 borders. The Syrians even threatened that, should the new government not accede to this demand, they would consider other options at their disposal, including the military option.[4]

But the roots of the difficulties that have plagued the peace process on the Syrian-Israeli track are far deeper than the mere change of government in Israel. This is borne out in 'Adil Hafiz's book, *Hafiz al-Asad: A Leader and a Nation.* The book was published in 1993, during the peace talks between Syria and the Labor government under Yitzhak Rabin. Totally ignoring the progress that had been made in those negotiations at that time, Hafiz clearly expressed Damascus' traditional attitude toward Israel, which attached no importance to the various shades along the Israeli political spectrum, and viewed Labor and Likud as merely two sides of the same coin and two faces of the same existential challenge—the State of Israel—with which the Arabs have been struggling for an entire generation. Hafiz wrote:

> [O]ver the years, Israel has tried to delude world public opinion. However, this propaganda failed. One of the reasons for this failure was the rise to power of the Likud government at the end of the 1980s [*sic.* the 1970s] together with a series of small religious parties. This revealed in even greater clarity just what its real aim was; the intentions of the Zionist entity cannot be hidden behind expressions in favor of peace made by present Israeli leaders [i.e., Rabin and Peres]. (p. 173)

Academic studies published in recent years in Syria and in Israel make it possible to examine the roots of the animosity that characterizes Syrian-Israeli relations. This historical enmity has made it difficult for the two countries to achieve a breakthrough in the lengthy and tortuous negotiations they began conducting with each other since 1991. The books under review examine relations between the two countries in recent years in light of regional and international changes and, of course, in light of the peace process. Careful reading opens a window through which one can perceive the basic concepts guiding each of the countries in their relations with one another. Considered together, these examples of recent Israeli and Syrian scholarship reveal that vast, perhaps unbridgeable, gaps exist between the two countries in everything that has to do with the basic concept of "the other" and with the manner and desirable direction the peace process must take. It may be assumed that these differences will continue to be a part of the fabric of relations between the two countries and will cast a heavy shadow over them into the future as well.

The following are the main impressions gained from both Syrian and Israeli studies regarding the basic conceptions that Syria and Israel have of one another. Syria still views Israel as an illegitimate entity that wants to subordinate the Arab world to its will. While Syria is committed to the peace process, it regards the process as a constraint, as the least evil of the alternatives it faces. Syria's dichotomous attitude regarding the peace process has its roots, inter alia, in its assessment that the peace agreement, which is the aim of this process, is designed to promote the idea of a "new Middle East," a Middle East that is politically, culturally, and economically controlled by Israel. Nevertheless, Syria wants to get as much as it can from the peace process on the political and economic planes, including the return of the Golan Heights to Syrian hands and the receipt of Western economic aid. Therefore Syria consistently reiterates its public commitment to the peace process, and in the past even displayed some readiness to hold substantive negotiations with Israel, but only on condition that they move in the direction Syria wants. Syria was, however, hesitant about unconditionally devoting its energy and will to achieving a peace agreement with Israel.

Israel's attitude toward Syria is not significantly different from that of Syria's toward Israel. Syria is viewed as an aggressive country whose long-term strategic goal is the destruction of the State of Israel. Therefore, Syria's "peace policy" is perceived in Israel with suspicion and considerable doubt. Thus, there are many in Israel who believe that is necessary to adopt a hard-line approach toward the Syrians and, in any event, to deal with them cautiously. It would thus appear that peace is still a long way off.

The Israel-Arab conflict is one of the longest and most complex that this generation has known. Its complexity arises to no small degree from its multilayered and multifaceted nature. One may also claim that it is not a single conflict but rather a collection of interconnected disputes, some of which have developed over the years and have but a weak connection to the original nucleus of this conflict. Indeed, it would appear that the development of the conflict into a conglomerate of various conflicts has obscured the original causes of the conflict. The prevalent assumption is that the core of the conflict is the Palestinian problem, and that so long as no solution to that problem is found—one acceptable to all sides—the Israeli-Arab conflict, in the broad and encompassing sense, will remain unresolved.[5]

The breakthrough in Israeli-Palestinian negotiations in the years 1993–96 did, however, raise some questions regarding this assumption. After all, the Palestinian problem finally appeared to be progressing toward a solution, while no like progress, in fact no progress at all, had been made in other aspects of the conflict, which remained far from being resolved. For example, the religious aspect of the Israeli-Arab conflict reached the dimensions of a holy war that Islamic fundamentalist extremists (e.g., Iran and its protégés Hizballah, Hamas, and Islamic Jihad) have mounted in Israel. The

Syrian front, that is, everything that had to do with relations between Israel and Syria, was another arena where the conflict was far from resolved.

The hostile relations that developed between these two countries over the years, and that exist to a great degree today as well, reflect the two central strata of the Arab-Israeli conflict in general: one pan-Arab, and the other territorial. In the pan-Arab aspect, Syria presents itself as the beating heart of the Arab nation, in other words, as the authentic, and possibly even the exclusive, representative of the pan-Arab vision. This approach translates into a Syrian commitment, absolute in the past and partial in the present, to the pan-Arab cause. Syria views itself as the vanguard of the pan-Arab struggle against Israel, in the name and on behalf of the Palestinians—even if the latter decides to bury the hatchet of war. This attitude is firmly rooted in Syrian history as well as in the personal and political biographies of its leaders. It must be accepted as authentic, although it can be at least partially explained on the basis of narrow political considerations, such as the attempt to satisfy public opinion in Syria and in the Arab world in general.

There is also the territorial aspect. Aside from the commitment to the pan-Arab cause, the Syrians are also guided by pure Syrian state interests. The inclination to prefer purely Syrian interests has increased to a considerable degree since the rise to power of President Hafiz al-Asad in Syria in November 1970. Asad has provided Syria with political stability the likes of which the country had not known since it gained independence, thus changing its image and making it a central player in the region and even a regional minipower. In view of all of this, it is clear why Syria attaches such importance to the Golan Heights, under Israeli occupation since 1967. This issue incorporates a clear component of national, and even personal, pride, since it was Hafiz al-Asad, as acting minister of defense, who bore the responsibility for the loss of the Golan to Israel in June 1967.[6]

However, as far as the Golan is concerned, Syria is guided also by security and economic considerations. In his book, 'Adil Hafiz refers to the importance of the Heights to Syria:

> [S]ince 1967, the Golan Heights have been controlled by the Zionists. The area is of strategic importance, and in Israel's view fit for Jewish settlement. The region has natural resources and allows control over the Huleh Valley, the Jordan Valley and Northern Israel. It is also capable of posing a threat to Damascus. There are also oil pipelines on the

Golan Heights leading to the Mediterranean Sea, and in addition, Israel views it as an important water reservoir. (p.174)

A series of studies published in Syria and in Israel in the course of the 1990s provides an opportunity to catch a glimpse of the respective Israeli and Syrian points of view—the fabric of relations between the two countries, that is, how Jerusalem and Damascus view one another: political leaders, army generals, intellectuals, academic experts, and finally, general public opinion. The importance of this issue is clear against the background of the peace negotiations, which the countries have been conducting since 1991. These negotiations, it would be appear, have not brought about the desired results and have not achieved even a minimal understanding regarding the peace process and its goals, on the basis of which the process could have moved forward.

However, before we enter into the discussion itself, a word of caution and clarification. The studies that are reviewed here are not official publications. They are pure research in the fields of foreign policy, national security, and regional studies, published by historians or researchers in the field of political science and representing their views on the fabric of Syrian-Israeli relations. Nevertheless, it should be borne in mind that Syrian society is a mobilized society in which intellectuals and academics are called upon to commit the fruits of their thinking and creativity to the national interest. Moreover, Hafiz al-Asad 's autocratic regime, which has ruled Syria for the past thirty years, discourages open public debate, especially the expression of ideas contrary to those on which it is based.[7] A powerful and striking example of this may be found in the introduction to 'Adil Hafiz's book, where the author states that

> this book is dedicated to President Asad, the leader and Arab warrior, who has adopted a clear and unbending line in all the decisions he has taken in all spheres of his activity, and whose activities have brought the Arabs to abandon the delusions and the dreams and to grapple with the true realities, so that we could bring about our inner renewal. (p. 5)

In Lebanon, unlike Syria, scholars have in the past enjoyed considerable freedom of thought and writing; however today Lebanon is for all practical purposes under full Syrian control. This situation puts clear limits on academics working in that country who have to adhere to the line dictated by Damascus. This can be seen in the introduction (written by Zuhayr al-Khatib, a deputy in the Lebanese House of Representatives) to Hamidi al-'Abdallah's book, *Asad's Strategy,* which states that

> Asad is the historic leader appearing before us and before the nation having behind him a quarter of a century of accomplishments and victories, in the midst of crises, wars and confrontations. All of this demonstrates the greatness of the historic leadership of this Arab leader, whose ideals are an example to us all. (pp. 9–10)

Academic studies in Syria and Lebanon should not, however, be dismissed as lacking any academic value. On the contrary, these studies reflect an authentic picture of the moods and even of the concepts and beliefs among broad sectors of the Syrian and of the general Arab public. Indeed, as far as Israel is concerned, it seems that the Syrian regime, because of its ideological and political nature, as well as its social roots, reflects better than any other Arab regime the moods within public opinion both in Syria itself and throughout the Arab world. This also holds true for Syrian intellectuals and academics.

Academic study of the Israel-Arab conflict or the Arab world in general in Israel has gradually divested itself of the traces of political "engagement" that had characterized it in the early days of the Jewish state. Today, studies published in Israel measure up to all recognized international academic standards. However, it must be recognized that Israeli scholars working in Israel will be influenced by public moods in everything that has to do with the country's relations with Syria and with the Arab world in general. It is also worth mentioning that one of the books under review here, *Syria and Israel's National Security*, was published by the Ministry of Defense Publishing House (Ma'arachot), and its target audience was, at least in part, the security community in Israel. Indeed, the book's main objective, according to its editors, is "to contribute to a deeper knowledge of Syria and the understanding of the constraints under which it functions and the considerations underlying its policies" (p. 9). Among the contributors to this publication are some former army generals who had served in senior positions in the intelligence community, although today they are better known as commentators in the Israeli media.

The studies included in this review under the general subtitle of "Syrian and Israeli perspectives" cover a broad spectrum of interests.

Since it is impossible within the scope of this essay to deal with all of them, this essay will examine Israeli and Syrian perspectives on several key issues:

- the mirror images, the basic conceptions of Syria about Israel and of Israel about Syria;
- historical memory, the manner in which the common past is viewed in Damascus and Jerusalem;
- strategic parity, as a key issue in relations between the two countries since the beginning of the 1980s;
- a look toward the future, the peace process: risks and prospects.

Mirror Images: Syria and Israel in the Eyes of One Another

Despite the peace process in which the two countries are engaged, almost nothing has changed in the manner in which Syria views Israel. A comparison between the studies on Israel published in Syria in the late 1960s and the 1970s, on the one hand, and those published today (two of which are reviewed here) shows that basic Syrian perceptions of Israel have remained unchanged, although they have been somewhat moderated and refined. Even today, Israel is viewed by Syria as an illegitimate and aggressive entity with expansionist ambitions. Moreover, its military might is believed to make it a real threat to the existence of Syria in particular and to the Arab nation in general.

First is the lack of legitimacy: Israel is seen as a spurious entity having no right to exist. This concept is based on a number of arguments, including the claim that the land on which Israel exists—Palestinian soil—is an Arab land belonging to the Arab-Palestinian people, stolen from it by force by Zionist invaders. According to this claim, Israel is the creation of the imperialist powers that ruled the region in the first half of the present century. However, as 'Adil Hafiz states in his book,

> despite the fact that the Arab nation had nothing to do with the persecution of Jews [in Europe] . . . the Great Powers forced it to pay the price for this persecution, and forcefully stole, in keeping with Zionist dictates, some of Palestine's soil on which the Zionist entity—the state of Israel—could arise and establish itself in order to expand further. (p. 173)

It should be noted that the Syrians also make use of the argument that most of the residents of Israel have no historic affinity with Palestinian soil, since these Jews—especially those who came from Europe—are descended from the Kuzars and therefore their historic homeland is not Palestine (Eretz-Israel), but Central Asia.[8]

Second, Israel is viewed as an aggressive entity with expansionist tendencies, whose aim is to realize the divine promise of establishing a Greater Israel from the Euphrates to the Nile. In his book, 'Adil Hafiz quotes parts of a speech made by President Asad in July 1985, according to which the Arab homeland was "facing the danger of a Zionist invasion whose aim is colonization. This invasion [was] to be organized by the racist Zionist movement, which relie[d] on the might of Western imperialism." The Zionist movement wanted "to conquer and expand in order to establish a Greater Israel from the Nile to the Euphrates" (p. 237, quoting *Tishrin*, 9 March 1990). According to the Syrians, on its way toward achieving its goal Israel is trying to harm and degrade the Arabs and to leave them in a state of continuous cultural and technological backwardness and military, economic, and political inferiority. Thus, Israel hopes to make it impossible for progressive Arab forces, led by Syria, to pose a threat to it or to prevent it from achieving its objectives.

It is worth noting in this context that Israel is also considered to be a regional power enjoying clear military, political, economic, and technological superiority over all the Arab states. Israel is viewed as a state with a nuclear capability, with a large army, and an especially strong air force. Israel also enjoys the full backing of the West. All of this makes Israel, in Syria's eyes, a real threat to the Arab world.[9]

Israel, for its part, views Syria as one of its bitter and most radical enemies in the Arab world, and in practical terms, the most concrete and significant enemy that it is facing, now that peace agreements with Egypt and Jordan and the Oslo Accords with the Palestinians have been signed. Israel's fears of Syria have their roots in the radical rhetoric emanating from Damascus, and mainly in that country's unprecedented military buildup. A clear expression of that approach can be seen in Amos Gilbo'a's article, "The [Syrian] National Security Concept," in the collection *Syria and Israel's Security*, edited by Avner Yaniv, Moshe Ma'oz, and Avi Kober, in which he states that

> Syria appears in Israeli consciousness, as well as in inter-Arab and international consciousness, as a radical and ag-

gressive country that has no compunctions about using its
army and behaving cruelly towards its enemies, both inside
and outside the country. Its image is one of a country that
finds itself in military conflicts with almost all of its neighbors, and has become one of the main terrorist centers in
the Middle East, and in short—a "trouble-making" country.
(p. 143)

The peace process has not changed this view. For many Israelis, Syria has remained an enigma, as is suggested in the title of Ma'oz's biographical study, published in 1987, *Asad: The Sphinx of Damascus*.[10] Their conclusion was, and still is, that in its heart of hearts Syria remains an enemy of Israel, and that Israel must be very cautious, forceful, and firm while dealing with Damascus.

Historical Memory

Syrian and Israeli attitudes toward one another are the results of the manner in which each of the countries looks at their joint past. On the Syrian side the picture is one of continuous Israeli aggression having its beginning in 1948, with the establishment of the State of Israel, the capture of most of Arab Palestine, and the dispossession of its Palestinian-Arab inhabitants. This continued, according to Syria, throughout the wars that Israel declared in 1956 and 1967 on its path toward achieving its vision of a "Greater Israel." From the Syrian point of view, the Six-Day War must be seen as a formative event, first and foremost for President Asad, who at the time served as acting minister of defense and commander of the air force. Indeed, as 'Adil Hafiz explains in his book, "the Zionist entity presented itself as a pursuer of peace, but the aggression of June 1967 proves to every honest person . . . that it is nothing but an aggressive, expansionist entity in its substance and objectives" (p. 173).

Historical memory in Israel is completely different. Israeli studies tend to emphasize Syria's role in fanning the flames of hostility toward Israel all these years, and especially its refusal to recognize Israel's right to exist and to hold peace talks with her. The Six-Day War, for example, is described in Israel as the necessary and unavoidable, albeit indirect, result of Syrian hostile actions initiated against Israel settlements along the border, as well as attempts by Damascus between the years 1964 and 1967 to divert the Jordan River waters. Even Moshe Ma'oz in his book *Israel and Syria: End of the Conflict?!*, a book that marks a turning point in the traditional Israel approach toward Syria, writes:

> [I]t appears that on the eve of the Six-Day war, most of the leaders of the Neo-Ba'th [leaders of the radical left faction of the Ba'th party who were in control in Syria at that time] believed that a popular war of liberation could bring about the collapse of Israel or at least a full-scale conventional pan-Arab war led by Egypt and Syria. (p. 91)

The October 1973 war, in which Syria launched an offensive against Israel, occupies a place of honor in the Israeli collective memory. Israeli research dealing with Israeli-Syrian relations over the past few years tends to underscore the attempts on the part of the Syrians to block the process of reconciliation between Israel and its Arab neighbors, as well as the assistance Syria grants to terrorist organizations operating from Syrian territory against Israel (pp. 102–24).[11]

Strategic Parity: Then and Now

The Syrians' view of Israel as an illegitimate and aggressive state, and at the same time as having absolute military superiority, created in Damascus a clear feeling of a genuine Israeli threat against Syria. President Asad has harbored this feeling ever since he rose to power in the mid-1960s. This feeling increased in intensity in the wake of accumulated experience, or more precisely, the way in which events such as the Six-Day War or the 1982 Lebanon war were interpreted in Syria.[12] This Syrian fear of an Israeli threat has been the basis of the Syrian efforts over the years to establish a strategic parity with the Jewish state. This parity was supposed to provide Syria with a defense shield against Israel and in the long run to allow the Syrians to impose on it, by force, a "Syrian solution" to the Arab-Israeli conflict. Such a concept can be seen or learned from Syria's slogan in the 1980s: *al-sumud w-al-tasaddi*—the firm stand (*sumud*) which will bring in its wake a rising to the challenge (*al-tasaddi*).[13]

This fierce Syrian view of Syrian-Israeli relations developed over the years in a number of stages. Until the end of the 1970s, the parity with Israel that Syria wanted to achieve was based on a pan-Arab coalition centered around Egypt, with Syria at its side. These two countries, together with a number of others such as Jordan, Iraq, or Saudi Arabia, were supposed to achieve a strategic parity with Israel that would deter it from attacking the Arabs, but that would also allow them to force Israel to accept Arab terms for a political solution to the Arab-Israeli conflict, or at least to appear at the negotiating table as equals. In *Israel and Syria,* Ma'oz explains this concept as follows:

> [E]ver since his rise to power, Asad has been trying, perhaps even obsessively, to achieve strategic parity with Israel. Aside from his declared ideological commitment to combat the Zionist entity and destroy it, his position had its roots in Asad's practical political position vis-a-vis Israel. . . . Asad, who saw the Jewish state as a regional power, wanted to create a counterbalance to Israel's superiority as a pre-condition both to an armed confrontation and a political settlement between the Arab world and Syria on the one side and Israel on the other. (p. 162)

The signing of the Israeli-Egyptian peace accord in 1979 and Egypt's withdrawal from the Arab camp were followed by the 1982 Lebanon War in which Syria found itself alone in a face-to-face confrontation with Israel. Drawing upon these lessons, Syria began building up its military capability with Soviet assistance. Indeed, in the early 1980s, the Syrian army doubled its size and procured advanced military equipment. However, the process of military buildup involved the diversion of all Syrian resources to this aim. The result was the collapse of the Syrian economy that could not withstand the burden of such heavy military expenditures. By 1986, President Asad was forced to stop the military buildup, thus abandoning the hope of achieving strategic parity with Israel. The collapse of the Soviet Union, Syria's main prop and arms supplier, was the last nail in the coffin of strategic parity. Nevertheless, the commitment to the concept of strategic parity still characterizes Syria thinking, even though, in order to realize it, Syria would be forced to adopt alternative—long and indirect—paths of action.

Syria tended to look at Israel through gun-sights, adopting a concept calling for the use of force in dealing with the Jewish state. However, this attitude is also characteristic of Israel's approach toward Syria. Such an approach can be seen in Amos Gilbo'a's article, "Syria and Israel's Security," which serves as an introduction to the Yaniv-Ma'oz-Kober collection, *Syria and Israel's National Security.*

Gilbo'a, who served as head of the Research Division in the Israeli Military Intelligence, writes that

> Syria is Israel's most serious security threat because of five main reasons: First, Syria has great conventional military might, that in any possible combination in a future war would be greater than that of the IDF operating against it. Second, Syria is more capable of surprising Israel than any other Arab state. Syria also has the ability to strike at Israel's hinterland—civilian and military alike. In this context it can use chemical weapons. In addition, Syria is the heart, engine and catalyst in any potential Arab war coalition against Israel, and the center of the Eastern Front. Without Syria, there is no Eastern Front. Finally, Syria has motivation and a conception involving the use of force. (p. 17)

Gilbo'a's conclusion is presented in no uncertain terms:

> With regard to Syria, Israel must operate according to the following rule: it must be optimistic while looking at the future, but pessimistic in its actions. Although it is ironic, the logical Israeli conclusion should be that in the foreseeable future the situation of "no war and no peace" will remain, while the border remains quiet and steady in view of the vast problems surrounding Syria. Israel must try and maximize each one of Syria's weak points and minimize its strong points, mainly its military might. (p. 19)

The Peace Process

For many years, relations between Syria and Israel were dominated by their mirror-image views of one another. The peace process that began in the wake of the Madrid Conference in October 1991 put these views to the test and opened a window of hope for change. This process was a clear result of changing regional and international realities in the early 1990s: the collapse of the Soviet Union, Syria's main ally until that time, and the destruction of Iraq's military power, which was considered even in Damascus (despite the hostile relations between the two countries) as Syria's strategic hinterland.

The new regional and international realities greatly weakened Syria, creating a strategic bind. The events of the period also demonstrated for Israel the limits of its own power. The Iraqi missile attacks on Israel in the course of the Gulf War, against which Israel was unable to provide a fully adequate response, and the Intifada, the Palestinian uprising in the West Bank and in Gaza, which exacted a heavy price from Israel, were eloquent illustrations of Israel's weak points. Ultimately, the Intifada caused many in Israel to change their minds about the future of those territories.

It would appear that the realities that formed the background to the Israeli and Syrian decisions to join the peace process in the fall of 1991 form the basis of some of the difficulties from which the process is suffering today. After all, both countries were led into the peace process, to a certain degree unwillingly, by the United States.[14] Thus, the process was considered, especially by Syria, as a constraint and even as a necessary evil. Indeed, the Syrian approach to the peace process, at least as projected through the Syrian media, was highly ambivalent. On the one hand, the Syrians stressed their desire for a just and lasting peace and their recognition that peace would serve Syria's security, political, and economic interests. The Syrians placed particular emphasis on the opportunity of gaining back the Golan Heights; in less obvious ways, they also recognized the economic advantages that would arise from concluding a peace agreement with Israel. It would also appear that, in the Syrian assessment, joining the peace process would remove, at least in the short run, a real Israeli (and maybe also an American) threat to Syrian national security.

Nevertheless, the Syrians frequently voiced criticism as well as suspicion and skepticism regarding the manner in which the process was proceeding and the direction it was taking.[15] The Syrians were dissatisfied, for example, with the fact that the process was based on a balance of power clearly favoring the Israeli side, the result of unqualified American support of Israel. This balance of power, remarked 'Adil Hafiz (pp. 244–46), allowed Israel to dictate its terms to the Arab partners to the negotiations and to make gains at their expense. Hafiz expressed special concern over the aims of the peace negotiations, quoting a speech made by President Asad as far back as March 1983:

> [T]he peace which Israel wants to achieve, and which the United States also adheres to, means the systematic expropriation of one Arab state after the other, of the traditions,

the history and mainly the hopes for the future of these states. Thus, they will become a bridgehead for Israel's gaining control, by the power of American arms and in the spirit of Israeli ambitions, over Arab lands. (p. 230)

It is thus possible to understand Syria's suspicion that the objective of the peace process, from the point of view of the United States and Israel, is to institute a Pax Americana, or perhaps even a Pax Israeliana, over the entire Middle East. In Syria's view such a peace would enforce Israeli or Western political, economic, and cultural hegemony over the Arab region. This would happen after attempts by Israel and the West to gain military control had been foiled by the Arabs for years. The choice, as Hamidi al-'Abdallah explains in *Asad's Strategy, A Comparative Study of Strategic Parity between Syria and Israel*, is "between the 'New Middle East' and the new 'Arab East' (*mashriq*)" (p. 273). Or, as Hafiz explains in it,

> the recognition which Israel wants is not diplomatic recognition, based on the right of each side to determine for itself the manner in which it is to behave and its relations with the other. The meaning of this recognition is the handing over of the economic keys of the region to the Zionists. This process is called by Zionist circles "normalization of relations." (p. 222)

Against the background of these fears, Syria has taken steps to strengthen its position in the region. First, it improved its ties with Iran (promoting and bolstering the strategic alliance with Tehran that it has been fostering since 1980). In this context, attention should be drawn to 'Abdallah's explanation:

> Iran is a Muslim country with a population of fifty million inhabitants and has considerable military capability and international position. Experience has proven that the alliance with Iran not only helped that country, but also lent strategic depth that Syria and the Arab nation need, in view of the weakness characterizing the Arab world. (p. 144)

In addition, the Syrians have taken steps to create an inter-Arab, Egyptian-Saudi-Syrian axis. This axis was reinforced in the wake of the Iraqi invasion of Kuwait and the outbreak of the Gulf Crisis. The strengthening of the alliance with Iran, and at the same time the promotion of a unified front of Arab states around it, was considered essential in Damascus' eyes, both in the event that the peace process reached an impasse, but also and mainly in the event that Israel and Syria concluded a peace agreement which, the Syrians feared, Israel might exploit in order to exert its will over the region.

Israel too views the peace process with suspicion, because of its doubts as to Syria's intentions regarding Israel. After all, for most Israelis, peace means reconciliation between peoples and should involve the recognition of Israel's right to exist in the region and the establishment of normal relations between countries: open borders, tourism, cultural, and commercial ties that allow Israel to become integrated into the region. The fact that Syria was unwilling to move toward Israel in these spheres influences the degree of Israel's trust in Syria's intentions, and thus the degree of willingness in Israeli public opinion to return the Golan Heights to Syria.

In *Israel and Syria* Ma'oz calls for the adoption of a more moderate approach toward Syria. Ma'oz even claims that Syria indeed wants peace, and that Israel should accede to Damascus' territorial demands in order to achieve that peace. However even Ma'oz writes that, despite his view that Syria is honest in its desire for peace, "one cannot totally discount the danger of a Syrian attack against Israel in the future, under certain circumstances and under the proper conditions." Given such a possibility, Ma'oz recognizes that "there are those who contend that Israel must continue to hold on the Golan." Although he does not agree with such an approach, Ma'oz admits: "it is impossible to say for certain that this approach is entirely groundless, since it impossible to know what developments will take place in Syria and the Arab region in the future" (p. 231).

Who Has Time on His Side?

In Israel and in the West, conventional wisdom holds that the regional and international changes of the late 1980s brought Syria to recognize that time was not on its side but rather on Israel's, and therefore it would do well to join the peace process. This assumption was based on an analysis of the socioeconomic and political conditions in which Syria, and indeed the Arab world in general, now found themselves. With regard to Syria, the accepted practice was to highlight the severe difficulties that country was facing and from which it did not seem likely to extricate itself in the foreseeable future: for instance, the issue of Asad's successor, and the power struggle in the top ranks causing instability in Syria's political system; the natural growth of the Syrian population being among the highest in the world, causing Syria severe economic difficulties.

Hafiz al-Asad has contradicted these Israeli and Western assumptions by not displaying any rush, in the negotiations conducted with Israel since Madrid, to move along the path to peace. His negotiations with Israel have proceeded at a very slow pace, and he constantly emphasized that he was not, in fact, operating under any time constraints. In retrospect, both Israelis and Americans have complained that Asad missed a golden opportunity to establish peace with Israel and thereby to regain the Golan Heights for Syria, an agreement that appeared achievable under the Rabin and Peres governments.

Asad's slow pace, to say nothing of the foot-dragging he practiced during the negotiations, teaches us that his perception of time is different from that in Israel and the West. In other words, Asad may have felt that, despite Israel's present relative advantage over Syria, in the final analysis and in the long term it is he who would gain the upper hand. According to this way of thinking, every day that passed did not necessarily strengthen Israel, but may rather erode its advantage, allowing the Arab position to gain in relative strength.

Such views frequently appear in the Arab studies published in recent years. For example, the Syrian minister of defense, Mustafa Tlas, stated in his book, *The Israeli Invasion of Lebanon*, published in the early 1980s, that the main loser in that war was Israel, since it had failed to realize its military objectives and to translate its military victories in the first weeks of that war into long-range strategic achievements.[16] The claim that time was on the side of the Arabs is also dealt with in Hamidi al-'Abdallah's book, which considers the strategic aspects of Israeli-Syrian relations. 'Abdallah points to the following steps in that process:

- *The continuous bloodshed in South Lebanon*: In south Lebanon Israel found itself facing an opponent (Hizballah) which forced upon it a struggle that it could not win. The guerrilla warfare practiced by the Hizballah allowed the latter to neutralize Israel's absolute military advantage, and to strike heavy blows against it. These blows undermined the stamina and resilience of Israeli society, and even led to internal debate in Israel over the continued presence of its forces in South Lebanon.

- *The Intifada*: The successful struggle against Israel in South Lebanon became a "source of inspiration for the Intifada fighters" (p. 138). This was another significant stage in the erosion of Israel's sense of power. The Jewish state, as it transpired, had no answer to the war of stones, Molotov cocktails, and knives which the Palestinians waged against it. The Intifada also exacted an economic price from Israel, and more important, caused the loss of lives. It undermined the will of the Israeli society and demonstrated to Israel just where its weakness lay. The change in Israel's position on the Palestinian question, that is, the readiness to recognize the PLO and to conduct negotiations with it, although insufficient in Syrian eyes, is nothing less than the direct result of the Intifada and of Israel's weakness that came to light as a result of it.

- *Missiles and chemical weapons*: The Iraqi missile attacks against Israel in the course of the Gulf War, and the achievement of such weapons capability by Syria and Iran, exposed a raw nerve and, in essence, Israel's "Achilles' Heel." By means of a relatively simple technology (certainly in comparison with that of the nuclear weapons that the Arabs believe Israel has), the latter were able to hit hard at Israeli population centers. The price that Israel paid in the Gulf War—the effect, even if only psychological, of the missile attacks against Israeli population centers—made it clear to everyone that in the next war the Arabs would be at a more advantageous starting point, and would be able to extract from Israel a far higher price than it had to pay in the past.

- *The American role in the Middle East*: The total commitment of the United States to Israel was considered an important, and even central, component in the buildup of Israel's power. This was especially true following the collapse of the Soviet Union, which created a lack of balance on the international as well as on the regional level. Against such a background, it is interesting to note Hamidi al-'Abdallah's assessment that the United States was undergoing a process of weakening, which would in turn affect the role it might play in the future in the Middle East and in world affairs. On the basis of an analysis of the main trends of the American economy (e.g., the growth of the deficit and the public debt) and of the American society (increasing gaps between the different social classes), 'Abdallah foresaw the twilight of America. (pp. 175–245).

From here the distance to the conclusion that the future looks bright for the Arabs is short. After all, according to 'Abdallah, the Arabs were maintaining, and even increasing, their quantitative advantage over Israel, and at the same time decreasing Israel's qualitative edge, especially in the technological sphere (pp. 45–46, 70). In truth, in the past the Syrians claimed that the balance of power between Israel and the Arabs was not only the result of the military balance between the two. President Asad explained in the late 1980s that

> strategic parity [did] not mean a parity of weapons, in other words tank for tank and plane for plane. Parity in weapons [was] a basic element in achieving overall parity, but the latter require[d] achieving parity in all spheres of life, first of all, cultural, economic and political. These spheres take precedence over the military. (p. 109)[17]

Indeed 'Abdallah's analysis presents a picture in which the scales in the military sphere, but in other spheres as well, have begun to tip in favor of the Arabs.

Conclusion

Syrian and Israeli studies published over the past several years reveal that the basic views that Syria and Israel had of each other have remained for the most part unchanged. This holds true for public opinion, but also and mainly for the elite—political, military, and intellectual. Israel has remained, in Syria's view, an illegitimate, aggressive, and expansionist entity, a constant source of threat. This situation exists despite, or perhaps precisely because of, the ongoing regional peace process. This process, as viewed by the Syrians, might grant Israel strategic gains at the their expense, and is therefore looked upon as a challenge and not necessarily as a "window of opportunity" for creating a new reality in the region to include friendly and close relations with Israel.

Israel's basic attitudes toward Syria have also remained substantially unchanged. Even in Ma'oz's book, which reflects a certain change in Israeli perceptions of Syria as a result of the peace process, one can still find the signs of suspicion and skepticism that had characterized Israel's attitude toward Syria in the past. For instance, Ma'oz writes that

> ever since [the] Rabin government rose to power in 1992 and expressed its readiness for territorial compromise, and in view of the disintegration of the Soviet Union and the rise of the United States as the sole superpower, Asad has apparently taken the strategic decision to arrive at a political settlement, i.e., a peace agreement with Israel. Nevertheless, no substantial change has occurred in Asad's political and ideological hostility towards Israel, and in his aim of achieving the withdrawal of Israeli forces from all of the Golan Heights and South Lebanon, and the solution of the Palestinian problem. (p. 228)

Ma'oz's book is indeed an indication of the fledgling change in, at least, part of the Israeli academic community toward Syria. This change is expressed, for example, in the author's call to Israel to pay the price of relinquishing the Golan Heights in return for a peace agreement with Syria (pp. 227–32). Such a change can be seen also, at least to some degree, in Israeli political circles—proof of which was the peace policy toward Syria adopted by both the Rabin and Peres governments. However, there is some doubt as to whether such a change has penetrated much deeper into broader strata of the Israeli political-military elite, or into Israeli public opinion.

Syria and Israel remain in disagreement on almost everything. Each side views its past, present, and therefore the future differently from the other. Their views are identical in terms of mutual suspicion and distrust, and therefore the basic hostility with which they perceive one another. Peace, it seems, is not just over the hill.

Notes

1. *Tishrin*, 2 January 1996.
2. Ibid., 3 December 1995.

3. See *ha-Aretz*, 11, 18 August 1996.

4. See Asad's interview with CNN, September 1996. The interview was published in all Syrian newspapers. *al-Thawra*, 29 September 1996. For first-hand Syrian and Israeli accounts of these negotiations, see "Fresh Light on the Syrian-Isreli Peace Negotiations," interview with Ambassador Walid al-Moualem, *Journal of Palestine Studies* 26:2 (Winter 1997), 81–94, and Itamar Rabinovich, *The Brink of Peace: The Israeli-Syrian Negotiations* (Princeton: Princeton University Press, 1998).

5. See Shimon Shamir, "The Arab-Israeli Conflict," in *The Middle East—Oil, Conflicts, Hope*, ed. A. l. Udovitch (Boulder CO: Westview, 1976), 195–230.

6. See Patrick Seale, *Asad: The Struggle for the Middle East* (London: I. B. Tauris, 1988), 117–41.

7. See Middle East Watch, *Syria Unmasked: The Suppression of Human Rights by the Asad Regime* (New Haven: Yale University Press, 1991).

8. See Asad speech, *Tishrin*, 9 March 1990.

9. See also, Eyal Zisser, "Syria and Israel: From War to Peace," *Orient* 36:3 (1995), 488–90.

10. Moshe Ma'oz, *Asad: The Sphinx of Damascus*, New York and London: Weidenfeld and Nicolson, 1987.

11. See also Zisser, "Syria and Israel," 491–93. Ma'oz's book under review was also published in English as *Syria and Israel: From War to Peace-Making* (New York: Oxford University Press, 1995). All page references in this essay are to the Hebrew edition.

12. See Seale, *Asad,* 117–41, 202–25, 364–91.

13. See Ma'oz, *Asad: the Sphinx of Damascus* (Tel Aviv: Dvir, 1988), 181–98. (Hebrew).

14. For an overview, with selected documents, see Laura Zittrain Eisenberg and Neil Caplan, *Negotiating Arab-Israeli Peace: Patterns, Problems, Possibilities* (Bloomington: Indiana University Press, 1998), 75–84, 196–204.

15. Ma'oz, *Syria and Israel: From War to Peace-Making*, 193–226; also Zisser, "Syria and Israel," 494–97.

16. Mustafa Tlas, *The Israeli Invasion of Lebanon*; Damascus: Mu'assasat Tishrin l-il-Sahafa w-al-Nashr, 1983. (Arabic)

17. See also *al-Safir*, 4 May 1990.

14. Egyptian Representation of Israeli Culture: Normalizing Propaganda or Propagandizing Normalization?

Deborah A. Starr

This essay examines the contents of three special issues of the important literary periodical Ibdāʿ (Creativity) which constitute the first collaborative public attempt in Egypt to discuss Israeli cultural production. The author shows that, despite the ideological anti-normalization rhetoric of the journal and the strictly enforced boycott of Israel in most Egyptian intellectual circles, there is evidence of some less-politicized ways of representing Israeli culture to Egyptian audiences among the Ibdāʿ contributors.

Israeli Culture: The Propaganda of Normalization and the Dimensions of the Confrontation; special issues of the journal *Ibdāʿ* (Creativity), January, February, March 1995. (Arabic)

Proper names common in English or with standard Romanizations appear in their familiar form. Otherwise, transliterations of names and words from Arabic and Hebrew conform to the Library of Congress system.

S ince *Ibdāᶜ*, an Egyptian monthly journal, first appeared in 1983, it has published works of contemporary literature and the fine arts, as well as critical studies and discussions. In 1995 *Ibdāᶜ* produced three consecutive special issues entitled "Israeli Culture: The Propaganda of Normalization and the Dimensions of the Confrontation."[1] The January issue was subtitled, "Poetry and Fine Arts"; February's was entitled "The Novel and the Short Story"; and the March issue (below) was devoted to "Academic Studies and the Humanities, Arab Jews, the Theater and the Cinema." The contents of the three issues can be divided into four categories: (a) scholarly articles by Egyptian professors of Hebrew; (b) editorials by Egyptian intellectuals; (c) translations of scholarly articles written in English and French; and (d) examples of Israeli literature and the arts.

Ibdāᶜ, March 1995. Reprinted by permission from the General Egyptian Book Organization.

Established Egyptian intellectuals, for reasons explained in the next section, continue to maintain publicly an intellectual boycott of Israel, refusing to "normalize" cultural relations with Israel and Israelis. Since the fear of appearing sympathetic to Israel has long reigned in the public sphere, these three issues of *Ibdāʿ* are significant, as they represent the first collaborative public attempt in Egypt to examine and discuss Israeli cultural production. The journal also offers insight into the perspectives and critical approach of the foremost Egyptian scholars of modern Hebrew. Although Hebrew studies has been an integral part of secular higher education in Egypt since 1908, the discipline has maintained a low public profile. The journal represents the first effort of Egyptian scholars of Hebrew to introduce the nonspecialist public to their field. Although the intended audience of the journal is the intellectual and literary-minded (yet uninformed) reader, the scholarly articles are a good indication of the current breadth of interest in Hebrew studies within the academic community.

This essay aims to demonstrate the complex set of relations that shape the terms of the normalization debate. The first section examines the various discursive spaces occupied by the notion of "normalization" as evidenced in the various contributions to *Ibdāʿ*, paying particular attention to pieces by academics who resist being enlisted into the service of public debates. The second section reviews the development of Hebrew studies as an academic discipline in Egypt in order to define the critical issues of concern to the scholars whose work appears in *Ibdāʿ*. The final section examines the contents of the journal issues under review to demonstrate two critical positions shared by the majority of contributors, specialists and nonspecialists alike: the essentially political nature of Israeli literature, and the absence of a single Jewish culture.[2]

Normalization Politics

Normalization in the context of Egyptian-Israeli relations is literally a negotiated term—a concept endorsed by the various protocols of the Camp David Accords as the result of Israeli demands for cultural exchange. For Israel, the implications of "normalization" run deep, denoting the legitimization of the Zionist project. In Zionist ideology, normalization signifies the dissolution of the inherently "abnormal" Diaspora and the establishment of a Jewish state on a "normal" (read Western) model fully integrated into the family of nations.[3]

The persistent Egyptian refusal to fully accept Israel on cultural terms continues to deny the fulfillment of the Zionist vision, even as some "post-Zionist" Israelis hail the end of that ideology. The terms of cultural exchange with Egypt were set by Israel on a Western model—a model not unfamiliar to Egypt, yet one that nevertheless requires Egypt to accept Israel's Westernized cultural hegemony.

Egyptian intellectuals, along with their counterparts in other Arab countries, maintain that they will continue to oppose normalization of relations with Israel as long as Israel does not withdraw from all occupied Arab territories. Resistance to normalization in Egypt also constitutes a protest against a separate peace between the two countries, as well as a demonstration of intellectuals' solidarity with the Palestinians, whose situation had been left unresolved by the 1979 Egyptian-Israeli Treaty. However, the context and shape of the Egyptian intellectuals' opposition to normalization reveals an underlying complex of power relations that extends beyond the issue of relations with Israel. Although in the West former president Anwar Sadat is remembered as a great leader and peacemaker, he was, at home, also a dictator who repressed opposition and whose policies of opening the economy fostered widespread corruption. Egyptian intellectuals also maintain that the peace treaty with Israel represented a sellout to American capital.[4] President Hosni Mubarak, who attempts to steer a moderate course both domestically and internationally, has had to operate under the shadow of the legacy he inherited from Sadat. Although freedoms have increased under Mubarak, direct criticism of the upper echelons of government remains taboo. While the administration maintains cool diplomatic relations with Israel, it allows for public debate and dissent that is far more aggressive than the government position. In this way anti-normalization remonstrations are a form of anti-government protest that at the same time serve government interests by maintaining pressure on Israel.

For Egyptian intellectuals, one outcome of the peace treaty was the immediate isolation from their colleagues throughout the Arab world. Within this context, opposition to normalization with Israel also functioned as a plea for normalizing severed cultural and intellectual relations with Arab countries and organizations. The Camp David accords led to the expulsion of the Egyptian Writers' Union (EWU) from the Arab Writers' Union (AWU). The EWU was only readmitted to the AWU after the April 1997 EWU elections that ousted several long-serving civil servants who, as government officials, were seen as pro-normalization. While the victorious candidates have on other occasions voiced their opposition to normalization of relations with Israel, they were elected as a referendum on a platform of institutional change and as an end to corrupt, ineffectual leadership. The readmission to the AWU nevertheless was a welcome outcome of the elections. In this case as in others, opposition to corruption and ineffectual leadership, characteristics of Egyptian government institutions at all levels, has also been intertwined with resistance to government-promoted normalization of relations with Israel.[5]

The journal *Ibdāʿ* sits in an ambiguous position between the government and the intellectual community. *Ibdāʿ*, published by the General Egyptian Book Organization, is one of several cultural journals launched by the state-run press during the early years of the Mubarak regime, signaling a rapprochement between the government and left-leaning intellectuals whose activities had been severely restricted under Sadat.[6] The poet Ahmad ʿAbd al-Muʿṭī Ḥijāzī, who had fled to Paris during the Sadat years, assumed the editorship of *Ibdāʿ* in 1991. Despite Ḥijāzī's former radicalism, the profile of *Ibdāʿ* aligns the journal and its editor with the organs of power in Egypt's government-sponsored cultural establishment, garnering respect in some circles and disdain among the avant-garde.

The three special issues under consideration appeared at a time when the lines of the anti-normalization battle were being redrawn. In the wake of the Oslo Accords and the establishment of relations on various levels between Israel and other Arab countries, the Egyptian government also began actively promoting the "creation of a culture of peace." In this air of reconciliation, the anti-normalization camp in Egypt began to fracture, as differing individual interpretations complicated the question of what "normalization" meant and at what stage in the peace process it might be warranted. One high-profile example was the 1994 visit of the playwright ʿAlī Sālim that he described for the Egyptian public in his book *Journey to Israel*.[7] Such a "breaking of rank" caused other Egyptian intellectuals to dig in their heels and stand fast in their anti-normalization positions.[8] Although contributors to the special issues of *Ibdāʿ* insist that the initial idea and the journal's ultimate content were not affected by political winds, it is in this atmosphere of renewed debate over what constitutes "normalization" that the journal appeared.

This public discourse on the issue of normalization, as well as the highly politicized title, "Israeli Culture: The Propaganda of Normalization and the Dimensions of the Confrontation," clearly shape the reader's expectations of the contents. Within the context of a debate characterized by the language of "holding the line" in an ongoing battle, the implications of the title are transparent—the reader on the home front must be briefed by experts on the dimensions of the conflict and apprised of the enemy's propaganda. While the title does not accurately reflect the contents, as we shall see, it nevertheless provides a discursive filter through which the articles can be read.

Opinion pieces by nonspecialist intellectuals introduce the first volume and conclude the final volume, supported by the editor's introduction to each issue, in effect outlining the various "dimensions of the confrontation." While the authors uniformly reject normalization, they differ in details of interpretation or application. For example, while Ḥijāzī ("National Culture or a Culture of Individuals?" January, pp. 4-5) calls for Israel to assimilate into the region, Maḥmūd Amīn al-ʿĀlim ("This Normalization with What Is Not Normal," January, pp. 6-11) criticizes Israel for having "stolen" from Arab and Palestinian culture in attempting to establish its own. The literary critic Salāḥ Faḍīl ("Nationalism of Enmity," January, pp. 12–15) cites the establishment of a Palestinian state with East Jerusalem as its capital and the destruction of Israeli nuclear weapons as preconditions, but does not describe what, in his opinion, constitutes normalization. Conversely, Edwār al-Kharrāṭ, a prolific critic and writer, clearly defines ("Yes to Knowledge, Of Course, But a Thousand Times No to Normalization," January, pp. 15–16) what activities he considers to constitute normalization, but neglects to define terms for a change in policy. These politicized articles discursively frame the contents of the journal.

The reader senses that the editors anticipated neither the overridingly nonbelligerent tone and perspective of the academic studies, nor their sheer weight. Ḥijāzī's introduction to the third and final issue effectively acknowledges the significance of the conceptual rift. In contrast to his unequivocal statement in volume 1, for example, that there is no Israeli culture, only individual artists and intellectuals ("National Culture or a Culture of Individuals?" January 1995, pp. 4–5), in the third volume he leaves the final word on the matter to scholars in the field:

> What I know is that the Israelis say that their language is alive—perhaps this is self-deception. We say that the Israeli language is dead—and perhaps this is self-deception. This issue requires an objective study to determine the conditions a living language must meet. Then we will see if these condi-

tions are applicable to Hebrew used now or not. ("Merely a Beginning," March 1995, p. 4)

This concession is an acknowledgment that some of the assumptions on which his political position is based may actually be open to debate, and thus require academic study to set the record straight. This admission undermines, to some extent, the authority of the nonspecialists and strengthens the voices of the experts.

The Egyptian scholars of Hebrew, who represent the majority of contributors to the special issues of *Ibdāʿ*, have a vested interest in distancing themselves from the terms of the public debate. As Rashād al-Shāmī, former chair of Hebrew studies at ʿAin Shams University, acknowledges, the department serves an important function in supplying governmental institutions with trained graduates. Yet scholars cannot ignore the public stigma attached to the contact with Israelis and Israeli institutions increasingly required by their research. Throughout 1994 and 1995, a number of Egyptian professors of Hebrew began participating in conferences in Israel or traveled there in order to conduct research, while others have long utilized resources at the Israeli Academic Center in Cairo, or have met or studied with Israelis overseas. However, in their writing, they avoid references to visits or contacts and refrain from expressing any views on normalization. As an analysis of their contributions to *Ibdāʿ* reveals, Egyptian academic discourse is careful to deflect their scholarly inquiries away from the weighty political stakes. It is understandable why al-Shāmī insists on the detached nature of academia, placing himself and his department's work outside of the volatile political and ideological winds in Egypt.[9] Indeed, historically speaking, Hebrew studies in Egypt has long steered clear of public political debates.

Hebrew Studies in Egypt

The inception of the study of Hebrew in Egypt is linked geopolitically to the British occupation and to the conscious modeling of Egyptian higher education on European universities. When the Egyptian University was established in 1908, the majority of the faculty were European, among them Orientalists who introduced the fields of linguistics and comparative literature, and thus the study of Semitic and Middle Eastern languages.

In other words, the study of Hebrew in Egypt predates the Arab-Israeli conflict and was carried out independently of political concerns over the rise of Jewish immigration to Palestine under the British Mandate. Indeed, in April 1925 Aḥmad Luṭfī al-Sayyid, then head of the Egyptian University (later renamed Fuad I, then Cairo University) attended the opening ceremonies of the Hebrew University of Jerusalem and the teachers' union of Dār al-ᶜUlūm wished their Jewish counterparts well in honor of the same occasion.[10] In reciprocation, Professor Selig Brodetsky, later president of the Hebrew University of Jerusalem, visited Cairo and delivered a public lecture at the Egyptian University.[11]

With the rechartering of the Egyptian University as a public institution in 1925, the Department of Arabic and Semitic Languages and Literatures was established, further institutionalizing the discipline.[12] Ṭāhā Ḥusayn, the great Egyptian thinker, writer, and educator, insisted in his 1938 comprehensive proposal on education, *The Future of Culture in Egypt,* that, among other requirements, students specializing in the Arabic language must also study either Hebrew or Persian, a university requirement maintained to this day.[13] It was in this context that Hebrew and other Middle Eastern languages became an integral part of modern, secular higher education in Egypt.

Throughout the 1930s and 1940s, the discipline of Middle Eastern languages remained relatively untouched by the tensions exacerbated by right-wing Egyptian nationalists and by the increasing violence in Palestine.[14] Until 1940 there was still a Jewish professor of Hebrew at Dār al-ᶜUlūm, Israel Wolfenson—an individual who bridged the gap between the study of Hebrew in Egypt and the study of Arabic in Jewish schools in Palestine and later Israel. Born in Jerusalem, Wolfenson began studying at the Egyptian University in 1922 and was granted his Ph.D. in 1929, which he followed by a second doctorate in Europe. He taught Hebrew at Dār al-ᶜUlūm from 1933 to 1940, when he was tapped to head the program for teaching Arabic for the Jewish Department of Education in Palestine.[15]

Egyptian academics initially focused on ancient and medieval Hebrew, but after the establishment of the State of Israel Egyptian administrative and political interest in modern Hebrew predictably grew. The first advanced degrees in modern Hebrew literature were awarded in the late 1960s from both ᶜAin Shams and Cairo universities. Since that time, approximately 54% of all advanced degrees awarded in Hebrew studies at these two universities have dealt with topics in modern literature.[16]

The idea for the special issues of *Ibdāᶜ* originated in the Department of Hebrew at ᶜAin Shams University, and the former department chair, Rashād al-Shāmī, solicited and edited the academic articles. Since contributors faced a very short production timetable, these articles represent academic research already completed or well in progress, offering a snapshot of contemporary interests and areas of study within the field.[17]

Dominant Critical Assumptions

The Political Nature of Israeli Literature

As evidenced by their contributions to *Ibdā'*, Egyptian scholars of Hebrew largely share the critical position that Israeli literature is essentially political in nature. In his introduction to a symposium entitled, "Arabic Influences on the Hebrew Language, Religious Thought and Hebrew Literature Throughout the Ages," Rashād al-Shāmī asserts that through the study of literature he and his colleagues can understand and analyze Israeli "social, political and cultural reality" and map Israeli intellectual trends. Several of the contributors to *Ibdā'* explicitly agree, citing the cultural platform of the Fifth Zionist Congress (held in Basle in 1901) which they interpret as a political endorsement of Hebrew literary and cultural activities in order to promote the movement's goals. From this historical basis, the Egyptians examine literary texts for their relationship to contemporary political ideologies.[18]

Such methodology enables Egyptian professors of Hebrew to access the sociopolitical developments of what still remains to them a largely inaccessible culture. While some Egyptian scholars of Hebrew have visited Israel and conducted research there, few have made repeat visits and none have stayed for an extended period of time. Some of those professors who would like to return report difficulties in securing the necessary permission from Egyptian university authorities.

The lack of direct contact with Israeli and Jewish culture, and the limitation of secondary sources, occasionally breeds disturbing factual errors, as can be seen from some of the contributions to the special issues of *Ibdā'*. For example, in her article tracing Jewish legends originating in the Old Testament, Suzanne al-Saʿīd Yūsuf misidentifies the major Jewish holidays, assigning them fixed dates according to the solar calendar ("Origins of Jewish Folklore," March 1995, pp. 46–51).

The short stories included in translation in *Ibdā'* also confirm the critical position that Israeli literature essentially fulfills a political function.[19] The translators who contributed to *Ibdā͑* agreed to select stories that would show the human side of Israeli characters, particularly in their relations with Arabs.[20] Four of the stories, for example, raise moral dilemmas and demonstrate the human toll of war and long-term militarism on both the victim and the victor. While Israeli representations of Arabs are understandably of interest to the Egyptian critic and reader, the choice of topic led to the inclusion of stories that are all transparent political statements. In addition, translators chose to include some obscure or atypical examples, giving a distorted impression to the uninformed reader of the extent to which these issues and this style are prevalent in Israeli literature.

Yoram Kaniuk's "Perets versus the State of Israel" is drawn from a series of semi-journalistic stories printed in the Israeli weekly *Sofshavū͑a* (the Friday supplement to *Ma͑arīv*). The author's ironic portrayal of Israeli society plays into an Egyptian reader's expectations of a flawed Israeli society. Two other stories included in translation represent interactions between Israeli soldiers and Arabs. Yitzḥak Orpaz's classic story, "On the Edge of a Bullet," describes the reflections of an Israeli soldier upon the wartime capture of a Palestinian in Gaza. Just as the narrator convinces his commander to release the prisoner, the Palestinian is killed by a shot fired by an IDF soldier using the prisoner's confiscated gun. "Qantara" represents one of a handful of stories written after the Six-Day War by the film critic Nissim Dayan. The story begins with the self-absorbed thoughts of exhausted soldiers on their way to the recently-captured Egyptian town of Qantara, and then describes the meaningless killing of an old Arab resident of the village.

The stories, "Hasan the Pilot" by Dror Green and "Akhziv" by Yoḥa Yuval, are introduced as representative samples of the portrayal of the Palestinian in Hebrew literature after the Intifada. "Hasan the Pilot" describes a young Palestinian boy who dreams of learning to fly, but is killed by a stray bullet shot into the air to disperse a crowd of stone-throwers. After his death, Hasan is sighted flying through the air throughout the Occupied territories, offering protection to his peers. "Akhziv" describes a meeting between friends, a Jew on leave from reserve duty and an Arab on his way to his father's village to assist his family in defending his brother who, attempting to slip into Israel by sea with a cell of guerrillas), was coincidentally captured by the soldier's unit. Yet neither story represents a significant trend in Israeli Hebrew literature. "Akhziv" won a short story competition for unknown writers sponsored by *haAretz*, while Green's collection of stories, *Tales of the Intifada*, received mixed reviews in Israel. On the one hand, the writer claims that major publishers refused his manuscript for political reasons, and that several stores refused to stock the book because the owners considered it too leftist. On the other hand, Green was criticized for contributing to the literary expression of "a further step in the direction of occupation" by attempting to speak for the Palestinians with no direct knowledge of his subject.[21]

In his introduction to these two stories, Professor Muḥammad Abu-Ghadīr ("Representation of the Palestinian in the Hebrew Short Story after the Intifada: A Study and Examples," February 1995, pp. 74–76) briefly traces the history of the representation of the Palestinian in Hebrew literature, demonstrating great sensitivity to shifts in the internal political and social environment for both Jews and Arabs. After 1967, he writes, both the crisis and the level of contact between Israeli Jews and Palestinians increased, with the Israeli writer-intellectual generally proactive and sympathetic to the plight of the Palestinians (a situation presumably reflected in the writing of this period). The Intifada raised the level of urgency of the crisis of occupation and pushed both the political right and left to extremes. Abu-Ghadīr's exposition implies that with increased contact the representation of Palestinians in Hebrew literature becomes both more realistic and more sympathetic. However, his analysis may be overly optimistic, since very few Israeli Hebrew writers address the Intifada in their literary works and the representation of Arab characters in Hebrew literature is more infrequent than Abu-Ghadīr's article suggests, and not indicative of any major trend in Israeli literature. Similarly, there has never been any parallel sustained interest in Arab or Egyptian culture in an Israeli publication of equal importance to *Ibdāʿ*.[22]

Thus, despite the goal of depicting the Israeli as human, the exclusion of a broad range of stories that would have represented other aspects of Israeli civilian life leaves the selected stories as a confirmation of the prevailing image of the Israeli as soldier. However, since the stories are critical of Israeli militarism, their writers (in absentia) are presented as conscientious and sensitive to the human costs of war and occupation.

Studies by Egyptian academics, as represented by the articles included in *Ibdāʿ*, also tend to favor transparently ideological or political texts. For example, in "The Political Function of Literature" (January 1995, 42–48), Aḥmad Ḥammād analyzes several poems from Natan Alterman's "Seventh Column" in *Davar*, which the poet used between 1943 and 1967 as a weekly forum for publicizing his political ideas. However, there are no articles on Natan Zach, for example, who led a revolution of poetic expression in Israel in the 1950s and who publicly took Alterman to task for, among other things, enlisting poetry to serve as patriotic propaganda.[23] Likewise, in his article "Ḥanoch Levin: An Israeli Theatrical Scream Against War and a Call for Peace" (March 1995, pp 112–21), Rashād al-Shāmī analyzes and translates large excerpts from Levin's explicitly political play, "You, Me and the Upcoming War." While not all of the texts analyzed are so explicitly ideological, the critics uniformly draw out inherent political ideologies through their readings.

An important source of this methodology is the work of the Israeli literary critic Gershon Shaked, whose writings have, to a great extent, shaped both the Egyptian and Israeli critical establishments. His four-volume *Hebrew Fiction 1880–1980* and his study of the writers of the 1960s, *A New Wave in Hebrew Fiction,* are standard reference works and pedagogical tools. Indeed, Shaked is the Israeli literary critic most frequently cited in Egyptian studies of Hebrew literature.[24] In his critical writing, Shaked perceives literature as a representation of society. His work is largely devoted to mapping individual literary texts onto the development of a uniquely Israeli society based on Zionist ideals. For Shaked, there is no escaping from the collectivity; in his analysis, even apparently apolitical texts represent a stage in the nation's collective development. In reviewing the psychological writing of the 1960s, Shaked claims:

> Inasmuch as fiction struggled for the spirit of the individual, nevertheless, collective problems returned and embraced it, and even occasionally strangled it. The freedom from the underlying plot of the dominant social model was, to a great extent, nothing but a fantasy.[25]

It is outside of the scope of this essay to closely analyze the implications of Shaked's critical position. Suffice it to say that he practices his own brand of "normalization": his criticism traces the development of Hebrew literature and "normalizes" it with respect to Western literature.

While perhaps the most influential, Shaked is certainly not the only Israeli critic to read Hebrew literature in the context of the development of national identity. In an article translated and included in *Ibdāʿ,* Menachem Perry offers a psychoanalytic reading of narratives by Amos Oz, David Grossman, and A. B. Yehoshua. He begins his discussion of the representation of the Arab-Israeli conflict in Israeli literature with texts that include Arab characters. He concludes his analysis with a reading of Yehoshua's book *A Late Divorce*—a narrative of a dysfunctional family which, Perry argues, functions as an extended symbolic representation of the state of the Arab-Israeli conflict after the 1967 war.[26]

In the final analysis, the gulf between Egyptian and Israeli literary critics is not so great. Both schools tease out the ideological underpinnings of the texts they analyze. The difference lies in the value placed on the findings. Shaked, and to some extent Perry, valorize the creation of a national literature through their criticism. Egyptian scholars are similarly prepared to situate Israeli literature within an ideological context, reading texts for their political allegory and symbolism. Yet, using the same evidence and methodology as their Israeli counterparts, Egyptian critics argue that ideology has hindered the development of Hebrew literature.

Absence of a Single Jewish Culture

When it comes to discussing the development of Diaspora Jewish culture, Egyptian critics, specialists and nonspecialists alike, stress the historical influence of the dominant host cultures and downplay the significance of shared Judaic texts and religious practices. In the introduction to the symposium, "Arabic Influences on the Hebrew Language, Religious Thought and Hebrew Literature Throughout the Ages," Rashād al-Shāmī outlines the shared premises of the papers presented—that there has never been a Jewish civilization, and that many Jewish cultures have developed and existed only under the influence of various host cultures.[27]

Certainly a vast variety of Jewish expressions, cultures, and identities exist and have existed throughout the ages. Yet the promotion of multiplicity over unity feeds into the normalization debate. Some Egyptian intellectuals assert that the fifty years of Israel's existence have not been sufficient for the creation of a single, shared Israeli culture. This assumption forms the basis of Ḥijāzī's claim, for example, that contact with individual Israeli thinkers would have no relevant impact since they do not represent a unified cultural constituency ("National Culture or a Culture of Individuals?" January 1995, pp. 4–5). Others view Israel as an anomaly in Jewish history, and therefore one that is inherently unstable. It is on the basis of this assumption that some Egyptian thinkers call for the assimilation of Israel into the region in which Jews have assimilated into their host cultures in the past. In effect, this call for "assimilation" advocates future cultural exchange on terms more amenable to Egyptian culture than the current format that appears, from their perspective, to be dictated by Israeli/Western cultural hegemony.

The selection of translated texts reproduced in *Ibdāʿ* supports these claims of the absence of a unitary and unique Israeli culture. Barry Chamish's short exposé on Israeli cinema and censorship in the 1970s quotes the Israeli director, Benjamin Hayim, as saying, "Israelis are still uncertain of their identity. Israel is a young country and there's no self-image yet."[28] Taken in context, Hayim is expressing hope for future improvement in Israeli cinematography, yet his comments are used to validate Egyptian claims of the absence of Israeli culture. Likewise, Bernhard Frank, in his introduction to the anthology *Modern Hebrew Poetry*, expresses concern over commercialization and Westernization, an issue that continues to occupy Egyptian intellectuals with respect to the future of their own culture. Frank writes:

> [Israeli Hebrew poet Dan] Pagis is writing what might be called "international poetry".... Is this kind of internationalization good? Bad? Had one applauded the Westernization of Japan? Does one applaud the McDonaldization of Europe? In the global village we share, Pagis' direction seems inevitable.[29]

The issues he raises here resonate with prevailing assumptions about Israel's wholesale adoption of Western culture and the country's privileged relationship with the United States. Such evidence by Western critics as to the absence of a unified or unique Israeli culture grants legitimacy to the Egyptian critical premise and, by extension, to its politicized conclusions. The assertion that the Diaspora condition is "normal" for most of the world's Jews inherently disrupts the Zionist discourse of normalization, which considers the Diaspora as profoundly "abnormal."

In emphasizing Jewish cultural diversity, Egyptian academic studies offer a contrast to Israeli literary criticism's partiality toward Ashkenazi culture. "Hebrew Literature: Introduction to the Ambiguities of Terminology" (January 1995, pp. 3–41), by ʿAyman Rifʿat, was originally written as a paper for an undergraduate class at the University of Alexandria, and reveals a great deal about the pedagogical emphasis of Hebrew studies in Egypt.[30] The essay attempts to isolate, define, and identify major contributors to Hebrew literary periods and trends. Within his discussion of Hebrew literature written in Israel, Rifʿat simultaneously traces developments in Ashkenazi, Sephardi-Mizraḥi, and Arab idioms. Such an integrationist approach is rare in criticism of Hebrew literature written in English and Hebrew.

The distribution of essays in these special issues of *Ibdāʿ* confirms that such a vision is not unique to the University of Alexandria. Six out of twenty-one essays on Israeli cultural production by Jews deal either exclusively with Sephardi-Mizraḥi culture or integrate it into the larger context of Israeli culture as just described. Additionally, essays about Palestinians add to, rather than detract from, the portrayal of Israeli culture, rounding out the representation of Israeli culture as a whole. In particular, the inclusion of an essay on Emile Habiby, who served as a Knesset member and who was awarded the 1992 Israel Prize for Literature for his writing in Arabic, attests to his own ambiguous cultural position between Israel and the Arab world (Faysal Darrāj, "Emile Habiby: The Lost Face among the Many Masks?" January 1995, 74–95).

In sum, this analysis of the denial of a unitary and unique Jewish culture once again distinguishes between the political positioning of the academics, on the one hand, and the anti-normalization advocates, on the other. The academic position also offers an integrated critical approach to the study of Israeli literature and culture that is significantly underrepresented in the Israeli and Western academies.

Conclusion

Contributions to *Ibdāʿ* by Palestinians help throw into relief the critical posturings of Egyptian intellectuals and academics. The difference between the Palestinian and Egyptian critical positions illustrates that the various forms of the normalization debate just discussed are based on culturally negotiated terms relevant specifically to Egyptian-Israeli relations. Unlike the vigilant separation between criticism and the political debates over normalization characteristic of Egyptian academic writing, the Palestinian contributions to *Ibdāʿ* integrate their political ideologies and their critical positions.

For example, in both the essay by Aḥmad Shāhīn, "The Contemporary Israeli Novel" (February 1995, pp. 13–22) and his translation of Frank's introduction to an anthology of modern Hebrew literature (January 1995, pp. 49–56), the critical object becomes subservient to the writer's political goals. For example, without indicating any changes in the text, Shāhīn selectively translates portions of Frank's introduction to *Modern Hebrew Literature*. The sections that appear in the following excerpt in bold were left out of the Arabic translation:

> The Liberation [War] Generation, as they were called, had either been born in Palestine, **now renamed Israel**, or had come there at a very young age, **to all intents and purposes they were *tsabras* (natives). They had all participated in the Liberation War, so that their love of the land was of immediate, first-hand nature.** Many of them had lived in kibbutzim.[31]

The translator's exclusion of Frank's distinction in the relationship to the land in this excerpt renders his definition of the generation ineffectual. Needless to say, Frank clearly betrays his own ideological sympathies in this passage—rhetoric one would expect the Arab reader to recognize because of its distinct contrast to the prevailing public discourse. However, this example demonstrates the translator's shaping of the object of study to meet his politically informed critical needs.

Two other articles written by Palestinians come out in favor of intercultural contact. Kamal Boullata, a Palestinian artist living in the United States at the time, describes trends in the development of Israeli and Palestinian art.[32] He frames his article with a description of acts of solidarity by Israeli-Jewish artists with their Palestinian peers during the early years of the Intifada. He closes his article on a very hopeful note, encouraging future joint projects such as a memorial erected by an Israeli artist and a Palestinian artist to commemorate six Palestinians killed on "Land Day" (1976) in the village of Sakhneen.

Ghānim Mazʿal of al-Najāḥ University in Nablus writes on Israeli protest poetry and on the history of attempts to sustain dialogue between Israeli and Palestinian writers and intellectuals. In closing "The Palestinian-Israeli Encounter and the Role of Hebrew Protest Poetry" (January 1995, 96–100), he takes a very clear stand in favor of contact between the cultures:

> The question here is: can literature and literati fill the role which politicians have failed [to play]? We do not posit that literature or writers have a magic formula that will solve the Arab-Israeli conflict. However, there is no doubt that writers

and literature are able to participate in one form or another in this arena. . . . Indeed, knowledge of the other side oftentimes fosters understanding of the rights of others. From this we can assert that proper cultural contact can assist in locating proper political solutions.

These Palestinian critics have negotiated discursive spaces different from those available to Egyptian academics and intellectuals—spaces that permit them to wed literary criticism with the terms of the political public debate.

As we have seen, Egyptian scholars of Hebrew effectively distance themselves from the position of anti-normalization advocates. The work of these academics as presented to the public in the three special issues of *Ibdā^c* not only fills in gaps in the public knowledge of the "other," but also provides a discursive reprieve from the contentious public debate.

Notes

1. Journalistic usage has created some confusion in Modern Standard Arabic over the word *da^cāwa,"* translated here as "propaganda." Spelled as it is in the title with an *alef maqsurah* rather than with a *tā marbūṭah*, the phrase should perhaps read "calls for normalization" rather than "propaganda of normalization." In his recent review of the journals, Sasson Somekh draws out the conflicting interpretations. However, he determines that even when translated as "calls for normalization," *da^cāwa* generally carries negative connotations. S. Somekh, "Normalization and What Is Not Normal: Israeli Culture through Egyptian Eyes," *Alpāyim* 16 (1998), 161. (Hebrew) When I informally circulated a volume of the journal among educated Egyptians who represent the target readership of the journal, they all independently read the title as "the propaganda of normalization." As I demonstrate in the next section, the editor of the journal explicitly states and reiterates his anti-normalization stance, thereby encouraging the translation of *"da^cāwa"* as "propaganda." One wonders, however, whether such ambiguity may not have been intentional.

2. Reference to the special issues of the journal will be denoted parenthetically in the text that follows by month and page numbers.

3. For a contemporary proponent of this notion, see A. B. Yehoshua, *Between Right and Right* (New York: Doubleday, 1981).

4. See, for example, Mohammed Hasanain Haykal, *Autumn of Fury: The Assassination of Sadat* (New York: Random, 1983); and Ghali Shukri,

Egypt, Portrait of a President 1971–1981: The Counter Revolution in Egypt, Sadat's Road to Jerusalem (London: Zed, 1981).

5. On the platform of the candidates see Wā'il ʿAbd al-Fattāḥ, "The Operation to Free the Writer's Union," *Rose al-Yūsef,* 31 March 1997, pp. 20–21. (Arabic) Information on the goals of the new board and the implications of the elections are from Baha' Ṭāhir, interview with author, 16 May 1997; Ibrāhīm Aṣlān, interview with author, 31 May 1997.

6. Other such Arabic journals include *ʿĀlam al-Kitāb* (1984) and *al-Qāhirah* (1985).

7. *Riḥlah Ila Isrā'īl,* Cairo: Dar Akhbār al-Yom, 1994. (Arabic)

8. For example, see the special file of twenty-one "anti-normalization" articles by high-profile Egyptian intellectuals in the independently published literary and cultural journal *al-Kitāba al-Ukhra*, 9, October 1994. (Arabic)

9. al-Shāmī, interview with author, 26 May 1997.

10. Lois Aroian, *The Nationalization of Arabic and Islamic Education in Egypt: Dar al-Ulum and Al-Azhar*, Cairo Papers in Social Science (Cairo: American University Press, 1983) 6:4.

11. Cited in Donald Malcolm Reid, *Cairo University and the Making of Modern Egypt* (Cambridge: Cambridge University Press, 1990), 78.

12. For a comprehensive study of Cairo University and of its role in recent history, see ibid. For details about Middle Eastern studies, refer to Al-Sibāʿī Muḥammad al-Sibāʿī, "Fifty Years of Middle Eastern Studies (Generation of Founders)," *Risālat al-Mashriq* (December 1993), 10. (Arabic) For a survey of more recent developments in Hebrew studies see Rashād al-Shāmī , Introduction to the papers of a symposium "Arabic Influences on the Hebrew Language, Religious Thought and Hebrew Literature Throughout the Ages," 26–28 December 1992, ʿAin Shams University, Faculty of Letters, Department of Hebrew Language and Literature. (Cairo: Dar al-Zahrah lil-Nashr, 1993), 9–10. (Arabic).

13. Reprint (Cairo: General Egyptian Book Organization, 1993), I: 216.

14. Aroian, *Nationalization of Arabic and Islamic Education*, 61; Reid, *Cairo University*, 154.

15. Wolfenson used semiticized versions of his name, Abū Dhu'ayb in Arabic and Ben Ze'ev in Hebrew. For a brief biography of Wolfenson, see Maḥmūd ʿAbbāsi's introduction to Ben Ze'ev, *Kaʿb al-Aḥbār: Jews and Judaism in the Islamic Tradition* (Jerusalem: Maṭbaʿat al-Sharq al-Taʿawuniyyah, 1976), 10–11. (Arabic).

16. Statistics valid through 1995. See ʿAin Shams, College of Arts, *Guide to Advanced Studies and Defended Theses from 1952 to February 1995*, 89–92; Cairo University, College of Arts, *Guide to University Theses*

Accepted by the College of Arts Since Its Founding to the End of 1995, I: 117–20. The other 46% of theses and dissertations covered topics in ancient or medieval Hebrew literature, language, and linguistics, or religion and Jewish thought. Through 1995 the two universities had awarded a total of thirty-eight Master's degrees and twenty-seven Ph.D.s in Hebrew studies.

17. Interview with author, 26 May 1997.

18. al-Shāmī, introduction to "Arabic Influences." This assumption is problematic on several levels. First, it overstates the relationship between institutions and literary development. Also it implies the uniform endorsement of the cultural platform at the Congress, despite evidence to the contrary. Additionally it assumes that neither institutions and prevailing ideologies nor writers' relationships to them have changed. For an in-depth discussion of the debates over culture within the Zionist movement from 1897 to 1903, see Shmuel Almog, *Zionism and History: The Rise of a New Jewish Consciousness* (Jerusalem: Magnes Press, 1987).

19. The stories translated from Hebrew are Nissim Dayan, "Qantara," *Keshet* 11 (Winter 1969), 82–86; Dror Green, "Hasan the Pilot," in his *Tales of the Intifada* (Jerusalem: Eikhut, 1989), 105–110 (Hebrew); Yoram Kaniuk, "Perets versus the State of Israel," in *Stories from Sofshavuʿa*, (Tel Aviv: Ma'ariv, 1986), 73–78 (Hebrew); and Yitzḥāk Orpāz, "On the Edge of a Bullet," in *Wild Grass* (Tel Aviv: ha-Kibbūtz ha-Meuchad, 1979), 59–69. (Hebrew)

20. Jamāl al-Rifāʿi, interview with author, 23 February 1997.

21. In general, the Israeli press portrayed Green as eccentric. His choice to self-publish caused some critics to doubt the literary merit of the work. In the course of the polemic, Green openly admitted that he had minimal contact with Palestinians and had not been to the Territories. See the interview by Liki Aginski, "The Small Leaves Have a Glass Eye," *Ḥadashot* (supplement), 3 May 1989, 12–13; Raḥel Ross, "The Embryo that Grew in a Jar of Salt Water," *Yerushalayim*, 24 March 1989; "Once There Was an Intifada," *Kol ha-ʿIr*, 24 March 1989; Roni Lipshitz, "Milmulīm," *Yerushalayim*, 28 April 1989, 22; and Amnon Raz, "Looking for the Anima," *ha-Aretz*, 28 July 1989, p. B9—all cited articles are in Hebrew.

22. Prof. Sasson Somekh's initial reaction to the first special issue of *Ibdāʿ* suggests that *Iton 77*, which has been an important vehicle for the translation of short pieces from Arabic as well as from other languages, should perhaps consider dedicating three of its future issues to Arabic literature. "What Isn't Normal" *Iton 77*, no.182 (March 1995), 2. (Hebrew) See also Ḥannah ʿAmīt-Kokhavi, "A Bridge Over Troubled Water: A Look at the Translation of Modern Arabic Literature into Hebrew," *Language International* 5:2 (1993), 12–13, which shows the very minor position that translations from Arabic have occupied in Israeli Hebrew culture.

23. See Natan Zach, "Reflections on Alterman's Poetry," ᶜAkhshāv 3–4 (1959), 109–22. (Hebrew)

24. Gershon Shaked, *Hebrew Fiction 1880–1980*, vols. 1–4 (Tel Aviv: ha-Kibbutz ha-Meuchad and Keter, 1977–1993) (Hebrew); and *A New Wave in Hebrew Fiction* (Jerusalem: Sifriyat ha-Poᶜalīm, 1971). (Hebrew)

25. *Hebrew Fiction 1880–1980*, III: 248–49.

26. Menachem Perry, "The Israeli-Palestinian Conflict as a Metaphor in Recent Israeli Fiction," *Poetics Today* 7:4 (1986), 609–19; translated in *Ibdāᶜ*, February 1995, pp. 61–73.

27. al-Shāmī, introduction to "Arabic Influences," 9–10.

28. Barry Chamish, "Sex, Religion and Satire in the Israeli Cinema: Black Banana," *Cineaste* 11:4 (1982), 27; translated in *Ibdāᶜ*, March 1995, pp. 137–40.

29. Bernhard Frank, introduction to *Modern Hebrew Poetry* (Iowa City: University of Iowa, 1980), xxiv; translated in *Ibdāᶜ*, January 1995, pp. 49–56.

30. Rifᶜat described his education in general and the article in particular in an interview with the author, 24 May 1997.

31. Frank, introduction to *Modern Hebrew Poetry*, xxxii; *Ibdāᶜ*, January 1995, p. 50.

32. "Facing the Forest: Israeli and Palestinian Artists," *Third Text* (Summer 1989), 77–91; *Ibdāᶜ*, January 1995, pp. 110–22.

15. Arab-Israeli Economic Relations and Relative Gains Concerns

Maen F. Nsour

This essay considers recent Arab analyses of the economic and political impact on the Arab states of an impetuous progression toward normal economic relations with Israel before reaching a comprehensive political settlement and ridding the region of the military buildup that threatens the national security of all states in the region. In contrast to the common expectation that regional economic relations will contribute to, and be reinforced by, the "peace process" (reflecting mainly the liberal approach to international relations), the author situates the works under review within a post-Madrid "alarmist" literature (reflecting the realist school of thought) which warns that economic relations with Israel under the current political, economic, and military asymmetries will foster Israeli economic and political hegemony over the Arab world.

Abdel-Fadil, Mahmoud, "Plans for the Middle Eastern Economic Arrangements: Prospects, Threats, and Methods of Confrontation," in Center for Arab Unity Studies, *The New Middle Eastern Challenges and the Arab World*, Beirut: Center for Arab Unity Studies, 1994, 127–66. (Arabic)

Abdullah, Ramadan, "Terminating the Arab Embargo on Israel: The Economic Consequences of the Settlement Process," *Qira'at Siyasiyah* 1:1 (Winter 1992), 160–67; and 1:2 (Spring 1992), 131–47. (Arabic)

Hilal, Jamil, *Israeli Economic Strategy for the Middle East*, Beirut: Institute for Palestine Studies, 1995. (Arabic)

Naqib, Fadle, *The Israeli Economy Within the Zionist Project*, Beirut: Institute for Palestine Studies, 1995. (Arabic)

Saba, Elias, "The Economic Aspects of the New Middle Eastern Challenges," in Center for Arab Unity Studies, *The New Middle Eastern Challenges and the Arab World*, Beirut: Center for Arab Unity Studies, 1994, 167–83. (Arabic)

Salamé, Ghassan, "Preliminary Views on the Middle Eastern Market," in Center for Arab Unity Studies, *The New Middle Eastern Challenges and the Arab World*, Beirut: Center for Arab Unity Studies, 1994, 32–58. (Arabic)

Introduction

*I*n the aftermath of the autumn 1991 Madrid Peace Conference, much of the literature on Middle East peace has propagated the notion that economic interdependence between Israel and the Arab states can enhance the economic welfare of states in the region, and at the same time reduce incentives to resort to force against one another to settle disputes. Interdependence and gains from economic relations, according to this line of thought, are the recipe for tranquillity in this beleaguered region. This argument finds its basis in Western Europe's evolution from a region of deadly conflicts to a zone of peaceful regional integration through the European Union. However, much of the literature in the Arab world, including the works reviewed in this essay, runs against the conventional wisdom in the "economics-of-peace" literature. These authors argue that Israel will attain higher relative gains as a result of economic cooperation with the Arab states, which it can easily use to achieve further economic and military supremacy, to intimidate its rivals, and thus to influence their political and economic policies. Israel's perpetual quest for national security has encouraged the development of an economy at the service of its military. Many Arabs perceive economic relations with Israel as an unwise and self-destructive policy, even if they realize some absolute gains. What counts most in this case of acute asymmetry and latent hostilities is *relative gains:* who is benefiting more, and what those who achieve higher relative gains will do with them.

If the final settlements between Israel and the Arab states reflect the severe imbalance in political, military, and economic capabilities, then relative gains will continue to be a major concern and economic relations will continue to suffer. (see tables 1 and 2 for comparative economic and military indicators.) Regional security and the Arab world's economic welfare, prosperity, and political stability, according to these authors, will be achieved not through economic cooperation with Israel, but by concentrating on their collective internal political and economic policies that invigorate democracy and economic efficiency, thus achieving equity and social welfare. Arriving at an acceptable comprehensive political settlement that leads to mutual confidence between the Arab states and Israel is seen as an essential prerequisite for any economic cooperation scheme in the Middle East. However, more often than not, these authors express skepticism about the possibility of reaching what a number of them have called "a fair settlement acceptable to the future Arab generations" under prevailing global and regional conditions.

Economics and Peace

Ever since Israel and Egypt signed a peace treaty in 1979, a wave of literature has emerged highlighting the "miraculous" impact of Arab-Israeli economic cooperation on prosperity, peace, and tranquillity in the region.[1] The Arab-Israeli conflict reached another milestone with the convening of the Madrid Peace Conference in October 1991, with its underlying assumption that promoting regional economic cooperation and integration could act as a strong foundation for peace and security in the Middle East.[2] Armand Hammer captures the gist of the Arab-Israeli "economics-of-peace" literature when he says:

> [E]conomic relations can contribute immeasurably and uniquely to the creation of peace among nations.... Equitable and mutually beneficial economic relations can bind nations together, creating conditions in which erstwhile enemies recognize a shared interest in the establishment and maintenance of peace.... The Middle East today stands to benefit from these peace-promoting functions of economics. In an area where binding ties are few, the most likely path to peace may be through shared economic interests.[3]

Table 1
Basic Economic Indicators for Selected Arab Countries and Israel—1995

	Population (millions)	GDP (million $)	GNP per capita ($)	Growth Rate (%)	Inflation Rate (%)	Trade (% of GDP)	GDP Average Annual Growth Rate (1990–1995)	Total Exports of Goods, Services, and Income (million $)	Total Imports of Goods, Services, and Income (million $)	Average Annual Growth Rate (%) of Exports of Goods and Services (1990–1995)	Total External Debt (million $)
Egypt	57.8	47,349	750	4.4	8.3	54	1.3	11,337	17,353	4.2	34,116
Jordan	4.2	6,105	1,510	6.3	2.3	121	8.2	3,606	5,200	8.2	7,944
Lebanon	4.0	11,143	2,660	6.0[a]	11.0[a]	70	—[b]	1,512	6,953	—[b]	2,966
Morocco	26.6	32,412	1,110	−5.5	6.1	62	1.2	9,118	12,900	3.1	22,147
Saudi Arabia	19.0	125,501	7,040	2.3	4.9	70	1.7	55,091	45,583	—[b]	16,600
Syria	14.1	16,783	1,120	4.0	13.0	..[b]	7.4	5,929	6,406	..[b]	21,318
Israel	5.5	91,965	15,920	6.9	10.1	69	6.4	28,659	39,750	9.5	45,000

Sources: World Bank, *World Development Report 1997: The State in a Changing World* (New York: Oxford University Press and the International Institute for Strategic Studies, 1996); *The Military Balance 1996/1997* (London: Oxford University Press, 1996).
[a] Estimates.
[b] Data unavailable

Table 2
Military Indicators for Selected Arab and Middle Eastern Countries

	Total Armed Forces 1995	Defense Expenditures 1994 (Billion $)	Defense Expenditures 1995 (Billion $)	Defense Budget 1996 (Billion $)	Defense Budget 1997 (Billion $)	Defense Percentage of Total Expenditure (%) 1995
Egypt	440,000	2.200[a]	2.400[a]	2.400[a]	—[b]	8.7
Iraq	382,500	2.700[a]	2.700[a]	—	—[b]	—[b]
Jordan	98,650[a]	0.433	0.440	0.537	—[b]	20.7
Lebanon	48,900	0.363	0.407	0.455	—[b]	—[b]
Libya	65,000	1.400[a]	1.400[a]	1.400[a]	—[b]	—[b]
Morocco	194,000	1.200[a]	1.300[a]	1.300[a]	—[b]	—[b]
Saudi Arabia	105,500	14.300	13.200	13.900[a]	—[b]	—[b]
Syria	421,000	2.100[a]	2.000[a]	1.800[a]	—[b]	28.2
Iran	345,000	2.300	2.500	3.400	—[b]	—[b]
Turkey	639,000	5.300	6.000	5.700	6.8	15.8
Israel	175,000	6.700	7.200	7.000	7.0	19.4

Sources: World Bank, *World Development Report 1997: The State in a Changing World* (New York: Oxford University Press and the International Institute for Strategic Studies, 1996); *The Military Balance 1996/1997* (London: Oxford University Press, 1996).

[a] Estimates
[b] Data unavailable

But this logic did not go unchallenged. An alarmist literature in the Arab world accompanied and followed the Madrid Conference, focusing on how Israel, which has the most advanced economy in the region, is poised to impose economic hegemony over the Arab states and thus maintain its political and military dominance.[4]

While the potential benefits of economic cooperation between the Arab states and Israel have been widely discussed, many of its attendant problems have not been adequately recognized in the Middle East "economics-of-peace" literature. Economic relations between Israel and its Arab neighbors and the possible associated compromise of national control over domestic economic activity lend an enormously important strategic dimension to economic relations between the Arab states and Israel, and to security arrangements in the Middle East in general. If a state or group of states allows its economic welfare to rest in the hands of foreign powers, its security position can be tremendously jeopardized. Alternatively, a state's national security is advanced to the degree it dominates economic forces in other countries while maintaining adequate control over its own economy—a basic tenet of the "realist school" of international relations, to which much of the Arabic scholarly literature on Middle Eastern regional cooperation closely adheres.

The Arab-Israeli conflict has already witnessed the strategic utilization of economic power; if normal economic relations unfold between the Arab states and Israel, attempts to manipulate these economic ties will undoubtedly intensify.

Concerns about Relative Gains in Regional Economic Relations

There has always been an intense theoretical debate on the relationship between security and economics between the two major schools of international relations, realism and liberal-institutionalism. The realist school emphasizes that political power, and hence security, are closely linked to the state's economic strength. Therefore, when a nation's security matters increase in importance, the relative standing of its economic strength becomes equally important. Kenneth Waltz speaks for this strain of realist thought when he says:

> When faced with the possibility of cooperating for mutual gain, states that feel insecure must ask how the gain will be divided. They are compelled to ask not "will both of us gain?"

but "Who will gain more?" If an expected gain is to be divided, say, in the ratio of two to one, one state may use its disproportionate gain to implement a policy intended to damage or destroy the other. Even the prospect of large absolute gains for both parties does not elicit their cooperation so long as each fears how the other will use its increased capabilities.[5]

Arab suspicions regarding Israel's intentions generate a deep feeling of insecurity. In "Preliminary Views on the Middle Eastern Market," Ghassan Salamé, professor of political science at the Institute of Political Science in Paris, speaks of five premonitions that currently dominate the Arabs' thinking on the subject. The first is the appending premonition (*hajis al-ilhaq*) under which Palestine and Jordan are gradually removed from the Arab sphere and constrained in a special partnership with Israel, which will firmly dominate their economies and use them as a bridge to the vast Arab markets. Israel has hindered the rise of a meaningful manufacturing sector in the West Bank and the Gaza Strip that can compete with the Israeli industrial sector, and has therefore maintained a captive market to which it exports around a billion dollars worth of products every year. Israel would not be willing to forsake this market; in fact, there are indications, according to Salamé, that it intends to make the Jordanian market captive as well. For example, Israeli exporters forcefully advocate the removal of customs duties on all goods traded among the three parties, except on agricultural products in which the Jordanians and the Palestinians enjoy a cost advantage. Israel's exporters also support the introduction of a sales tax on Jordanian and Palestinian products. Furthermore, Salamé points out that Israel suddenly has become interested in the welfare and well-being of Palestinian laborers, calling for the introduction of comprehensive welfare and health insurance schemes. This issue had never arisen prior to the establishment of the Palestinian Authority, but now it is seen as a way to raise the cost of Palestinian products and thus to reduce their ability to compete with the Israeli goods (pp. 33–38).

The second is the penetration premonition (*hajis al-ikhtirak*) in the Arab world. For Salamé, the World Bank's *Mid-East Peace Talks, Regional Cooperation and Economic Development*[6] is standing proof of malevolent intentions behind the promotion of regional projects such as roads, harbors, airports, and oil and gas pipelines, from which Israel will be the ultimate beneficiary transforming it into an indispensable hub for all regional economic activity (pp. 38–40).

The third premonition is that of strangulation (*hajis al-ikhtinaq*), whose argument is that political and economic arrangements in the region will eventually expand to include countries such as Turkey, Iran, Ethiopia, and Eritrea, creating a belt of non-Arab-League nations that have as a common denominator a certain degree of hostility to the Arabs. The new arrangements, according to Salamé, will constitute a siege under which the Arab League will be dismantled or significantly weakened, giving way to new regional organizations in which the Arabs have marginal influence (pp. 40–42).

Fourth, a suppression premonition (*hajis al-insihaq*) infuses Arab perceptions of vigorous Israeli indulgence not only in further enhancing its overwhelming military capabilities but also in accumulating all kinds of weapons of mass destruction, including nuclear arms. Therefore, the nuclear deterrence afforded by Israel and the gross imbalance in conventional military capabilities allow Israel wider margins in conducting its foreign policy vis-à-vis the conflict with the Arab world, including the threat or use of force. Moreover, the technological gap between the Arab world and Israel is wide, with no signs of a genuine Israeli willingness to transfer technology even to Arab neighbors with which Israel has peace treaties. Salamé sees a correlation between the persisting imbalance in military and technological capabilities and the rise of the "Middle Eastern market"; Israel will resort to calculated transfers of advanced technology and limited sales of military goods to some Arab countries for policies perceived to be compatible with Israel's national interests. Israel will gradually turn from being the focus of Arab apprehension to serving as a referee in their internal disputes, castigating "undisciplined" states and rewarding others for positions and policies it perceives as favorable (pp. 42–46).

The fifth is the cleavage premonition (*hajis al-inshiqaq*). There has always been a fundamental difference between Arab and Western strategists in defining the Arab Middle East. Arabs rely on a common history and culture as the foundation for an Arab nation, while the West focuses on geography and strategic considerations in defining a "Middle East" in which individual Arab states exist alongside their non-Arab neighbors. To Salamé, pan-Arabism is a worthy political and civilizational worldview, while the other is nothing but a set of arrangements that will lead to further fragmentation and division in the Arab world. Although the author sees no real prospects for upholding the Arab economic boycott of Israel, he calls for adherence to Arab nationalism while, at the same time, following a realistic path in dealing with the unfavorable circumstances by which Israel maintains superiority and pushes for unacceptable political solutions and a set of economic arrangements which, from the Arab perspective, are potentially counterproductive in the long run (pp. 46–47). Salamé forcefully advocates that

> Arabs should relinquish fighting geography with ideology. On the contrary, they must arrive at a certain balance between the two. While the final decision on taking a position regarding the "Middle East market" should be left up to the Arab states adjacent to Israel, it is the responsibility of the rest of the Arab states not to undertake any action that might create additional pressures on the Arabs directly involved in negotiating a political settlement; they should not call for an end to the Arab boycott, they should refrain from rushing to normalization, they should not attempt to play a reconciliatory role between Israel and the "confrontation states." (p. 50)

In his two-part article entitled, "Terminating the Arab Embargo on Israel: The Economic Consequences of the Settlement Process," Ramadan Abdullah, an economics professor at the Islamic University in Gaza, examines the accuracy of the argument that unprecedented regional prosperity will result from closer Arab-Israeli economic relations and studiously discusses the economic and political effects of terminating the Arab boycott on Israel. On the economic front, Abdullah argues that bringing the boycott to an end will have the following impacts:

- *Various sectors of the Israeli economy will experience a huge flow of foreign capital and technology transfers.* This flow will enable the Israeli economy to accommodate further waves of Jewish immigrants, many of whom will probably settle in Arab land occupied during the 1967 war. Newly injected capital and know-how will have a positive effect on Israel's trade balance, balance of payments, and debt burden.
- *Israeli penetration of the huge Arab market and development of commercial relations in which the balance of trade between the Arab countries and Israel will be to the latter's advantage.* Market penetration can lead to the disappearance of infant high-tech, high-value-added Arab industries, and a threat to established industries due to imminent

Israeli dumping and fierce competition. This penetration will help Israel in revitalizing its private sector. Israeli companies will gain negotiating advantage with foreign companies, and the economy's efficiency will be enhanced, thus allowing the diversion of more resources to the military establishment. Furthermore, Israel's produce will make its way into the Arab markets, eventually leading to the growth of a more diversified agricultural sector. A further growth of this sector will give Israel an increased incentive to solve its water problems at the expense of neighboring Arab states that are also suffering from water shortages.

- *Arab labor will not benefit from the termination of the boycott.* First, Jewish immigration, especially from the former Soviet Union, has saturated the labor market in Israel with both skilled and unskilled labor. This demographic shift, together with the tremendous security complications that will result from integrating more Arab labor in the Israeli economy will act as serious hurdles to reducing unemployment in Arab countries (Winter 1992, pp. 160–67; Spring 1992, pp. 131–47).

According to Abdullah, the call to terminate the boycott on Israel and to settle for an Israeli-dictated political and economic arrangement has strategic, political, cultural, social, historical, and civilizational implications that surmount in their importance any economic or commercial considerations (p. 147). Ideological and historical considerations have always had a significant influence on the ways in which Israeli leaders conduct the conflict with the Arab states. Economic normalization will mandate that the Arabs abandon their own ideological and historical imperatives, which will deepen the persisting imbalance of power to Israel's advantage. Termination of the boycott would not reflect any real need on the Arab side but rather an economic retreat in keeping with similar retreats on the political and military fronts under an increasingly unfavorable balance of power in the region. Cultural normalization will follow, changing once and for all the general perception of Israel in the Arab world. For Abdullah, this will create the appropriate circumstances for further political, economic, and cultural penetrations (pp. 147–53).

Jamil Hilal, a sociologist by training, active in Palestinian politics, notes in his *Israeli Economic Strategy for the Middle East* that the "shallow understanding of the West European experience" that dominates the discourse in the literature on Mideast peace that argues that tightly intertwined economic relations between Israel and the Arab states will bring about economic prosperity and regional security, had a brief tranquilizing effect on the Arab masses (pp. 4–5). But the anticipated economic prosperity did not materialize; in fact, economic failures are still common features throughout the region, especially within the Palestinian entity. The marketing of the peace agreements and accords as miracles that will bring about prosperity, welfare, and stability in the region and that will eliminate all chronic problems in the Arab world soon appeared to the Arab masses as nothing but a mirage. Like many strategists and political economists in the Arab world, Hilal maintains that the roots of the economic and social problems lie elsewhere, and that even a just and reciprocal peace can be, at best, a palliative for these problems (p. 7). According to Hilal, the Arab fear of Israeli economic hegemony will hinder the establishment of a Middle Eastern common market (p. 30).

In *The Israeli Economy Within the Zionist Project,* Fadle Naqib, professor of economics at the University of Waterloo in Canada, argues that economic normalization in Arab-Israeli relations will not lead to beneficial cooperation, but will rebound solely to Israel's advantage— and to the disadvantage of Arab strategic interests. He reports a deep belief among the vast majority of Arabs that Israel's motivation for cooperation is economic expansion, which will fuel her geographic and demographic expansionism as well (pp. 2, 4). However, the author falls short (as does Abdullah) in not responding to some sophisticated arguments in favor of free trade between Israel and its economically less-developed neighbors based on neoclassical international trade theory which, in turn, has the principle of comparative advantage at its core. In short, neoclassical literature suggests that a country can gain from free trade as long as the relative cost of goods in some other country (or countries) is different from that which would be in the domestic market in the absence of free trade. The smaller the country the greater the potential gains. Perhaps, for Naqib (and for Abdullah), political arguments based on realism are sufficient to support their positions against economic normalization with Israel.

In "Plans for the Middle Eastern Economic Arrangements: Prospects, Threats, and Methods of Confrontation," Mahmoud Abdel-Fadil, professor of economics at Cairo University, argues that there seem to be intense, orchestrated efforts to put pressure on the Arab countries to abandon the economic boycott of Israel, despite the fact that "a comprehensive and just settlement for the Arab-Israeli conflict has not been reached" (p. 154). He argues that the boycott should not be looked at from a purely economic perspective, in which only the gains from trade are considered. According to Abdel-Fadil, this would be a gross oversimplification and an unwarranted underestimation of the Arab mind and sensitivities. The economic boycott was devised not only to inflict damage on the Israeli economy, but also as an effective symbolic weapon in a conflict rife with symbolism. In Abdel-Fadil's view, reciprocal compromise should be at the core of the Arab negotiation strategy; relaxation of the Arab economic boycott should occur in proportion to the speed with which Israel moves toward an acceptable final settlement to the conflict—not one that is prompted merely by the current global and regional imbalance of power which favors Israel (ibid.)

In "The Economic Aspects of the New Middle Eastern Challenges," Elias Saba, a former minister of economics in Lebanon, proclaims that Israel has opted for a political settlement because it realizes that the new global and regional balances of power are conducive to a conclusion to the conflict that meets its requirements, especially in bringing the economic boycott to an end and reaching a complete political normalization with the Arab states. In the "New Middle East," Israel will be the focal point, assisted by the Palestinians, without whom Israel cannot engage the Arab countries' economies. Jordan and Egypt will play a pivotal role. Jordan will become Israel's economic gate to Iraq and the Gulf states, while Egypt will serve as its gateway to the markets of North Africa. "The new regional regime will become the latest imperialist offense on the Arab world's human and material resources and potentials. The immediate outcome will be an integration of the Arab economies with that of Israel and in such a way that will serve the latter's interests" (pp. 171, 175). The expected loss of economic sovereignty will inevitably lead to a loss of political sovereignty. Saba argues that the most important leverage Arabs have in their negotiations with Israel is economic. Therefore, proper use of the economic weapon is necessary for reaching an acceptable comprehensive political settlement. As long as negotiations are underway and a final settlement has not been reached, Saba advocates the position that the Arabs should maintain the economic boycott. He then concludes: "In addition to the continuation of the boycott and the stringency in adhering to its clauses and conditions, we see it as our duty to come up with innovative means and mechanisms to halt normalization in the shadow of a partial Arab-Israeli settlement" (p. 179).

"Realists" versus "Liberal-Institutionalists"

Realist theory argues, that under conditions of international anarchy, states are sometimes reluctant to cooperate even when they have shared interests, and that international institutions are incapable of promoting international cooperation.[7] This proposition is eloquently stated by Kenneth Waltz in his celebrated work *Man, the State, and War: A Theoretical Analysis:*

> To achieve a favorable outcome from [any possible] conflict a state has to rely on its own devices, the relative efficiency of which must be its constant concern. . . . In anarchy there is no automatic harmony. . . . Because each state is the final judge of its own cause, any state may at any time use force to implement its policies. Because any state may at any time use force, all states must constantly be ready either to counter force with force or to pay the cost of weakness. The requirements of state action are, in this view, imposed by the circumstances in which all states exist.[8]

Realism recognizes the fact that states strive to maximize their survival and independence and therefore guard their position vigilantly in the system of world politics, most notably through achieving high relative gains. If a state has the slightest notion that its partner in any cooperative arrangement is a potential threat, concerns over relative gains determine whether that state will continue such cooperation. In other words, a state will sacrifice its absolute gains in a cooperative venture if its partner-state—and potential future foe—reaps higher relative gains. Survival and independence predominate states' priorities, and can be preserved by sustaining high relative capabilities. When states experience deteriorating relative capabilities they recognize that their own existence could well be on the line; hence, the seemingly exaggerated reactions by states scoring modestly on the relative-capabilities scale, especially if they are surrounded by hostile actors. Economic, military, and political resources are decisive in a state's ability to influence policy decisions of other states and, at the same time, to keep their own course of action unencumbered. Therefore, when states interact with a threatening partner, they forgo individual absolute gains, irrespective of the distribution of the relative gains, and astutely act as defensive positionalists.[9]

Conversely, liberal institutionalists argue that the role that conflict plays in realist reasoning is significantly inflated, while the potential impact that international institutions can have on cooperation is unduly discounted. Liberals maintain that assuming anarchy does, in fact, have an inhibiting effect on cooperation, institutions can play a remedial role in states' tendency to forge cooperative schemes in an effort to advance their national interests. However, the difference between the two schools appears to be irreconcilable, with the realist position stating that in an anarchic world system states are primarily preoccupied with achieving higher relative gains, while liberal-institutionalists insist that states tend to maximize their absolute gains, even if this means that higher relative gains accrue to their partners as a result of cooperation.

Liberal theorists consider interdependence as a means by which security can be enhanced. They have carried out extensive modeling exercises to downplay the inhibiting role of relative-gains concerns on states' propensities to cooperate with each other. However, their assumptions have been largely unrealistic and consequently their scenarios have led to fallacious conclusions. Without exception, liberal scholars have had no choice but to concede the supremacy of the realist relative-gains-concerns argument once they introduce the facts of world politics into their working models.

In his attempt to investigate the impeding effect of relative gains concerns on trade, James Morrow accuses realists of ignoring the disadvantaged partner's option to arm itself as a response to perceived threats from its more advantaged trade partner.[10] Morrow contends that "[i]f a state does not spend its entire gain from trade on the military, it is better off with trade than without."[11] The main point in Morrow's argument is that if higher relative gains allow one state to spend more on its military forces, the other state can draw on its absolute gain to enhance its military capabilities and thus to reduce the threat of the partner. In this case, both trade partners emerge as winners, since a state spending only part of its gain from trade on its military could devote the rest to other sectors. However, for this argument to hold, each state must have the capability to manufacture arms.[12] Morrow himself lists three limitations to his assertion. First, the model regards military allocations not as flows but as stocks that depreciate to zero in every round. The model does not give any attention to timing and thus considers current military power an outcome of current military spending. Second, the model presumes that all parties function in an environment where complete information is available. Third, the model assumes that trading with a specific country will confer benefits; it ignores the possible existence of other trading partners with which a country could reap the benefits of a comparative advantage. Thus, we may conclude that the limitations of Morrow's model are sufficient to brand it as irrelevant to real-world politics.[13]

In a frequently cited article, Robert Powell assumes that states strive to maximize their overall economic welfare within the limitations brought about by an anarchic international system in which force is an option. Although Powell starts with liberal assumptions, his initial conclusions are in total congruence with the realist line of thought. When the use of force is inexpensive and a viable option, cooperative schemes that result in unequal absolute gains will not materialize, even though the states' preferences revolve around economic welfare through higher absolute gains. This outcome conforms with the expectations of realist theories. However, Powell argues, if the use of force is inconceivable due to its high cost, then cooperation can emerge in accordance with neoliberal institutionalist expectations. Thus the applicability of many aspects of neoliberal institutionalism and structural realism depend to a great extent on the special prevailing circumstances.[14] Powell correctly maintains that

> If the nature of military technology is such that one state can turn a relative gain to its advantage and the disadvantage of others, then these constraints will induce a concern for relative gains and this may impede cooperation absent any superior authority to ensure that these gains not be used in this way. . . . The prospects for cooperation are . . . sensitive to the costs of fighting.[15]

Duncan Snidal, author of some major works on relative-gains concerns, acknowledges that the relative-gains argument is significant in two- or few-actor situations—an unlikely real-world case—and, most importantly, when there exist serious asymmetries among a fairly large group of states.[16] "In this way the relative gains argument may find an important place in international relations theory."[17] He recognizes that some states pose a higher threat because of geopolitical reasons, "or because of their seemingly aggressive character or ideological differences or a history of grievances between the two states. Or a state may be inherently more threatening simply because it has greater capabilities."[18] Snidal concludes that unless cooperating countries enjoy ample symmetry, relative-gains concerns determine whether cooperation among them can be a favorable route.[19] For precisely the same reasons that Snidal and Powell report, the authors of the works under review argue that Israel should not be allowed to reap high relative gains as a result of economic normalization with the Arabs.

Some researchers have shown that, under a simulated integration arrangement involving highly asymmetric countries, faster growth takes place in the innovating economy with greater endowments of skilled and unskilled labor than in the non-innovative economy.[20] This is because when a "chronically non-innovative" country integrates with an industrially advanced one, the former will not be on an exact balanced-growth path, and an obvious migration of unskilled labor will take place into the advanced economy. Migration of unskilled labor can give rise to two main effects. First, there will be an increase in the marginal productivity of human capital in the advanced economy's manufacturing sector as a result of an increase in unskilled labor. Second, the demand for durable goods increases in the advanced economy as a direct impact of an increase in the unskilled labor. The solution is "to systematically encourage the flow of capital and technology from the more developed to the less developed economies."[21]

In the Arab-Israeli arena, however, we find Israel—after the commencement of the Madrid peace process in 1991—resorting to force against Lebanon and the Palestinians and hinting at the possible use of force against the Syrian military. Furthermore, Israel continues to maintain and enhance a military force equipped with both conventional and unconventional weaponry. Clearly, with several Arab parties, resort to force has modest costs for Israel. Even if Israel considers the use of force to be relatively costly, its military deterrence and the threat to act militarily give the country great flexibility in interacting with neighbors who cannot afford to utilize these instruments of foreign policy. This leads Naqib to argue that Arabs in general and Palestinians in particular are not so enthusiastic about the peace process because it involves major Arab concessions, despite the fact that Israel still occupies Arab land in Syria, Lebanon, and Palestine, has not yet recognized the rights of the Palestinian people, and constitutes a serious source of military threat to their security. Hence, he disagrees with the conclusions of the liberal advocates who believe that if citizens feel that the peace process has some positive impacts on their livelihood and welfare they will eventually accept it by virtue of their direct economic interests (p. 2). Relative gains are of absolute importance.

Although liberals imply that economic cooperation and a positive impact on their livelihood and welfare will lead individual Arabs and Arab governments to accept a politically compromised settlement with Israel, in fact the opposite is true: vigorous economic cooperation between Israel and the Arabs can only follow a political settlement that fully satisfies Arab demands for an Israeli withdrawal from occupied Arab land and the creation of a Palestinian state with Arab Jerusalem as its capital.

Increased economic relations enable Israel to strengthen its security position not only by accelerating its rate of economic growth but also by creating dependency relationships on the part of the Arab states through trade and investment ties.[22] Indeed, realism offers a more convincing explanation than liberalism of the effects of security concerns on cooperation among states and, consequently, the impact of concerns over relative gains on regional cooperation. In the absence of institutions capable of enforcing civility among states in the international arena, security and survival—a state's raison d'être—will always be the highest priorities.

Hilal maintains that the Israeli idea of a "new Middle East" is a settlement that would make Israel a regionally integrated state and a major decision-maker with regard to political and security matters (p. 46). He also argues that economic and security cooperation schemes and the creation of this "new Middle East" include a suppression of the principle of reciprocity in state relations and a unilateral perspective based on Israel's desire for regional acceptance without any real regard for the completely different needs and requirements of the Arab world. For example, the call for arms reduction and a halt to arms races is unconvincing in the shadow of Israel's nuclear dominance and its insistence on qualitative supremacy. Talk about "peace" is necessarily distorted in light of Israel's insistence on imposing its sovereignty over Arab Jerusalem, its rejection of an independent Palestinian state, its refusal to withdraw from the Golan Heights and South Lebanon, and in the shadow of a policy that encourages the addition and expansion of settlements in the West Bank and the Gaza Strip (p. 111).

In "Plans for the Middle Eastern Economic Arrangements: Prospects, Threats, and Methods of Confrontation," Abdel-Fadil asserts that an evaluation of the dividends of peace should not be an exclusively cost-benefit economic analysis without any consideration given to the historical, strategic, psychological, and cultural dimensions of the Arab-Israeli conflict. Abdel-Fadil argues that Israel is not like any other state that seeks economic partnership with Arab states. He maintains that it is a state with its own "project," and that there will always be sensitivities and complications of an historic, strategic, cultural, and psychological nature that make decisions to establish normal relations with it based on pure economic calculations inconsistent with Arab interests. Political and strategic considerations in this case should have precedence over purely economic considerations because, according to the author, the potential for Israeli economic and technological hegemony is high. Abdel-Fadil goes even further:

> "Peace" for Israel is the resumption of its war against the Arabs on economic, financial, technological, and cultural fronts. . . . [I]n the shadow of a new Middle East and the inequitable distribution of the dividends of peace, Israel could well become the focal point [of the economic activity] while the Arab countries will become the periphery in the absence of a collective Arab system that can preserve the minimum requirements for independent and balanced development. This is apart from the tremendous political losses that would materialize as an outcome of the dismantling of the Arab regime and the liquidation of its collective security. (p. 141)

Abdel-Fadil argues that a "new Middle East" must include free-trade arrangements with conditions that will improve the welfare of people in the region and promote the equitable distribution of benefits among the various participants. But there is no sufficient compatibility in the economic structures of Israel and its neighbors and there is no mechanism to reduce the negative impacts on the disadvantaged economies. In fact, the new politico-economic arrangements are part of an Israeli security scheme that would allow it to create "defensible dimensions" as opposed to "defensible borders," or, in other words, a web of tight political relations that ensures the suppression of any threat against which mere military capabilities will be incapable of defending. The new Israeli borders, according to this plan, will not be defined by geography, but by economics and politics. Put differently, Israel's security will be preserved by controlling politics and economics in neighboring countries. Surely the conventional conception, based on the understanding of preserving national security by defending geographic boundaries and the creation of "security belts," cannot be useful any more in the age of long-range ballistic missiles that can be mounted with conventional and unconventional warheads (pp. 145–46).

Do Institutions Matter?

The realist theory in international relations assumes that nation-states are involved in a struggle for power in a state of anarchy. This assumption leads to two major realist propositions concerning cooperation among nation-states. First, states are primarily concerned with amassing power and preserving their national security, the implication of which is the inevitability of competition and conflict. In other words, even if states' common interests can be realized, cooperation can be forsaken.

A second realist proposition is that international institutions cannot have a substantial effect in moderating anarchy's inhibiting effect on states' propensity to cooperate. In fact, institutions in a realist world are creations of the most powerful states, through which they maximize their power-based gains. In John Mearsheimer's words, international organizations "mirror the distribution of power in the system."[23]

Abdel-Fadil assumes that the establishment of two parallel routes in the Madrid Conference, namely, the bilateral and multilateral negotiating tracks, was meant to ensure that any minimal Israeli compromise on land or cosmetic relinquishment of direct control over Palestinians on the bilateral tracks would be reciprocated on the Arab side by yielding to new regional arrangements on the multilateral track. The multilateral negotiation mechanisms are designed to bring about a set of new institutions that will take the place of existing Arab institutions, and in which Israel will become a dominant actor. This, according to Abdel-Fadil, will turn the Arabs into a "cultural phenomenon" with no political or economic context. (pp. 146–47).

Liberals argue that, in the presence of international organizations, states should no longer fear for their security and that, therefore, there is no real reason to pursue a path of power acquisition. For Robert Keohane and Joseph Nye, international institutions "help set the international agenda, and act as catalysts for coalition-formation and as arenas for political initiatives and linkage by weak states,"[24] which annul the need for pursuing peace through the balance of power. However, Keohane and Martin acknowledge that "th[e] necessity for institutions does not mean that they are always valuable, much less that they operate without respect to power and interests, constitute a panacea for violent conflict, or always reduce the likelihood of war."[25]

The inadequacy of international organizations in maintaining world peace and the lack of a central authority capable of enforcing agreements make it crucial for states to fend for themselves and to strive to amass power in an arduous quest for prosperity and security. For a state to be powerful, or to continue to survive, possessing a strong economy—which is manifested by a relatively high GNP, advanced high-technology industries, and an abundance of human and natural resources—is inevitable.[26] Or, as Raymond Aron put it,

> [s]ecurity, in a world of autonomous political units, can be based either on the weakness of rivals (total or partial disarmament) or on force itself. If we suppose that security is the final goal of state policy, the effective means will be to establish a new relation of forces or to modify the old one so that potential enemies, by reason of their inferiority, will not be tempted to take the initiative of aggression.[27]

A strong economy is a vital element in a state's ability to defend itself and to pursue its national interests. The power of the state can be greatly enhanced through economic means. The doctrine of the relationship between a strong economy and state power relies on two basic principles. First, politics and commerce are the chief concerns of the state, and, second, the state should continuously attempt to maximize its external power.[28] The purpose of economic consolidation between politics and commerce is to fulfill the social and political gains linked with the unification of the economy and the state. The second, and far more important, principle is the indispensable role that economic factors play in significantly enhancing the power of the state. Fredrich List points out that "[t]he prosperity of a nation is not . . . greater in proportion in which it has amassed more wealth . . . but in the proportion in which it has more developed its power of production."[29]

The international position of the state compared to other states, especially its rivals, is the driving force behind the state's adoption and implementation of security-conscious policies. After all, a state's ability to establish and sustain an agile military force depends, to a great extent, on its continuous ability to divert adequate resources to such an endeavor. Military strength—in certain circumstances—is also a means by which the state can preserve its national wealth and prosperity. For some states, it is not mere strength that is sought but dominance over their potential military and political rivals. As the power of the state is measured by its relative standing in comparison to other states, a nation might enhance its power not only by expanding its own capabilities, but also by conspiring to weaken its potential enemies. Either course would improve its relative strategic standing among nations.[30]

Abdel-Fadil advances two options for a future Arab course. The first option is a "tactical retreat" with an intent to "reorganize" for a strategic leap. This option takes into consideration the difficulty of resisting the imposition of a "new Middle East" in the region under current regional and global circumstances and the appropriateness of serenely reorganizing the currently enfeebled Arab nation for a comeback under a favorable change in the global balance of power. However, Abdel-Fadil cautions that the extent of any tactical retreats should not be allowed to have a future negative impact on the strategic interests and objectives of the Arab states. He also draws attention to the adverse implications that a relatively long period of "tactical retreat" would have on the Arabs by creating new realities, new interests, and new alliances, which will eventually hinder their strategic goals (pp. 152).

A second option for the Arab states relies on the assumption that, under the current circumstances, a military encounter with rival powers is a kind of "national suicide," and this dictates strategic disengagement to save the nation's economic and military capabilities from destruction. However, this disengagement should be accompanied by serious efforts to acquire the essential elements for future reemergence as an independent and prosperous nation (pp. 152–53).

Conclusion

Once again, liberal optimism has receded in the wake of discordant realities in the Middle East; political realism can only console us with grievous rationalism. Winds of optimism originally blew out of research centers outside the Arab world, promising unprecedented economic welfare stimulated by free commerce and intense economic relations between Israel and the Arab states. The evolving economic order was expected to forge interest-based connections that no state could afford to ignore. In the "new Middle East," Israel would be the base of high-technology production and a financial-services center, while its Arab partners would be responsible for fostering the new arrangements with cheap labor and capital. To almost all Arab economists and strategic analysts, this utopian scenario, with all the "bounties" that it promises, does not meet the basic requirements of economic security and political independence.

Economic and financial capabilities are a paramount component of national power. To assert their prominence in the international system, nations frequently exploit their economic advantages in the diplomatic and military arenas.[31] Under crisis conditions, vulnerable states become targets of foreign economic coercion and their policies fall hostage to the dominant actors in the system. Once in a dominant position, states usually embrace economic coercion as an integral element of their foreign policy and grand strategy, thus jeopardizing the security and stability of the system simply because conflict escalation may well take place as a result of coercion through economic means. Economic sanctions against rival states can be significantly effective as conflict among states intensifies. However, the degree of effectiveness relies to a great extent on the level of dependence of the target state on the sanction-imposing state. The more dependent a state is on external states, the more vulnerable it is.

In a region where the balance of power is likely to effect a final political settlement that severely compromises the minimum requirements of the vanquished, and where tremendous structural economic differences exist among the "ex-belligerents," relative gains from any scheme of economic cooperation will continue to be major concerns for Arab actors. Since Israel is poised to reap higher relative gains, the Arab states will hesitate to be involved in intensive economic regional cooperation arrangements with Israel, lest the latter evolve into an economic colossus, in addition to consolidating its already established political and, most importantly, military hegemony. A preferred course currently debated among the Arab intelligentsia is that the security and economic welfare of the Arab world would be best served not by regional cooperation with Israel, but by the adoption of internal political and economic policies that invigorate democracy, economic efficiency, and social welfare.

Notes

1. See, for example, Ruth Arad, Seev Hirsch, and Alfred Tovias, *The Economics of Peacemaking: Focus on the Egyptian-Israeli Situation* (New York: St. Martin's, 1983); and Haim Ben-Shahar, Gideon Fishelson, and Seev Hirsch, *Economic Cooperation and Middle East Peace* (London: Weidenfeld and Nicolson, 1989).

2. See, for example, *The Economics of Middle East Peace: Views from the Region,* eds. Stanley Fischer, Dani Rodrik, and Elias Tuma (Cambridge MA: MIT Press, 1993); and Stanley Fischer and Thomas Schelling, *Securing Peace in the Middle East: Project on Economic Transition* (Cambridge MA: Institute for Social and Economic Policy in the Middle East of John F. Kennedy School of Government, Harvard University, 1993).

3. Armand Hammer, introduction to Haim Ben-Shahar et al., *Economic Cooperation and Middle East Peace* (London: Weidenfeld and Nicholson, 1989), xv.

4. See, for example, Mahmoud Abdel-Fadil, "The Paradox of MENA," *al-Ahram Weekly*, 14–20 November 1996; Ahmed Yusif Ahmed, "The Arabs and the Challenges of the (New) Middle Eastern Regime: A Discussion of Some Political Dimensions" (Arabic), in Center for Arab Unity Studies, *The New Middle Eastern Challenges and the Arab World* (Beirut: Center for Arab Unity Studies, 1994), 17–31; Inaam Raad, "The New Middle East Is an Expansion of the Zionist Project in the Region," *al-Hayat*, 11 November 1995; and Ahmed Abul-Fat'h, "Yes . . . Normalization [with Israel] Is the Twenty-first Century Colonialism," *al-Sharq al-Awsat*, 3 November 1996.

5. Kenneth Waltz, *Theory of International Politics* (Reading MA: Addison-Wesley, 1979), 105.

6. World Bank, *Mid-East Peace Talks, Regional Cooperation and Economic Development: A Note on Priority Regional Projects* (Washington, DC: Middle East and North Africa Region, Technical Development: World Bank, 1993).

7. Joseph Grieco, *Cooperation among Nations: Europe, America, and Non-Tariff Barriers to Trade* (Ithaca NY: Cornell University Press, 1990), 38.

8. Kenneth Waltz, *Man, the State and War: A Theoretical Analysis* (New York: Columbia University Press, 1959), 160.

9. Defensive positionalism, Grieco asserts "may act as a constraint on the willingness of states to work together even in the face of common interests. This is because states fear that partners may achieve relatively greater gains; that, as a result, the partners could surge ahead of them in relative capabilities; and, finally, that these increasingly powerful partners in the

present could use their additional power to pressure them or, at the extreme, to become all the more formidable foes at some point in the future." *Cooperation among Nations*, 40.

10. James Morrow, " When Do 'Relative Gains' Impede Trade?" *Journal of Conflict Resolution* 41:1 (February 1997), 12–37.

11. Ibid., 12.

12. Ibid., 13.

13. Ibid., 33–34.

14. Robert Powell, "Absolute and Relative Gains in International Relations Theory," *American Political Science Review* 85:4 (December 1991), 1303–20.

15. Ibid., 1306, 1316.

16. Duncan Snidal, "Relative Gains and the Pattern of International Cooperation," *American Political Science Review,* 85:3 (September 1991), 701–726; Snidal, "International Cooperation among Relative Gains Maximizers," *International Studies Quarterly* 35 (1991), 387–402.

17. Snidal, "Relative Gains," 702.

18. Ibid., 716.

19. Snidal, "International Cooperation," 388.

20. Luis Rivera-Batiz and Dangyang Xie, "Integration Among Unequals," *Regional Science and Urban Economics* 23 (1993), 337–54.

21. Ingrid Rima, "Trade among Partners Who Differ in Their Economic Development," in *Economic Integration Between Unequal Partners*, eds. Theodore Georgakopoulis et al. (Aldershot, England: Edward Elgar, 1994), 168.

22. See Robert Baldwin and David Kay, "International Trade and International Relations," *International Organization* 29:1 (Winter 1975), 127.

23. John Mearsheimer, "The False Promise of International Institutions," *International Security* 19:3 (Winter 1994–95), 7, 13.

24. Robert Keohane and Joseph Nye, *Power and Interdependence* (Glenview IL.: Scott, Forseman and Company, 1989), 35.

25. Keohane and Lisa Martin, "The Promise of Institutionalist Theory," *International Security* 20:1 (Summer 1995), 50.

26. Ethen Barnaby Kapstein, *The Political Economy of National Security: A Global Perspective* (New York: McGraw-Hill, 1992), 2–5.

27. Raymond Aron, *Peace and War: A Theory of International Relations* (Malabar FL: Robert Krieger, 1966), 72.

28. Gordon McCormick, "Strategic Considerations in the Development of Economic Thought," in *Strategic Dimensions of Economic Behavior*, eds. Gordon McCormick and Richard Bissell (New York: Praeger, 1984), 4.

29. Fredrich List, *The National System of Political Economy* (New York: Augustus M. Kelley, 1966).

30. McCormick, "Strategic Considerations," 5.

31. A state can use foreign economic relations as a source of power by extending or denying elements of economic value to another state or to non-state actors such as rebels. See Klaus Knorr, "Economic Relations as an Instrument of National Power," in *Strategic Dimensions,* 184.

16. The Debate over Normalization: Adonis and His Arab Critics

Muhammad Muslih

Departing from our regular format of a formal review of scholarly Arabic publications, Muhammad Muslih's essay considers Arab reactions to several comments, apparently condoning cultural normalization between the Arab states and Israel, made by the internationally known Syrian poet and cultural critic Adonis in the immediate wake of the signing of the Oslo Accords. The author discerns three sorts of responses to the question of normalization: one fearful for the maintenance of Arab cultural authenticity, a second confident in Arab cultural resilience, and a third opposed to normalization because of its view of continuing Israeli violations of the spirit of peace and normalization.

Almost three months after the signing of the Oslo agreement between Israel and the PLO in September 1993, Adonis—the internationally acclaimed Syrian poet and essayist, whose real name is Ali Ahmad Sa'id—participated in a UNICEF-sponsored conference in Granada, Spain, attended by Arab and Israeli intellectuals. In his conference statement, Adonis offered two observations with respect to Israel. The first was his suggestion that "Israel geographically belongs to a region of the world whose culture has been based on an interaction and diversity since the days of the Sumarians, the Canaanites, and the Pharaohs."[1] Second, he queried whether or not Israel might give Judaism a pluralistic dimension by legitimizing intermarriages and by adopting a multicultural approach toward education.[2]

Adonis's remarks were brief and in no way fully developed. Yet, his references to the inherent pluralism of the Middle East and his hopes for multiculturalism within the Israeli state were interpreted as support for the normalization of Arab-Israeli relations and led, on 27 January 1995, to his dismissal from the Arab Writers Union of Syria. Some of the 90 (out of a total of 115) Arab writers who voted for his dismissal were expressing their opposition to any form of cultural normalization with Israel, irrespective of the outcome of the peace process. "We will reject cultural normalization," stressed Ali Uqla Irsan, president of the Arab Writers Union, "and we will preserve our cultural citadel, a citadel that has safeguarded throughout history the irrevocable principles and moral values of our nation, and protected our rights and our land."[3]

Adonis's suggestions also sparked a debate among Arab intellectuals, a debate that revolved around the following questions: If Israel still occupies Arab land, and if it still follows hegemonic policies in the region, then why did Adonis not focus in his Granada speech on those policies instead of prematurely raising questions about cultural diversity and pluralism? If Israel had not accepted international legitimacy with respect to the question of withdrawal from all occupied Arab territories, then why should Adonis consider political and cultural normalization with the Jewish state?[4]

The answers to these questions were reflected in articles and editorials published in Arab newspapers and magazines. On the basis of a careful reading of these articles and editorials, one can identify three opinions. Although the ideas expressed by the writers were not all necessarily penned in direct response to Adonis, they give us a more in-depth idea about the thinking of Arab intellectuals on the question of normalization, and allow us to situate the influential Adonis within the framework of this debate.

Cultural Authenticity

Advocates of the first view object to Adonis's suggestions in the name of cultural authenticity. They argue that developments in the post-1973 era, particularly the 1982 Israeli invasion of Lebanon, proved to Israeli policymakers that the cost of imposing hegemony through military power was unaffordable given Israel's size and population.

Adonis (Ali Ahmad Sa'id)

To offset this disadvantage, Israel, according to this view, has embarked on a new strategy of economic and cultural penetration. The implication of Adonis's proposals, according to this view, is that Israel will find it easier to pursue its new strategy encouraged on the one hand by its military supremacy, and on the other by its interaction with certain Arab governments and by certain prominent individuals in the field of Arab culture and arts.

The new Israeli strategy is seen as being more dangerous in the long run than military power because it pursues penetration behind a veil of economic and cultural disguises. In other words, Israel's aim behind seeking normalization is not in the main cultural or economic; rather, it is hegemonic and may acquire an imperialistic character if the state of Arab disarray and weakness persists. The role of the Arabs in the political and cultural spheres would be marginalized by an aggressively dominant Israel. In this context, the power of Israel, which is the power of an ascendant political and economic entity supported by the West, forces Arabs to look for means of resistance. This sentiment was captured by Muhammad Kishli, in an essay entitled "No to Normalization, Yes to a Development Project." Here are Kishli's words:

> We should say "no" to normalization, and "yes" to a real and effective program of development in the economic, social, political, and cultural spheres. A weak party will be always vulnerable to any invasion and to any attempt aimed at imposing hegemony or domination. If we fail to mobilize our resources and our capabilities which are abundant in all domains in order to develop our societies in every sphere, our future will be uncertain in the face of this serious Israeli challenge which infringes upon our very national existence.[5]

Nizar Qabbani, the Beirut-based Syrian poet who died in April 1998, applied his considerable artistic skills to make his political point. His poem, *"al-Muharwilun"* (Those who scurry [to normalization]), won acclaim throughout the Arab world for its mockery of those who sacrificed their dignity in the rush to peace with Israel. The following lines are taken from the middle section of Qabbani's eighteen-stanza poem:

> After this secret flirtation in Oslo
> we emerged barren. . . .
> They granted us a homeland smaller than a grain of wheat . . .
> a homeland that we swallow without water
> like an aspirin tablet!! . . .
> After fifty years . . .
> we sit on this wasteland
> without residence . . . like thousands of dogs!! . . .
> After fifty years . . .
> we can't find a homeland to dwell in
> except illusory visions.
> It is not peace [*sulhan*] . . .
> That peace which was plunged into us like a dagger. . . .
> It is rather an act of rape!! . . .
> What good is scurrying [to normalization]?
> What good is scurrying?

> When the conscience of the people is alive
> like the fuse of a bomb . . .
> All the Oslo signatures are not worth . . .
> one mustard seed!! . . .[6]

A longtime opponent of normalization, Qabbani used the poem as not only a frontal attack on Arabs who opened the door to relations with Israel, but also as an implicit criticism of Adonis and other intellectuals who shared his views.

Cultural Interaction Based on Arab Strength

Proponents of the second view adopt a position that is not inconsistent with the thrust of Adonis's suggestions. Implicitly or explicitly, they are receptive to the idea of cultural interaction with Israel. They stress the fact that the civilization and culture of the Arabs will not be compromised when they interact with Israel, even though Israel is superior in the military and technological spheres. In an interdependent world, all societies interact. This is as true of the most sophisticated societies as it is of the least technologically developed. Moreover, those who subscribe to this view argue that once a process of political normalization has started between Arabs and Israelis, cultural normalization will have to follow, and the Arabs need not fear that process; no one is asking them to disavow their civilization or heritage. As the Palestinian writer Safi Safi has put it:

> Life goes on. Different peoples in different parts of the world are open to each other. We can develop ourselves by reaching out to others and by learning from their experiences in all fields of life, including the cultural field. I am absolutely sure that our mission as intellectuals is to call for cultural openness. Our first priority should be the fight against introversion. Introversion will not protect our culture even if the culture of Israel were superior.[7]

The meeting ground—the relationship between a vanquished party and a victorious party—is a common thread running through this debate among Arab intellectuals. Advocates of the first view are concerned about Israeli domination in all domains of life. "Even Arab oil," wrote Abd al-Karim Ghallab, "will be influenced by normalization and therefore will become Israeli oil."[8] Other advocates of this first position also express their fear that interaction with Israel, especially in the cultural and social spheres, may corrupt the moral fabric of Arab society through the infiltration of ideas and practices alien to the Arab Muslim social code.[9]

By contrast, advocates of the second view begin with a different premise. They are sure of the strength of their culture, and for this reason they do not feel apprehensive about contact with Israeli culture. After all, they argue, cultural interaction is a road that the Arabs will have to travel, but with open eyes.[10] Arab arts and civilization have encountered many others in the centuries since the rise of Islam and have not only retained their distinctiveness but indeed flourished.

Israel as an Unworthy Partner

The third perspective is that of Arab intellectuals and politicians who object to normalization and to the kind of observations made by Adonis, not because they have not come to terms with the reality of Israel, nor because they are concerned about Israeli domination, but because they believe that Israel pursues policies that are inconsistent with peace. They cite several problems which, in their view, should discourage the Arabs, especially Arab literary figures of the highest caliber like Adonis, from advocating or engaging in normal relations with Israel, including:

- Israel's refusal to recognize the right of the Palestinians to establish their own independent state in the West Bank and Gaza;
- Israel's insistence on retaining Arab East Jerusalem;
- Israel's refusal to withdraw from the Golan and South Lebanon;
- Israel's refusal to subscribe to the policy of a nuclear-free Middle East.

The general feeling of this third school is that normalization will become a practical proposition only when all aspects of the Palestinian question, including Jerusalem, are resolved, and when there is a breakthrough on the Syrian and Lebanese fronts. The success of normalization, they also believe, requires more than just agreements between governments. Above all, success requires peace-building activities, most notably concrete policies that demonstrate to the broad

Arab public as well at to its elite that Israel harbors no territorial ambitions beyond the lines of 4 June 1967.[11]

Conclusion

Neither Adonis nor the writers who disagreed with him offered a systematic analysis of their positions on the peace process, and especially on the question of normalization with Israel. The debate just summarized has been reconstructed by a careful reading of scattered articles and essays published over a short period of time (1993–96), during which Israeli Prime Minister Yitzhak Rabin and then acting Prime Minister Shimon Peres made breakthroughs with the Arab world. Not all of these writers were of the highest caliber and many of them were of only second or third rank of importance. Yet, despite these shortcomings, there is a certain consistency in what they write about normalization. It is useful to consider and understand their views because, on the one hand, they are not without influence on the readers of their own generation and, on the other, they reflect the mood of a significant number of people in the Arab world.

In many ways, it is these writers, aware as they are of the coming of "mass politics" and the information revolution, who are least likely to be swayed by what Arab governments involved in the peace process say or do, and who continue to work diligently to attract literate men and women to their positions along the spectrum of Arab political thought about the important topic of normalization with Israel. Although the unresolved debate was relegated to secondary status during the tenure of Prime Minister Benjamin Netanyahu [1996–99], it is sure to resume in full if and when the peace process is resuscitated.

Notes*

1. Quoted in *al-Adab* (Beirut) 42: 8–9 (August–September 1994), 14.

2. See *al-Adab* 43: 3–4 (March–April 1995), 21.

3. *al-Hayat* (Beirut), 29 January 1995, 1, 4.

4. For this point see "Three Responses to Adonis," *al-Adab* 43:3–4 (March–April 1995), 21ff.; see also *al-Safir* (Beirut), 5 January 1994; *al-*

---

*All sources are in Arabic.

Nahar (Beirut), 19 April 1994; and the nine issues of *al-Adab* from September to October 1993 through October 1994.

5. *"La lil-Tatbi', Na'm li-Mashru' Tanmawi,"* paper delivered by Muhammad Kishli [Lebanon] at the Constituent Assembly of the National Conference against Normalization, Beirut, 28 January 1995, in *al-Manabir* 9:77 (April–May 1995), 129. For similar views see articles in *al-Adab* 41:11 (1993); *al-Muwajaha* (Cairo), 3 (June 1992); and *al-Yasar* (Cairo) 30 (August 1992) and 31 (September 1992).

6. Nizar Qabbani, "Those Who Scurry [to Normalization]," *al-Hayat*, 28 September 1995.

7. Safi Safi, "Cultural Normalization," *al-Katib* (Jerusalem) 15:159 (31 December 1994), 6. For similar views, see the comments of 'Abd al-Qadir Salih and Ahmad Barqawi in *al-Adab* 41:11 (November 1993), as well as articles in *al-Arabi* (Kuwait), March 1995.

8. Quoted in *al-Arabi* 449 (April 1996), 12.

9. See Hamid 'Ammar, "Penetration Has Its Limits, Zionization Has Its Limits Too!!" *al-Ahali* (Cairo), 6 May 1992; see also, the view of the Jordanian writer Wahib al-Sha'ir as outlined by 'Abd al-Qadir Salih, "The Cultural Course of the Gaza-Jericho Agreement and the Methods for Confronting It," *al-Adab* 41:11 (November 1993), 47. This view is expressed in detail in the literature of radical Islamists, particularly in Egypt.

10. A brief but telling exposition of this view can be found in the essay written by Muhammad al-Rumayhi, editor of the Kuwaiti monthly magazine *al-Arabi*, under the title "The Cultural Dimension of the State of No War and No Peace," *al-Arabi* 449 (April 1996).

11. For arguments expressing this view, see the editorial in the Egyptian publication *al-Muwajaha* 3 (June 1992), 2; see also the statement of al-Sayyid Yasin, Egyptian intellectual and secretary-general of the Forum on Arab Thought, in *al-Ahali* 551 (29 April 1992).

Contributors

Hemda Ben-Yehuda is a Lecturer in the Department of Political Science at Bar Ilan University, specializing in international relations theory and the analysis of state behavior in crises. Her research, with its particular emphasis on leaders' attitudes in the Arab-Israeli conflict, has appeared in the *Journal of Conflict Resolution, International Interactions, Review of International Studies, Journal of Peace Research,* and *Israel Affairs.*

Hanita Brand is a Lecturer in Hebrew and Comparative Literature in the Department of Asian and Middle Eastern Studies at the University of Pennsylvania. She has published articles on Hebrew and Arabic literature in English, Hebrew, and Arabic periodicals, among them the *Journal of Arabic Literature, Edebiyat, New Observations, Masa,* and *Noga.*

Nitza Druyan is the Director of the Long Island Center for Jewish Studies and teaches in the Jewish Studies Program of Hofstra University. She is the author of *Without a Magic Carpet: Yemenite Settlement in Eretz-Israel, 1881–1914* (Jerusalem: Yad Yizhak Ben-Zvi and the Hebrew University of Jerusalem, 1981, in Hebrew) and of numerous articles in Hebrew and English on Yemenite Jewry and on ethnic and cultural issues in Israeli society.

David C. Jacobson is Associate Professor of Judaic Studies at Brown University. He is the author of *Modern Midrash: The Retelling of Traditional Jewish Narratives by Twentieth Century Hebrew Writers* (Albany: State University of New York Press, 1987) and *Does David Still Play Before You?: Israeli Poetry and the Bible* (Detroit: Wayne State University Press, 1997). He is co-editor, with Kamal Abdel-Malek, of *Israeli and Palestinian Identities in History and Literature* (New York: St. Martin's Press, 1999).

Muhammad Muslih is Associate Professor of Political Science and Middle Eastern Studies at Long Island University, C.W. Post Campus. His publications include *The Origins of Palestinian Nationalism*

(New York: Columbia University Press,1988), *Towards Coexistence: An Analysis of the Resolutions of the Palestine National Council* (Washington, DC: Institute for Palestine Studies, 1990), and, with A.R. Norton, *Political Tides in the Arab World* (New York: Foreign Policy Association, 1991).

Maen F. Nsour is the Director of the Economic Aid Coordination Department at the Ministry of Planning, Amman, Jordan. He is a senior fellow at the Institute of Public Policy, George Mason University and an adjunct faculty member of the Political Science Department, University of Jordan. His book *Economic Cooperation Under the Security Dilemma: The Case of Israel and the Arab States* is forthcoming in Arabic.

Ilan Peleg is Charles A. Dana Professor of Government and Law at Lafayette College. He is the author and editor of several works, including *Begin's Foreign Policy, 1977–1983* (Westport, CT: Greenwood, 1987), *The Emergence of Binational Israel: The Second Republic in the Making,* co-edited with Ofira Seliktar (Boulder, CO: Westview Press, 1989), *Human Rights in the West Bank and Gaza* (New York: Syracuse University Press, 1996), and *The Arab-Israeli Peace Process: Interdisciplinary Perspectives* (Albany: State University of New York Press, 1997). He is a past president of the Association for Israel Studies (1995–1997).

David Rodman is free-lance writer whose articles and reviews have appeared in *Israel Affairs, International Journal of Intelligence and Counterintelligence, Armed Forces and Society, SAIS Review, Jerusalem Journal of International Relations,* and *Midstream.*

Yaakova Sacerdoti is a Lecturer in Hebrew Language and Literature at the University of Michigan, Ann Arbor. Her articles on children's literature have appeared in *Sifrut Yeladim ve-Noar.* She is the author of *On the Crossroad: Research on Dialogue Structure in Children's Literature* (Tel Aviv: ha-Kibbutz ha-Meuchad, 1999). (Hebrew)

Ofira Seliktar is Ann and Bernard Cohen Associate Professor of Israel Studies at Gratz College and a consultant on the Middle East Water Resources Project at the University of Pennsylvania. Her publications on Israel, the Arab-Israeli conflict, and water issues in the Middle East include *New Zionism and the Foreign Policy System of*

Israel (London: Croom Helm, 1986) and *The Emergence of Binational Israel: The Second Republic in the Making,* co-edited with Ilan Peleg (Boulder, CO: Westview Press, 1989). Her most recent book is *Failing the Crystal Ball Test: The Fundamentalist Revolution in Iran* (Westport, CT: Praeger, forthcoming).

Tobe Shanok is an independent scholar and has been engaged in research on pre-Mandate Eretz Yisrael/Palestine through the Center for Middle Eastern Studies at Harvard University. Her research interests are the organization and development of institutions, leadership, and economic expansion within the yishuv, 1914–1918.

Jeffrey Sosland has lectured in the Department of Government at Georgetown University and conducted research in Israel as a Post-Doctoral Fellow at the Hebrew University of Jerusalem (1997–1998). He is a Visiting Professor at the University of Missouri-Columbia (1999–2000).

Deborah A. Starr is a doctoral candidate in comparative literature at the University of Michigan. She conducted the research for this article in Cairo as a Fellow of the Council of American Overseas Research Centers. She is also the author of "Reterritorializing the Dream: Orly Castel-Bloom's Remapping of Israeli Identity," in *Mapping Jewish Identities*, Laurence Silberstein, ed. (New York: New York University Press, forthcoming).

Naomi Weinberger is an Associate Research Scholar at the Middle East Institute of Columbia University and an Adjunct Professor of Political Science at Yeshiva University. Dr. Weinberger is the author of *Syrian Intervention in Lebanon* (New York: Oxford University Press, 1996) and of several scholarly articles on international peacekeeping operations. She is a past vice-president of the Association for Israel Studies (1995–97).

Eyal Zisser is a Research Fellow at the Moshe Dayan Center for Middle Eastern and African Studies and a Lecturer in the Department of Middle Eastern and African History at Tel Aviv University. His articles on Syria, Lebanon, and Hizbullah have appeared in *Middle Eastern Studies, Orient, Middle East Quarterly, The World Today, Terrorism and Political Violence, ha-Mizrah he-Hadash, Iyyunim bi-Tkumat Israel,* and other journals. He is the author of *Asad's Syria— At a Crossroads* (Tel Aviv: ha-Kibbutz ha-Meuchad, 1999). (Hebrew).

The Editors

Laura Zittrain Eisenberg is a Visiting Associate Professor in the History Department at Carnegie Mellon University. She is the author of *My Enemy's Enemy: Lebanon in the Early Zionist Imagination, 1900–1948* (Detroit: Wayne State University Press, 1994) and co-author, with Neil Caplan, of *Negotiating Arab-Israeli Peace: Patterns, Problems, Possibilities* (Bloomington: Indiana University Press, 1998).

Neil Caplan teaches in the Humanities Department of Vanier College, Montreal, Canada. His publications include *Palestine Jewry and the Arab Question, 1917–1925* (London: Frank Cass, 1978), *The Lausanne Conference, 1949: A Case Study in Middle East Peacemaking* (Tel Aviv University, Moshe Dayan Center for Middle Eastern and African Studies, 1993), *Futile Diplomacy*, a multi-volume documentary history of the Arab-Israeli conflict (London: Frank Cass, vol. 1, 1983; vol. 2, 1986; vols. 3–4, 1997), and, with Laura Zittrain Eisenberg, *Negotiating Arab-Israeli Peace: Patterns, Problems, Possibilities* (Bloomington: Indiana University Press, 1998).